Book Ownership in Stuart England

Book Ownership in Stuart England

The Lyell Lectures, 2018

DAVID PEARSON

OXFORD
UNIVERSITY PRESS

OXFORD
UNIVERSITY PRESS

Great Clarendon Street, Oxford, OX2 6DP,
United Kingdom

Oxford University Press is a department of the University of Oxford.
It furthers the University's objective of excellence in research, scholarship,
and education by publishing worldwide. Oxford is a registered trade mark of
Oxford University Press in the UK and in certain other countries

© David Pearson 2021

The moral rights of the author have been asserted

First Edition published in 2021

Impression: 1

Published in the United States of America by Oxford University Press
198 Madison Avenue, New York, NY 10016, United States of America

British Library Cataloguing in Publication Data
Data available

Library of Congress Control Number: 2020949090

ISBN 978-0-19-887012-8

DOI: 10.1093/oso/9780198870128.001.0001

Printed and bound by
CPI Group (UK) Ltd, Croydon, CR0 4YY

Preface

This book distils the fruits of long years of observation and evidence-gathering on patterns of early modern book ownership, derived not least from looking at many thousands of books, in many libraries. The impetus to bring it together like this was provided by the invitation to be Lyell Reader in Bibliography at the University of Oxford in 2017–18, and to give the annual Lyell Lectures; I am very grateful to the Lyell Electors for that privilege, and also for their financial input towards the costs of illustrating this volume. The Electors have also supported the development of the free online database *Book Owners Online*, which is intended to be an ongoing legacy and reference source arising from this work, and I appreciate their vision in extending their activities in this forward-looking direction. I hope the precedent thus set will not be the last.

There is a lot of information in this book, and it is written partly in the hope that it will become a useful quarry for other book-historical researchers. It bases much of its analysis on the material evidence of books themselves, including bookbindings, and in that sense it is meant both to add to and to develop the growing body of book-historical work which recognizes the importance of that approach. It is also a polemical book, in challenging ways in which the topic which is more commonly called book collecting is approached and written about; and if I can influence our broader thinking around terminologies, methodologies, and the kinds of questions which we should bring both to individual historic books and to whole libraries, I will be glad.

There have of course been many people who have helped me along the way. Looking at books is the most fundamental prerequisite of book-historical research, and although I cannot list all the librarians and other custodians who have, over all those years, facilitated my evidence-gathering by giving access to their books, I hope they know it was appreciated. In the more immediate run-up to the Lectures, various members of Bodleian Library staff gave indispensable help, and I would particularly like to thank Alex Franklin, Andrew Honey, Richard Ovenden, Jennifer Varallo, and Sarah Wheale and her colleagues in Rare Books. Others who helped in various ways included Karen Attar, Elizabethanne Boran, Linda Crosby, Sarah Cusk, Anthony Davis, Daryl Green, Onesimus Ngundu, Jean-Pascal Pouzet, Mark Purcell, Nigel Ramsay, Emma Smith, Joanna Snelling, and Bill Zachs. My colleagues on the *Book Owners Online* database project are also part of this journey, and I would like to say thank you to Robyn Adams, Clodagh Murphy, and Matt Symonds for their contributions. For reading my entire text in draft, and providing many helpful suggestions, I am very grateful to Giles

Mandelbrote, Scott Mandelbrote, and Will Poole. Ellie Collins, Aimee Wright, Sarah Barrett and their colleagues at Oxford University Press kept me on the straight and narrow through the publishing process. Of course, this list must end in the way that such things usually do: errors, omissions and other failings remain the responsibility of the author alone.

I also owe a number of formal acknowledgements to the owners of books reproduced as images, for their permission to do so: the Bodleian Library, University of Oxford (Figs 3.1, 3.2C, 3.5, 3.7, 3.11A and B, 4.2, 4.12A and B, 4.13A and B, 5.1–5.3, 6.1–6.4, 7.1, 7.2B, 7.5); the Syndics of Cambridge University Library (Figs 3.4, 4.5–4.8C, 7.3A–C); the Trustees of Thomas Plume's Library (Figs 3.6, 5.7); Guildhall Library, City of London (Fig. 3.10); Mr Anthony Davis (Figs 3.13A and B); the Wellcome Trust (Figs 3.15A and B); Thomas Fisher Rare Book Library, University of Toronto (Fig. 4.3); Senate House Library, University of London (Figs 4.9–4.11); the Pepys Library, Magdalene College, Cambridge (Fig. 5.4); the Master and Fellows of Balliol College, Oxford (Fig. 6.6); the Master and Fellows of Magdalen College, Oxford (Figs 6.7, 6.8); the President and Fellows of Corpus Christi College, Oxford (Figs 5.6, 6.9); the Folger Shakespeare Library (Figs 7.4A and B).

Contents

List of figures

1

Introduction

Private libraries in Stuart England

This book is about the private library and the ownership of books in England during the seventeenth century, between the end of the Tudor period and the beginning of the Hanoverian. It considers questions of evolution and development, contents and size, and motives for book ownership. It covers a century during which the production and circulation of print expanded considerably, alongside an equally growing market in second-hand books, and when book ownership was very widespread; when books might be found, in varying numbers, in the homes of all kinds of people from the humble to the wealthy.

The theme should not need much intellectual justification, given the importance of printed and written books as communicators of ideas, as storehouses and preservers of knowledge, as influencers in society. Our minds are tuned to a world in which scholarship depends much more upon institutional libraries than individual ones; but throughout the early modern period the balance was different, and significant collections were equally likely to be found in, and passing between, private hands. Private libraries were also the tributaries of the public ones, which have become our collective documentary heritage, so the record of the past that has come down to us, that has shaped our perceptions and understanding of history, has been significantly shaped by what people have gathered and placed in libraries. Things which people did not own and preserve have disappeared into an unknowable void. Book ownership has also helped to shape our values around disciplinary canons, around what is important or less important material across many subject areas—what is fashionable to own becomes desirable, becomes perceived to be of higher value than that which is not collected.

Methodologies

Jason Scott-Warren began an article on the book buying of a late sixteenth-century Suffolk gentleman, Sir Thomas Cornwallis, with a helpful overview of approaches taken in this field, between the detailed study of the annotations of an individual reader and the gathering of many library catalogues from many

Book Ownership in Stuart England: The Lyell Lectures, 2018. David Pearson, Oxford University Press (2021).
© David Pearson.
DOI: 10.1093/oso/9780198870128.003.0001

people.[1] He concluded that each has its place, with an ongoing need for both qualitative and quantitative evidence, and that 'parachutists and truffle-hunters must work together to write the history of the book'.[2] Methodologically, this book is the work of a parachutist, interested in mapping trends and patterns. It refers to numerous case studies and individual owners, but its aim is to create an overview. Private library history can be written through a detailed analysis of one particular library, exploring groups of books in turn and placing the owner and his or her interests in their contemporary context, but I am more interested in the bigger picture.

The backbone of the book is the list of seventeenth-century book owners which constitutes the Appendix, and whose rationale is set out more fully on p. 165. It seeks to bring together the names of people who died between 1610 and 1715 for whom we have appreciable evidence of book ownership, beyond a single book or a small handful identified from inscriptions. They include people who used book-plates or armorial binding stamps, those whose books were dispersed in a recorded sale, whose probate documents reveal libraries through wills or inven-tories, or who gave libraries which they had accumulated to institutions; and also some whose books may today be scattered around the world, but which survive in sufficient numbers to deduce the existence of a critical mass. The list cannot pretend to be complete even within its own terms of reference, but with 1,374 names in all I believe it to be sufficient to be representative, and to enable meaningful trend analysis.

The people on the list are categorized by their primary occupation or back-ground, while acknowledging that this is an imprecise science with areas of overlap. There are 160 entries for aristocrats and 276 for members of gentry families (including knights, baronets, and people with estates, usually inherited, such that they fit that rather vaguely defined but broadly recognizable mould). The largest category, perhaps unsurprisingly, is that of the clergy, 149 vicars and rectors plus 100 Nonconformist ministers, ordained men who were ejected after 1660 and often licensed as Presbyterians or other denominations under the 1672 Declaration of Indulgence, and who constitute a noticeable proportion of the serious clerical book-owning sector after the Restoration. To that clergy category can be added senior clergy—22 deans, 58 canons, 13 archdeacons, 49 bishops, and 16 archbishops, another 158 in all.

There are 148 people classed as academics, including 61 senior academics (heads of colleges or similar). There is a fluidity and possible ambiguity between academics and clergymen, as ordination was often a college requirement and many people used livings effectively as income streams to support a primarily

---

[1] Jason Scott-Warren, 'News, sociability, and bookbuying in early modern England: the letters of Sir Thomas Cornwallis', *The Library*, 7th ser. 1 (2000), pp. 381–402.

[2] Ibid. 386.

academic career. The academic lists aim to include only those who had university positions or clearly spent some or all of their careers in Oxford or Cambridge; I believe the size of the sample mitigates any margin of error. I have 111 lawyers, including judges and barristers, and 88 medics, comprising 74 physicians, 11 surgeons, 2 apothecaries, and an oculist. There are only 36 women in the list, who are considered more specifically in Chapter 3. After 15 heralds, 19 schoolmasters, 29 civil servants, small numbers of miscellaneous other classifications (including authors, scientists, engravers and gardeners), that leaves 70 names who either were definitely merchants or tradesmen of various kinds, or who are grouped there for lack of further knowledge. Fig. 1.1 shows these statistics expressed as a pie chart, which both reminds us of the spread of book ownership at this time and suggests a picture of ratios across that spread.

The other key evidence base underpinning this book is that of books themselves. It draws upon a range of documentary sources, including wills, letters, and diaries, but it is rooted very much in the experience of looking at many thousands of books in many libraries around the world. This may seem too obvious to need saying, but perhaps not; people do write about book history without having examined a lot of books. A few years ago a serious university press published a book on *Galileo's reading*, professing to use 'the material history of Galileo's library to examine the interplay of natural philosophy and epic poetry in making knowledge', but it does not reference a single original book in a library today

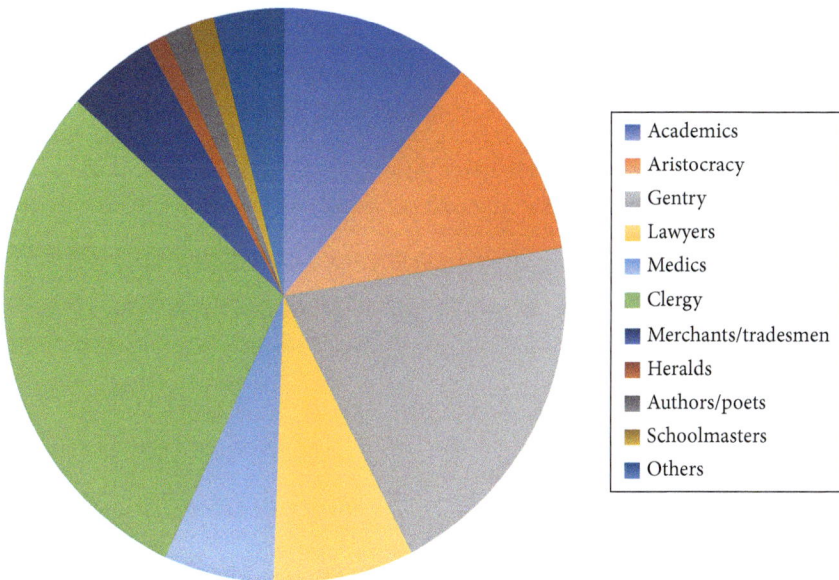

Fig. 1.1 The breakdown of book owners in the list in the Appendix, by profession or background.

known to have belonged to him, and use of material evidence from his books (as opposed to words from the pages of books he is believed to have owned or read) is noticeably scarce.[3] At a time when we talk much about the material culture of the book, about the importance of considering the book as a whole artefact, it is surely essential to develop a rounder view and draw on evidence of the ways in which books have been marked, used, and bound to help understand what they meant to their owners, and why they may have owned them.

Received wisdom

The topic of the seventeenth-century private library is hardly an untilled furrow, but one which has been explored from many angles. There have been countless studies of individual owners and editions of library catalogues, and consolidated series of library lists have been brought together, some of them still growing, to help us compare and contrast. We have moved on from the horizons of Seymour de Ricci, whose *English collectors of books and manuscripts* dealt with the second half of the seventeenth century by mentioning Francis Bernard, Sir Godfrey Copley, John Evelyn, Narcissus Luttrell, Samuel Pepys, George Thomason, Richard Smith, and James Sotheby, and suggesting that 'the choice might easily have been made more comprehensive: I fancy, however, that most of the more significant names have been quoted.'[4] That said, those famous names can still be said to cast a disproportionately large shadow over the landscape as a whole—as David McKitterick has observed, 'Pepys has become the best remembered—and most quoted—bibliophile in seventeenth-century London.'[5] Pepys was, however, only one of many hundreds of his contemporaries buying and owning books in Restoration London. His library was not the largest or grandest of its time, and his bindings—which have received much attention—were typical of work being turned out day after day by numerous good-quality workshops, for many customers.

We should also recognize that our approach to the subject is often skewed by the academic or collecting fashions of the time of writing, which may focus disproportionately on the books which later generations think are the interesting ones, irrespective of the values of the time under consideration. Writing about Horace Walpole's library in the middle of the twentieth century, Wilmarth Lewis felt the need to say rather apologetically that 'there were few books at Strawberry

---

[3] Crystal Hall, *Galileo's reading* (Cambridge: Cambridge University Press, 2013).
[4] Seymour de Ricci, *English collectors of books and manuscripts* (Cambridge: Cambridge University Press, 1930), 32.
[5] David McKitterick, *The invention of rare books* (Cambridge: Cambridge University Press, 2018), 89.

Hill which would today reach four figures in a New York saleroom'.[6] Historical bibliography as was, book history as is, has often been allowed its place at the academic feast as a handmaid to literary scholarship, and a lot of work in this area has had as its wellspring a focus on a small and narrow part of the overall content spectrum. Our copy-censuses have been undertaken on the First Folio and on Sidney's *Arcadia*, or on famous scientific books, not on Hooker's *Lawes of ecclesiastical politie*. The way to become famous as a seventeenth-century book owner is to have owned some Shakespeare: to quote de Ricci again, 'the name of Edward Gwynn . . . deserves to be rescued from oblivion as the owner of at least one volume of paramount importance: the bound collection of nine Shakespeare quartos.'[7] But Stuart-era book owners were far more likely to possess John Barclay's *Argenis* than Shakespeare, or Donne's sermons rather than his poems. When looking in detail at the contents of five late seventeenth-century libraries as recorded in sale catalogues, I was struck by how little the works which we have come to define as the really significant books of the time turn up on contemporary shelves, in comparison with the ones which we now consider much less important.[8]

The issue was noted by Andrew Cambers in his book on *Godly reading*, where he observes, 'the history of devotional reading has been one area in the history of reading which has suffered relative neglect', noting: 'Heidi Hackel's otherwise excellent study of the reading of Frances Bridgewater excludes religious books on the basis that they raise separate issues to other books.'[9] 'Separate issues' is of course a euphemistic shorthand for the sentiment that literary texts are thought to be interesting while theological ones are dull, but remaining in that mindset will never achieve an objective overview of seventeenth-century libraries. I would echo Cambers's praise of Heidi Hackel's work in this field, but she has herself acknowledged the literary blinkers: in her book *Reading material in early modern England* she describes her eye-opening visit to the stacks in the Huntington Library to discover the range of material that took up Bridgewater Library shelves: 'I was struck immediately by all the sermons, handbooks and pamphlets that are mere footnotes to the literary canon that must have taken up so much of the space in . . . private libraries . . . their physical presence, shelf after shelf, made a deep impression upon me and forcefully altered my sense of early modern print.'[10]

Does this matter? I believe it does, in the interests of understanding history as it was. This is not the place to debate the principles and aspirations which should underpin humanities scholarship, but if we assess or overlay the past too much

[6] W. S. Lewis, 'Horace Walpole's library', *The Library*, 5th ser. 2 (1947), pp. 45–52, 45.
[7] de Ricci, *English collectors*, 28.
[8] David Pearson, 'Patterns of book ownership in late seventeenth-century England', *The Library*, 7th ser. 11 (2010), pp. 139–67, 158.
[9] Andrew Cambers, *Godly reading* (Cambridge: Cambridge University Press, 2011), 32.
[10] Heidi Brayman Hackel, *Reading material in early modern England* (Cambridge: Cambridge University Press, 2005), 14.

through the values of the present, we will be in danger of imposing meaning rather than discovering it. This book is therefore unapologetic in talking rather more about theological and devotional books than literary or scientific ones, because they occupied so much more space on the average seventeenth-century bookshelf. In doing so it echoes studies that have been undertaken of what was printed: 'the output of the majority of publishers for the first century or so of printing was heavily dominated by religious works of one sort or another. Indeed, in his influential study of English books and readers, Stanley Bennett estimated that, in this period, printers, as a body, gave something like half their output to this side of their business.'[11] *The whole duty of man*, which went through over 80 editions between its first publication in 1658 and 1730, was 'so frequently reprinted that enough copies had been published by the end of Queen Anne's reign for every tenth household to have owned a copy'.[12]

'The contents of a private library have been described as a projection of the owner's mind.'[13] This commonly encountered sentiment, if not entirely fallacious, needs to be unpicked with care. It all too easily slips into an assumption that the books people owned were ones that reflected the ideas they were particularly interested in or agreed with, so that they sought to own primarily texts which fitted that landscape. In reality people came to own, lose, or fail to acquire books for all kinds of reasons, and they certainly did not only own books that they agreed with or admired. When looking at the libraries of English bishops in the early seventeenth century, I was struck by the regular appearance of works by Roman Catholic authors whose doctrine they spent much of their time refuting; in a world in which print was such an important medium for disputing and defending ideas, it was essential to know the enemy in order to confound him.[14] Quite apart from that, there was a widespread respect for serious scholarship, and a recognition that valuable exegesis was produced by Catholic as well as Protestant authors. 'Rather than offering us a sharply defined picture of its last owner's personal intellectual orientation, [a library] reveals instead his larger intellectual inheritance and the range of texts he might have used to think with, or against' is a much better way of recrafting that idea at the beginning of this paragraph.[15]

Our contemporary book-historical landscape has seen a growing focus on areas like marginalia and the history of reading, and there have been valuable pieces

---

[11] Andrew Murphy, 'The history of the book in Britain, *c.*1475–1800', in M. F Suarez and H. Woudhuysen (eds), *The book: a global history* (Oxford: Oxford Univeristy Press, 2013), 293.

[12] Ian Green, *Print and Protestantism in early modern England* (Oxford: Oxford University Press, 2000), 353.

[13] Jennie Challoner, 'A new manuscript compilation of Katherine Philips', *The Library*, 7th ser. 17 (2016), pp. 287–316, 299.

[14] David Pearson, 'The libraries of English bishops 1600–1640', *The Library*, 6th ser. 14 (1992), pp. 221–57, 229.

[15] Philip Benedict and Pierre-Olivier Léchot, 'The library of Élie Bouhéreau', in M. McCarthy and A. Simmons (eds), *Marsh's Library: a mirror on the world* (Dublin: Four Courts Press, 2009), pp. 165–84, 183.

published in recent years reflecting on methodologies, and caveats for the unwary. Will Poole, in the context of an anonymous library list which may be attributed to John Hales, has written about the many forms and purposes which lists of books can take, the questions to be asked, the dynamic nature of such things, and the point that a catalogue made at a particular time does not reflect all the books a person ever owned.[16] Many writers have stressed the recognition that a book owned is not necessarily a book read, that people read books they did not own, and that there are various reasons why books we would expect to find on certain shelves are not locatable there. Puzzlement has been expressed over the absence of Newton from Thomas Plume's Library, or the relatively small holdings of Aristotle by John Locke.[17] But there are all kinds of reasons why books which would seem to fit in a particular library are not there; they may have been once, but have been lost, stolen, or removed at some point after the owner's death. They may have loaned out to a friend, and never returned. Or they may never have been acquired because opportunities were missed, or because they were known to be available somewhere else.

The key point here is to adopt the parachutist, rather than truffle-hunting, methodology. If we focus on one particular library, and use it too much to make broader observations, our evidence base will be too narrow. One text in, or not in, a particular library is not something upon which to build a thesis; that text regularly found in many libraries, or seldom found, gives us something more concrete. Adrian Johns, in a book-historical essay, talks about 'resisting the temptation to assign significance disproportionately to phenomena that happen to look significant in retrospect while neglecting phenomena more representative of the period and place in question'.[18] Finding something unusual and discussing it as though it were not, or vice versa, because only a few examples have been considered when hundreds should have been, is a trap we need to avoid. One of the aims of this book is to map the typical, by taking enough of an overview, to help us to recognize better what really is unusual when we see it.

The national context

All the book-focused activities described in this book took place across a period which was hardly static in social, political, or cultural terms. During a century in

---

[16] William Poole, 'Analysing a private library, with a shelflist attributable to John Hales of Eton, c.1624', in E. Jones (ed.), *A concise companion to the study of manuscripts, printed books, and the production of early modern texts* (Chichester: Wiley Blackwell, 2015), pp. 41–65.

[17] W. J. Petchey, *The intentions of Thomas Plume* (Maldon: Trustees of the Plume Library, 2004), 3; John Harrison and Peter Laslett, *The library of John Locke* (Oxford: Oxford University Press, 1971), 21.

[18] Adrian Johns, 'The coming of print to Europe', in L. Howsam (ed.), *The Cambridge companion to the history of the book* (Cambridge: Cambridge University Press, 2015), 108.

which England gave the world Bacon, Boyle, Harvey, Hobbes, Milton, Newton, and Shakespeare, and the most-read English language book of all time (the King James Bible), its population grew from four to five million, it underwent tumultuous political upheaval and strife, and it evolved itself from a rather marginal European country into a world power to be reckoned with. None of these things, individually, can be seen to have had a directly transformative effect on the story told in this book—or, to put it another way, there is no particular event in the wider landscape that was a milestone in changing the way that private libraries were assembled, or in shaping their contents. There is no seventeenth-century equivalent to the invention of printing, or of the internet, or of the mechanization of processes that so changed book production in the nineteenth century. People owned Bibles before the Authorized Version appeared, and they owned scientific books (or, in the classification of the time, natural philosophy books) before they had the opportunity to buy Boyle and Newton. The authors who produced the most popular devotional books of their generation were different at the two ends of the century, but such books were widely owned in 1620 as they were in 1680.

The narrative is more one of continuous growth, against the backdrop of commercial expansion in the wider national context. Libraries on average got bigger and book ownership became more widespread, as the century progressed. It is well known that the number of printers and books produced in Britain increased significantly between the two ends of the century, as did the number of books imported.[19] The economic development of the book trade through this period has been presented by James Raven, who describes a growing seventeenth-century book market responding to increasing demand from the middling, propertied classes, increased standards of living relative to those in Continental Europe, and diversification of retail activities via book auctions and book-lending opportunities.[20] He also notes the difficulties of chronicling these changes in any simple or linear way, recognizing the multiple threads which produce the tapestry of economic history: 'our modelling of [spending power] is very difficult', 'we can . . . attempt to characterize change only from very rough and ready statistics'.[21] The middle decades of the century, dominated by the Civil War and Interregnum, were hugely disruptive for the lives of many individuals, and many books were destroyed through military action, or lost to owners who suffered ejection or sequestration. These decades were also a time of markedly increased output from the printing presses, when the fuelling of warfare by tract and newsbook became

[19]   See e.g. the statistics in D. F. McKenzie, 'Printing and publishing 1557–1700', in J. Barnard and D. F. McKenzie (eds), *The Cambridge history of the book in Britain*, vol. 4 (Cambridge: Cambridge University Press, 2002), pp. 553–67, 557.

[20]   James Raven, 'The economic context', in Barnard and McKenzie, *The Cambridge history*, vol. 4, pp. 562–82; see also James Raven, *The business of books* (New Haven, CT: Yale University Press, 2007), esp. ch. 4 ('The late Stuart trade').

[21]   Raven, 'The economic context', 572–3.

part of the conflict. But behind the front lines, as it were, scholars and gentlemen continued to develop their libraries, booksellers continued to trade, and the value of books was recognized by the protection or reassignment of libraries, as long as the looters and despoilers did not get there first.[22] Numerous significant bequests were made in the 1650s or 1660s of libraries by owners who were fortunate enough to avoid the dispersal and loss which were much lamented by those who had been more dangerously close to the edge of the parapet.

As regards the relationship between private and public libraries, the importance of the role which the former have played in feeding the latter has already been emphasized. The seventeenth century was a time of gradual and steady development in institutional and civic libraries, but one which started from a low base and which by the end of the period was still a wholly different landscape from the kind of universally available infrastructure which we take for granted today. The previous century had been largely a time of dispersal and fragmentation of such libraries as had existed in the pre-Reformation world, mostly in ecclesiastical or educational places. By the beginning of the seventeenth the pieces were beginning to be picked up, but most English cathedrals and churches were bibliothecally moribund. The Bodleian Library, opened in 1602, expanded steadily and provided a well-acknowledged model of the benefits of creating such resources, but attempts to establish any kind of national library always failed.[23] Many colleges at Oxford and Cambridge built new and increasingly grand library spaces during the century, but the growth of their holdings depended primarily on gifts and bequests, not purchase.

For clergymen in London, the foundation of Sion College in 1630 created what became a significant accessible library for them.[24] Elsewhere, town libraries, which often had local clergy largely but not exclusively in mind, were gradually founded across the country, with accelerating enthusiasm as the century progressed. The town libraries of Ipswich (1599), Norwich (1608), and Bristol (1613) are the earliest examples; Archbishop Harsnett bequeathed his books to create a town library for Colchester in 1631, and in 1654 Humphrey Chetham established an unusually well-endowed public library for Manchester, distinguished by having dedicated funds for new acquisitions.[25] This is not an exhaustive list of such libraries from the first half of the century, but the pace gathered considerably

[22] A number of cathedral libraries were dispersed or partly destroyed in the 1640s, but many were protected, or ordered to be repurposed (e.g. Canterbury, Durham, St Paul's, York); the story is summarized in Sheila Hingley, 'Ecclesiastical libraries', in G. Mandelbrote and K. Manley (eds), *The Cambridge history of libraries in Britain and Ireland*, vol. 2 (Cambridge: Cambridge University Press, 2006), pp. 122–33. Although Lambeth Palace Library was exiled to Cambridge for a while, its value as a resource was recognized and defended as soon as Laud fell (p. 128).

[23] Thomas Kelly, *Early public libraries* (London: Library Association, 1966), 152.

[24] C. B. L. Barr and David Selwyn, 'Major ecclesiastical libraries', in E. S. Leedham-Green and T. Webber (eds), *The Cambridge history of libraries in Britain and Ireland*, vol. 1 (Cambridge: Cambridge University Press, 2006), pp. 363–99, 393–4.

[25] Kelly, *Early public libraries*, 68ff.

after the Restoration; Thomas Kelly noted that over a third of all the endowed libraries in Britain were founded between 1680 and 1720.[26] Part of this momentum was fuelled by the drive of men like Barnabas Oley and Thomas Bray to create working collections of up-to-date books for poor clergymen, in the interests of ensuring doctrinal soundness and the effective cure of souls.[27] A number of English cathedrals began the re-establishing of their libraries around the 1620s and 1630s but most suffered disruption during the Civil War period, and it was often post-Restoration philanthropy that effectively refounded them in the later decades of the century.[28]

All of this activity notwithstanding, it is clear that private libraries constituted a significant part of the country's overall book landscape throughout this period. The largest institutional libraries depended in no small part on having ingested great private ones—Lambeth Palace Library and the Bodleian being obvious examples—and most of them were built on private origins. The tradition of bequeathing books to colleges, universities, cathedrals, and parishes was a strong one throughout the century, taken for granted on both sides as a good thing to do for the benefit of posterity, the reputation of the donor, and the permanent stewarding of a cherished asset built up over a lifetime. In 1685, Chetham's Library held just under 3,000 volumes; ten years later, Trinity College, Cambridge had 3,750.[29] These would have been good-sized private libraries for their time, but not outstandingly so; Lazarus Seaman (d. 1675) had over 5,000 volumes recorded in the first book auction sale in England, in 1676, and the physician Francis Bernard (1627–98) had well over 10,000. Several writers have commented on the importance of early private libraries as resources for wider communities than the owners and their immediate families, arguing that they could sometimes function in effect as public or institutional libraries do today.[30]

Destruction and loss

While this book can, and does, use surviving books as a key part of its evidence base, it can only guess at the ones which no longer exist. The destruction and loss of books over time is a seriously under-explored area, but one which has a huge

[26] Ibid. 90.
[27] Michael Perkin, *A directory of the parochial libraries of the Church of England* (London: Bibliographical Society, 2004), 33–8.
[28] Hingley, 'Ecclesiastical libraries', 124–7.
[29] Matthew Yeo, *The acquisition of books by Chetham's Library, 1655–1700* (Leiden: Brill, 2011), 20; Philip Gaskell, *Trinity College Library: the first 150 years* (Cambridge: Cambridge University Press, 1980), 128.
[30] A number of such references are brought together in L. Gwynn, *The library of Sir Thomas Browne*, PhD thesis, Queen Mary College, University of London, 2016: https://qmro.qmul.ac.uk/xmlui/handle/123456789/25850 (accessed 1 Feb. 2019), pp. 100–101.

impact on the documentary testimony.[31] The theme is visited by Adam Smyth in one of the chapters in his book *Material texts in early modern England*, where he points out: 'if book destruction as censorship and punishment is one noisy tradition, then accidental book loss was another refrain throughout the early modern period.'[32] The only thing I would disagree with there is the word 'refrain': words like cacophony, deluge, cannon roar would be nearer the mark.

Throughout history, books have been destroyed because they were unwanted, worn out, superseded, recycled, or otherwise surplus to requirements. Numerous studies have been undertaken on survival rates for early printed books, particularly incunabula, where the average rate has been estimated as being as low as one in 500.[33] James Raven, while looking at the very large edition sizes of some popular books of the seventeenth century, refers to a school primer of 1676–7 known to have been printed in 84,000 copies, of which only one can be traced today.[34] Survival has often depended on that flow from the private to the public; as Paul Needham observed, 'books that do not enter institutional libraries often become rare so quickly that age or antiquity alone is not a very important factor—an eighteenth-century edition, being two or three hundred years younger than an incunable, does not for that reason alone have any greater chance of survival.'[35] The hunt for cheap or waste paper for a wide variety of uses, from wrapping groceries to furnishing the house of necessity, is also being increasingly documented, and Lord Chesterfield's advice on ways in which books can become multi-tasking devices is well known.[36]

In the seventeenth century there are some obvious high points of destruction, like the Great Fire of London, which consumed numerous libraries in 1666.[37] During the Civil War, many libraries were not only sequestered and redistributed, but destroyed as victims of military activity; the soldiers who plundered the home of the Devon clergyman Thomas Jones (d. *c*.1655) in 1645 were said to have

[31] There have been a number of published studies and collections of essays on the topic, but they tend to concentrate on well-known times of mass destruction through war or disaster; some are listed in the Bibliography on p. 304.

[32] Adam Smyth, *Material texts in early modern England* (Cambridge: Cambridge University Press, 2018), 60.

[33] Paul Needham, 'The late use of incunables and the paths of book survival', *Wolfenbütteler Notizen der Buchgeschichte* 29 (2004), pp. 35–59; for references to other work in this area, see David McKitterick, *The invention of rare books* (Cambridge: Cambridge University Press, 2018), 41.

[34] Raven, *Business of books*, 93.   [35] Needham, 'The late use', 40.

[36] E.g. Susan Morrison, *The literature of waste* (New York: Palgrave Macmillan, 2015); Amélie Junqua and Geoffrey Day, *Too good to waste: paper in eighteenth-century England* (forthcoming), and the growing list of resources returned by a Google search on fragmentology; Bonamy Dobrée (ed.), *The letters of Philip Dormer Stanhope, 4th Earl of Chesterfield*, vol. 3 (London: Eyre and Spottiswood, 1932), pp. 1066–7.

[37] Examples noted in the lists in the Appendix include Stephen Charnock (1628–80), Thomas Goodwin (1600–80), and the library of William Harvey (1578–1657) in the Royal College of Physicians. The Fire also, of course, consumed huge numbers of books not yet owned, waiting to be bought from the booksellers whose stock in the cellars of St Paul's Cathedral were 'consumed burning for a weeke': E. S. de Beer (ed.), *The diary of John Evelyn* (Oxford: Clarendon Press, 1955), vol. 3, 459.

defiled and torn his books into pieces, and scattered the leaves across the roads and fields.[38] The books of Henry King, Bishop of Chichester (1592–1669) were reputedly rent in pieces with torn leaves scattered over the church and pavement when the Cathedral was sacked.[39] John Riland (d. 1673), fellow of Magdalen College, Oxford, described how his study was broken up during the 1640s, with the loss of all his books and papers.[40]

We must recognize, though, that these particular times of concentrated destruction are only spikes in a graph of constant activity. Everyone has heard of the Great Fire of 1666, but fire was a constant hazard in seventeenth-century towns with wooden structures, and London was regularly burning. Quite apart from serious fires in 1633 (London Bridge) and 1676 (Southwark), buildings which burnt down or were fire-damaged during the century included the Globe and Fortune theatres (1613, 1621), the Banqueting House (1619), Exeter House (1627), the Theatre Royal (1672), the Navy Office (1673), the Middle Temple (1679), Gray's Inn (1680), and Whitehall Palace (1698).[41] Books are likely to have been lost in most if not all these conflagrations (some of Ashmole's collections were destroyed in the Middle Temple fire in 1679), but again, any specific and identifiable incidents are only drops in a large ocean. Books may cease to exist through fire, war, and natural disaster, but most of all by becoming simply unwanted and unsaleable.

There are many names on the list in the Appendix where we have evidence of library ownership, where we know from inventories, catalogues, or other evidence that someone had hundreds of books, but not a single one can be identified today. That may be because they did not mark their books—a common frustration of provenance research—but it may equally be because the books no longer survive. The quest for books owned by Shakespeare has a long history which has generated many forgeries, but despite the obvious rewards of such a literary El Dorado, nobody has ever convincingly discovered one.[42] There is no secondary evidence like book bills or probate inventories, but Shakespeare certainly read books, and it seems likely that he owned some. Why can we not find them? It may be that he was a non-inscriber, and his books are hiding in plain but undiscoverable sight in a library today. But it is equally likely that they disappeared into the trackless sea of second-hand books some time after his death, and did not end up with the minority that found themselves preserved into the twenty-first century. For the names on the list with catalogue-type evidence, but no books, we do at least know

---

[38] John Walker, *An attempt towards recovering an account of the . . . sufferings of the clergy* (London, 1714), pt 2, 280.

[39] Geoffrey Keynes, *A bibliography of Henry King* (London: Douglas Cleverdon, 1977), p. xvi.

[40] A. G. Matthews, *Walker revised* (Oxford: Clarendon Press, 1948), 365.

[41] John Richardson, *The annals of London* (London: Cassell, 2000), pp. 116–67. This year-by-year chronology of London also notes numerous floods, gunpowder explosions, and other disasters.

[42] Stephen Greenblatt, *Will in the world* (New York: Norton, 2005), 173. Stuart Kells, *Shakespeare's library* (Berkeley, CA: Counterpoint, 2018) adds no new discoveries.

something about what and how much was owned; for countless others, we have less—a stray inscription or bookplate, without being able to know what it was once a part of, or not even that. The landscape of early modern book history is a jigsaw whose pieces have mostly been thrown away over time, and we often have to use the pieces we have to infer what the whole picture once looked like.

The structure of this book: inclusions and exclusions

The following three chapters provide a summary overview of the kinds of libraries owned by various categories of people, beginning with the academic, professional, and middling to upper end of society where so much of the discoverable evidence of the time is concentrated. I then consider women and books during the seventeenth century, and the patterns of ownership found beyond the boundaries of the polite society covered in Chapter 2. The following chapter looks at the storage and housing of libraries, and the range of formats in which books were used.

The two final chapters focus on questions of motivation, which I see as a lode of intellectual enquiry running through this study. Why did people own books? A question to which many people will readily respond: they owned them because they wanted to read them, or at least thought they did, and they wanted continued access to the knowledge or ideas that they contain. But the picture is more complex than that, because books have been owned for a multiplicity, or perhaps a matrix, of reasons, which may include making a personal statement, furnishing a room, forming an investment, or creating a legacy for posterity. Books and libraries, 'and the manner in which they were displayed', as Lucy Gwynn observed, 'conveyed a set of messages to the viewer about the owner and his understanding of the world'.[43] The psychological drivers behind collecting have led people to acquire books more as collections than as libraries, seeking some kind of perceived completeness, or something bigger than anyone else's, to gather books as trophies, or as objects of taste and fashion. We know that trends in all these areas have changed over time. Chapter 6 focuses on books beyond their textual utility, to ask how far people owned books partly or solely as objects of display, as projections of their wealth and status. The final chapter look at attitudes to collecting in the seventeenth century, compared with those that came later, and asks whether the terminology that we commonly use in this field is appropriate. It surveys a range of evidence including bindings, manuscripts, subject collecting, and the relationship between libraries and museums.

---

[43] Lucy Gwynn, 'The design of the English domestic library in the seventeenth century', *Library Trends* 69 (2011), pp. 43–53, 44.

My approach to content analysis is based more on subjects than on formats, as there is nothing unusual in finding a mixture of printed and manuscript material at this time in libraries of all kinds. This might encompass pamphlets and ephemeral items, as well as more substantial ones. As Harold Love observed, the fact 'that many of the texts known to an educated English reader in the seventeenth century would have been encountered in manuscript rather than in print is hardly news'.[44] Since the publication of his landmark book in 1993, numerous studies have appeared which flesh out our understanding of the extent of scribal publication in the early modern period, including the circulation of literary and political works in manuscript forms.[45] The 'paper books' which appear so commonly in inventories will often have included notebooks and commonplace books, or manuscript compilations of professionally relevant texts, which were all part of what made a library useful to its owner.

Other angles to this subject could be brought in, and might be expected, but are well covered elsewhere. My focus is on the history of ownership, rather than reading; I have not sought to delve into the various forms of advice on the study and absorption of books which were produced, or the evidence of their take-up via commonplace books and marginalia, but there is a plentiful literature in this area which I have selectively included in the Bibliography. There is clearly a dynamic interplay between ownership, and the book trade, but I have no new discoveries to add to the plentiful work published by those who are the specialists in this area, and to whom any enquirers can more effectively turn. The mapping of the printing industry and its outputs, and of bookselling, has a long history. As David McKitterick has recently pointed out, the weakness in our armoury lies with our knowledge of the second-hand trade in the early modern period, where the paucity of documentary evidence can make it easy to overlook the fact that there were always more pre-owned books in circulation than there were new ones.[46] Once printed auction and retail sale catalogues come along in the last quarter of the seventeenth century we have more to work with, but for the first three quarters of that century we have only snippets which have often been referred to, but rarely augmented. It is well known that a list of around 40 booksellers who 'deale in old libraryes' was drawn up for the Privy Council in 1628, and that at the other end of the century John Bagford told us that the bookseller Christopher Bateman 'hath had more libraries go through his hands within this twenty years than all those at Paris put together', but in between we

[44] Harold Love, *Scribal publication in seventeenth-century England* (Oxford: Clarendon Press, 1993), 3.

[45] Most recently, e.g. Noah Millstone, *Manuscript circulation and the invention of politics in early modern England* (Cambridge: Cambridge University Press, 2016), or Angus Vine, *Miscellaneous order: manuscript culture and the early modern organization of knowledge* (Oxford: Oxford University Press, 2019).

[46] McKitterick, *The invention of rare books*, 33.

largely have a vacuum.[47] What we know, or can safely infer, is that throughout the century there must have been no end of transactions involving second-hand books and whole libraries, many of them generating some kinds of lists, accounts, or other documentation, whose records have disappeared into the void. All that remains is a peppering of prices, notes, and booksellers' codes spread around old books the world over whose systematic mapping and decipherment appears to offer a path only to fools and mad (to borrow from Swift), though the challenge may one day be taken up. But not here, or by me.

Key conclusions

A number of wider observations emerge from this book, which might usefully be summarized here. The next chapter notes, unsurprisingly, how libraries grew in size (both the biggest and the average ones) as time progressed, and emphasizes the proportion of theological material (broadly defined) which commonly constituted so many academic or professional libraries. Devotional and doctrinal books will also be extensively found on the shelves of the gentry and aristocracy, but perhaps in smaller concentrations, alongside a range of more recreational or practical books, embracing languages and intellectual horizons which reflect their education and their interests. Breadth of subject coverage is usually a feature of any seventeenth-century library of any size, whatever the owner's background. It is also observable that the average proportion of English-language material, and English-printed books, steadily increases as the century progresses. At the beginning of the seventeenth century, a scholarly or clerical library would almost certainly be numerically dominated by Latin books printed on the Continent, but by the end of the century the ratios might be nearer half-and-half English to non-English.

Much of the documentation that we have on libraries of this time relates to male owners, but the possession and reading of books by women was also very widespread, and neither remarkable nor subversive. Well-educated ladies might have books in French, Italian, or other European languages, but most volumes owned or given to women will be found to be in English, much less commonly in Latin. Evidence of this pattern turns up very commonly in contemporary wills. The extent to which some of the products of the book trade were directly targeted towards women has not commonly been recognized.

Similarly, book ownership across a wide sweep of society, in rural, less educated, and less wealthy households, was more ubiquitous than documentary

---

[47] W. W. Greg (ed.), *A companion to Arber* (Oxford: Clarendon Press, 1967), pp. 240–41; 'An account of the several libraries public and private, in and about London... from Mr. John Bagford's collections', *The Gentleman's Magazine* (Dec. 1816), 510.

sources might suggest, but is hard to capture because the evidence is so dispersed. Books often remained within particular localities over many generations, and there is a noticeable pattern of the movement of serious and relatively expensive books from wealthy households to humbler ones over time. Many better-off homes would have had studies or closets, small shelved spaces where books could be both stored and read; but the drive to create larger library rooms in grander houses is detectable from the beginning of the century, and a standard feature of any such property by the end of the Stuart period. Although we tend to think of libraries as rows of bound books standing on shelves, there is manifold evidence to remind us that they were actually circulated and used in a variety of cheaper or more transitory formats. Large numbers of stitched pamphlets often sat alongside leather-bound volumes in seventeenth-century libraries.

There have always been multiple possible reasons for owning books; they do furnish a room, and there is plentiful evidence of people spending more money on their books than they needed to in order to have functioning texts. Many seventeenth-century books incorporate various ways of marking or binding which clearly make a statement about their owners, but the teasing out of books for show rather than for use is rarely a simple either/or kind of exercise. There are examples of aristocratic owners whose books indicate, via their material characteristics, that they were intended at least as much for purposes of display and the creation of an impression as they were for reading. Unread books—revealed as such by their physical condition—invite us to ask why they were thus neglected. We should go on to ask whether 'neglected' is an appropriate word; we tend to assume that books are for reading, and that other uses are secondary or frivolous, but if a book fulfils its intended function through its material rather than verbal qualities, it is surely not neglected?

Many of the people whose activities around owning books are described in these pages are regularly referred to as book collectors. We are familiar, today, with the idea of book collecting, which carries with it a set of broadly understood ideas and values, but at least some of that mindset would be alien to formers of private libraries in the seventeenth century. I believe we should avoid the 'c' word in this early modern context, unless there is good reason not to, and refer to owners rather than collectors. Similarly, although much of our book-historical research focuses on the history of reading, and the wish to explore the reader experience as the key interface between a book and its owner, the 'r' word is too narrow to embrace the totality of the relationship between books and people. We should talk about owners and users, rather than collectors and readers.

2

Libraries for the studious, professional, and wealthy

Of the 1,370 or so private libraries listed in the Appendix, around 1,150, or a little under 90 per cent, are those of academics, clergymen, professional people like physicians or lawyers, or of the wealthier classes of society who constituted its governing layer, at local or national level. Many of the latter, while also devoting time to the running of estates, were magistrates, Members of Parliament, states-men, or courtiers. All of these men—and, in the seventeenth century, the gender-specificity is historically accurate—were given a book-based education to develop their fitness for their roles, understood the importance of books as quarries of knowledge and communicators of new ideas, and needed access to both those things in pursuit of their activities and their social interactions. They were commonly book acquirers throughout their lives, from their student days onwards, building up their libraries as adjuncts and tools for their working careers, or for recreation, and the expansion of intellectual horizons, in the spaces in between. This chapter seeks to present and summarize trends and typical charac-teristics of these kinds of libraries throughout the seventeenth century.

The size of libraries

In the majority of cases, we do not have precise figures for the sizes of these libraries. Unless there are detailed inventories, or the books survive in one place, it is usually impossible to know. The existence of sale catalogues in the last quarter of the period adds significantly to this kind of evidence base, but there are numerous caveats even then because many sales combined books from multiple sources without distinction, or may constitute only a part of one library. There are plenty of examples where a sale catalogue mentions a subsequent portion to be exposed to sale at a later date, for which no catalogue survives. There are also the challenges which bedevil all kinds of lists, probate inventories as well as sale catalogues, of distinguishing between titles and volumes, estimating the extent of bundles of pamphlets, knowing whether any books were taken out by friends and family before any listing was begun, and of interpreting throw-away notes about 'sundry other volumes'. All of which notwithstanding, for at least a fifth of the list in the Appendix, it is possible to know in round numbers how big the libraries were—a large enough sample from which to draw out some trends.

Book Ownership in Stuart England: The Lyell Lectures, 2018. David Pearson, Oxford University Press (2021).
© David Pearson.
DOI: 10.1093/oso/9780198870128.003.0002

Unsurprisingly, libraries got bigger as the century progressed, as regards both potential maxima and averages. In the first quarter of the seventeenth century, the library of Richard Bancroft, Archbishop of Canterbury (1544–1610), was the largest of its day at around 6,000 volumes, but he was given a head start with 2,000 passed on by his predecessor John Whitgift.[1] More remarkable perhaps is the achievement of the Yorkshire clergyman William Crashawe (1572–1626), whose claim in 1613 that his library of 4,000 books was one of the most complete libraries in Europe was not unreasonable, at least in a British context.[2] At this time, any library counted in four figures was unusually big and there are not many documented examples; Toby Matthew (1546–1628) left 3,000 to York Minster in 1628, via his widow, while Philip Bisse (1541?–1613) gave about 2,000 to Wadham College, Oxford shortly before his death.[3] The library of 1,500 books of Sir Thomas Knyvett (d. 1618) was uncommonly large for its time for a gentry library, and the 300 owned by his East Anglian contemporary Sir Nathaniel Bacon of Stiffkey (1549–1622) was more typical of those kinds of shelves then.[4] Libraries counted in the tens rather than the hundreds are typical of the book lists around the turn of the seventeenth century in Elisabeth Leedham-Green's Cambridge inventories, and the collections of the Oxford academics Walter Browne and John English, who both died in 1613 with a little over 500 books each, are substantial academic libraries of their day.[5]

By the middle of the century it was possible to have libraries of 10,000 books or therabouts, at the upper end of the scale, as with the Cambridge head of house Richard Holdsworth (d. 1649), the peer Edward, 2nd Viscount Conway (1594–1655), and John Selden (1584–1654), whose 8,000 or so books in the Bodleian constitute not quite his entire library.[6] But there were not many on that scale; Robert Ashley (1565–1641) gave 5,000 books to the Middle Temple in

[1] James Carley, 'The libraries of Archbishops Whitgift and Bancroft', *The Book Collector* 62 (2013), pp. 209–28.

[2] P. J. Wallis, 'The library of William Crashawe', *Transactions of the Cambridge Bibliographical Society* 2 (1956), pp. 213–28.

[3] C. B. L. Barr, 'The Minster Library', in G. Aylmer and R. Cant (eds), *A history of York Minster* (Oxford: Oxford University Press, 1977), pp. 487–538, 500–502; William Poole, *Wadham College books in the age of John Wilkins* (Oxford: Wadham College, 2014), pp. 31–7.

[4] David McKitterick, *The library of Sir Thomas Knyvett of Ashwellthorpe* (Cambridge: Cambridge University Library, 1978); R. J. Fehrenbach, 'Sir Roger Townshend's books', in R. J. Fehrenbach and E. S. Leedham-Green (eds), *Private libraries in Renaissance England*, vol. 1 (Binghamton, NY: Medieval and Renaissance Texts and Studies, 1992), pp. 79–135, 79–83.

[5] E. S. Leedham-Green, *Books in Cambridge inventories* (Cambridge: Cambridge University Press, 1986); J. Black, 'Walter Brown', in R. J. Fehrenbach and J. Black (eds), *Private libraries in Renaissance England*, vol. 7 (Tempe: Arizona Center for Medieval and Renaissance Studies, 2009), pp. 113–209; W. Costin, 'The inventory of John English', *Oxoniensia* 11–12 (1946–7), pp. 106–16.

[6] J. C. T. Oates, *Cambridge University Library: a history... to the copyright act of Queen Anne* (Cambridge: Cambridge University Press, 1986), pp. 314–48; I. Roy, 'The libraries of Edward, 2nd Viscount Conway, and others', *Bulletin of the Institute of Historical Research* 41(103) (1968), pp. 35–47; Sandra Naiman, 'John Selden', in W. Baker (ed.), *Pre-nineteenth century British book collectors* (Detroit, MI: Gale, 1999), pp. 297–306.

1641, Henry Lucas (d. 1663) gave 4,000 to Cambridge in 1663.[7] The library of Robert Burton (1577–1640), divided between the Bodleian and Christ Church, was a little under 1,800.[8] There are many more libraries counted in the hundreds not thousands; there are numerous academic libraries in that range, and the schoolmaster Thomas Hayne (1582–1645) could give about 600 books to Leicester Town Library in 1645.[9] Archbishop Samuel Harsnett (1561–1631) gave 900 books to Colchester, and Sir John Kedermister (d. 1631), who spent years building up a collection to create a vicar's library for Langley Marish, did so with only 300.[10] John Holles, 2nd Earl of Clare (1595–1666), listed about 500 books in his possession in the 1650s.[11]

After the Restoration, opportunities and aspirations to build libraries grew, and at least thirty can be identified that ran to four figures, for people who died between 1670 and 1690; there were certainly more. The 1686 sale catalogue of Arthur Annesley, Earl of Anglesey (1614–86), includes over 6,500 lots, and there were over 4,000 books at Penshurst Place when Robert Sidney, 2nd Earl of Leicester, died there in 1677.[12] John Cosin, Bishop of Durham (1595–1672), endowed his library in Durham in 1669 with about 5,500 books.[13] The ownership of collections of this size was noticeably spreading outwards at this time, across sectors of society, and the library of Richard Smith, whom we would now classify as a civil servant and who died in 1675, was reckoned to comprise 8,000 titles.[14] Two of the largest libraries to go through the first decade of book auctions in England belonged to Nonconformist clergy—Lazarus Seaman (d. 1675), the very first auction in 1676, with over 5,600 lots, and Thomas Jacombe (1624?–87) ten years later, with 5,007.[15] The judge John Godolphin (1617–78) had around 2,000 books, as did the physician Nathan Paget (1615–79) who died the following year.[16]

Turning the corner into the eighteenth century, at the very end of the Stuart period John Moore, Bishop of Ely (1646–1714), pushed the boundaries with his celebrated collection of around 30,000 books, now one of the glories of Cambridge

---

[7] K. Whitlock, 'The Robert Ashley founding bequest to the Middle Temple Library', *Sederi* 14 (2004), pp. 153–75; Oates, *Cambridge University Library*, 349–67.

[8] Nicholas Kiessling, *The library of Robert Burton* (Oxford: Oxford Bibliographical Society, 1988).

[9] C. Deedes et al., *The Old Town Hall library of Leicester* (Oxford: Corporation of Leicester, 1919), pp. xvi–xvii.

[10] Gordon Goodwin, *A catalogue of the Harsnett Library* (London: Richard Amer, 1888); Jane Francis, 'The Kedermister Library', *Records of Buckimnghamshire* 36 (1996), pp. 62–85.

[11] University of Nottingham, Portland MSS Pw V 4, 185–92 (and see below, p. 32).

[12] *Bibliotheca Anglesiana, sive catalogus variorum librorum* (London, 1686); Germaine Warkentin et al., *The library of the Sidneys of Penshurst Place* (Toronto: University of Toronto Press, 2013), 7.

[13] A. I. Doyle, 'John Cosin (1595–1672) as a library maker', *The Book Collector* 24 (1975), pp. 25–32.

[14] *Bibliotheca Smithiana: sive catalogus librorum*, London, 1682; see also David McKitterick, *The invention of rare books* (Cambridge: Cambridge University Press, 2018), pp. 106–7.

[15] *Catalogus variorum et insigniorum librorum…Lazare Seaman* (London, 1676); *Bibliotheca Jacombiana, sive catalogus variorum librorum* (London, 1687).

[16] *Catalogus variorum et insignium librorum…D. Johannis Godolphin…et D. Owen Phillips* (London, 1678); *Bibliotheca medica viri clarissimi Nathanis Paget* (London, 1681).

University Library via the munificence of George I.[17] Other five-figure libraries, reckoned to have been around 10,000 volumes strong, were those of the physician Francis Bernard (1627–98), auctioned in the year of his death, and Edward Stillingfleet, Bishop of Worcester (1635–99), whose printed books went to help found Marsh's Library in Dublin, and whose manuscripts went to Harley.[18] But by this time it was possible for substantial four-figure libraries to be assembled by people from a wide range of backgrounds: clergymen like George Ashwell, rector of Hanwell (1612–94), whose library of about 3,000 books was auctioned in Oxford in 1694; gentry families with literary leanings, like Sir William Boothby (1638?–1707) who talked of his books as the joy of his life, and who had about 6,000. Even a surgeon (though admittedly serjeant-surgeon to the Queen), Charles Bernard (1650–1711), could own over 3,500.[19] Thomas Plume, archdeacon of Rochester (1630–1704), built up a library of nearly 8,000 books to leave to his native town in Essex.[20] At the same time, countless academic and professional libraries of several hundred books would be found in studies up and down the country, and collections like that could be enough to set off a parish library, like the 300 books left by John Okes (d. 1710) to his parish of Wotton under Edge, or the 440 given to King's Lynn by Thomas Thurlin (d. 1714), vicar of Gaywood.[21]

By way of comparison between England and Continental Europe, it may be noted that these statistics, and the pattern of growth in averages and at the larger end of the scale, are broadly in step with what might be found on both sides of the English Channel, though the largest European libraries of their day commonly exceeded their English equivalents. The French statesman Jacques-Auguste de Thou (1553–1617) had over 8,000 titles in about 5,600 volumes, roughly similar in size to Archbishop Bancroft's library.[22] The 40,000 books of Cardinal Jules Mazarin (1602–61) certainly constituted a larger library than anything accumulated by any Englishman of his generation, and the same can be said of the library of the Austrian nobleman Joachim von Windhag (1600–1678), estimated to be around 30,000 volumes.[23] This was the approximate size of John Moore's library

[17] David McKitterick, *Cambridge University Library: a history*, vol. 2: *The eighteenth and nineteenth centuries* (Cambridge: Cambridge University Press, 1986), pp. 47–152.

[18] *A catalogue of the library of the late learned Dr. Francis Bernard*, London, 1698; W. N. Osborough, '6 Anne, chapter 19', in M. McCarthy and A. Simmons (eds), *Marsh's Library: a mirror on the world* (Dublin: Four Courts Press, 2009), pp. 39–61, 45–7.

[19] *Catalogus librorum tam antiquorum quam recentium in omni facultate* (Oxford, 1696); Peter Beal, 'My books are the great joy of my life', *The Book Collector* 46 (1997), pp. 350–78; *Bibliotheca Bernardiana: or, a catalogue of the library of the late Charles Bernard* (London, 1711).

[20] David Pearson, 'Thomas Plume's library in its contemporary context', in Christopher Thornton and Tony Doe (eds), *Dr Thomas Plume, 1630–1704: his life and legacies* (forthcoming).

[21] Michael Perkin, *A directory of the parochial libraries of the Church of England* (London: Bibliographical Society, 2004), pp. 402, 254–5.

[22] Ingird de Smet, *Thuanus: the making of Jacques-Auguste de Thou* (Geneva: Droz, 2006).

[23] P. Gasnaulty, 'De la bibliothèque de Mazarin à la bibliothèque Mazarine', in C. Jolly (ed.), *Histoire des bibliothèques françaises. Les bibliothèques sous l'Ancien Régime* (Paris: Promodis, 1989), pp. 167–80; L. Buźas, *German library history, 800–1945* (Jefferson, NC: McFarland, 1986), 234, 234.

some decades later; that of the German classical scholar Johann Albert Fabricius (1668–1736), thought to comprise 32,000 volumes, was a comparable European library of Moore's own generation.[24]

Contents

What did these libraries contain? This may, with good reason, look like territory where generalization is dangerous, but there are trends and common patterns which can usefully be observed. Writing about private libraries in an article in *The Library* in 2012, I said,

> we have a broad understanding of the shape taken by many seventeenth-century libraries of any size, of the kinds of things we are not surprised to find in the collection of a cleric, an academic, or a gentleman. At least half its contents would comprise what we would call theology of some shape or form, but it would otherwise be wide ranging as regards recorded knowledge, and would embrace some coverage of history, literature, geography and travel, classics, science, medicine, and law.[25]

After further analysis, I would say that remains true for clergymen and academics, while for gentlemen a quarter to a half of theological content is a common pattern. For everyone, I would continue to emphasize the idea of a spread of subjects; vicars didn't own just divinity books, physicians didn't own just medical books, country squires didn't own just plays and books on farriery. It makes sense in the context of their ideas about the breadth of learning needed to make a well-rounded man, honed through Renaissance thinking so that 'by the seventeenth century the idea of the general scholar had reached its apogee... Educators championed this model of education, insisting on the need to survey the vast boundaries of learning'.[26] It was only towards the end of the century that the growing size of those boundaries led to a growing acceptance of depth rather than breadth, of a pragmatic need for selectivity over comprehensiveness.[27]

---

[24] Ibid. 227.

[25] David Pearson, 'The English private library in the seventeenth century', *The Library*, 7th ser. 13 (2012), pp. 379–99, 382–3.

[26] Mordechai Feingold, 'The humanities', in N. Tyacke (ed.), *The history of the University of Oxford*, vol. 4: *Seventeenth-century Oxford* (Oxford: Clarendon Press, 1997), pp. 211–357, 219.

[27] Ibid. 238–9.

Clerical, academic, and professional libraries

Some years ago I published an analysis of the libraries of English bishops from the first four decades of the seventeenth century, which conform to those norms.[28] Where we know the contents, it is typical to find theological works comprising at least half the titles, embracing the biblical, liturgical, patristic, doctrinal, controversial, and devotional. The combined libraries of Archbishops Bancroft and Abbot contained a little under 60 per cent of theological material, with a further 19 per cent classified as history, 11 per cent as law, and the remaining 12 per cent embracing a range of subjects including classics, literature, philosophy, and geography.[29] Other episcopal libraries whose contents are known and which provide similar evidence, give or take some variations under the broader umbrella, are those of Francis Dee (d. 1638), Arthur Lake (1569–1626), and Toby Matthew (1548–1626).[30] The works which turn up repeatedly in these kinds of libraries, apart from Bibles and liturgies, are the writings of the Church Fathers, classical authors, Biblical commentators (both Roman Catholic and Protestant), and contributions to contemporary doctrinal debates.[31] Beyond this inevitable core these men would broaden their thinking from a wide range of publications reflecting their available heritage of knowledge and ideas; Abbot owned works by Sidney, Spenser, Drayton, Montaigne, Petrarch, Tasso, and Boccaccio, while Lake's gift to New College, Oxford, included scientific and mathematical books, as well as a set of Hakluyt's *Voyages*.

The smaller library of a little over 300 books assembled by Sir John Kedermister (d. 1631), with the deliberate intention of creating a working toolkit for the clergy of Langley Marish, is almost entirely theological, with strong holdings of patristics and medieval theologians. Continental Reformed writers are well represented, like Calvin, Chemnitz, Luther, Pareus, and Zanchius, but there are also numerous volumes of Biblical commentaries by the Jesuit Jean de Lorin. The handful of non-theological texts in this library include a manuscript pharmacopoeia, Johann Scapula's Greek and Latin dictionary, some compilations of aphorisms, Holinshed's *Chronicle*, and Gower's *De confessio amantis*.

Turning to the other end of the century, the 8,000 books assembled by Thomas Plume and given to Maldon in 1704 display similar proportions: about 65 per cent are theological, with 15 per cent history and current affairs, 4 per cent literature and classics, 1 per cent lexicons and philology, but in this case much less law. What Plume had instead was nearly a tenth of the whole made up of science, mathematics, medicine, and astronomy, reflecting partly his interests and the

---

[28] David Pearson, 'The libraries of English bishops, 1600–1640', *The Library*, 6th ser. 14 (1992), pp. 221–57.
[29] Ann Cox-Johnson, 'Lambeth Palace Library 1610–1664', *Transactions of the Cambridge Bibliographical Society* 2 (1955), pp. 105–26.
[30] Pearson, 'English bishops', 227, 248.   [31] Ibid. 228.

growth of publication in these fields during the seventeenth century.[32] We can look at many printed sale catalogues of the last quarter of the century and see broadly similar distributions; the large library of the Nonconformist Thomas Jacombe, which went under the hammer in 1687, was subdivided as theology 68 per cent, Latin miscellaneous 21 per cent, English miscellaneous 11 per cent. The books of the clergyman George Ashwell, also mentioned earlier, were classified as 53 per cent theology, 27 per cent Latin miscellaneous, 14 per cent English miscellaneous, and 6 per cent tracts, in 1694; another rector's library, that of William Bassett (1645?–96), auctioned two years later, was 50 per cent theology, 24 per cent Latin miscellaneous, 26 per cent English miscellaneous.[33]

Drawing distinctions between clerical and academic libraries at this time can be difficult, or artificial, because the spheres were so closely connected and men moved between them with a foot on each side. Many of the parochial clergy were apppointed to those livings as a natural progression from years spent as a student and then a fellow of a college, and the more senior figures in the landscape commonly held multiple positions simultaneously. Humphrey Tyndall (d. 1614) had one of those parallel academic and clerical careers which was so common; he progressed through the degree structure at Cambridge from Bachelor to Doctor between 1567 and 1582, became a fellow of Pembroke College from 1567, and was elected President of Queens' College in 1579, a post he held for the rest of his life. He was Vice-Chancellor of the University in 1585. He was also vicar of Soham, archdeacon of Stafford, a prebendary of Lichfield and of Southwell, and dean of Ely, most of these being positions he held in plurality for many years until his death. He was buried in Ely but left his books to Queens', where he had his main residence in the President's Lodge, and where his books and other possessions were inventoried.[34] His 90 titles in about twice as many volumes were almost entirely theological, with a noted predominance of Calvinist writers once the Bibles and patristic texts were accounted for.

Richard Holdsworth (1590–1649) began his career with a similar progression up the academic ladder at Cambridge, Bachelor in 1611 and Doctor in 1637.[35] As a fellow of St John's (from 1613), his skills as a tutor gained him much respect, and the professorship of divinity at Gresham College (1629). He was equally regarded as a preacher, and while his main church base was as rector of St Peter-le-Poer, London (from 1623), he was also a prebendary of Lincoln and archdeacon of

---

[32] Pearson, 'Thomas Plume's Library'.

[33] *Bibliotheca Bassetiana: or a catalogue of Greek, Latin and English books* (London, 1697).

[34] J. Venn and J. A. Venn, *Alumni Cantabrigienses...from the earliest times to 1751*, vol. 4 (Cambridge: Cambridge University Press, 1927), 284; Leedham-Green, *Books in Cambridge inventories*, 569–72.

[35] P. Collinson (3 Jan. 2008), 'Holdsworth, Richard (1590–1649), Church of England clergyman and college head', *Oxford Dictionary of National Biography*. Retrieved 19 Dec. 2018 from: http://www.oxforddnb.com/view/10.1093/ref:odnb/9780198614128.001.0001/odnb-9780198614128-e-13499; Venn and Venn, *Alumni*, vol. 2, 391.

Huntingdon. He died in his London rectory, but most of his books were kept in Cambridge. He was master of Emmanuel College, Cambridge from 1637 and if his career had not been disrupted by the ejections of the 1640s he would have died combining his college mastership with the deanery of Worcester, to which he was appointed in a notional and futile way shortly before his death. He owned what was possibly the largest private library in England of his generation, around 10,000 books, whose fate after his death became a legal tussle between Emmanuel College and the University Library, settled in the latter's favour. A listing of his books at that time includes a numerical summary by subject breakdown, showing that familiar pattern: just over half, 56 per cent, count as theological, with 13 per cent history, 9 per cent 'philology' (a catch-all including literature, classics, and anything 'which the classifiers had failed to place more suitably elsewhere'), and smaller percentages of law, geography, medicine, and mathematics.[36] 'Libri controversiarum' constitute the largest single section of the theological books (nearly 1,000 works), and there were significant holdings of Church Fathers (656 'patres'); as with the libraries of the bishops of the earlier part of the century, it is noteworthy that commentaries and scholarly theological works by Roman Catholic authors are strongly represented, with 'scriptores pont[ificales]' outnumbering 'scriptores prot[estantes]' (952 to 619). Although there can be no doubting the subject areas where Holdsworth would have seen the core and foundation of his library to have been, Oates's overview of its contents includes many authors and titles more familiar to modern audiences, including Bacon, Camden, Chaucer, Fabyan, Holinshed, Montaigne, Ortelius, Sidney, Spenser, and Vesalius.

This was one of the largest private libraries of its day, and its breadth and comprehensiveness can hardly be taken as representative. A more typical example of a mid-century clerical/academic library might be the books of Mark Frank (1612–64), who spent much of his life associated with Pembroke College, Cambridge, where he was student, fellow, administrator, and ultimately master between his matriculation in 1627 and his death, although his career was interrupted by the Civil War.[37] He was ejected from his fellowship in 1643, spent the Interregnum in unknown circumstances, and was rewarded for royalist loyalty at the Restoration not only with the mastership of the college but also with several ecclesiastical preferments. Apart from a group of books by Cornelius a Lapide (a Jesuit author whose Biblical commentaries were greatly respected by seventeenth-century theologians of all denominations, and whose writings will be found extensively owned in Anglican personal and institutional libraries) left to a clerical friend, Frank bequeathed all his books to Pembroke College, where they are listed

[36] Oates, *Cambridge University Library*, 304–10, 327–31.
[37] K. Stevenson (21 May 2009), 'Frank, Mark (bap. 1612, d. 1664), college head and theologian', *Oxford Dictionary of National Biography*. Retrieved 20 Jan. 2019 from: http://www.oxforddnb.com/view/10.1093/ref:odnb/9780198614128.001.0001/odnb-9780198614128-e-10082.

in the donors' book.[38] There are 360 items on the list, representing over 500 actual volumes when multi-volume sets are taken into account. As always with such lists, we need to bear in mind the possibility that some books did not make it into the institutional donation, or that some books were lost along the way (often an issue for those who suffered ejection or sequestration during the 1640s). There is however no such lament for lost books in Frank's will, of the kind that can be found in numerous other wills of this time, and being unmarried he had no wife or children to take into account. Its middling size, for the period, and contents suggest that what he left in 1664 can be taken to be the bulk of the library that he built up over preceding decades and that he managed to keep together through his years in the wilderness.[39]

Frank's library was predominantly theological in content, with only about a quarter of the 360 items describable as something else. The theology included numerous Bibles and liturgical books (including the Roman Catholic and Greek Orthodox Churches), patristic writings, and a range of doctrinal, controversial, and devotional titles such as would be found in countless other similar libraries of his generation. His shelves were not weighed down by the kinds of sixteenth-century Reformed Protestant authors who commonly feature in the libraries of those of a generation or so earlier, like Humphrey Tyndall or the bishops of James I's time, and there is a noticeable absence of (for example) Bucer, Bullinger, Melanchthon, Walther, and Zanchius.[40] His Calvinist theology was represented instead through the lens of early seventeenth-century English writers like John Boys, George Downame, and John King. He had books on the doctrinal controversies of the earlier part of the century (proceedings of the Synod of Dort, titles relating to Arminianism), and numerous books by doctrinal theologians of his own time, like John Bramhall, Edward Stillingfleet, and Herbert Thorndike. He had sets of sermons by Anthony Farindon, Robert Sanderson, Jeremy Taylor, and other well-known contemporary publishers in that genre, and his devotional works included popular bestsellers like *The whole duty of man* and *The gentleman's calling* as well as Sir Richard Baker's *Meditations* and works by Henry Hammond. He had a copy of the 1649 English version of the Koran, and a 1621 Cologne edition of the *Summa theologia* of St Thomas Aquinas. A number of his historical books had an obvious relevance to the study of the church, like Fuller's *Holy warre* and an English translation of Josephus.

---

[38] Pembroke College, Cambridge MS LC.II.77, available in full-text digital facsimile at https://cudl. lib.cam.ac.uk/view/MS-LC-II-00077/314 (accessed 19 Jan. 2019). Frank's donation is on pp. 279–88 and 313–19 of the digital version. Frank's will is The National Archives PROB 11/314/176.

[39] Examples of those whose wills note the loss of books during the 1640s and 1650s include John Hales and Robert Mapletoft.

[40] All writers who were noted as commonly owned by early 17th-c. bishops: Pearson, 'The libraries of English bishops', 228. Calvin (the other name noted there as regularly owned) was held by Frank in an edition of his Biblical harmony, and his commentary on the Pentateuch.

Beyond theology, Frank had books on medicine, law, and history, besides works of classical authors and miscellaneous other titles. His ancient texts included Lucian, Pliny the Elder, Plutarch, Quintilian, Seneca, and Terence (though not Cicero, Horace, Ovid, Tacitus, Virgil, and others who might be expected). For medicine he had a copy of the works of Hippocrates, Bartholin's *Anatomia*, the *Schola Salernitana*, the *English physitians guide* and a few other works; for law he could turn to Pulton's *Statutes*, *Parsons law* by William Hughes, Richard Zouch's *Elementa iurisprudentiae*, and a copy of the *Corpus iuris canonici*. He had Montagu, Selden, and Spelman on the subject of tithes. His historical titles, beyond those specifically focused on ecclesiastical history, included Samuel Daniel on English history, Guicciardini on Italian, and Edward, Lord Herbert's *Life and reign of King Henry the eighth*. He also had an extensive set of the small-format histories and geographical overviews of many European countries, published by the Elzevirs, summarized in the donors' register with a one-line entry for 'Republiq. books 46 vol'. He had a number of books on the history and affairs of his own times, including William Younger's *Brief view of the late troubles and confusions in England* (1660), Peter Heylyn's *Observations on the historie of the reign of King Charles* (1656), and Thomas Bayly's *Royal charter granted unto kings* (1649).

Frank owned Hobbes's *De cive*, in its original Latin version, though not *Leviathan*; he also had a copy of Seth Ward's critique of Hobbes, *In Thomae Hobbii philosophiam exercitatio epistolica* (1656). His coverage of the natural world was enhanced with a copy of Athanasius Kircher's *Mundus subterraneus*, and he also had Kircher's survey of *China illustrata monumentis*. A number of his books might be categorized as a ready-reference section, including John Rider's *Dictionary*, Henry Spelman's *Villare Anglicum: or a view of the townes of England*, Henry Phillipps's *The purchasers pattern. Shewing the true value of any land or houses... Also new tables of interest*, and a small group of almanacs. He had very little on his shelves which we would construe as literature, except George Herbert's *Remains* (1652) and that ubiquitous seventeenth-century fable found again and again in libraries of the time, John Barclay's *Argenis*.

Overall, Frank's books provide a fairly representative example of the kind of library which might be found mid-century on the shelves of many successful academics and clerics. At around 500 volumes it was significantly bigger than Tyndall's (a college head of the beginning of the century), but less than half the size of that of his next successor but one as master of Pembroke, Nathaniel Coga, who had over 1,500 books when he died in 1693. Around half of Frank's books were in English, with 45 per cent in Latin and a small smattering of French and Greek; at the beginning of the century, the proportion of Latin titles would be significantly higher. It has already been noted that there are some standard authors missing from Frank's list and there are various titles beyond the classical ones which we might have expected to find; he would surely have read not only Cicero but also Hooker's *Laws of ecclesiastical politie*, or writings of Francis Bacon, neither of which feature in his list. He did own Kenelm Digby's *Two treatises... of... the nature of bodies*, which is his nearest match to evolving seventeenth-century scientific philosophy.

It is quite likely that Pembroke exercised the liberty expressed in Frank's will to sell or exchange some of his books, if they were duplicates, so the list in the donors' book may not be his complete library. However, if we stand back and observe the contents that are recorded, we can see that it would have provided him with a fairly comprehensive view of what he would have felt he needed to know. His core Biblical, liturgical, and patristic texts were all provided, with an extensive apparatus of doctrinal interpretation from several generations. His devotional works would help to keep him on the straight and narrow road to salvation, and if he needed legal or medical information he had a small but well-chosen selection of key texts. His historical and geographical books are more restricted than might be found in a wealthier or more cosmopolitan household, and it is easy to think of other popular large-format books which might have sat alongside Daniel and Guicciardini.[41] Between those and his Elzevir republics, though, he could have turned to his shelves to find information about many of the countries of the known world and their histories. The difference between Frank and Holdsworth is not so much the range of subjects represented as the depth of authors and ideas within those fields covered. Frank could find something out across a spectrum of knowledge, while Holdsworth could access a much deeper seam of historical and contemporary writing at any point on the spectrum.

Looking to gain a fuller insight into books which were commonly owned (or not) across different social groups, I published an analysis of five private libraries from the end of the century as recorded in sale catalogues.[42] Two of these were Cambridge academics, Humphrey Babington (1615–92), fellow and vice-master of Trinity College, and Nathaniel Coga (1637?–93), master of Pembroke. They both spent most of their careers in Cambridge, but as usual were also ordained clergymen, appointed to livings as part of their income base (Babington held rectories in Lincolnshire and Nottinghamshire, Coga in East Anglia). Both libraries, containing around 1,000–1,500 books, include a solid core of theological material, and a wide spread of other subjects, conforming to that typical pattern. Three-quarters of Coga's books were in Latin, and around the same proportion were published during his lifetime, reflecting a library built up as a working tool to support his teaching, preaching, and study. Recreation and other pursuits can also be found in these libraries, as both men had music books, and

---

[41] Books like Richard Knolles's *Generall historie of the Turkes*, Edward Grimeston's *Generall historie of the Netherlands*, Philippe de Comines's *Historie* (in Danett's English translation), or Walter Raleigh's *History of the world* went through numerous folio editions in the early 17th c. and regularly turn up in libraries of the time.

[42] David Pearson, 'Patterns of book ownership in late seventeenth-century England', *The Library*, 7th ser. 11 (2010), pp. 139–67.

titles on falconry or foreign travels; Babington owned a copy of *The legend of Captaine Jones: relating his adventure at sea ... and strange combate with a mightie beare* (1631). Comparing these late seventeenth-century libraries with those of the bishops at the beginning of the century, it was noticeable how the proportion of English language books, and English-printed ones, changed from a small percentage to something more like half and half.

These examples are of course all larger libraries of their day, and at the smaller end of the scale we may find bookshelves which are more focused, or less wide-ranging. A handful of the names in the Appendix are what might be called young academics, men who had graduated and become college fellows but who died in their late 20s before their libraries had developed very far, with around 60–100 books apiece (e.g. Edward Homer, 1581?–1614, Alexander Clugh, d.1621, Henry Gostling, 1646?–75). Will Poole has edited a mid-century one from New College, Oxford, John Hutton (1627/8–52); as he points out, collections like this largely reflect the curriculum study necessary to obtain a degree, and a symbiosis between what they could (or needed to) own themselves and what they could find on their college library shelves.[43]

Professional libraries are, unsurprisingly, usually reflective of their owners' working lives, but the broad spread principle still typically applies to larger ones. Of the 15,000 lots in the 1698 sale catalogue of Francis Bernard, royal physician, only 30 per cent were classified as medical, with 11 per cent Latin theology, 33 per cent Latin miscellaneous, and 14 per cent English miscellaneous. Percentage-wise, there was twice as much theology as law in the library of Chief Justice Sir Edward Coke (1552–1634).[44] These are both at the larger end of the spectrum for their generations; more medium-sized is the library of Nathan Paget (1615–79), London physician and friend of Milton, whose library was auctioned after his death.[45] Thirty-eight per cent of the lots were *libri medici*, the remainder covering the usual miscellaneous spread of subjects, mostly in Latin or English. The books of the York lawyer Roger Belwood (d. 1694) were auctioned in London after his death and his 25 per cent of law books, including a section of legal manuscripts, is a greater proportion than would be found in a non-legal owner.[46] But 17 per cent of his books were theological, including many Latin and English ones such as would be found in all kinds of libraries of the time, and he had many titles in history, biography, classics, geography, and more besides. He had copies of Evelyn's *Sylva* and Hooke's *Micrographia*, and a chronologically wide range of English poets from Chaucer to Aphra Behn. Overall, the library suggests a

[43] William Poole, 'Book economy in New College, Oxford in the later 17th century', *History of Universities* 25 (2010), pp. 56–127, 85–102.
[44] William Hassall, *A catalogue of the library of Sir Edward Coke* (New Haven, CT: Yale University Press, 1950).
[45] *Bibliotheca medici viri clarissimi Nathanis Paget.*
[46] *Bibliotheca Belwoodiana, or, a catalogue of the library of Roger Belwood* (London, 1695).

resource which was partly geared to professional needs, but was also a support for life more generally, providing opportunities for recreation, education, and horizon-broadening. Belwood's manuscripts, mostly seventeenth-century transcripts of statutes and case reports, remind us that professional men like lawyers and physicians relied significantly on this kind of material for their daily work.

Turning to the other end of the century, a similar pattern, on a smaller scale, can be seen in the books of Philip Stringer, a Cambridge lawyer who died in 1605. This is one of the inventories edited by Elisabeth Leedham-Green in her calendar of the book lists from the records of the Cambridge Vice-Chancellor's Court, and it rather stands out in the middle of a concentration of very academic lists dominated by doctrinal and controversial Latin theology.[47] Stringer was a graduate of St John's College and a fellow there around 1570, before leaving mainstream academia to be a practising lawyer, holding various offices including University solicitor, registrar for the diocese of Peterborough, and Justice of the Peace for Cambridge. Leedham-Green noted that his list of appraised goods 'do not suggest affluence, giving rather a rustic impression, and the books indicate a gentleman rather than an academic'. His book list is short—about 40 named titles, then references to a dozen quarto books stitched, two paper books, 11 octavo books stitched, and the like; he seems to have had maybe 100 books in all, of which half were solidly leather-bound, and the rest pamphlets in wrappers. There were law books—abridgements of statutes, Rastell's exposition of *Termes of the lawes*, and 'divers old statute books', but most of the titles were non-legal. Two Bibles are listed, and a number of other theological or devotional books—Hooker's *Ecclesiastical polity*, Ursinus's *Doctrinae Christianae compendium*, Joseph Hall's *Meditations*, Fenner's *Sacred doctrine of divinity*—and he also owned Camden's *Britannia*, William Warner's *Albion's England*, and a few other historical works. He had Legh's *Accidence of armory*, Record's *Whetstone of wit*, an Italian book of emblems, and Platt's *Jewel house of art and nature*, a practical book on husbandry and distilling. He needed some law books to do his job, and he needed his theological texts to help assure his salvation; he also wanted a wider set of books which, on their much smaller scale, fit the same kinds of purposes as we saw with Belwood— recreational, horizon-broadening, and helping to equip for life.

There are many libraries of divines, lawyers, and doctors to consider, but fewer from other professions with detailed records. The books of the painter Henry Cook (1642–1700), who executed numerous large-scale wall paintings, were auctioned after he died; there were about 250 lots, so a modest collection, and there is a concentration of volumes which clearly supported his business, with titles on architecture, anatomy, painting, perspective, and physiognomy.[48] Some

---

[47] E. S. Leedham-Green, *Books in Cambridge inventories*, vol. 1 (Cambridge: Cambridge University Press, 1986), pp. 552–4.
[48] *A catalogue of the library of Mr. Henry Cook, painter* (London, 1700).

of his less obviously specialist titles may have been acquired because illustrated (e.g. 'Milton's poetical works, with sculptures, 1695'). Nineteen per cent of his books were in French, and 18 per cent in Italian; most of his evidently professional books were in those languages, or in Latin, and as he spent a period in exile in Italy it seems likely that many of these were acquired abroad (although books in modern foreign languages could also be bought in London in the seventeenth century).[49] He had Vasari's lives of the painters in Italian and du Fresnoy's *L'art de peinture* in French; he also had Montaigne in French, and *Orlando furioso* in Italian. Less intuitively, he had John Barclay's *Argenis* in French, and *Don Quixote* in Italian. But half his books were English, with a wide variety of dictionaries, histories, poetry, and of course theology; he had various standard devotional works and commentaries of his own generation, as well as works of William Ames and St Augustine in Latin. He had Ogilby's road book (an early road atlas of Britain), several of Robert Boyle's books on experiments, and Burton's *Anatomy of melancholy*.

George London, Queen Anne's gardener (d. 1714), whose books were auctioned after his death in 1714, had 750 lots in his sale, largely in English but with a few Latin and French titles.[50] He had books on gardening and husbandry, alongside a typical mix of history and current affairs, travel, theology and literature, with a sprinkling of medicine and law. He owned Chaucer, Milton, and Dryden as well as Hooker, Stillingfleet, and Jeremy Taylor, and a volume of tracts for and against Dr Sacheverell, which may be classified as theology, or politics (or, more meaningfully, an indication of their centrality and interconnectivity in contemporary thinking).

Libraries of the gentry and aristocracy

These are all the serious libraries of serious men. What about those which might have had a more recreational flavour? Or, to put it another way, what is typically found in aristocratic and gentry libraries, rather than those of clergymen and lawyers? Ian Green thought that there was a 'simple but fairly fundamental divide between clerical and lay libraries'; I would put it less strongly (or more ambivalently) than that, but there are observable trends.[51] Peers and gentry families made up nearly 32 per cent of the names in the Appendix, a sizeable proportion; many were spread around the manor and grander houses of England, an important and

---

[49] K. Barron (8 Jan. 2015), 'Cook, Henry (1642?–1700), decorative painter', *Oxford Dictionary of National Biography*. Retrieved 19 Dec. 2018 from: http://www.oxforddnb.com/view/10.1093/ref:odnb/9780198614128.001.0001/odnb-9780198614128-e-6138.
[50] *A catalogue of the library of George London* (London, 1714).
[51] Ian Green, *Print and Protestantism in early modern England* (Oxford: Oxford University Press, 2000), 27.

easily overlooked point which Mark Purcell has rightly stressed.[52] These kinds of libraries often contained a wider or differently balanced spread of subjects, and commonly reflected in their range of languages the education in broader European culture which families like this received both in the classroom and via their travelling itineraries. Theological or devotional material commonly constituted a significant element, but less prominently than it typically did on academic and clerical shelves. They were often accumulated over multiple generations, more so than would typically be the case in academic and clerical libraries. They are also more likely to have served a range of purposes beyond reading, around displaying the wealth, learning or status of their owners, as explored in Chapter 6.

The library of the Norfolk gentleman Sir Thomas Knyvett (d. 1618)—unusually large, for its day, with nearly 1,500 books—has been analysed in detail by David McKitterick, who pointed out its particular strengths in medicine, botany, and numismatics.[53] Knyvett's classified library catalogue shows 22 per cent of the whole as theology, 14 per cent as medicine (strikingly high), 18 per cent as history, politics, and geography, and 31 per cent, the largest subdivision, as 'philosophy and other humanities'. Most of his categories have separate sections of French, Italian, and Spanish books, as well as Latin and English ones, exemplifying that point about linguistic spread and proficiency. When Sir Thomas Bromley of Holt Castle in Worcestershire died in 1641, his more modest library, valued at £4, was noted as 'mostly French and Italian'.[54] Another Norfolk gentleman, Sir Edward Paston, who died in 1630, has been studied particularly for his outstanding collection of music; we don't know how big his library of books was, but his will refers to 'many Latin, Spanish and French books' in his study.[55] The mid-century catalogue of the Earl of Leicester's library at Penshurst shows that it was stronger in its holdings of Italian poetry and drama than it was for English literature.[56]

The published analysis of the Penshurst library also stresses its breadth of subjects: 'one of the most attractive features of this collection is its eclecticism.'[57] This sentence is followed by an impressive reeling-off of the many topics on which 'the Sidneys owned the most up-to-date books in several languages', including beekeeping, drainage, forestry, military strategy, heraldry, optics, and surgery. Subject breadth, and extensive holdings of French books, is similarly commented upon in an account of the library of the Duke of Lauderdale (1616–82).[58] When looking at the five late seventeenth-century sale catalogues mentioned earlier, it

---

[52] Mark Purcell, *The country house library* (New Haven, CT: Yale University Press, 2017), 17.

[53] McKitterick, *The library of Sir Thomas Knyvett.*

[54] Malcolm Wanklyn (ed.), *Inventories of Worcestershire landed gentry, 1637–1786* (Worcester: Worcestershire Historical Society, 1998), 167.

[55] Philip Brett, 'Edward Paston...and his musical collection', *Transactions of the Cambridge Bibliographical Society* 4 (1964), pp. 51–69.

[56] Warkentin et al., *The library of the Sidneys*, 9.   [57] Ibid.

[58] Giles Mandelbrote, 'The library of the Duke of Lauderdale', in C. Rowell (ed.), *Ham House: 400 years of collecting and patronage* (New Haven, CT: Yale University Press, 2013), pp. 222–31, 225.

was noticeable that the gentry one (Sir Norton Knatchbull, 1602–85), though on a smaller scale than these aristocratic libraries and belonging to a seriously scholarly gentleman who published a Latin work of New Testament textual studies, was more wide-ranging on several fronts than those of the clergymen. Putting it another way, I thought that Knatchbull's library was 'probably the one that a collector today would most like to take home'.[59]

A number of mid-century library lists made by John Holles, 2nd Earl of Clare (1595–1666) survive in the Portland papers at Nottingham University, including 'a note of my books at Haughton, in my upper closet and in an ould trunk in the great chamber', dated 1654, and 'an ancient note of my books...this 20. of Jan. 1657'.[60] The former comprises 387 titles, the latter 403; there is some overlap between them, but some books appear on one list and not the other, so the total size of his library at this time is not clear, perhaps something upwards of 500 books. Again, there is a strong showing of European languages; in the 1654 list, 39 per cent are English, 28 per cent French, 23 per cent Greek and Latin, and the rest Italian or Spanish. His French books included many romances, plays, and similar works (e.g. a multi-volume *Amadis de Gaule*, a similar set of *Cassandre* by Gualtier de Coste, Tabourot's *Les bigarrures*), as well as historical works by D'Aubigny, Matthieu, Villeroy, and others chronicling the affairs of France in the sixteenth and early seventeenth centuries. He also had devotional literature in French, including Bibles and psalters, Pierre de la Place's *De l'excellence de l'homme chrestien*, and Pierre du Moulin's *Defense de la foy*. He had Cervantes in Spanish, and Machiavelli in Italian (as well as in English). All these books were supported by grammars and dictionaries for the various languages.

Although his range of theological literature was not as extensive as would be found in a typical clerical or academic library, he had more than enough material to ensure a well-read and thoroughly orthodox position according to the kind of modified Calvinism in which the English Church of first half of the seventeenth century was steeped. As well as Bibles and prayer books, he had copies of the works of William Perkins, John Dod, and Robert Cleaver on the Commandments and the Eucharist, Henry Smith's sermons, John Preston's *Saints qualification*, Jeremiah Dyke's *Good conscience*, and Nicholas Byfield's *Principles*. Other contemporary theological authors found on Holles's shelves included William Ames, Joseph Hall, Thomas Hooker, William Sedgwick, Richard Sibbes, and Thomas Taylor.

Holles had extensive holdings of classical authors, both Greek and Latin, with most in their original languages and some in English translation.[61] He owned many historical works, covering both England and the world more widely, with

---

[59] Pearson, 'Patterns', 155.   [60] University of Nottingham MS Pw V 4.

[61] Including: Aristotle, Aulus Gellius, Caesar, Cato, Cicero, Dionysius of Halicarnassus, Heliodorus, Herodian, Homer, Ovid, Polybius, Plato, Pliny, Sallust, Seneca, Suetonius, Tacitus, Terence, Thucydides, Valerius Maximus, Xenophon.

well-known authors like William Camden, Samuel Daniel, Raphael Holinshed, and Walter Raleigh all represented; he had copies of Carew's *Survey of Cornwall*, Dallington's *View of Fraunce*, and Knolles's *Generall historie of the Turkes*. Although many of the books on his lists were published during the lifetime of his also bookish father, the 1st Earl (1564–1637, see p. 115 below), and may have been inherited from him, his copy of James Howell's *Exact historie of the late revolutions in Naples*, a translation from Alessandro Giraffi first published in 1650, reflects ongoing book buying (he also had a copy of Howell's *Dodona's grove*, which cannot have been earlier than 1640). His literary holdings were certainly closer to modern tastes than those of many more academic libraries of this time; not only did he have a folio Shakespeare, but he also had several volumes described as '9 playes', '6 plays', or the like, Sidney's *Arcadia*, and works by Spenser. He had numerous books on warfare, heraldry, and arithmetic, and nearly twenty volumes of statutes from vaious periods; medicine was more thinly represented, by Hippocrates and a copy of a popular household guide, Philip Barrow's *Methode of physicke*.

Putting Holles's library against Mark Frank's, of similar date and size, we can see the broader comparative patterns between a gentry and an academic library all manifested; more languages, literature and books relevant to his social responsibilities in the former, and more material that might be considered recreational. A final section of manuscripts in the 1657 list includes a number of music and song books. Both contain theology, though a much higher proportion of Holles's was in English, and the weight of patristic and controversial doctrinal material found on Frank's shelves was not needed at Haughton. Both men had relatively small smatterings of law and medicine, appropriate to their needs, and neither had much that we would describe as scientific (beyond mathematics). Holles's holdings of classical authors was stronger, but all those writers would have been known to Frank and they may have been weeded out from his shelves before the books were taken in to Pembroke. Frank had texts which we would describe as history, but Holles's coverage of this area was wider and deeper.

The library catalogue which the antiquarian Cheshire squire Sir Peter Leycester (1614–78) compiled in 1670 lists a little over 1,300 books; he had more history than literature, and his books were mostly English and Latin, with a little French.[62] The catalogue shows us how he classified the books, 'how my books stand placed in my study', with presses A to S assigned a subject, including law, history, divinity, miscellaneous, and so forth. There were five presses of divinity, two of law, three of English history, and two of foreign histories. This catalogue also has separate lists of books used daily in the parlour, kept outside the study (which were not only prayer books but also dictionaries and law manuals), of music books

[62] Elizabeth Halcrow (ed.), *Charges to the grand jury ... by Sir Peter Leicester*, Chetham Society 3rd ser. 5 (Manchester, 1953), pp. 106–52.

in the music room adjoining the study, and of school books, about 30 books which were evidently kept apart for everyday educational purposes.

Just over 100 books bought by the Essex baronet Sir Thomas Barrington (c.1585–1644) from a London bookseller in the 1630s are known from a surviving bill; they were mostly English and Latin, with 42 per cent theological.[63] He was buying multiple copies of devotional works by Richard Sibbes, some presumably to give away, as well as similar favourites from the early seventeenth-century English Calvinist stable like William Pemble and John Preston. He was also buying books on falconry and farriery, Henry Blount's *Voyage into the Levant*, an Ortelius atlas, the poems of Fulke Greville, and the works of Shakespeare. This is yet another, smaller snapshot of that common thread found running through so many of these aristocratic and gentry libraries: the divinity remains an important concern, which we must not overlook, alongside a wide spread of urbane, civilized, cultured interests, a mixture of the practical, the spiritually necessary, and the recreational. Looking at a library list of 60 years later, 240 books owned by the heir to the Newdegate baronetcy in Warwickshire in 1696, J. T. Cliffe talks about 'the kind of publications which could have been found in hundreds of gentlemen's collections', Joseph Hall and Edward Stillingfleet, Ben Jonson, Cowley, Dryden and Otway, Gerard's *Herbal*, and Dalton's *Country justice*.[64]

Conclusions

The kinds of book owners covered in this chapter constitute the most obvious, the most expected, and the most immediately documented of this period. Some of the key trends brought out—that libraries get bigger, on average, as time proceeds, and that broad subject coverage is commonly encountered—may not be surprising, but are worth analysing in an evidence-based way. Books were obviously ubiquitous among academics, clergymen, and professions which relied upon them, and in these cases deciding what constitutes a library worth describing as such is a moot point; it could be argued that a a list of book owners should start with the membership directories of the universities and inns of court, as everyone in there is likely to have owned at least some books. The statistics on aristocratic and gentry libraries highlight the significant proportion of national bookstock which sat on such shelves, a point which is perhaps less self-evident today. Book ownership in the seventeenth century was widespread both geographically and socially, and the following chapters will pursue this point with some of the less well-recorded, but no less important, parts of that landscape.

[63] M. Bohannon, 'A London bookseller's bill, 1635–1639', *The Library*, 4th ser. 18 (1938), pp. 432–46.
[64] J. T. Cliffe, *The world of the country house in seventeenth-century England* (New Haven, CT: Yale University Press, 1999), pp. 166–7.

3

Women and books in the seventeenth century

There is a marked and obvious gender imbalance in many accounts of historic book ownership, reflecting the nature of much of the surviving documentary evidence. Of the more than 1,370 names in the lists of seventeenth-century owners in the Appendix to this book, only 36 are women (mostly from the aristocratic and gentry classes), which might be interpreted as a sign that men were readers and women were not. This is emphatically not true; the distorted statistical lens is an unavoidable consequence of early modern property law, whereby the goods of married women were technically vested in their husbands.[1] The result of this is that so much of the source material upon which such lists depend, including wills, inventories, and sale catalogues, are in the names of men, although they include material which to modern minds belonged to women. Wives made wills only with their husbands' consent, and rarely did so; only 1 per cent of surviving wills between 1558 and 1700 are those of wives.[2] Probate documentation relating to women is typically associated with widows, unmarried at the time of their death. A study of women and consumer behaviour in the late seventeenth and early eighteenth centuries, based on an analysis of nearly 3,000 probate inventories, noted that the ratio of female inventories in the overall sample (15 per cent) closely matches the proportion of households headed by widows (13 per cent).[3] The same study went on to observe that where women's inventories do survive, 'books ... were recorded in equal proportions in both men's and women's inventories'.[4]

The paucity of primary evidence, combined with traditions of prioritization in academic study, has meant that until fairly recently, women's book ownership in the early modern period has been a neglected topic. There are no women at all in William Fletcher's *English book collectors* (1902), apart from a brief passing mention of Elizabeth I; the first woman, chronologically, to feature in Seymour de Ricci's *English collectors of books and manuscripts* is Frances Currer (1785–1861), in

---

[1] Anne Laurence, *Women in England 1500–1760: a social history* (London: Weidenfeld and Nicolson, 1994), pp. 228–30.
[2] M. Prior, 'Wives and wills 1558–1700', in J. Chartres and D. Hey (eds), *English rural society, 1500–1800* (Cambridge: Cambridge University Press, 1990), ch. 8.
[3] Lorna Weatherill, 'A possession of one's own: women and consumer behavior in England, 1660–1740', *Journal of British Studies* 25 (1986), pp. 131–56, 133.
[4] Ibid. 142.

Book Ownership in Stuart England: The Lyell Lectures, 2018. David Pearson, Oxford University Press (2021).
© David Pearson.
DOI: 10.1093/oso/9780198870128.003.0003

his view 'England's earliest female bibliophile'.[5] A survey of over 100 articles on private libraries, published in *The Library* from the start of the journal in 1892 to 2015, found only one, until 1989, which focused on a woman's library (a short article on the books of Diane de Poitiers written in 1926).[6] There are hardly any women's lists in Sears Jayne's *Library catalogues of the English Renaissance*, and *Private libraries in Renaissance England*, of its 279 library lists published to date, has only 17 that belonged to women.[7]

The unbalanced account which these statistics reflect has been increasingly explored, understood, and reshaped during the last 40 years or so in a wide range of books and articles which have looked at seventeenth-century women's access to and use of books from many angles, and the picture is now very different. Scholars have looked at literature produced primarily for a female market, following on from Suzanne Hull's pioneering study of 1982, and there have been several exemplary and regularly cited studies of particular women's collections, such as Paul Morgan on Frances Wolfreston, David McKitterick on Elizabeth Puckering, and Heidi Hackel on the Countess of Bridgewater.[8] Kate Loveman has opened up for us Elizabeth Pepys's reading alongside that of her diarist husband, and the subject has been considered in the obvious wider context of women's writing at that time.[9] More recently, essays on the ownership and reading of books by women in early modern Britain has significantly explored and documented this landscape, and a website dedicated to illustrating interesting examples of early modern female book ownership has been set up.[10] In 2005, the Beinecke Library at Yale mounted an exhibition devoted to books owned by women before 1700, and there is a more popular book, all about women and books in art, to sit alongside the annually published calendars of *Reading women* produced for a broad market.[11]

[5] W. Y. Fletcher, *English book collectors* (London: Kegan Paul, 1902); Seymour de Ricci, *English collectors of books and manuscripts* (Cambridge: Cambridge University Press, 1930), 141.

[6] George Bushnell, 'Diane de Poitiers and her books', *The Library*, 4th ser. 7 (1926), pp. 283–302; the survey was undertaken for the virtual issue on Private Libraries, https://academic.oup.com/library/pages/Library_on_Private_Libraries (accessed 8 Feb. 2019).

[7] Sears Jayne, *Library catalogues of the English Renaissance*, 2nd edn (Godalming: St Paul's Bibliographies, 1983), 46.

[8] Suzanne Hull, *Chaste, silent, and obedient: English books for women, 1475–1640* (San Marino, CA: Huntington Library, 1982); Paul Morgan, 'Frances Wolfreston and "Hor Bouks"', *The Library*, 6th ser. 11 (1989), pp. 197–219; David McKitterick, 'Women and their books in the seventeenth century: the case of Elizabeth Puckering', *The Library*, 7th ser. 1 (2000), pp. 359–80; Heidi Hackel, 'The Countess of Bridgewater's London library', in J. Andersen and E. Sauer (eds), *Books and readers in early modern England* (Philadelphia: University of Pennsylvania Press, 2002), pp. 138–59.

[9] Kate Loveman, *Samuel Pepys and his books* (Oxford: Oxford University Press, 2015).

[10] Leah Knight et al. (eds), *Women's bookscapes in early modern Britain* (Ann Arbor: University of Michigan Press, 2018) Georgianna Ziegler, 'Patterns in women's book ownership, 1500-1700', in Valerie Wayne (ed.), *Women's labour and the history of the book in early modern England* (London: Arden Shakespeare, 2020), pp.207-24; https://earlymodernfemalebookownership.wordpress.com/contact/ (accessed 12 Nov. 2019).

[11] Robert G. Babcock et al., *A book of her own* (New Haven, CT: Beinecke Rare Book and Manuscript Library, 2005); Christiane Inmann, *Forbidden fruit: a history of women and books in art* (Munich: Prestel, 2009).

We therefore now have a fuller picture which might be summarized as follows. Yes, of course women owned books in the seventeenth century. They constituted over half the population, and although the proportion of women who could read was lower than that of men, it was one which was steadily growing. Estimates of female literacy at the time have been debated; a 1980 study which reckoned that 90 per cent of women were illiterate in 1640, falling to 70 per cent by 1714, has been questioned by several later writers, who point out that statistics like this, based on evidence of being able to write, overlook the fact that reading and writing skills were separately taught, and women who could only mark their name with a cross might still have been able to read.[12] In many larger and more affluent households, it was common practice for women to have their own closets or private spaces in which books would often be kept and read, and many records of these survive. Beyond that, to quote from a list made by Heidi Hackel, the evidence for women's libraries survives in many forms: 'ownership stamps and signatures in extant copies of books, references in journals and letters, passages in commonplace books, representations in portraits, bequests in wills, and lists in probate and household inventories'.[13]

Ladies' closets

The closet activities of aristocratic and gentry ladies perhaps constitute the most accessibly documented of those categories, and there are numerous examples, some of them now well known, like Lady Anne Clifford (1590–1676), whose surviving library inventory and diary, with accounts of books being read or read to her in the 1610s, are supplemented by the famous triptych of 1646 which is full of books.[14] That picture has been ingeniously used to try to reconstruct the libraries of Anne and her mother.[15] Not many books from her library survive today, but several that do, including her copy of Sidney's *Arcadia* now in the Bodleian, are richly annotated with marginalia and her note of starting and finishing her

---

[12] That estimate from David Cressy, *Literacy and the social order* (Cambridge: Cambridge University Press, 1980), pp. 121–2, has been queried by (inter alia) Jacqueline Pearson, in 'Women reading, reading women', in Helen Wilcox (ed.), *Women and literature in Britain* (Cambridge: Cambridge University Press, 1996), pp. 80–99, 80–81; Margaret Ezell, 'The politics of the past', in Sigrid King (ed.), *Pilgrimage for love* (Tempe: Arizona Center for Medieval and Renaissance Studies, 1999), pp. 19–40, 23; Heidi Hackel, *Reading material in early modern England* (Cambridge: Cambridge University Press, 2005), 57.

[13] Hackel, 'The Countess of Bridgewater's London library', 139.

[14] Hackel, *Reading material*, 222–40, where the picture is reproduced; to see it in colour, visit https://www.abbothall.org.uk/great-picture (accessed 6 Oct. 2018).

[15] Leah Knight, 'Margaret Clifford, Countess of Cumberland', and Leah Knight, 'Anne Clifford, Countess of Pembroke', PLRE 268 and 277 in R. J. Fehrenbach and J. L. Black (eds), *Private libraries in Renaissance England*, vol. 9 (Tempe: Arizona Center for Medieval and Renaissance Studies, 2017), pp. 157–61, 347–63.

reading.[16] Andrew Cambers has written extensively about the closet reading of the Yorkshirewoman Lady Margaret Hoby, who has been described as having a 'life saturated by print' and who died in 1633, but his book on *Godly reading* reveals a number of similar examples, and observes the different customs that characterized male and female closet book use.[17] Heidi Hackel has edited the library inventory of Frances Egerton, Countess of Bridgewater, listing 241 books and made between 1627 and 1632.[18]

An inventory which has more recently been edited, and which is typical of the contents of these kinds of closets around the middle of the century, is that of Margaret Heath (1578–1647), made after her death; the original survives among the Heath family papers in the British Library.[19] Born Margaret Miller, she married Robert Heath in 1600 and lived through his early career as a courtier seeking favours, until he became Recorder of London in 1618, Solicitor-General and a knight in 1621, and Chief Justice of Common Pleas in 1631.[20] His political fortunes had ups and downs and when she died he was in exile in France; they had six children, and her 1631 portrait by Cornelius Johnson makes it clear that she was a lady of wealth and fashion.[21] The inventory lists 82 titles, all in English. She had both a coloured and an uncoloured copy of Gerard's *Herbal*, Parkinson's *Garden of flowers*, and a few other books relating to gardening, husbandry, and medicine, but over 80 per cent of the contents are what we would classify as theological or devotional. She had Bibles and prayer books, sermons and expository works, and many books giving guidance on spiritual matters—Byfield's *Rules of holy life*, Bolton's *Directions for comfortable walking with God*, Baynes's *Holy soliloquies*, Sibbes's *Soul's conflict*. More books are in quarto than any other format, but other formats feature too, and fourteen of her books were sixteenmos, presumably a handy size to carry around and use for reflection and meditation whenever sought. But she was clearly not afraid of digesting larger works, as Joseph Hall's *Works* in folio is a book which by the time of its 1647 edition ran to over 1,350 pages. The only literary work, as we would think of these things, was a copy of Herbert's *Poems*, although Sylvester's translation of the *Divine weeks and*

---

[16] P. Sidney, *The Countesse of Pembroke's Arcadia* (London, 1605), Bodleian Library J-J Sidney 13. Another similarly annotated book of hers is illustrated in Richard Kuhta, ' "I beegane, to ovrloke this booke...".: Lady Anne Clifford's copy of *Titles of honor*', in Thomas Tanselle (ed.), *Other people's books* (Chicago, IL: Caxton Club, 2011), pp. 42–5.

[17] Andrew Cambers, *Godly reading* (Cambridge: Cambridge University Press, 2011), pp. 43–54.

[18] Hackel, 'The Countess of Bridgewater's London library'.

[19] M. Empey, 'Margaret Heath', in *Private libraries in Renaissance England* 11 (forthcoming); see also M.-L. Coolahan and M. Empey, 'Women's book ownership and the reception of early modern women's texts', in Knight et al., *Women's bookscapes*, 231–52, 234–5.

[20] Paul E. Kopperman (2008), 'Heath, Sir Robert (1575–1649), judge', *Oxford Dictionary of National Biography*. Retrieved 6 Oct. 2018 from: http://www.oxforddnb.com/view/10.1093/ref:odnb/9780198614128.001.0001/odnb-9780198614128-e-12842. See also P. E. Kopperman, *Sir Robert Heath, 1575–1649* (London, 1989).

[21] http://www.nationaltrustcollections.org.uk/object/922330 (accessed 6 Oct. 2018).

works of Du Bartas would have been thought of in that way at the time; both are verse, but also have devotional or biblical roots.

A very similar, if smaller, inventory is the almost exactly contemporary one of Elizabeth Sleigh (later Elizabeth Ireton), made in May 1647 and now in a manuscript in the Wellcome Library.[22] This list of 52 titles, again all in English apart from four French books, and more in quarto than any other format, includes a few books relating to medicine and household duties, but is otherwise entirely religious in content. There is a noticeable preponderance of books by popular English devotional authors of the late sixteenth and early seventeenth centuries, writing books of guidance on godly living, conscience, faith, and prayer in the Calvinist tradition—William Perkins, Richard Rogers, Richard Bolton, Paul Baynes, Arthur Hildersham. When Lady Sleigh retired to her closet she, like Lady Heath, was surrounded by books like John Preston's *Golden scepter* and *The saints daily exercise*, Perkins on the creed, Bolton on the four last things, and Jeremiah Dyke's *Good conscience*, all much-read works in their day.[23] Ann Sadleir (1585–1670), the daughter of Sir Edward Coke, is another example of an educated lady of this social class with an extensive and well-studied library, much of which she donated to the Inner Temple; most of those books were theological, and Arnold Hunt observed that 'she was extremely well read in contemporary English protestant divinity'.[24] Ladies like this spent more time pondering questions of election, uprightness of heart, and temporary faith than the average twenty-first century audience can easily truly understand.

There are evident parallels between Lady Heath's books and the larger library of Frances Egerton, whose books were also almost all in English, apparently acquired new or at least not long after publication, and with a significant if lesser emphasis on theology and devotion.[25] About half the Bridgewater list comprises religious books, including books by Bolton, Perkins, Rogers, and others of that stable, but she also had a wider range of reading on her shelves, with literature, history, and accounts of foreign countries. As well as Herbert, Lady Frances had titles by Spenser, Shakespeare, Jonson, and Drayton. Her knowledge of the wider world could be developed with books like Richard Knolles's *Generall historie of the Turkes*, José de Acosta's *Naturall and morall historie of the East and West Indies*, and an English translation of Philippe de Commines's history of late

[22] R. J. Fehrenbach, 'Lady Elizabeth Ireton', in R. J. Fenrenbach and J. L. Black (eds), *Private libraries in Renaissance England*, vol. 8 (Tempe: Arizona Center for Medieval and Renaissance Studies, 2014), pp. 281–92.

[23] For the authoritative overview of the relative popularity and distribution of devotional texts at this period, see Ian Green, *Print and Protestantism in early modern England* (Oxford: Oxford University Press, 2000).

[24] Arnold Hunt, 'The books, manuscripts and literary patronage of Mrs Anne Sadleir', in V. Burke and J. Gibson (eds), *Early modern women's manuscript writing* (Oxford: Oxford University Press, 2004), pp. 242–79.

[25] Hackel, 'The Countess of Bridgewater's London library'.

medieval France. That broader range fits her profile as an educated, fashionable, and wealthy lady from the upper strata of society. It is noteworthy that most of the books associated with Elizabeth Grey, Countess of Kent (1581–1651), by the presence of her armorial badge of a talbot passant on the covers, are sixteenth- and seventeenth-century books in Italian, covering a range of mostly historical or literary subjects; she was another aristocratic and well-educated lady, noted for her literary patronage and association with John Selden.[26]

The broader picture

There is, however, plentiful other evidence that women from a wider range of backgrounds read extensively in what we would classify as literature. It has often been pointed out that early modern conduct books talk about the undesirability of women reading romances or what Thomas Salter, in *The mirror of modesty*, called the pestilent infection of lascivious poetry; but it is equally often observed that the existence of such warnings is a reflection of how common the practice must have been.[27] Sidney's *Arcadia* was originally written for the entertainment of his sister, and Heidi Hackel has noted that half the surviving copies of pre-1700 editions, which carry ownership inscriptions, have those of women.[28] The evidence is more plentiful later in the century than earlier; several writers have commented on the references in Dorothy Osborne's letters to Sir William Temple in the 1650s and 1660s to her enthusiasm for French romances, and her advice on which ones to read.[29] Kate Loveman has looked closely at Elizabeth Pepys's reading in the 1660s; she was an attentive reader of the *Arcadia*, but was apparently most fond of French heroic romances, which she spent many hours reading in the original language.[30] David McKitterick observed the evident interest of Elizabeth Puckering, who died in 1689, in poetry and drama, as testified by books that she marked.[31]

Another female library from this end of the century which reflects that broader range is that of Cary Coke of Holkham, daughter of a Gloucestershire baronet who in 1696, aged 16, married Edward Coke, who had inherited the hall and estate of Holkham in Norfolk. They became the parents of Thomas Coke, 1st Earl of Leicester, and were a bright and fashionable young couple who died cruelly

---

[26] J. Considine (2006), 'Grey, Elizabeth [née Lady Elizabeth Talbot], countess of Kent (1582–1651)', *Oxford Dictionary of National Biography*. Retrieved 15 Oct. 2018 from: http://www.oxforddnb.com/view/10.1093/ref:odnb/9780198614128.001.0001/odnb-9780198614128-e-11530?rskey=6WlwB8&result=3; eleven of her books thus stamped are listed on the British Armorial Bindings database, of which nine fit that description.

[27] E.g. by Amy Erickson, *Women and property in early modern England* (London: Routledge, 1993), 9.

[28] Hackel, *Reading material*, 159.   [29] Pearson, 'Women reading', 92.

[30] Loveman, *Samuel Pepys and his books*, 142.   [31] McKitterick, 'Women and their books', 375.

Fig. 3.1 The bookplate of Cary Coke (1680–1707). Bodleian Library Holk.d.28 (Elkanah Settle, *Reflections*, 1687). By permission of the Bodleian Libraries, The University of Oxford.

young, within a few months of each other, in 1707.[32] In 1701 they each had a bookplate made, and I am very grateful to Mac Graham, the Librarian at Holkham Hall, for sending me a list of the 120 books still at Holkham today which carry Cary's plate (Fig. 3.1). Half are theological and devotional, with those earlier heavyweights Preston and Sibbes represented alongside more contemporary guides like Allestree, Hammond, and Stillingfleet, but there is also a wide spread

---

[32] On their books, see D. P. Mortlock, *The Holkham Library: a history and description* (Cambridge: Roxburghe Club, 2006), 31.

of history, conduct books, current affairs like the *Turkish Spy*, and literature including Boccaccio, Butler, Cowley, Killigrew, Philips, Rochester, and Spenser. She had several classics in translation and all her books were in English. To the books at Holkham we should add a group of 30 volumes of contemporary plays, uniformly bound up around the beginning of the eighteenth century and book-plated with either hers or his; they are all now in the Bodleian Library, part of a purchase of interesting books from Holkham in 1955.[33]

However, when Elizabeth Freke, a gentry lady whose life is unusually well documented via a manuscript autobiography, listed the 78 books she put into the deal box by the fireside in her closet, in 1711, her library had many similarities with the ladies Heath and Sleigh.[34] Like Lady Heath, she owned Joseph Hall's works in folio, and had a wide range of devotional literature including sermons by Lancelot Andrewes and Henry Smith, St Augustine's meditations, Jeremy Taylor's *Life of Jesus*, Thomas à Kempis, and *The whole duty of man*. She also had a sprinkling of household gardening and medical books, with titles like *The family physician* and *The husbandman's instructor*, while her most obviously literary text was Cowley's *Poems*. She had rather more historical texts than the mid-seventeenth-century ladies, but on the whole the profile and size of her collection matches theirs quite strikingly. There is plentiful evidence of a continuing asso-ciation of devotional books with women throughout the Stuart period; their access to wider ranges of books was enhanced when their domestic circumstances meant that they were within households where their own books coexisted with those of male relatives.[35]

Evidence from wills

The kinds of ownership patterns we see from these inventories are very much substantiated and amplified by the evidence which can be drawn from wills, where there are rich seams which have been mentioned but not systematically drawn upon by other writers on seventeenth-century female libraries. This evidence lies not so much in women's wills, which as already noted are few and far between, but in those of men who regularly bestowed particular books on their wives, daugh-ters, and nieces. Throughout the century, there are many examples of standard patterns, the simplest of which is the direction that all English-language books go to female relatives. When Sir Nathaniel Bacon of Stiffkey died in 1622, he directed that all his English books, either printed or manuscript, be divided between his

---

[33] David Rogers, 'The Holkham collection', *Bodleian Library Record* 4 (1953), pp. 255–67.
[34] R. A. Anselment (ed.), *The remembrance of Elizabeth Freke 1671–1714*, Camden Society 5th ser. 18 (Cambridge, 2001), pp. 172–5.
[35] A point which is well expanded under the heading 'Collective ownership' in Coolahan and Empey, 'Women's book ownership', 237–9.

wife and daughters; a few years later, the lexicographer John Florio left all his English books to his wife.[36] Hannah Dickinson, the woman with whom the ever-memorable John Hales was living when he died in 1656, was bequeathed his English books, and the lawyer Sir Matthew Hale left English books in divinity, medicine, and history to his wife in 1676.[37] William Burkitt, celebrated for his expository notes on the New Testament, left his English devotional books to his wife, before the bulk of his library went to become a parish library for Milden.[38]

Choice was often a theme in these bequests, presumably to avoid women being given material which they either would not or should not want. The widow of the lawyer Paul Croke, who died in 1631, was to have such English books 'as she shall choose', a formula which is found many times, as for example in the wills of David Stokes, canon of Windsor, who died in 1669, the academic philosopher Ralph Cudworth who died in 1688, the physician John Lawson in 1705, the lawyer Sir John Franklin in 1707.[39] Choice was generally expressed as unencumbered, but occasionally there is a requirement of male approval: John Davenant, the Bishop of Salisbury who died in 1641, left English books to his nieces 'as his brother thought fit', and in 1710 the lawyer and judge George Bramston directed that his daughter Theodosia should have such English books as she shall choose, 'and which my executors think proper for her to have'.[40]

The other pattern which is encountered very commonly is the giving of particular books to female relatives, most obviously but by no means always Bibles. Andrew Cotton, a Cheshire gentleman who died in 1640, bequeathed a large English Bible to his cousin's wife 'in confidence that she will daily bestow some time in reading'.[41] Bishop John Prideaux of Worcester left a great gilt Bible and prayer book to his wife in 1650, Thomas Holbech of Emmanuel College left a quarto English Bible to his niece in 1680, the Southwark rector Richard Hook left a great Bible with the apocrypha in two volumes, printed in Cambridge, to his daughter in 1715.[42] This specifying of particular editions or special copies is not unusual, and in 1684 the daughter of the antiquary Thomas Gore received 'the English testament with the common prayer with the curious cuts, having a cover of crimson velvet laid over with plates of carved silver', together with his 'Bible

---

[36] R. J. Fehrenbach, 'Sir Roger Townshend's books', in R. J. Fehrenbach and E. S. Leedham-Green (eds), *Private libraries in Renaissance England*, vol. 1 (Binghamton, NY: Center for Medieval and Early Renaissance Studies, 1992), pp. 79–135, 81; The National Archives (TNA) PROB 11/149/97.

[37] John Hales, *Works* (London, 1765), vol. 1, pp. 203–6; J. B. Williams, *Memoirs of the life, character and writings of Sir Matthew Hale* (London, 1835), pp. 327–58.

[38] TNA PROB 11/473, sig. 232.

[39] The relevant wills will all be found at TNA: PROB 11/160/489 (Croke); PROB 11/330/182 (Stokes); PROB 11/392/116 (Cudworth); PROB 11/483/225 (Lawson); PROB 11/495/440 (Franklin).

[40] TNA PROB 11/186/499 (Davenant); PROB 11/518/153 (Bramston).

[41] Paul Pixton, *Wrenbury wills and inventories 1542-1661* (Chester: Record Society of Lancashire and Cheshire, 2009), pp. 341–4.

[42] TNA PROB 11/213/611 (Prideaux); PROB 11/364/342 (Holbech); PROB 11/544/313 (Hook).

covered with white satin wrought in divers coloured silks'.[43] In 1642 Thomas
Sanderson of Gainsborough left his wife a Bible with silver clasps, a quarto Bible in
carnation velvet to his daughter Mildred, and a folio Cambridge Bible to his
daughter Lucy; his daughters were also to receive six prayer books or other
books of divinity tending to devotion.[44]

That phrase about books of divinity tending to devotion is one which chimes
very much with the kinds of books we met in ladies' closets, and there is a good
correlation between the titles which feature so often in those inventories and ones
which are regularly met with as specific bequests in wills. Thomas Sanderson's
wife also received works by Richard Sibbes, while Izaak Walton (author of *The
compleat angler*) left a copy of Sibbes's *Bruised reed and smoking flax* to his
daughter in 1683, along with a copy of the works of Joseph Hall.[45] Edward
Veel's sister could remember her Nonconformist minister brother with the set
of Poole's *Annotations upon the Holy Bible* which he left her in 1708, and the
works of William Perkins, that 'prince of puritan theologians, and the most
eagerly read' (in the words of Patrick Collinson), feature in several seventeenth-
century bequests to women.[46] In 1618 John Blythe, a fellow of Peterhouse, died
and left £5 to his 'little god-daughter' Sara Giles, 'to buy for her these good books
following', a list of fifteen titles including works by Beza, Calvin, Downame, Hall,
Luther, Perkins, and Rogers, all in English, and all very clearly setting her on the
road for a godly life.[47] There are exceptions to the general trend, but they do stand
out as such within the majority of devotional works; Edmund Castell, the orientalist, left books by Raleigh, Heylyn, and Culpeper to his female relatives, although
none of them would look out of place in a lady's closet, nor would the copy of
Parkinson's Herbal left to his cousin Sara Hobart by the clergyman Barnabas
Barlow in 1657.[48] He also left a copy of works by Cicero to another female cousin,
which is more unusual, but which may well have been an English translation.

Evidence from inscriptions

As others have observed, evidence of the scale and nature of women's ownership
of books is scattered widely around the libraries of the world, in inscriptions and
other kinds of ownership markings in surviving books. There is no simple route
to the discovery of these, although the quantity of provenance data in library

---

[43] J. E. Jackson, 'The last will of Thomas Gore, the antiquary', *Wiltshire Magazine* 14 (1874), pp. 1–12.
[44] TNA PROB 11/190/438.   [45] TNA PROB 11/375/139 (Walton).
[46] TNA PROB 11/502/234 (Veel); Patrick Collinson, *The Elizabethan Puritan movement* (London: Methuen, 1967), p. 125; Edmund Staunton (1600–1671) left Perkins's works to Anne Lomax (TNA PROB 11/337/134); Walter Snell (d. 1677) left the same text to Olympia Robartes (TNA PROB 11/356/57).
[47] Cambridge University Library, VCCt Wills III.
[48] TNA PROB 11/382/24 (Castell); PROB 11/266/63 (Barlow).

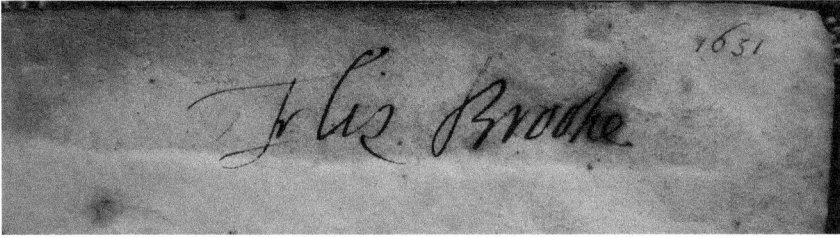

Fig. 3.2A The inscription of [Lady] Elizabeth Brooke (1602?–83), on the flyleaf of a copy of John Preston, *Life eternall*, 1631. Author's collection.

Fig.3.2B The inscription of Elinor Archer, dated 1709, on the flyleaf of a copy of Thomas à Kempis, *The Christian's pattern*, 1708. Author's collection.

catalogues is steadily growing, and they can sometimes be searched by different genres of owner. Anyone who has spent any time browsing the shelves of historic libraries is likely to have seen plenty of instances, of simple inscriptions and more complex ones which may tell us a little bit more. Fig. 3.2 shows some typical examples, names on title pages and flyleaves, sometimes with dates reflecting the time of acquisition, stray survivals from what may once have been a handful or some dozens of books similarly inscribed. They will be found more commonly in devotional books than anything else, but there are plenty of recorded female inscriptions in literary, historical, and other kinds of texts.[49] Sometimes, inscriptions reflect gifts within families, more often, in my observation, of women to

[49] Babcock, *A book of her own*, includes (pp. 67–76) a list of 172 printed books used in the exhibition, with 17th-c. women's inscriptions; the great majority are devotional/theological, but they also include literary texts by Chaucer, Cleveland, Drayton, Shakespeare, and Waller, and copies of Noy's *Compleat lawyer*, Walton's *Compleat angler*, and *Hodder's arithmetick*.

Fig. 3.2C The inscription of Katherein Spurwaie, dated 1658, on the flyleaf of a copy of Richard Baxter, *The saints' everlasting rest*, 1658. Bodleian Library Vet.A3.e.556. By permission of the Bodleian Libraries, The University of Oxford.

women than men to women—Fig. 3.3 shows a late seventeenth-century Bible given to a girl in 1735 by her grandmother, then aged 85. In Fig. 3.4, an aristocratic lady patron is giving a devotional book to another woman, perhaps an acquaintance or someone in a position felt worthy of reward. Handsome copies of devotional books passing down the female side of family lines through several generations is a commonly encountered model, noted by Natalie Zemon Davis as books becoming 'carriers of relationships'.[50] Florid and more decorative inscriptions are more often

---

[50] Natalie Zemon Davis, *Society and culture in early modern France* (London: Duckworth, 1975), 192.

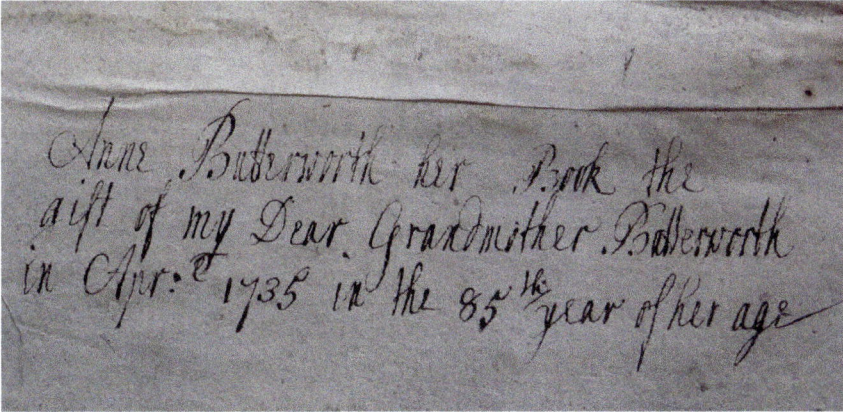

Fig. 3.3 'Anne Butterworth her Book the gift of my Dear Grandmother Butterworth in Apr: 1735 in the 85th year of her age', on the flyleaf of a copy of *The holy Bible*, 1689. Author's collection.

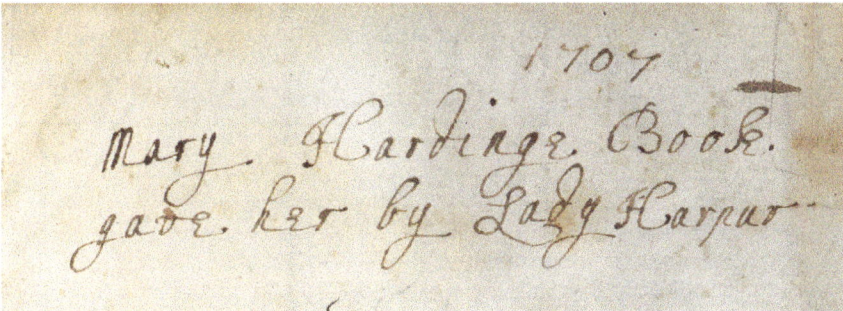

Fig. 3.4 '1707 Mary Hardinge Book gave her by Lady Harpur', on the flyleaf of a copy of Symon Patrick, *The Christian sacrifice*, 1701. Cambridge University Library Rel. d.70.5. Reproduced by permission of the Syndics of Cambridge University Library.

found in female inscriptions than in male ones, and examples like that in Fig. 3.5 (or 3.2C) are not unusual. Women could also sometimes have more inventive fun on their flyleaves, as Joyce Swingfeild did in Fig. 3.6 in the middle of the century. These kinds of inscriptions are most commonly, but not invariably, found in English language books, fitting that common trope of female ownership.

Joint inscriptions

An intriguing subset of the category of female inscriptions in books is that of joint ones, where a woman's name appears alongside a man's. The best-known example

Fig. 3.5 The more florid inscription of Anne Paule, dated 1660, on the flyleaf of a copy of St Augustine, *Certeine select prayers*, 1575. Bodleian Library Don.f.328. By permission of the Bodleian Libraries, The University of Oxford.

is probably that of Thomas and Isabella Hervey, of Ickworth House in Suffolk; there are over 200 books there today, and others scattered around the world, which carry the distinctive inscription 'Tho: & Isabella Hervey', or close variants. Thomas (1625–94) was the last of a line of sub-aristocratic Herveys, before his descendants started becoming Earls of Bristol; he was married to Isabella (1625–86, née May) for nearly 30 years before she predeceased him. Their library has been studied by Emma Smith, who has asked all the obvious questions of these books, to work out what the inscription signifies, whether they are his books, her books, their books, or a mixture.[51] It is evident that the inscriptions are all in Thomas's hand, many probably written in simultaneous batches, and they seem to manifest affectionate acknowledgment of a happy union, rather than any more

---

[51] Emma Smith, 'Marital marginalia: the seventeenth-century library of Thomas and Isabella Hervey', in Katharine Acheson (ed.), *Early modern English marginalia* (London: Routledge, 2019), ch. 8.

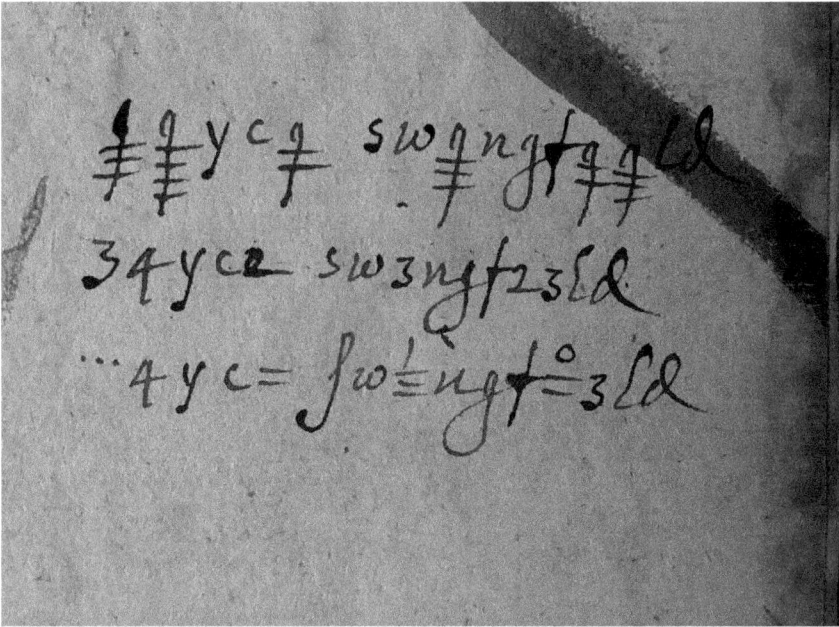

Fig. 3.6 The inscription of Joyce Swingfeild, in codes of her own devising, on the flyleaf of a copy of Georges de Scudéry, *Curia politiae*, 1654. Plume Library, Maldon. By permission of the Trustees of Thomas Plume's Library.

subtle statement about shared reading activity. This interpretation is strengthened by the existence of a small batch of books which seem to have originally been Isabella's own, which Thomas annotated with a mournful quotation from Virgil after her death.[52]

The Herveys are the best-known example of this kind of joint inscription, but such things are not uncommon, though usually encountered as one-off examples. There are also some seventeenth-century book labels like this, and an embroidered binding in the Henry Davis Collection at the British Library, with the arms of Henry Norreys on the front and those of his wife, Margaret, on the back.[53] Thomas Rawlinson rather unhelpfully cut the inscription in Fig. 3.7 out of what was probably a sixteenth-century edition of Chaucer, and mounted it in one of his autograph albums; here, the late sixteenth- or early seventeenth-century inscriptions 'Anne Barlee' and 'Will[ia]m Barlee' do appear to be in different hands, with Anne's in both an italic hand and a smudged secretary, and William's in secretary.

---

[52] Ibid.

[53] B. N. Lee, *Early printed book labels* (Pinner: Private Libraries Association, 1976), nos 192, 256; M. M. Foot, *The Henry Davis gift: a collection of bookbindings*, vol. 2 (London: British Library, 1983), pp. 92–3.

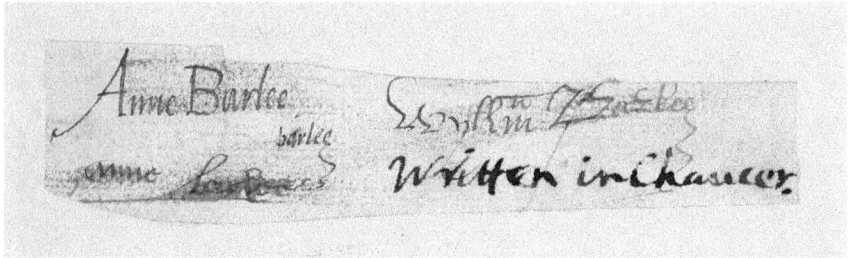

Fig. 3.7 Inscriptions 'Anne Barlee' and 'Will[ia]m Barlee', cut out of an early edition of Chaucer. Bodleian Library MS Rawl.D.1386/38. By permission of the Bodleian Libraries, The University of Oxford.

There is rather more to go on in a 1550 edition of Chaucer now in the Folger Library, where there are late sixteenth-century inscriptions of Thomas Vernon and Dorothy Vernon, certainly in the same hand, just below the note, 'A good woman is a crown of gold to her husband and an evell woman is the sting of a serpent.' As Alison Wiggins has pointed out, writing about this book, that was probably written by a man.[54] The Vernons are identifiable; they married around 1578 and headed a gentry household in Cheshire. The book first belonged to Dorothy, who also inscribed the book with her maiden name of Egerton, and there are annotations in the book by other family members.

No single pattern emerges from these various examples of joint inscriptions as regards whether they represent joint use of the books, or joint ownership in the minds of the individuals. Kate Loveman, in her study of reading in the Pepys household, observed that it is sometimes not clear whether books belonged to Samuel, or Elizabeth, or both of them; Elizabeth never marked the books, but Samuel's diary records her reading of some of them.[55] Under English law of the time, joint ownership of moveable goods within a married household, including any brought by the woman at the time of marriage, was not technically recognized. Are these people just enlightened, and ahead of their time? The embroidered armorial binding may remind us that the bringing together of male and female signs of identity happened all the time in heraldry, through the marshalling of arms when people married, and that is not usually ascribed to sentiment or ideas of sharing; as one of the standard heraldic textbooks puts it, marshalling indicates 'sovereignty, dominion, alliance, descent, or pretension'.[56] Each case needs to be assessed on its evidence, but without forgetting the contemporary context.

[54] Alison Wiggins, 'What did Renaissance readers write in their printed copies of Chaucer?', *The Library*, 7th ser. 9 (2008), pp. 3–36, 26.
[55] Loveman, *Samuel Pepys and his books*, 143.
[56] A. C. Fox-Davies, *A complete guide to heraldry* (London: Jack, 1909), 523.

Bookplates and armorials

As discussed more fully in Chapter 6, two key ways of marking the ownership of books emerged or matured during the seventeenth century: the use of armorial binding stamps, and bookplates. An obvious question to ask is how extensively these were taken up by women during this period. The answer is, not much: disproportionately little, in light of the extent to which women did have books of their own (or, to turn that around, perhaps another reason why female book ownership has been so much below the radar). Bookplate use became popular in England at the end of the seventeenth century, and many were made in the so-called Early Armorial design which was popular until about 1720.[57] Alongside several hundred such plates made for men, there is only a small handful made for women. The 'Brighton Album' in the Franks Collection of bookplates in the British Museum contains over 600 bookplates from this period, of which only 24 belonged to women.[58] Most of them were commissioned for the wives of peers or baronets (there is a notable paucity of bookplates made for women in families below these social ranks, although there are plenty made for men), and where there is a female plate it is usually the case that one was also made for the husband, or for other members of the same family.

A clutch of bookplates was made for members of the Brownlow household, of Belton House in Lincolnshire, all dated 1698, and all engraved by William Jackson.[59] There is one for the head of the household, Sir William, but also ones for his wife, Dorothy, and for his sister-in-law Dame Alice, widow of the third baronet, which was made for her in two sizes, large and small. Dorothy's mother, Anna Mason (d. 1717), widow of Sir Richard Mason (c.1633–85), Controller of the Green Cloth for James II, also had a bookplate made by Jackson, dated 1701 (Fig. 3.8).[60] This family were early adopters of the idea of the bookplate, and clearly had books within the house in separate personal closets. The Cokes of Holkham Hall, Edward and Cary, have already been mentioned; their his and hers bookplates are not of identical design but both dated 1701.[61] She is described on her bookplate as his wife, but there is of course no corresponding wording on Edward's plate.[62] Baptist Noel, third Earl of Gainsborough, had a

---

[57] See p. 124 below.

[58] British Museum, Dept of Prints and Drawings, Franks Collection vol. LVI; David Pearson, 'The Brighton Album revisited', *The Bookplate Journal* (forthcoming).

[59] E. R. J. Gambier Howe, *Franks bequest: Catalogue of British and American book plates*, vol. 1 (London: British Museum, 1903), pp. 140–41; Peter Hoare, 'The perils of provenance', *Library History* 18 (2002), pp. 225–34.

[60] B. N. Lee, *British bookplates* (Newton Abbot: David & Charles, 1979), pp. 44–5.

[61] John Blatchly, *Some Suffolk and Norfolk ex-libris* (London: Bookplate Society, 2000), pp. 12–13.

[62] These early female bookplates commonly use this kind of wording to describe their owner: 'Dame Ann Barnardiston wife to Sr Thomas Barnardiston...' (Franks *120), 'Dame Alice Brownlowe relict of Sr John Brownlowe...and daughter of Richard Sherard...' (Franks *139).

Fig. 3.8 The bookplate of Dame Anna Margaretta Mason (d. 1717). By permission of The British Museum.

bookplate made for him dated 1700, and the catalyst for making a separate one for his wife, Dorothy, dated 1707, is clearly their marriage in February of that year; it seems likely that this was commissioned more out of motives of status and family achievement than bibliophily, but again signifies a discrete collection of books.[63]

---

[63] Howe, *Franks bequest*, vol. 2, 302.

There are similarly fewer than a dozen armorial binding stamps used by women throughout the seventeenth century, nearly all of them from the peerage. Some are associated with gifts rather than ownership; books stamped with the arms of Rachel Bourchier, Countess of Bath (1613–80), indicate books bought with money she gave to academic institutions, not books she owned.[64] Women's armorial tools are typically small and modest, based on crests rather than full armorial achievements, unlike many of the armorial stamps used by men. There are half a dozen surviving books with one of two similar armorial crest tools put on Lady Anne Clifford's books, and a similarly small handful of books with one of three coronetted initial tools used for Mary Dormer, Countess of Carnarvon (1655–1709), who sometimes inscribed her books M Carnarvon (Fig. 3.9).[65]

In the context of armorial bindings it may be noted that there is one Elkanah Settle book which stands out among his voluminous output as having been regularly given to women rather than men. Settle is an unusual and interesting figure in the early eighteenth-century book-historical landscape, well known for commissioning bindings on copies of his poems carrying the coats of arms of prospective patrons, who sometimes returned them unwanted, when the binding might be recycled as a palimpsest with another coat of arms pasted over.[66] Over 350 of his bindings survive, almost invariably presented to men. Of around 120 separate poems making up this corpus, there is one which was regularly dispatched with a coat of arms on the cover on a lozenge, not a shield, showing that it was intended for a woman.[67] Settle's *Pindaric poem, on the propagation of the Gospel in foreign parts*, was printed in 1711, and celebrates the work of the recently founded Society for the Propagation of the Gospel; it is not immediately clear why it was thought to be so suitable a target for female recipients. Part of its purpose was to encourage fund-raising for missionary work, and perhaps Settle hoped that women would be particularly sympathetic, and able to influence the holders of purse strings; but maybe he merely wanted an opportunity to send his poems to women as well as men, and thought this was suitable.[68] Over half the known surviving copies—seventeen are recorded in the *English Short-Title*

---

[64] https://armorial.library.utoronto.ca/stamps/IBOU002_s1 (accessed 21 Oct. 2018).

[65] https://armorial.library.utoronto.ca/stamp-owners/CLI001 (accessed 21 Oct. 2018); https://armorial.library.utoronto.ca/stamp-owners/DOR001 (accessed 21 Oct. 2018).

[66] David Pearson, 'Elkanah Settle revisited', *Papers of the Bibliographical Society of America* 114 (2020), pp. 71–95.

[67] Unmarried and widowed women always display their arms on a lozenge, not a shield: Fox-Davies, *Complete guide*, 533–4. Some of the copies of this book sent out by Settle with apparently male arms on the covers, using a shield, may of course also have been intended for the lady of the house, as married women use a shield with their husband's arms.

[68] The text is a typical Settle panegyric, full of hyperbole and patriotic bombast. It is dedicated to Queen Anne, so there is a female connection there, but she was his dedicatee on other occasions, e.g. his *Carmen irenicum* (1707), which is not found with lozenges on his presentation copies.

Fig. 3.9A The coronetted binding stamp of Mary Dormer, Countess of Carnarvon (1655–1709), from a copy of Edward Sparke, *Scintilla altaris*, 1678. Author's collection.

Fig. 3.9B Mary Dormer's inscription from the flyleaf of the same book.

Catalogue—retain their original presentation bindings, with arms on a lozenge, like the example in Fig. 3.10.[69]

The market for fine books for women

Personalized fancy bindings for ladies are more commonly encountered in the form of luxury bindings tooled with their names or initials, such as the example in Fig. 3.11, a 1660 Bible with the initials of Elizabeth Brodridge added in engraved silverware and incorporated in full in the contemporary fore-edge painting. A key point which has not hitherto been explicitly noted by book historians, but for which there is plentiful surviving evidence, is that there was clearly a part of the book trade throughout this period producing attractive books with women, rather than men, very much in mind. There are many published reproductions of the kinds of embroidered bindings which were popular in the first half of the seventeenth century, typically found on smaller-format Bibles and devotional books, which nowadays are usually the worse for wear but which in their day

---

[69] Other examples are British Library C.66.f.24, Winchester College Library Eccles 8C, Princeton University Library RHT 17th-777, New York Public Library Berg Coll 77–664, Maggs catalogue 1075 no.126 (now at McMaster University).

Fig. 3.10 One of the numerous copies of Elkanah Settle's *Pindaric poem*, 1711, presented to a woman (as is evident from the lozenge used for the coat of arms). Guildhall Library, London Settle 45. By permission of Guildhall Library, City of London.

would have been bright and attractive.[70] They were produced in great numbers between about 1600 and 1640, and we know from a 1638 petition presented by London milliners that there was a professional operation behind the production of ready-made covers for such books.[71] Alexandra Walsham has written an article about these 'jewels for gentlewomen', interested particularly in their manifesting of 'the shape and texture of piety in early modern England'.[72] They were of course owned primarily by women, as is regularly demonstrated by those which have contemporary ownership inscriptions, and would often have been gifts.

The heyday for such bindings passed in the middle of the century, but the production of ready-made fine books for ladies did not. The Restoration period has sometimes been marked as the high point of fine English bookbinding, partly because binders like Samuel Mearne exercised exquisite craftsmanship, and partly because the period was well studied and written up by Howard Nixon who remains a standard authority in this field.[73] Nixon separated out the various workshops and helped us to distinguish Queens' Binder A from the Small Carnation Binder and the Centre-Rectangle Binder, but one point he did not bring out is how often these upmarket bindings of the late seventeenth-century are found on books given to or owned by women. There are countless copies of *The whole duty of man*, *The ladies' calling*, Bibles, prayers books, and similar devotional titles in these kinds of bindings with female inscriptions. It seems clear that they were produced—often, I think, ready-made in advance of sale—for a steady market in the supply of gifts and books which ladies of the better sort were meant to have, partly for their spiritual wellbeing and partly to have about their persons in church and closet to demonstrate their social standing. When they survive in good condition, as many do, we may surmise that the latter purpose took precedence over the former. Books like this can be found in every grade of fineness, from the relatively modest to the most luxurious. Fig. 3.12 shows a small Thomas Ken catechism text in quite simply tooled black goatskin, given to a woman in 1686 by her cousin Frances, and passed on to her own daughter in 1704; Fig. 3.13 shows something a little more elaborate and expensive, on a 1700 edition of one of Jeremy Taylor's devotional texts, with a contemporary inscription noting the gift to a woman from her aunt. We do not have any engravings of fashionable shopping outlets in seventeenth-century England quite like Abraham

---

[70] E.g. Foot, *Henry Davis gift* vol. 2, nos 65, 80–82, 85, 87–8, 96; F. Bearman et al., *Fine and historic bookbindings from the Folger Shakespeare Library* (Washington, DC: Folger Library, 1992), pp. 135–7, 140–44; M. Foot, *Pictorial bookbindings* (London: British Library, 1986), pp. 56–9.

[71] H. M. Nixon and M. Foot, *The history of decorated bookbinding in England* (Oxford: Clarendon Press, 1992), pp. 54–5.

[72] Alexandra Walsham, 'Jewels for gentlewomen: religious books as artefacts in late medieval and early modern England', in R. Swanson (ed.), *The church and the book* (Woodbridge: Boydell and Brewer, 2004), pp. 123–42.

[73] H. M. Nixon, *English Restoration bookbindings: Samuel Mearne and his contemporaries* (London: British Library, 1974).

Fig. 3.11A The front cover of a handsomely bound copy of *The holy Bible*, 1660, with engraved silverware incorporating the initials of the owner, Elizabeth Brodridge. Bodleian Library Broxb.42.9. By permission of the Bodleian Libraries, The University of Oxford.

Fig. 3.11B The painted fore-edge of the same book, incorporating Elizabeth's name in the central wreath. By permission of the Bodleian Libraries, The University of Oxford.

Bosse's well-known depictions of the Galerie du Palais in Paris around 1640 (Fig. 3.14), but I believe that customers of both sexes would have frequented upmarket bookshops in late seventeenth-century London to find places like that at the left of the picture, where the rows of ready-bound books with gilt backs behind the counter would have included these kinds of books made with ladies in mind.

Household books

Another category of book which is likely to have been in the hands of women at least as much as men, and probably more so, is that of the recipe or household book. These may have been printed, but more commonly manuscript, perhaps augmented over generations, and a reminder to us that for women as well as men, books meant the handwritten alongside the published. Great numbers of these survive, and they can be found in many research libraries and record offices; there is a particularly good collection in the Wellcome Library, made readily accessible by a digitization programme.[74] As a genre they have recently begun to be seriously explored by social and culinary historians and to have their own dedicated literature; one such source defines a recipe book, 'whether printed or manuscript, [as] one which collects together and communicates information about the preparation of foodstuffs, drink, medications, cosmetics, household substances and other materials, including veterinary treatments, paints and occupationally specific materials'.[75] As is pointed out there, books like this are often multigenerational,

---

[74] https://wellcomelibrary.org/collections/digital-collections/recipe-books/ (accessed 28 Oct. 2018). A search of the Wellcome online catalogue for recipe books, 1600–1699, returns over 150 items.

[75] M. DiMeo and S. Pennell (eds), *Reading and writing recipe books, 1550–1800* (Manchester: Manchester University Press, 2013), 6. See also E. Leong, *Recipes and everyday knowledge: medicine, science and the household in early modern England* (Chicago: University of Chicago Press, 2018).

Fig. 3.12A A simple but elegant gilt-tooled goatskin binding, on a copy of Thomas Ken, *An exposition of the church-catechism*, 1685. Author's collection.

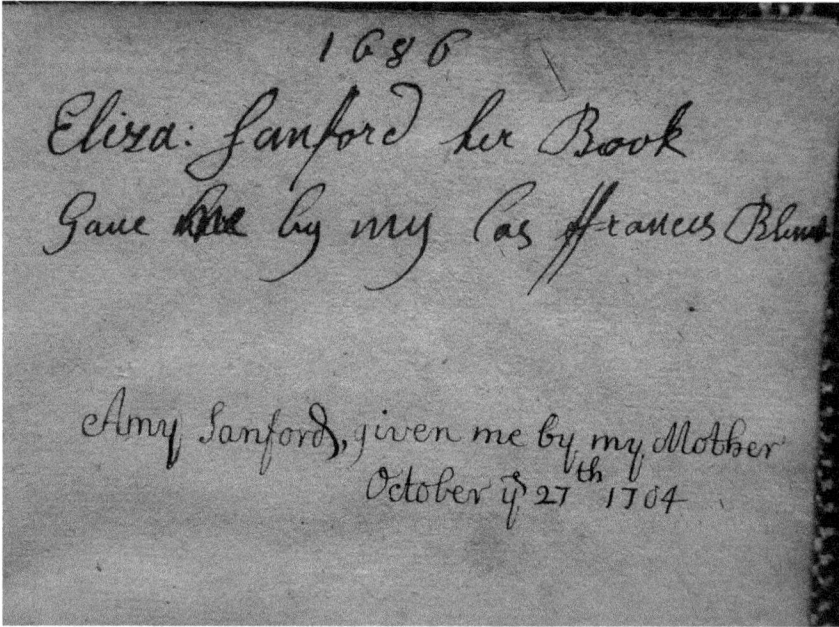

Fig. 3.12B Inscriptions from the flyleaf of the same book: '1686 Eliza: Sanford her Book Gaue by my Cos Frances Blunt'; 'Amy Sanford, giuen me by my Mother, October y^e 27th 1704'.

passing down families and being augmented along the way, more commonly descending through female lines than male ones; they may be entirely manuscript, or hybrid assemblages of printed books with annotations, or scrapbook-like manuscripts with bits of print inserted.[76] They were kept in households of many kinds, from the humble to the grand, though the realities of survival mean that a disproportionate number of those which have come down to us emanate from aristocratic or gentry families, where they may actually have been initially created by scribes or amanuenses. Richard Aspin has written about one such linked pair of manuscript recipe books now in the Wellcome Library, one in the hand of Elizabeth Okeover of Okeover Hall, Staffordshire (b. 1644) and another associated with her aunt of the same name (1629–c.1671), written out by a professional scribe.[77] Fig. 3.15 shows openings from a recipe book which passed through hands more of the middling sort; this blank book in a simple and minimally decorated contemporary calfskin binding was first owned by an Amy Eyton, who

---

[76] Domestic manuscripts frequently passed down through a female lineage": DiMeo and Pennell, *Reading and writing recipe books*, p. 35.

[77] R. Aspin, 'Who was Elizabeth Okeover?', *Medical History* 44 (2000), pp. 531–40; Wellcome Library MSS 3712 and 7391.

Fig. 3.13A A more upmarket gilt-tooled goatskin binding, on a copy of Jeremy Taylor, *The rule and exercise of holy living*, 1700. Collection of Mr Anthony Davis.

Fig. 3.13B The contemporary inscription from the flyleaf, 'Sarah Adeane Her Book Given me by my Aunt Fleetwood'.

Fig. 3.14 Abraham Bosse, *La Galerie du Palais*, an etching of *c*.1637–40 showing the shopping arcade at the Palais de Justice in Paris. By permission of The British Museum.

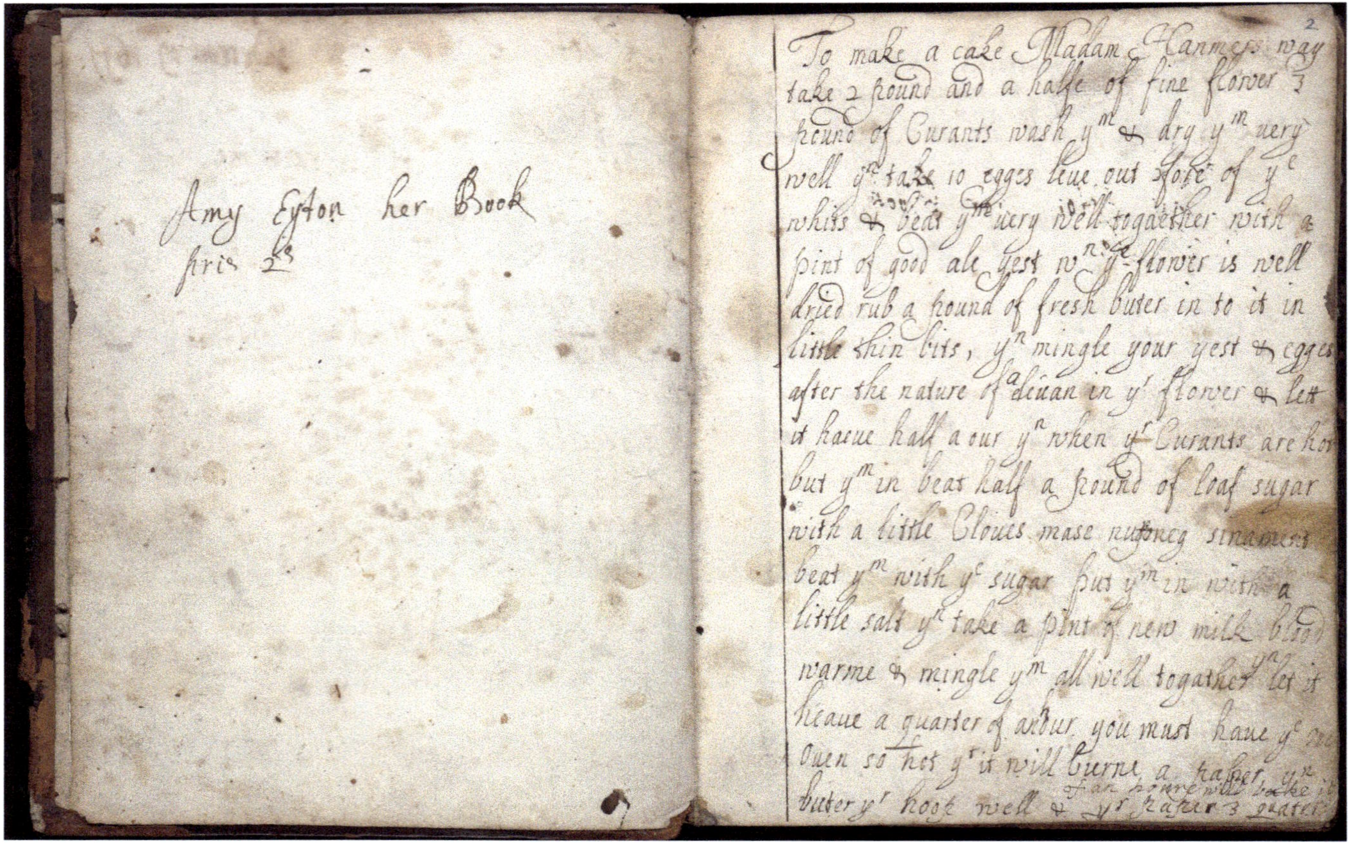

To make a cake Madam Carnes way
take 2 pound and a halfe of fine flower 3
pound of Currans wash ym & dry ym very
well & take 10 eggs leue out fore of ye
whites & beat ym very well togather with a
pint of good ale yest rub ye flower is well
dryed rub a pound of fresh buter on it in
little thin bits, ye mingle your yest & eggs
after the nature of Pancan ye flower & let
it haue halfe a ... when ye Currans are ...
but ym in leas half a pound of loaf sugar
with a little Cloues mace nutmeg sinamon
beat ym with ye sugar ... ym in with a
little salt & haue a pint of new milk ...
warme & mingle ym all will togather lay it
& leaue a quarter of a howr you must haue ...
oun so het yt it will Burne a toast ...
buter yr hott will & ... paper 3 ...

Amy Eyton her Book

pris 2s

Fig. 3.15A A late seventeenth-century household recipe book, begun by Amy Eyton, who noted that the book cost her two shillings. Wellcome Library MS 2323.

Fig. 3.15B The first flyleaf of the same book, on which Amy Eyton made a list of her clothes, including 'shifts', 'tuckers', and 'quaifs'.

bought it for two shillings around 1677, and who part-filled it with numerous cookery and medical recipes while also noting on the flyleaf 'a note of my close [clothes]'.[78] Written from both ends, it carries the inscription of another Ayton (Mary), and was clearly used over several generations as a growing household compendium of useful information.

Conclusions

This chapter has exemplified and enhanced the central point which others have made, and on which various academic projects are actively focused: that the ownership of books by women was widespread and ubiquitous throughout the Stuart period. Such ownership embraced books of all kinds and formats, and can be evidenced via many channels. What is much harder to do is to fill the gap identified by David McKitterick in his article on Elizabeth Puckering: 'as a subject, book ownership amongst women awaits its historian.'[79] It is easy enough to produce overviews like this based on exemplars, but if that historian's role is to produce a comprehensive chronicle or reference base of all the women who owned books at that time, I doubt it can be done, because the evidence is too dispersed, elusive, or lost. It is possible to list, in the Appendix, the names of over 1,300 seventeenth-century men who were book owners of what could reasonably be called private libraries, but I cannot do it for women, although I am sure there were many more than we currently have documented. Should we just add the names of all the female members of the households of those men, on the assumption that they could have had access to, and use of, those books? That would be an oversimplification, ignoring social and educational realities, and losing sight of the many instances of genuinely female libraries.

These questions will continue to be explored, but meanwhile, in conclusion, we might also reflect on some of the ways in which modern cultural historians have focused on the reading woman as something subversive or controversial. Various recent writers in this field have looked for sharp edges: James Conlon, for example, tells us that 'faced with a reading woman, man is, at least on some unconscious level, facing a scene that threatens his cultural hegemony'.[80] Jacqueline Pearson built an article about women's reading around the sense that this 'was an area of conflict in the sixteenth and seventeenth centuries', pointing out that 'Shakespeare tends to depict acts of reading by women in a range of suggestive and sinister ways'.[81] The

---

[78] Wellcome Library MS 2323: https://wellcomelibrary.org/item/b19567820#?c=0&m=0&s=0&cv=1&z=-0.074 per cent2C-0.036 per cent2C1.1478 per cent2C0.721 (accessed 28 Oct. 2018).

[79] McKitterick, 'Women and their books', 363.

[80] J. Conlon, 'Men reading women reading: interpreting images of women readers', *Frontiers: A Journal of Women Studies* 26 (2005), pp. 37–58.

[81] Jacqueline Pearson, 'Women reading, reading women', in H. Wilcox (ed.), *Women and literature in Britain* (Cambridge: Cambridge University Press, 1996), pp. 80–99.

evidence set out in this chapter surely suggests that these people perhaps protest too much. Suzanne Hull pointed out: 'by 1640 reading by women was seldom attacked. Instead, it was even seen as a necessity', and men may have felt less threatened by a woman with a book in her hands than some gender politicians might wish. Women owning books in the seventeenth century was not adversarial, contentious, or an undermining of the social order; it was entirely ordinary.

4

Books for the common man

Book ownership outside academic, professional, and wealthy circles

Fig. 4.1 shows a number of pages from a copy of the 1638 London edition of *The soules exaltation*, a set of sermons by Thomas Hooker, a Puritan preacher who was very popular with his East Anglian congregations, but whose views were not at all harmonious with Laudian Anglicanism, and who by the time that book was published had already fled first to Holland and then to New England.[1] It is a very imperfect copy; it lacks its title page and other leaves, is ragged, torn, and stained, and whatever binding it once had has been completely lost by an early twentieth-century rebinding. It is not the kind of book which normally commands much attention from bibliophile collectors, and would be described by a modern bookseller apologetically, but it has very interesting testimony to its early life manifested in the many annotations running throughout its pages. Its provenance is not found neatly contained on its flyleaf or title page, but in names and inscriptions written all the way through, up and down margins, at the ends of chapters, wherever there is blank space; they are written in several hands, with varying degrees of neatness or apparent education, and there are scribbles and pen trials interspersed. One of the neater hands is that of a man called Robert Fisher, who tells us that he owned the book in 1660, and elsewhere that he was the curate of Thornthwaite; scattered throughout the book there are inscriptions of Daniel, Edward, and James Stanger, and at one point a woman's name, Jannet Thompson. On one blank verso a helpful note tells us that the book belongs to James Stanger, having been given him by Robert Fisher in 1662 'in steade of one that he had of mine', when Fisher went away from Thornthwaite, having been Reader there for fifteen years.

Thornthwaite is a tiny village in the Lake District, at the south end of Bassenthwaite Lake, a little to the north-west of Keswick and nestling at the foot of the Whinlatter Pass. It is a very scenic part of the world though not one which is regularly associated with books and learning, especially in the seventeenth century, when it was most certainly at the back of beyond. But this book was there, and very actively used; the pattern of inscriptions, stains, and tears suggests use of

---

[1] S. Bush (3 Jan. 2008), 'Hooker, Thomas (1586?–1647)', *Oxford Dictionary of National Biography*. Retrieved 31 Oct. 2018 from: http://www.oxforddnb.com/view/10.1093/ref:odnb/9780198614128.001.0001/odnb-9780198614128-e-13697.

Book Ownership in Stuart England: The Lyell Lectures, 2018. David Pearson, Oxford University Press (2021).
© David Pearson.
DOI: 10.1093/oso/9780198870128.003.0004

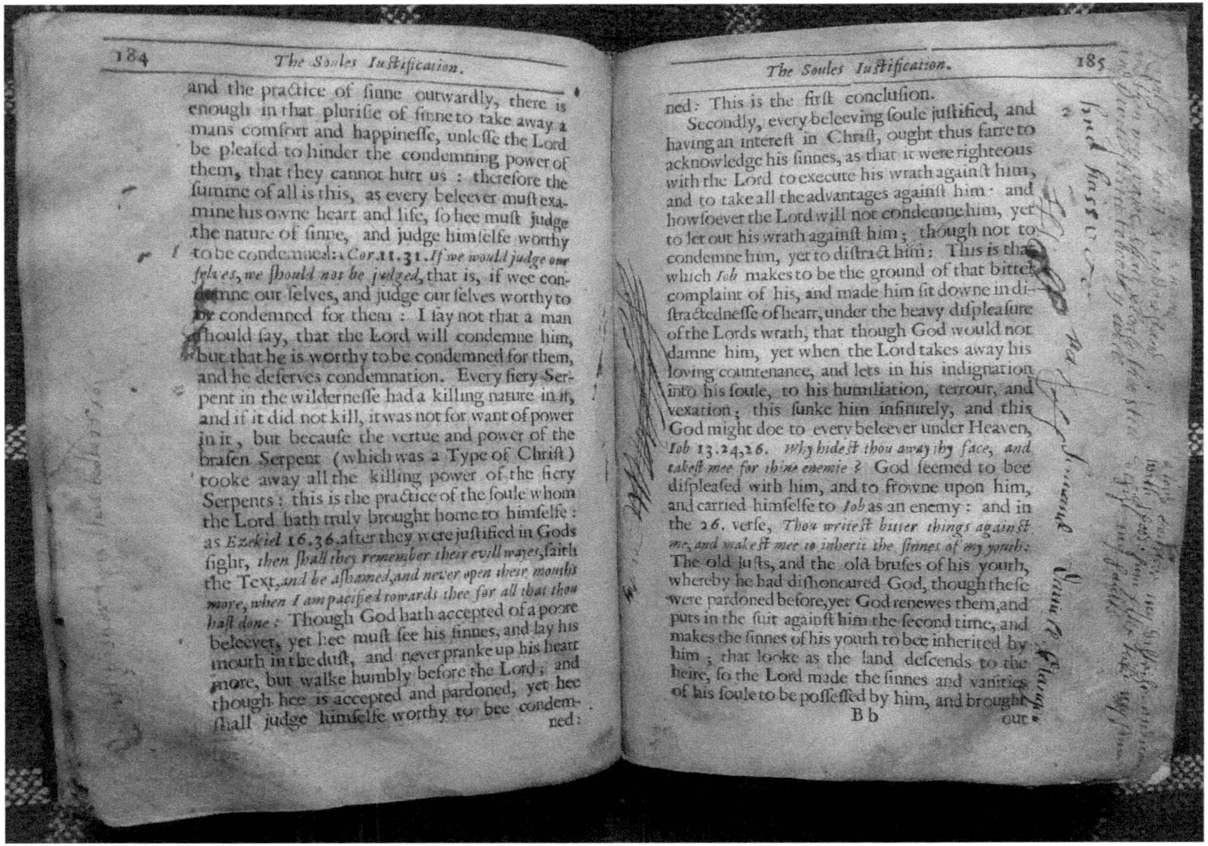
184 The Soules Justification.

and the practice of sinne outwardly, there is enough in that plurisie of sinne to take away a mans comfort and happinesse, unlesse the Lord be pleased to hinder the condemning power of them, that they cannot hurt us: therefore the summe of all is this, as every beleever must examine his owne heart and life, so hee must judge the nature of sinne, and judge himselfe worthy to be condemned: 1 Cor. 11.31. *If we would judge our selves, we should not be judged*, that is, if wee condemne our selves, and judge our selves worthy to be condemned for them: I say not that a man should say, that the Lord will condemne him, but that he is worthy to be condemned for them, and he deserves condemnation. Every fiery Serpent in the wildernesse had a killing nature in it, and if it did not kill, it was not for want of power in it, but because the vertue and power of the brasen Serpent (which was a Type of Christ) tooke away all the killing power of the fiery Serpents: this is the practice of the soule whom the Lord hath truly brought home to himselfe: as *Ezekiel* 16.36. after they were justified in Gods sight, *then shall they remember their evill wayes*, saith the Text, *and be ashamed, and never open their mouths more, when I am pacified towards thee for all that thou hast done*: Though God hath accepted of a poore beleever, yet hee must see his sinnes, and lay his mouth in the dust, and never pranke up his heart more, but walke humbly before the Lord; and though hee is accepted and pardoned, yet hee shall judge himselfe worthy to bee condemned:

The Soules Justification. 185

ned: This is the first conclusion.

Secondly, every beleeving soule justified, and having an interest in Christ, ought thus farre to acknowledge his sinnes, as that it were righteous with the Lord to execute his wrath against him, and to take all the advantages against him: and howsoever the Lord will not condemne him, yet to let out his wrath against him; though not to condemne him, yet to distract him: This is that which *Job* makes to be the ground of that bitter complaint of his, and made him sit downe in distractednesse of heart, under the heavy displeasure of the Lords wrath, that though God would not damne him, yet when the Lord takes away his loving countenance, and lets in his indignation into his soule, to his humiliation, terrour, and vexation; this sunke him infinitely, and this God might doe to every beleever under Heaven, *Job* 13.24,26. *Why hidest thou away thy face, and takest mee for thine enemie?* God seemed to bee displeased with him, and to frowne upon him, and carried himselfe to *Job* as an enemy: and in the 26. verse, *Thou writest bitter things against me, and makest mee to inherit the sinnes of my youth*: The old lusts, and the old bruses of his youth, whereby he had dishonoured God, though these were pardoned before, yet God renewes them, and puts in the suit against him the second time, and makes the sinnes of his youth to bee inherited by him; that looke as the land descends to the heire, so the Lord made the sinnes and vanities of his soule to be possessed by him, and brought out

Bb

Fig. 4.1A A An opening from a copy of Thomas Hooker, *The soules exaltation*, 1638, with annotations and marks of use by a late seventeenth-century Cumbrian yeoman family. Author's collection.

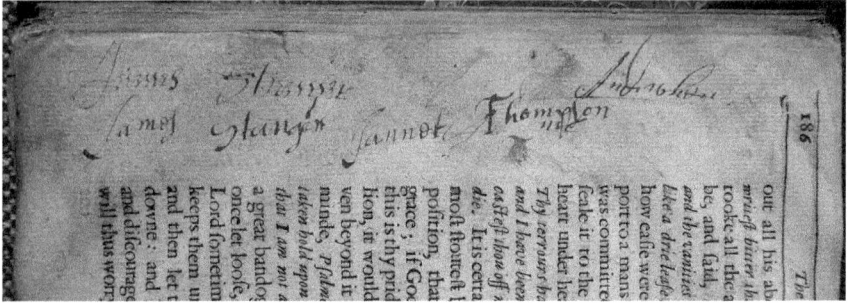

Fig. 4.1B The names of James Stanger and Jannet Thompson written up a margin (they were married in 1676).

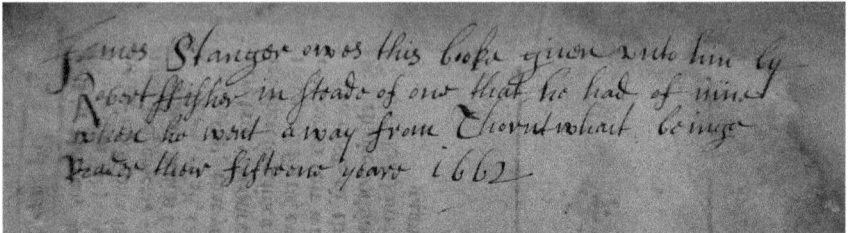

Fig.4.1C An inscription in the book noting that James Stanger was given the book in 1662 by Robert Fisher, Reader at Thornthwaite, 'in steade of one that he had of mine'.

the pages not only for writing practice and doodling but also for serious reading and the recording of devotional sentiments. Fisher may have had a university education, but the Stangers are probably best classified as yeomen farmers. None of them are is easy to trace; Fisher being Reader for fifteen years to 1662 suggests an ejected Puritan, but he is not listed in *Calamy revised* or the Church of England database. A Robert Fisher was vicar of Penrith in the early 1660s but he only graduated from Cambridge in 1662; he could conceivably have been this man's son. The university lists have a Robert Fisher graduating from Emmanuel (Cambridge) in 1623, or one matriculating from Queen's (Oxford) in 1631, with no further details of their careers; either is possible.[2] Numerous Fishers and Stangers are recorded in the Keswick area in the late sixteenth century, in the records associated with the German miners who were brought over to mine copper and lead there in the 1560s, so they were families long established in the region.[3] Some of these Stangers can be found in parochial records; the James Stanger and Jannet Thompson whose names appear in this book were married at

---

[2] J. Venn and J. A. Venn, *Alumni Cantabrigienses...to 1751*, vol. 2 (Cambridge: Cambridge University Press, 1922), 143; J. Foster, *Alumni Oxonienses* (Oxford: James Parker & Co., 1891), 501.

[3] W. G. Collingwood, *Elizabethan Keswick* (Kendal: Titus Wilson, 1912); see the numerous Fishers/Visschers, and Stangers, in the index. There is a Stanger Street in Keswick today.

Threlkeld in 1676.[4] The latest date in any of these inscriptions is 1712 associated with a Daniel Stanger, and I assume that these other Stangers are James and Jannet's children, suggesting that the book stayed in the family for at least a couple of generations. It was bought in a bookshop in Whitehaven in 2012, and although it is silent on its whereabouts between the early eighteenth and early twenty-first centuries, I suspect it never left Cumbria during that time.

The point here, of course, is that this book was owned in the seventeenth century by people who were not members of the educated, professional classes associated with the capital or other centres of civilized activity, or of the upper strata of society. It was owned in a remote rural place by people of humbler background who are not the kind which come most immediately to mind when we talk about book ownership in the seventeenth century, and certainly not if we talk about book collecting. However, anyone who has handled seventeenth-century books in any quantity will know that this kind of evidence is not uncommon; the challenge lies around investigating how widespread this kind of ownership was. How far beyond those professional and educated circles can we go and still find people owning and reading books, and what kinds of books would they would be?

It is a challenge not unlike that mentioned at the end of the preceding chapter, of mapping book ownership by women; there is a lack of documentary evidence, beyond inscriptions scattered in books in libraries across the world. Of the 1,370 or so people in the list of seventeenth-century book owners in the Appendix, the great majority are educated, professional men, or members of the aristocracy and gentry, such as we might obviously expect to have had books in their lives, or to have needed them for their regular business; they account for at least 90 per cent of the whole. The list includes some schoolmasters or apothecaries, who were often in the less wealthy quartiles of society, but for whom there is still an obvious rationale for book ownership. It also includes a number of people classified as merchants or businessmen, and there was surely no end of homes across the country where middling prosperous (or better) people like this, whose education would have relied on schooling and apprenticeship without university, would have had books in their possession. Anthony Abdy, a successful East India merchant who died in 1640 having been an alderman of London, had books in his little parlour in his house at Lime Street, valued at £12, and also had some books in his house in Leytonstone, including Pliny (probably in English) and Knolles's *Turkish history*.[5] Thomas Craddock, a merchant who died in Port Royal, Jamaica in 1684, left behind just over 100 books, including plays, pamphlets, and songs as well as a not unusual mix of English devotional and historical texts.[6] Early eighteenth-century sale catalogues

---

[4] Precise family details can be established via https://www.ancestry.co.uk/.
[5] As recorded in his probate inventory, London Metropolitan Archives CLC/521/MS03760.
[6] Roderick Cave, 'Thomas Craddock's books: a West India merchant's stock', *The Book Collector* 25 (1976), pp. 481–90.

survive for a painter (Henry Cook) and a gardener (George London), and we have records of library sales, though without surviving catalogues, for several people of that time described as merchants, such as Nathaniel Shepheard in 1709 and John Burgess in the same year.[7] But this takes us back into the territory of the relatively prosperous and the metropolitan, not the rural or less well-off.

Documented examples

This is not uncharted territory and I am not the first to ask such questions. There is quite an extensive literature of exploration in this field, coming at it from various directions. The widespread distribution and consumption of cheap print throughout the Stuart period, of ballads and chapbooks as well as pamphlets and newsbooks, has seen numerous researchers building on the foundations laid by Margaret Spufford's *Small books and pleasant histories*, and a multi-volume Oxford University Press series on Popular Print Culture is in progress.[8] The boundary is grey and arguably meaningless, but for the current study I am more interested in books than chapbooks, about how many there were in average homes, and I take for granted that we understand that anyone who could read in the seventeenth century was 'exposed to a steady hail of printed pamphlets of news, political and religious propaganda, astrological prediction and advice, songs, sensation, sex and fantasy', as Spufford put it.[9]

Abigail Williams's *Social history of books* looks at many of these questions in the context of the eighteenth century, and draws on a range of sources to produce an overview of the ways in which books were owned, read, and regarded in what she calls the homes of the middling sort then.[10] She uses probate inventories, diaries and journals, statistics on literacy and book production, images, and evidence in surviving volumes to assemble a picture of the ubiquity of books in the social fabric and as possessions in many households. All of these things exist for the seventeenth century, though generally in lesser quantities, and have been variously drawn upon. Peter Clark looked at probate inventories in Kent from the late sixteenth and first half of the seventeenth century to find that by 1640, book ownership in towns across all sections of society turned up in about 40 per cent

---

[7] See Appendix, p. 206.
[8] Margaret Spufford, *Small books and pleasant histories: popular fiction and its readership in seventeenth-century England* (London: Methuen, 1981); G. Kelly (gen. ed.), *The Oxford history of popular print culture* (Oxford: Oxford University Press, 2011–) (vols. 1 and 6 have so far appeared).
[9] Spufford, *Small books*, p. xviii.
[10] Abigail Williams, *The social life of books: reading together in the eighteenth-century home* (New Haven, CT: Yale University Press, 2017).

of cases.[11] Spufford, in the *Cambridge history of libraries*, while noting the scarcity of these kinds of lists, refers to an inventory of 1614 for a labourer in the Forest of Arden, who left ten shillings' worth of 'certain small books' as part of an estate valued at just under £9.[12] Robert Tudman, a Cheshire yeoman who died in 1632, had six books valued at £1; John Parker, a Lichfield apothecary who died in 1655, owned 'sixteen books little and big'; Thomas Lawrence, a yeoman of Trumpington just outside Cambridge, had at least ten books in his study when he died in 1669; there are plenty of other examples like this.[13] John Tayer, a Gloucestershire shoemaker and glover, noted lists of his books in his account books in the late 1620s showing that he owned Bibles and devotional books, practical household texts and almanacs, and books on law and history.[14]

A recent volume of *Private libraries in Renaissance England* has a number of lists that fit under this heading, including Christopher Harrison, a Kendal merchant who died in 1612, whose inventory includes about thirty books, and Nathaniel Brading, a merchant adventurer, who had a library of similar size in 1645.[15] Harrison is described as 'a comfortable landowner with livestock and property', possibly in the clothing business; his books were almost entirely theological, and probably in English (the descriptions of some individual volumes are ambiguous), though he did have at least one book of husbandry alongside John Dod's exposition of the ten commandments, and the sermons of George Gifford and Henry Smith. Brading's inventory, apparently listing books which he took with him on a trading voyage to Madagascar, where he died, is also predominantly theological in content, though he also had a book of music, and a copy of Henry Peacham's *Compleat gentleman*. The diary of the London turner Nehemiah Wallington, who died in 1658, has been drawn on by numerous writers not only as evidence of the theological struggles of an ordinary artisan but also for its references to his reading, buying, and spending too much money on books.[16]

Mark Purcell has written about the library at Townend, near Windermere, an unusual survival of over 1,000 books accumulated over many centuries by the Browne family, in a remote yeoman farmhouse which is similar to that of the

---

[11] Peter Clark, 'The ownership of books in England, 1560–1640', in Laurence Stone (ed.), *Schooling and society: studies in the history of education* (Baltimore, MD: Johns Hopkins University Press, 1976), pp. 95–111.

[12] Margaret Spufford, 'Libraries of the "common sort"', in E. Leedham-Green and T. Webber (eds), *The Cambridge history of libraries in Britain and Ireland*, vol. 1 (Cambridge: Cambridge University Press, 2006), pp. 520–26, 522.

[13] Paul Pixton (ed.), *Wrenbury wills and inventories* (Chester: Record Society of Lancashire and Cheshire, 2009), 284; David Vaisey (ed.), *Probate inventories of Lichfield and district, 1568–1680* (Stafford: Staffordshire Record Society, 1969), 99; Spufford, 'Libraries', 524.

[14] Ibid. 523.

[15] R. Fehrenbach and J. Black (eds), *Private libraries in Renaissance England*, vol. 9 (Tempe: Arizona Center for Medieval and Renaissance Studies, 2017), pp. 149–55, 309–17.

[16] Paul Seaver, *Wallington's world: a Puritan artisan in seventeenth-century London* (London: Methuen, 1985), 5.

Stangers at Thornthwaite.[17] The Brownes began accumulating books there certainly by 1600, and the two Benjamins who were born in the second half of the seventeenth century and died in the middle of the eighteenth were keen book buyers, sourcing many of them from local booksellers and auction sales. That article begins with an account of a 1707 auction at Troutbeck, where 80 per cent of the 108 lots were books, which were bought not only by Browne but by numerous other local people. Purcell's book on the country house library also reminds us that houses with large numbers of servants might maintain small collections of books specifically for them, or that the other books in those libraries would at least provide exposure or opportunities for reading.[18] As many people have pointed out, seventeenth-century people across the whole social spectrum experienced print in all kinds of ways, from shops to the many uses to which waste paper was put, without having to own books. Poorer people 'might acquire books in various ways other than purchase: through borrowing from a local minister or school-teacher or a neighbour'.[19]

Evidence in books

Beyond the various kinds of secondary evidence, there is of course a huge reservoir of the primary sort to be found in surviving books, comprising not only names and identities but also patterns of annotation and use that can be typically found. An obvious place to start this line of enquiry is the Bible, the book most likely to be found in the broadest cross-section of seventeenth-century households, and whose widespread circulation is well documented. Ian Green used the phrase 'flooding the market' for English language Bibles in the decades leading up to the Civil War, and estimated that perhaps 30,000 Bibles were sold every year in the 1670s.[20] Abigail Williams, looking at eighteenth-century inventories, confirmed that the Bible is the book that turns up more than any other, though she also rightly flags up the close second that is run by popular devotional texts like *The whole duty of man*.[21] We know that many editions of English Bibles in the

---

[17] Mark Purcell, 'Books and reading in eighteenth-century Westmorland', *Library History* 18 (2001), pp. 91–106.

[18] Mark Purcell, *The country house library* (New Haven, CT: Yale University Press, 2017), 123, 231.

[19] I. Green and K. Peters, 'Religious publishing in England 1640–1695', in J. Barnard and D. F. McKenzie (eds), *The Cambridge history of the book in Britain*, vol. 4 (Cambridge: Cambridge University Press, 2002), pp. 67–93, 90.

[20] Ian Green, *Print and Protestantism in early modern England* (Oxford: Oxford University Press, 2000), 55.

[21] Williams, *Social life*, 99, 245. On the widespread distribution of popular devotional works, it has been pointed out that 20,000 copies of Richard Baxter's *Call to the unconverted* were printed in its year of publication (1658), and that at least 30,000 copies of *Pilgrim's progress* were printed in the late 17th c.: F. Donoghue, 'Colonizing readers', in A. Bermingham and J. Brewer (eds), *The consumption of culture 1600–1800* (London: Routledge, 1995), pp. 54–74, 59. Nearly 20,000 copies of Baxter's *Saints'*

seventeenth century ran to thousands of copies.[22] Where did they all go, and where do we find the evidential trail? There are plenty of surviving Bibles whose inscriptions and annotations reflect their use and study by scholarly owners, but for this purpose the quest is for those in households outside educated professional circles. Green recognized that 'many lay people . . . owned a Bible, and some even had a special place in their houses to keep it', but he wondered 'how often that Bible was read and used, as opposed to being kept'.[23] The answer, as demonstrated by the evidence in many surviving Bibles, is: often.

Andrew Cambers, in his book *Godly reading*, is one of several people who have commented on the use of Bibles as holy or totemic objects as well as things to read, used in ceremonies and exorcisms.[24] An extension of the sense of that book as a sacred place is seen in the well-known practice of writing lists of births, marriages, and deaths into Bibles, a tradition with a long history. Large-format nineteenth-century Bibles, which were often issued with specially printed pages for the filling in of family trees, have long been a curse for antiquarian booksellers, but there are plentiful examples from earlier centuries, including the seventeenth.[25] Fig. 4.2 shows an example from the Bodleian Library, which belonged in the middle of the century to a Yorkshire gentleman, Matthew Hall of Leventhorpe; his hand-written genealogy covers the births of himself and his children, and a note of his ancestry in the male line back to the fifteenth century.[26] There is no record of his being university-educated, but he was clearly competent in Latin. The habit was practised at all levels of society, as the Bodleian also has a Bible which belonged to Gilbert Sheldon, the Restoration Archbishop of Canterbury, whose leaves are strikingly clean and unread, but which has three pages of his manuscript notes at the end recording not only births, marriages and deaths in his own family but

---

everlasting rest were printed between 1650 and 1688 (Isabel Rivers, 'Dissenting and methodist books of practical divinity', in I. Rivers (ed.), *Books and their readers in eighteenth-century England* (Leicester: Leicester University Press, 1982), pp. 127–64, 141).

[22]   Green, *Print and Protestantism*, 56. See also Scott Mandelbrote, 'The Bible press', in I. Gadd (ed), *The history of Oxford University Press*, vol. 1 (Oxford: Oxford University Press, 2013), pp. 481–509, 490–95.

[23]   Green, *Print and Protestantism*, 79.

[24]   Andrew Cambers, *Godly reading* (Cambridge: Cambridge University Press, 2011), 3.

[25]   Despite its ubiquity, the family Bible as a topic has not been systematically studied or documented in Britain (but for Italy, see A. Cicchetti and R. Mordenti (eds), *I libri di famiglia in Italia*, vol. 1 (Rome: Edizioni di storia e letteratura, 1985)). Peter Stallybrass touches on some early examples in 'Books and scrolls: navigating the Bible', in J. Andersen and E. Sauer (eds), *Books and readers in early modern England* (Philadelphia: University of Pennsylvania Press, 2002), pp. 42–79, but his focus is more on marginalia. Margaret Connolly describes some 16th-c. examples in MS devotional books in her *Sixteenth-century readers, fifteenth-century books* (Cambridge: Cambridge University Press, 2019), pp. 168–70. There are descriptions of individual case studies, and a popular guide for family historians, which contains references to many examples: Rena King, *The family Bible: a priceless heirloom* (Bury: Family History Partnership, 2014).

[26]   Matthew is not in the university lists, but he sent his son, Philip, to Christ's College, Cambridge in 1668 (Venn and Venn, *Alumni Cantabrigienses . . . to 1751*, vol. 2, 287).

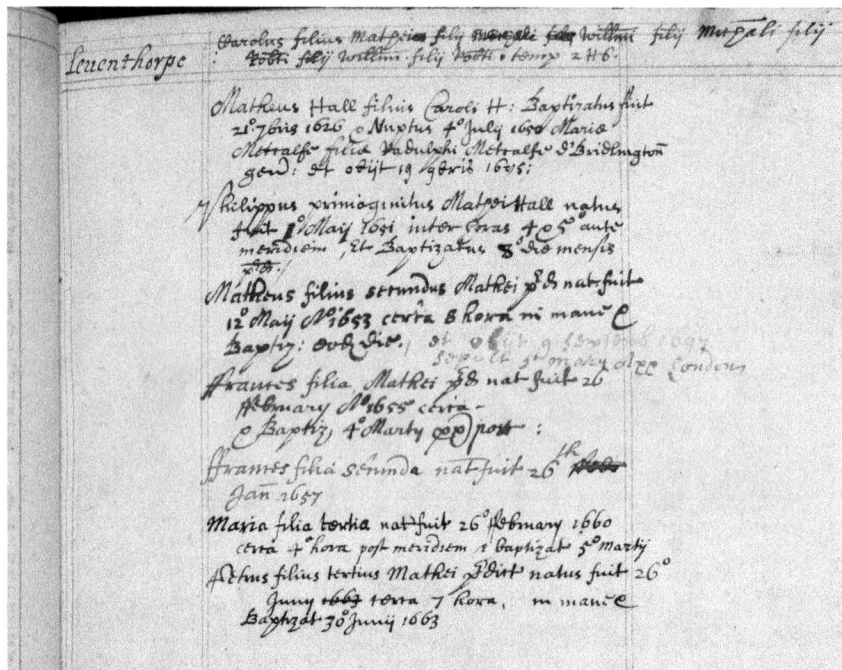

Fig. 4.2 A family inscription in a Bible made by Matthew Hall, a Yorkshire gentleman, noting his own birth in 1626 before a list of his children; at the head, he traces his lineage back through seven generations to the time of Henry VI. Bodleian Library Bib. Eng.1606.d.1. By permission of the Bodleian Libraries, The University of Oxford.

also some of those in the royal family at which he officiated or was a godfather.[27] Fig. 4.3 shows an example more germane to the theme of the common man, a 1612 Bible bound with a 1639 Book of Common Prayer, extensively genealogically annotated by a line of families beginning with William Rutland, citizen and apothecary of London, who tells us he was born in 1627.

The Bible Society Collection, now in Cambridge University Library, is particularly fertile hunting ground for this line of enquiry; it offers a concentrated and chronologically arranged group of Bibles, with multiple copies of many editions.[28] I have looked at several hundred Bibles there from the late sixteenth to the late seventeenth century, for evidence not only of these kinds of inscriptions but also of the names and markings which are typically to be found. Looking at these books *in toto* one is struck by some general observations about the internal scruffiness of

[27] Bodleian Library Bib.Eng.1638.d.2, *The Holy Bible*, London, 1648 (bound with *The book of common prayer*, Cambridge, 1638, and *The whole book of psalmes*, Cambridge, 1638).

[28] http://www.lib.cam.ac.uk/collections/departments/bible-societys-library (accessed 7 Nov. 2018); its only limitation, which has to be recognized, is that as it is essentially a collection formed in the 19th c., a number of its Bibles have been through the hands of washers and makers-up of perfected copies.

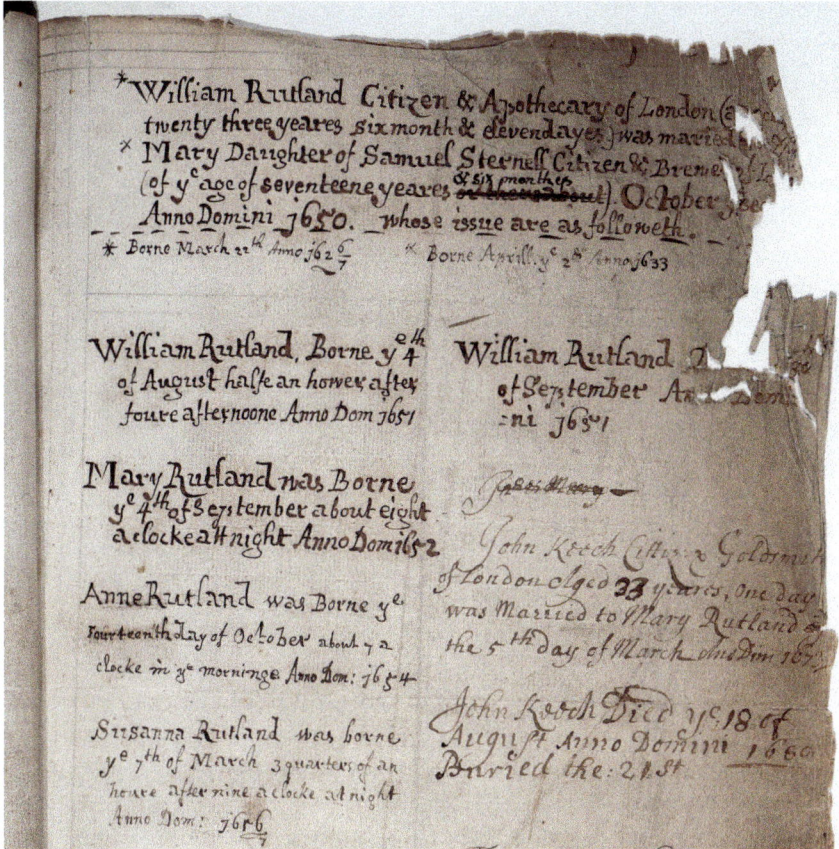

Fig. 4.3 A series of family inscriptions in a Bible, begun by William Rutland, citizen and apothecary of London (b. 1627), and continued by his descendants. Thomas Fisher Rare Book Library, University of Toronto, STC f00071.

the books (i.e. evidence of use), and the wide variation of bindings—or rather, of variation in the average gap between the date of binding and the date of printing. In a typical historic library, such as a college or cathedral library, there is nothing unusual in finding books bound long after they were printed, but as a proportion of the whole (when looking at 'working' books and not those which became collectors' trophies) they are likely to be a minority. What is observable about Bibles is that they were books which often remained in active use for many generations, longer than was commonly the case for many volumes. If we examine a random range of seventeenth-century books from the shelves of the Bodleian, or the Folger, or a National Trust Library, a pattern which commonly emerges is one with evidence of use, of marginalia and inscriptions, in the first century or so of their lives, but less thereafter. Of course, there are exceptions, but a statistically significant sample is likely to reveal that trend: new books are read, and old books sit on shelves for more occasional use. Bibles are different, and it is not unusual to find a seventeenth-century Bible clearly read and engaged with over many generations. Fig. 4.4 shows a 1677 Cambridge quarto Bible which belonged first to Joseph Pratt (d. 1701), physician to Queen Mary, but which descended down a family line of Pratts, Pilkingtons, and Sandifords in Ireland and was inscribed by many generations down to the children of Thomas Sandiford, who died in 1820, and who inserted a little essay into the book on the history of the family. Seventeenth-century Bibles may have generational inscriptions of nineteenth-century families, demonstrating that such people were using an old edition, rather than a contemporary one, as their working Bible.

Early Bibles will regularly be found not only with these characteristic kinds of family inscriptions, but also with a wide range of other things suggesting differing levels of education and motivation, but all reflecting the books passing through hands whose names are not likely to enter a list of documentable owners. John Cheesman, who would rather be a doorkeeper in the house of God than to dwell in the tents of wickedness in 1668, had a clearly educated hand, but whether it was his child or someone completely unconnected writing 'God with us' we can only speculate (Fig. 4.5). A variety of tags regularly crop up in inscriptions like this— John Mills asking that the Lord of Heaven upon him look (Fig. 4.6) is a variation on the more commonly encountered 'X his book God give him grace therein to look'; but all manner of doodles, scribbles, drawings, and pen trials will be found in books like this. A 1613 Bible in the Bible Society collection has inscriptions of several owners, of both sexes, between the early seventeenth and early nineteenth centuries, and towards the end a half torn-off leaf with the names of ten people, possibly but not definitely in the same seventeenth-century hand—all men except for Doroty Hudson, who seems likely to be the wife of William Hudson, who I further guess to be related to the Thomas Hudson who wrote his name around the margin of the title page in an early to mid-seventeenth-century hand (Fig. 4.7). Is this a group of neighbours, or the members of some decision-making group, or people who were gathered together for some purpose? We don't know, but this book exemplifies patterns which are regularly found with these kinds of inscriptions, including the scattering of names and scribbles all through the book, often in places with no apparent rationale. Grace and Henry Procter, together with other members of the Procter family, wrote their names many times up and down the margins of a 1611 quarto Bible, with various spellings of the surname and different writing hands, sometimes dated around the 1690s, and there are numerous other names in the book (Fig. 4.8). The book is a particularly battered example, its pages stained, dirty, and torn, its corners rounded down because they were so frayed; it is clearly a volume which has passed through many hands over a long period of time, before it was rescued into the nineteenth-century binding in which it now lives, heavily used and read throughout.

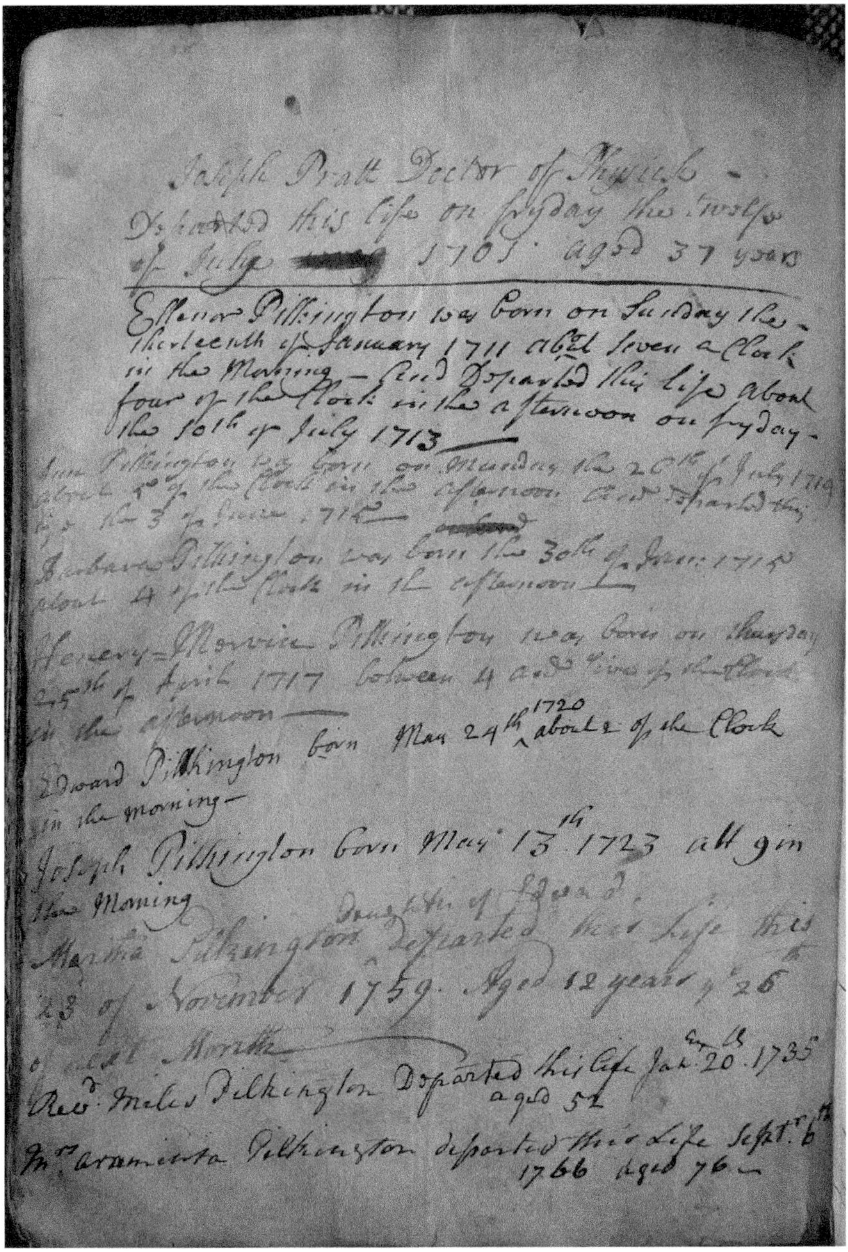

Fig. 4.4 A 1677 Bible in which the family inscriptions, which continue to the nineteenth century, begin with Joseph Pratt (1664/5–1701, physician to Queen Mary). Author's collection.

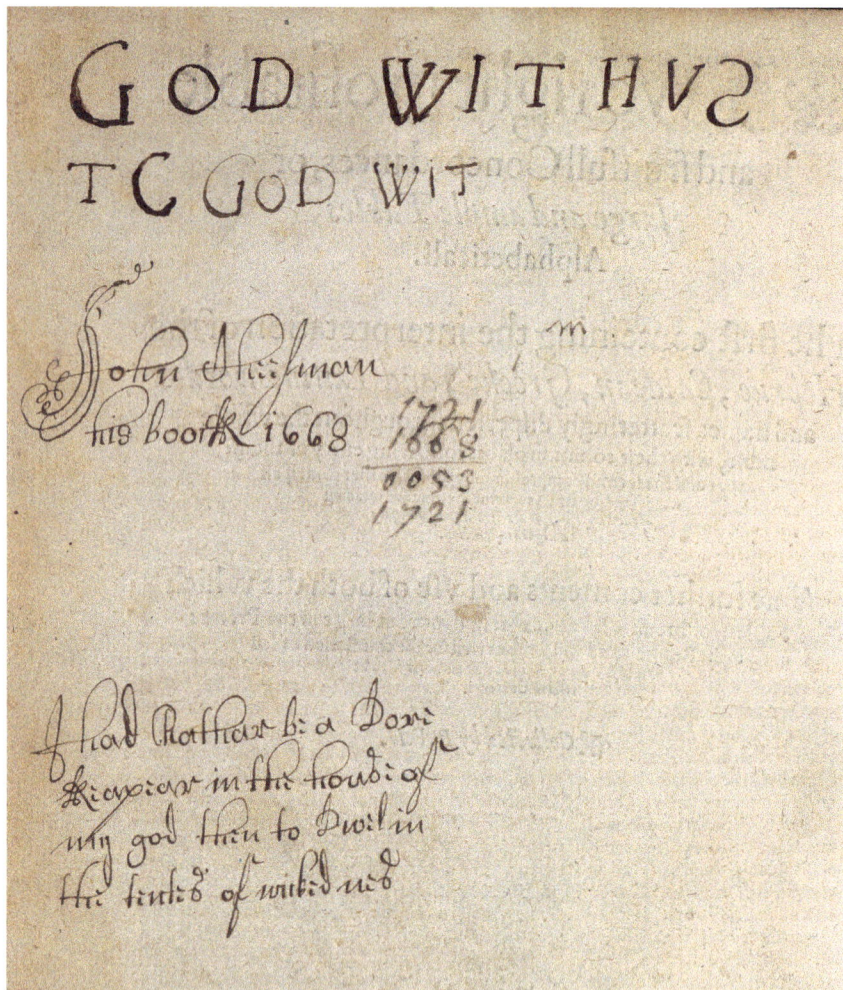

Fig. 4.5 A 1607 Bible inscribed in 1668 by John Cheesman; 'God with us', above, is clearly in a less practised hand. Cambridge University Library BSS 201.c.07.3. Reproduced by permission of the Syndics of Cambridge University Library.

One of the earliest examples of a family-inscribed Bible which I have seen is a mid-sixteenth century one now in Senate House Library in London, with inscriptions of the Haldenby family of Lincolnshire and Yorkshire, starting in the 1550s (Fig. 4.9).[29] From a book-historical perspective, it is an example that has just about everything, except a title page; it has layer upon layer of ownership history

---

[29] I am grateful to Bonnie Walker, who first drew this to my attention.

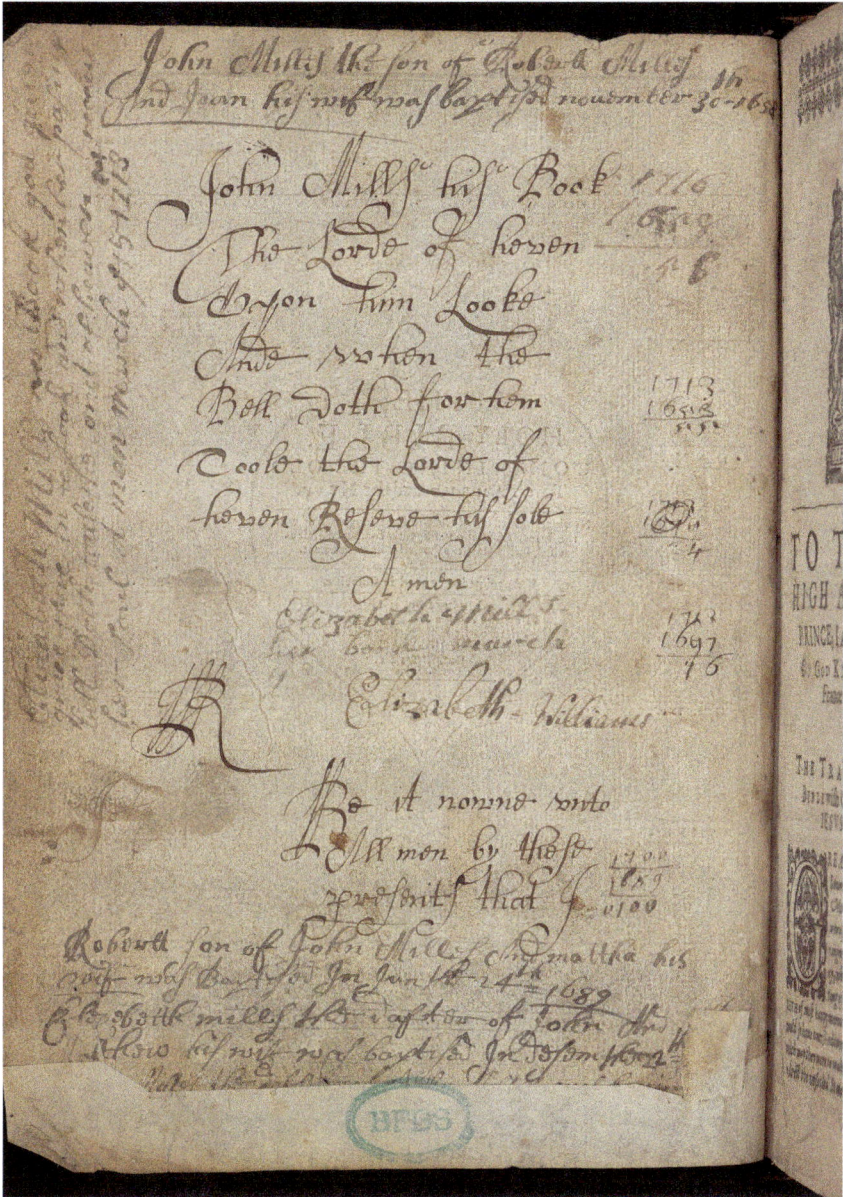

Fig. 4.6 A heavily inscribed blank leaf from a 1634 Bible, including variants on wordings commonly encountered in books like this. Cambridge University Library BSS 201.c.34.3. Reproduced by permission of the Syndics of Cambridge University Library.

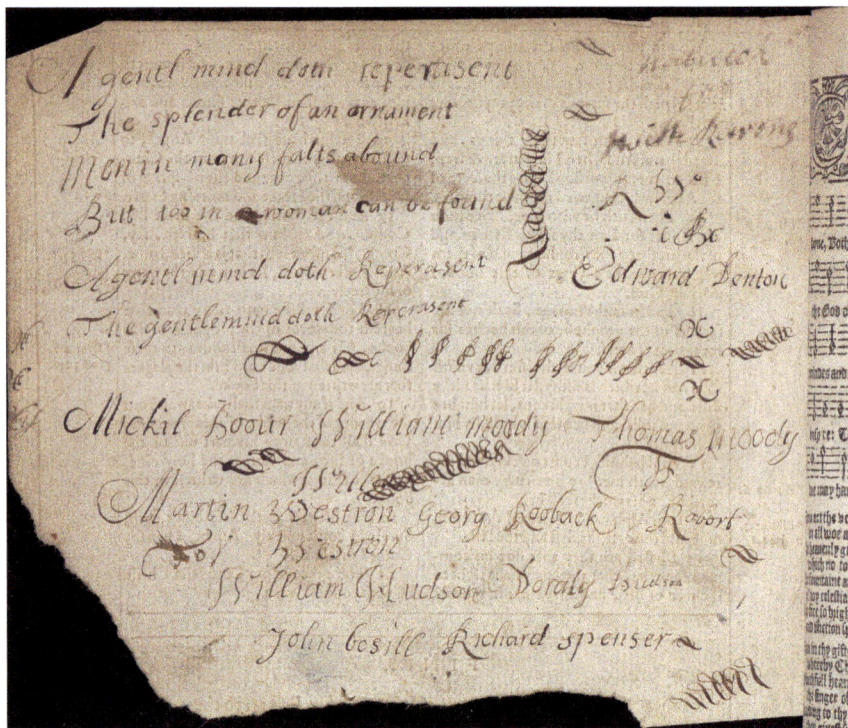

Fig. 4.7 A partly torn-away leaf in this 1613 Bible includes many names, as well as aphorisms and pen trials. Cambridge University Library BSS 201.c.13.16. Reproduced by permission of the Syndics of Cambridge University Library.

manifested in inscriptions from various points on the spectrum of sophistication. It has several sixteenth-century lists of members of the Haldenby family and the beginnings of an early seventeenth-century genealogical list of another family, that of Robert Seaton. It has a number of later names who appear in multiple places, particularly Jonathan Brunyee, who also started a family list in the middle of the eighteenth century, but also including William Aldam, John Hobson, John Jeeve, William Peacock, James Romley and Daniel Yole, variously dating from the second half of the seventeenth century or the first half of the eighteenth. They are mostly male names, except for one Mary, who may be the wife, sister, or daughter of Daniel Yole. There are different kinds of marginalia, including some early cropped notes highlighting or commenting on textual points, and more trivial ones noting the size of Goliath, or repeating common devotional sentiments; the inscriptions include drawings, and more than one person asking God for grace. There are missing leaves at the front which have been supplied in eighteenth-century manuscript, and the book is throughout in that grubby, thumbed, scruffy condition consistent with centuries of use.

Fig. 4.8A–C Various members of the Proctor family wrote in the margins of this 1611 Bible in the last three decades of the seventeenth century. Cambridge University Library BSS 201.c.11.5. Reproduced by permission of the Syndics of Cambridge University Library.

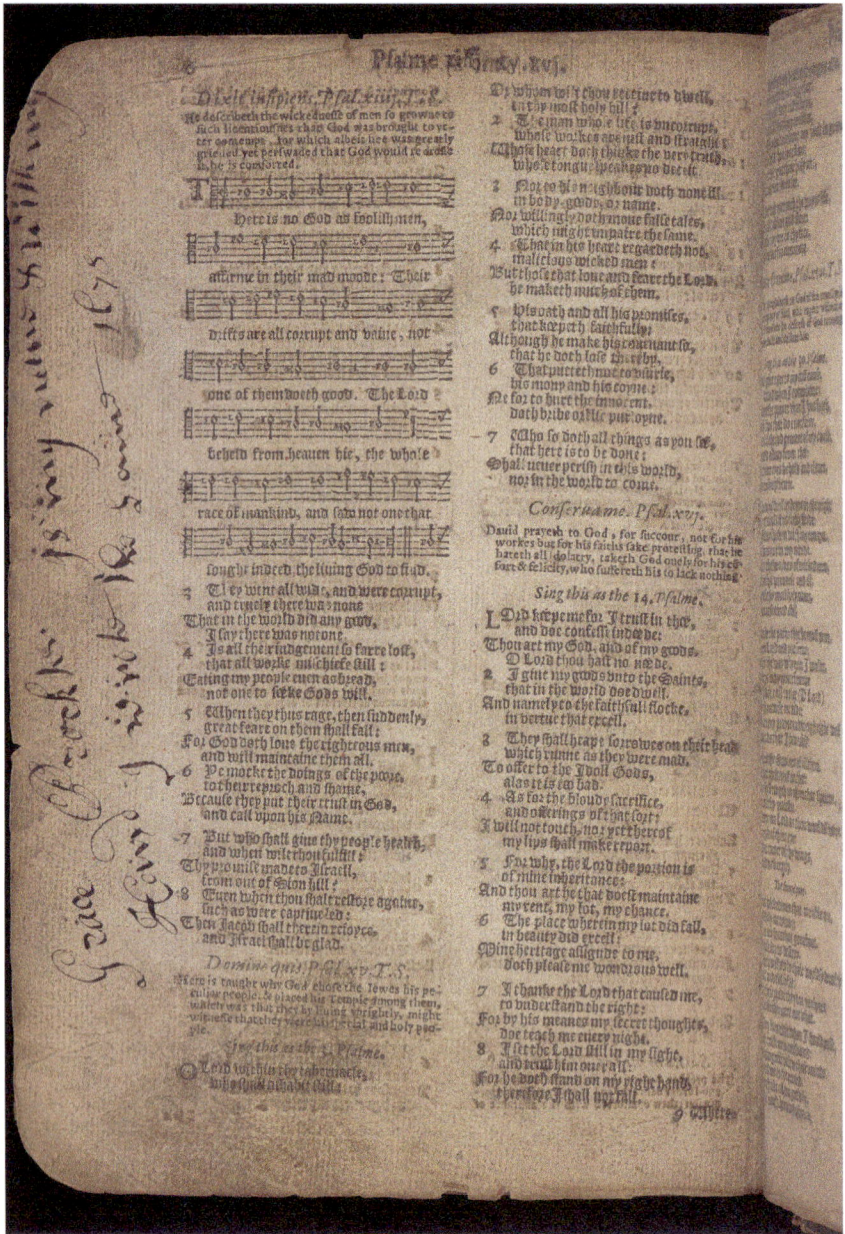

Fig. 4.8B Continued.

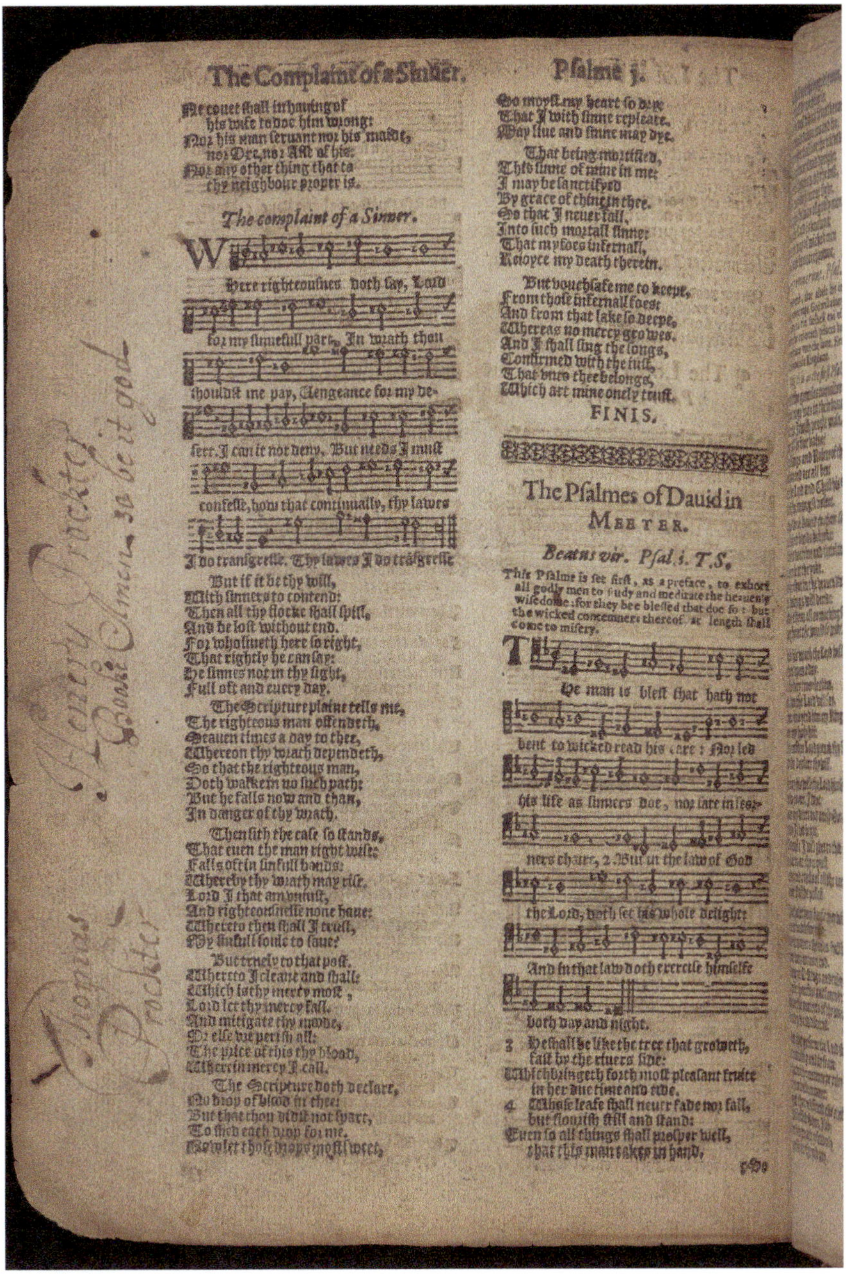

Fig. 4.8C Continued.

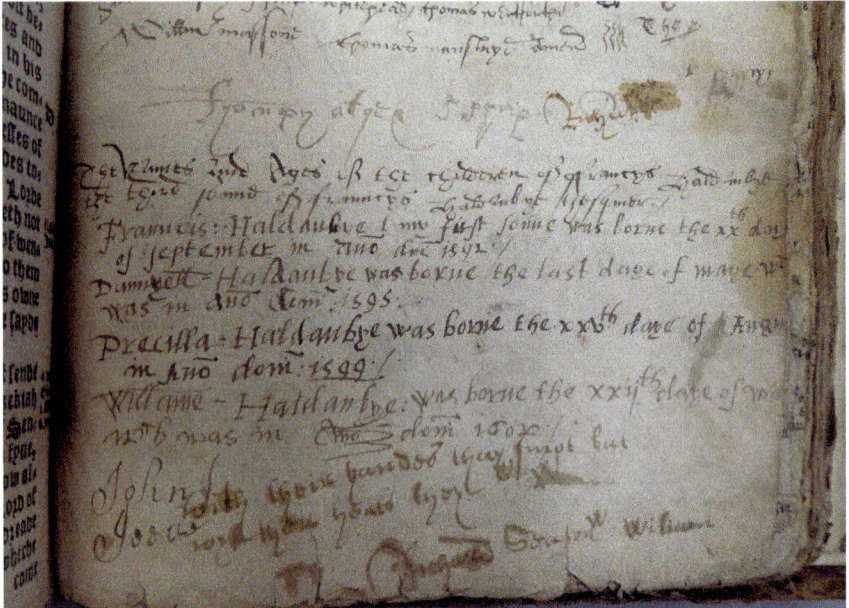

Fig. 4.9 Late sixteenth-century inscriptions of the Haldenby family in a 1551 Bible, the earliest of many annotations made in this book by different hands over succeeding centuries. Senate House Library, University of London [Rare] G9 [English-1551] fol.

It has a couple of other characteristics which are not uncommon with this kind of book: firstly, it evidently started life in a better-off household, as the Haldenbys were Tudor gentry, but within a generation or so was circulating in less socially elevated families. Secondly, like the Cumbrian book at the beginning of this chapter, it remained in a particular geographical locality for many centuries, though moving from hand to hand. The Haldenbys were based in Lincolnshire and East Yorkshire, and in the nineteenth century the book was in the hands of a solicitor in Epworth, Lincolnshire. In between I doubt that it travelled far; Jonathan Brunyee, who owned it in the eighteenth century, lived at Ealand, in Lincolnshire, and can be traced being married at Crowle, nearby, in 1748, and buried there ten years later (Crowle is also the burial place of Christopher Haldenby, in 1572). Daniel Yole who dated his inscription in 1673 could possibly be a man of that name who was buried in Hull in 1695, which is only the other side of the Humber estuary from where Francis Haldenby is buried at Adlingfleet.[30] Many of the other names in the book are too common to be identified, but I would be surprised if any of them lived far from north Lincolnshire.

---

[30] These identifications mostly rely on Ancestry.com; see also https://www.findagrave.com/memor ial/85871858/francis-de–haldenby (accessed 25 Nov. 2018).

Although Bibles provide good hunting ground for evidence of this sort, they are by no means the only place to look. It is not unusual to find family record inscriptions in other kinds of books, as in the list of the children of William Kynning of Leyton, in Essex, found in a 1674 edition of Thomas Brooks's *Apples of gold* (Fig. 4.10). This is another popular devotional work by a Nonconformist minister, in the vernacular, like the book being read in Thornthwaite, and English language editions of influential theological works are likewise an obvious place to look. A 1583 edition of John Jewel's sermons (Fig. 4.11) was still being actively read and used through the seventeenth century and into the eighteenth, when an Edward Ellis recorded the birth of his daughter and the death of his wife in the 1710s. During the seventeenth century it was variously annotated and used for writing and drawing practice by at least five other people of both sexes who all left names in the book, along with doggerel, trivia, and many notes which are clearly not text-related.

A Lichfield apothecary was mentioned earlier, who died in 1655 leaving sixteen books little and big, which are likely to have been a mixture of devotional and professional material, with perhaps some accessible historical books, chronicles relating to English or world history. That pattern can regularly be seen in the lists in *Private libraries in Renaissance England* which were also cited above. The copy of the 1609 English translation of Josephus in Fig. 4.12 is perhaps the kind of book to have been commonly found in homes like that; like the Haldenby Bible, it follows that pattern of a large-format and therefore relatively expensive book which began life in a better-off household, but before too long found itself in humbler hands. On the title page it has a faded contemporary inscription of John Errington of Hexham, a member of a well-established gentry family there, but before the seventeenth century was out it was in the hands of a Garret Starkey, who inscribed his name multiple times in variant spellings, along with some others. Starkey is not readily uniquely identifiable, but a man of that name was buried in Morpeth in 1684, another was buried in Newcastle in 1710, and another was a hostman (a coal trader) on the Tyne in 1714, all situated in the north-east not far from Hexham.[31] The book is scruffy, torn, dog-eared, mutilated, and today has a macaronic binding put together from two different boards, one seventeenth-century and one eighteenth, with a twentieth-century reback, and has clearly had an active and interesting individual history, despite the fact that it would today be described apologetically in a booksellers' catalogue.

These are all books which we can imagine being read, as well as written in, by these various generations of users, but it is also not hard to find less obviously accessible texts with these kinds of evidences. Fig. 4.13 shows a late fifteenth-century Latin Bible, now in the Bodleian, with a contemporary English panel-stamped binding. Its earliest identifiable owner is a Richard Moore, around the middle or end of the sixteenth century; it has a modest amount of textual

---

[31] The Starkeys can be identified through Ancestry.com; there is an account of the Erringtons of Hexham in *The Gentleman's Magazine* 102(1) (1832), 581.

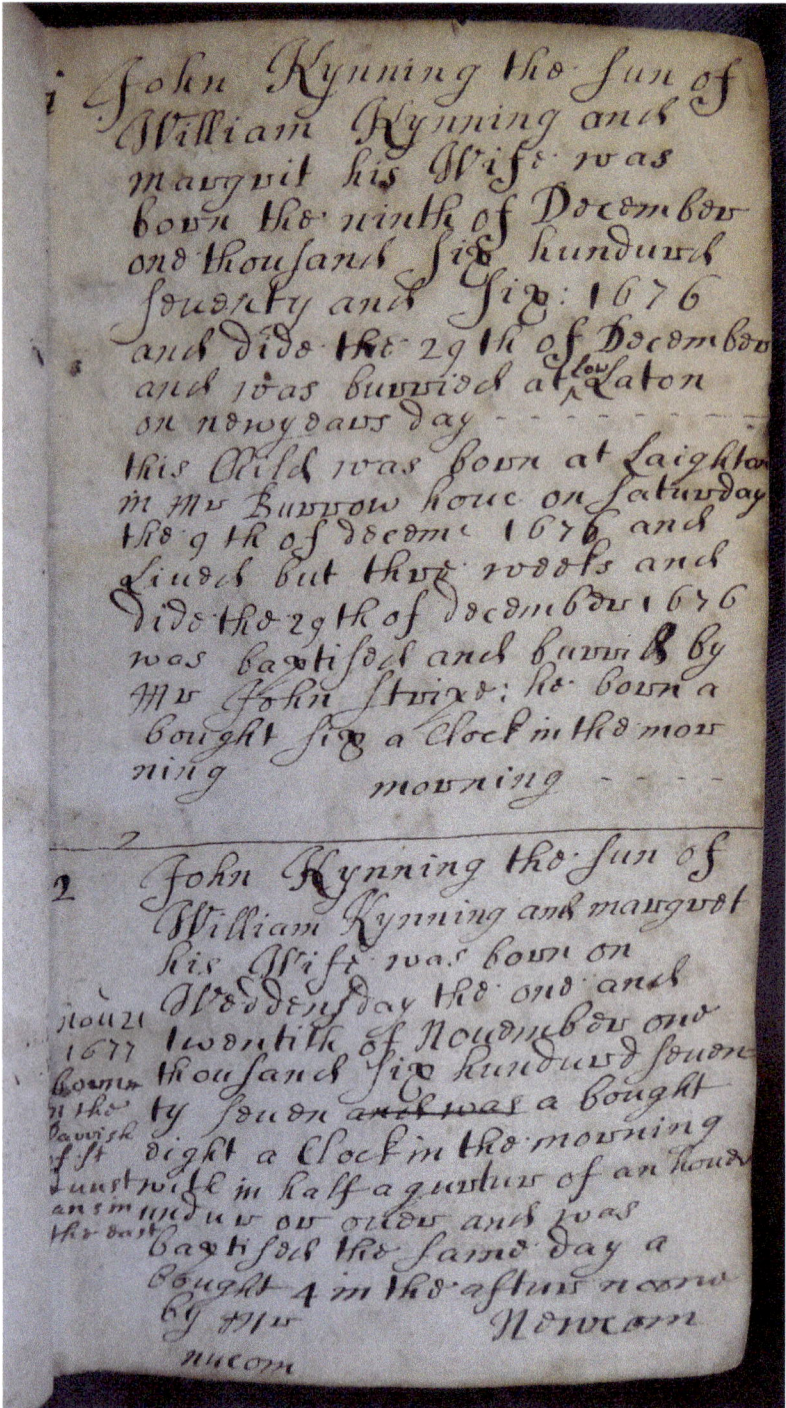

Fig. 4.10 Family inscriptions of the Kynning family, of Leyton (Essex), on the flyleaves of a copy of Thomas Brookes, *Apples of gold*, 1674. Senate House Library, University of London G855 [Brookes] SR.

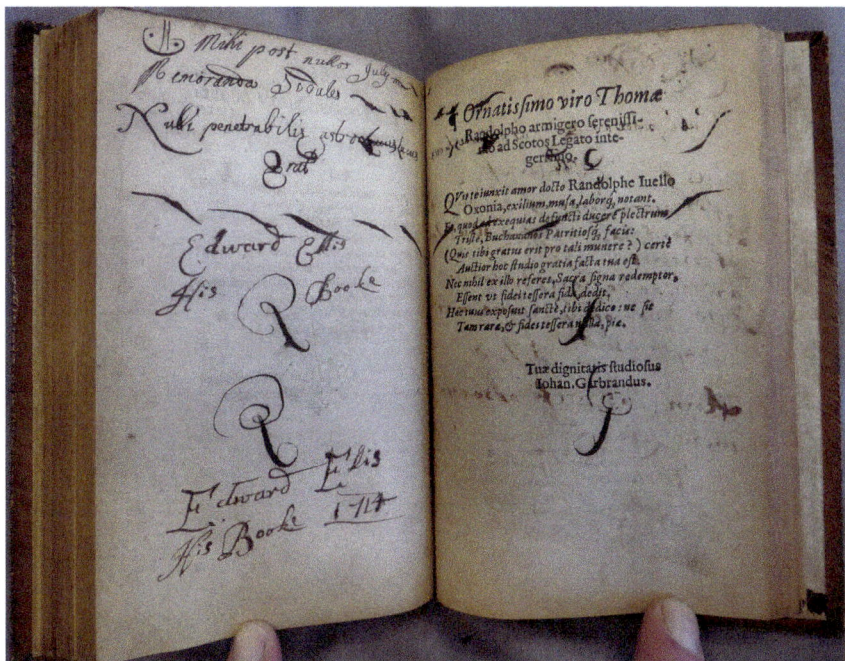

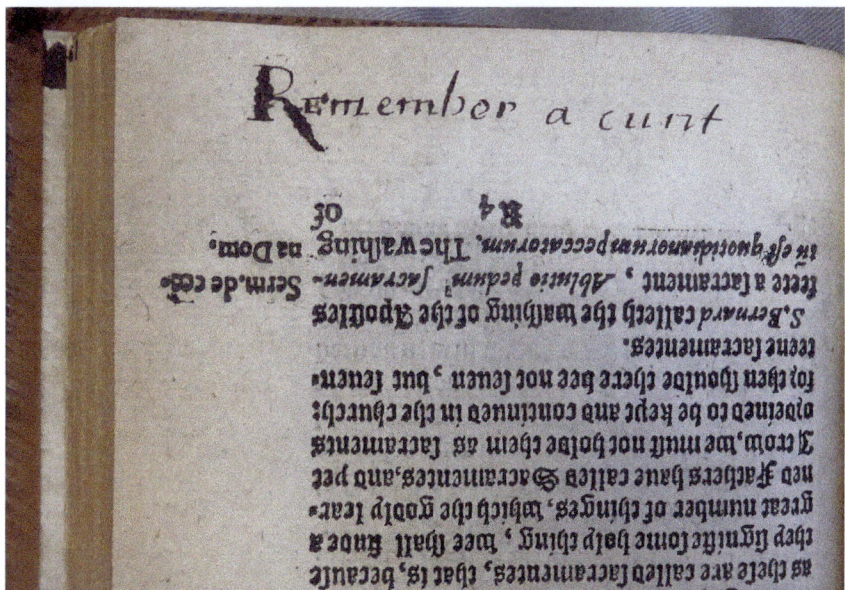

Fig. 4.11 Many scribbles, in numerous hands, in a copy of John Jewel, *Certaine sermons*, include some unexpected marginalia. Senate House Library, University of London [D.-L.L.] G8 [Jewel].

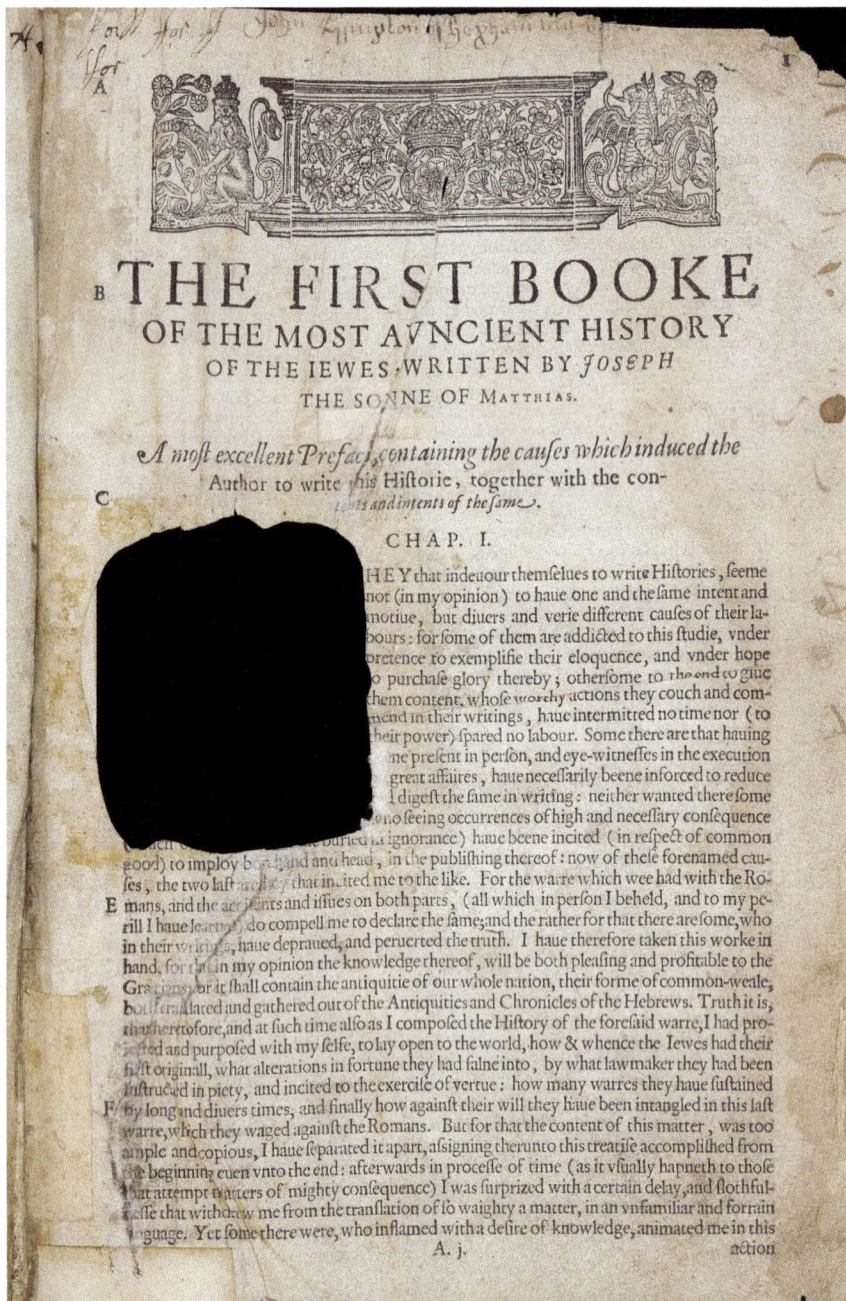

Fig. 4.12A The mutilated first leaf of a copy of *The famous and memorable workes* of Josephus, 1609, which began life in a gentry household near Hexham. Bodleian Library Lawn.c.152. By permission of the Bodleian Libraries, The University of Oxford.

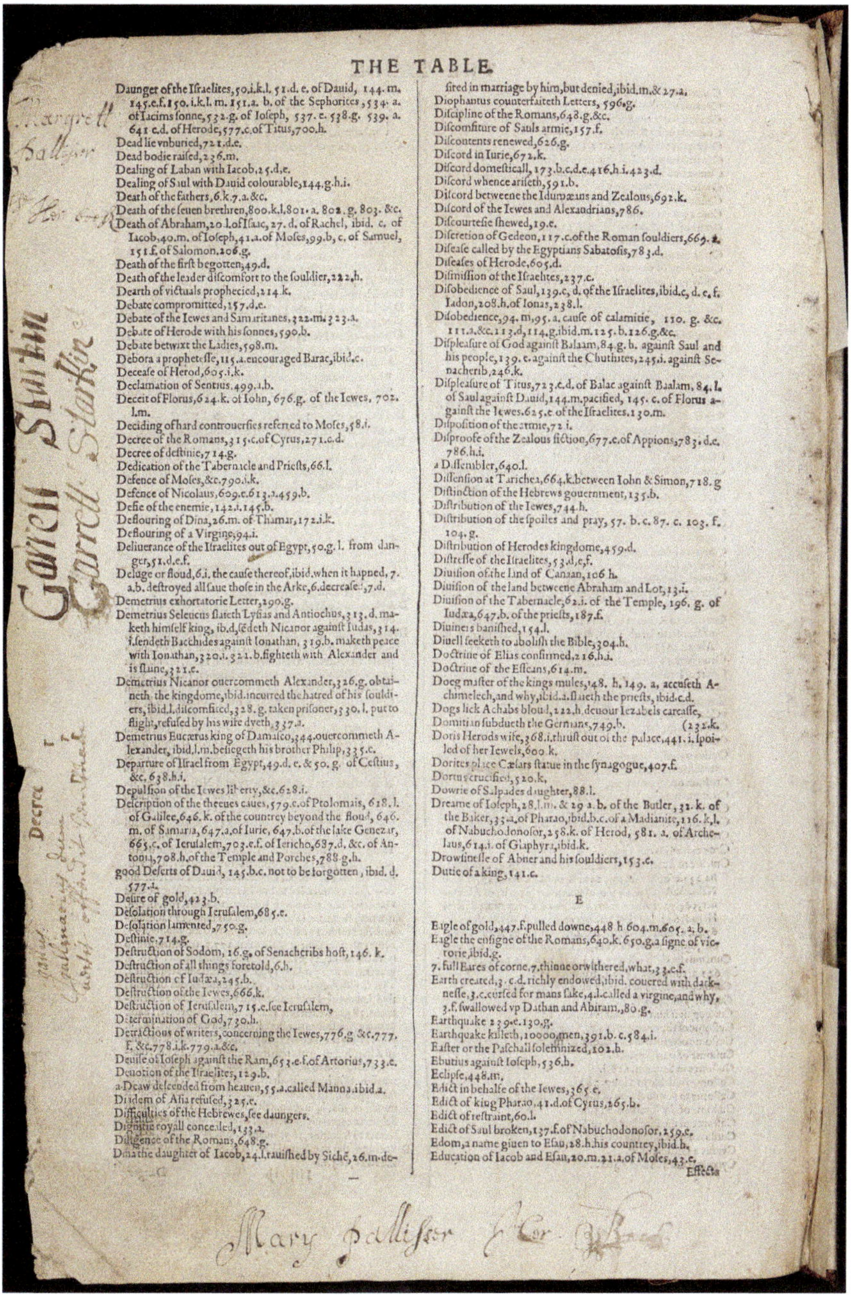

THE TABLE.

Fig. 4.12B By the end of the seventeenth century, this Josephus was being written in by a Garret Starkin, among others. By permission of the Bodleian Libraries, The University of Oxford.

Fig. 4.13A The inscription of John Evans, dated 1674, at the beginning of a 1495 Latin Bible. Bodleian Library Inc.fGS2.1495.1. By permission of the Bodleian Libraries, The University of Oxford.

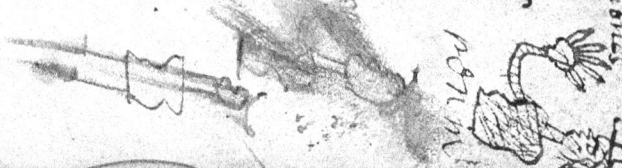

Fig. 4.13B Evans's inscription from a page in the middle of the book, accompanied by drawings and scribbles. By permission of the Bodleian Libraries, The University of Oxford.

marginalia which is perhaps a generation or so after Moore, and by 1674 it was in the hands of a John Evans, who wrote a fairly literate-looking inscription beneath the woodcut of Jerome at the beginning of the book, and up a margin in the Book of Wisdom. The drawing and scribbles around the latter are surely not his, but added perhaps by some of the other people who wrote in the book around the end of the seventeenth century, including a Thomas Evans in 1701, a William Thomas in the same year, a James Jones, and a Thomas Williams. In the second half of the eighteenth century it was being inscribed by a James Larwill. None of these later hands look well-formed or suggestive of readers of the Vulgate; perhaps Evans of 1674, with his rather legalistic-sounding inscription, was some kind of lawyer or notary, using the book as a swearing-in tool, and his children and their friends practised their writing on wet days in Wales, where this book surely was then if circulating in families called Evans, Jones, Thomas, and Williams. This may be crossing the line into speculation or story-spinning; sticking to the evidence, what we can be sure of is that this book was annotated by several generations of people who do not look as though they were reading it.

Conclusions

More examples like this could be produced *ad infinitum*. Several patterns and observations emerge from these kinds of books. Firstly, it is evident that books were owned and circulating in a wide variety of families in the seventeenth century, not by any means only in the kinds of professional, educated, and relatively wealthy classes whose libraries make it into a listing like that in the Appendix. Weavers as well as merchants, journeymen as well as liverymen, were all likely to have books in their homes which could run beyond a Bible, a prayer book, and a copy of Baxter's *Saints' everlasting rest* to books on history, travel, home guidance, and anything more besides. Books in such households are commonly in the vernacular, but not always. Academic owners often inscribed their books with neat notes of ownership on the opening leaves and tidy marginalia, but it is very typical to find these wider circles of people being less disciplined. Regularly encountered patterns include names written repeatedly throughout books, on apparently random leaves, up and around margins, and a fondness for doggerel devotional, patriotic and similar phrases, or sums—time and again we encounter notes working out the age of the book against the year of writing, like that which can be seen in Fig. 4.5. Books often remain within geographical localities over several centuries, even when not remaining within a family, and relatively expensive ones which start their life in a better-off household may often find themselves a couple of generations later in humbler circumstances. This is quite an important point, which helps to explain the breadth of circulation. Writers on this kind of subject often put together statistics on the income of labourers and squires, the costs of books as opposed to loaves of bread, and the number of books being published each year. What they tend to leave out, not least because it is so hard to quantify, is the extent of second-hand traffic, or something beneath even that, what Abigail Williams envisaged in a well-chosen phrase about 'tattered old books that had been knocking around a whole village or a family'.[32] In rural Lincolnshire, or Essex, or even in London, it is not hard to envisage scenarios in which books start leaking out of libraries when circumstances change, through a death or some other event, and move around without the formality of commercial trade.

Joad Raymond, in the introduction to the first volume of the *Oxford history of popular print culture*, mentions some of the well-known names in the annals of humbler book ownership, including Nehemiah Wallington, Frances Wolfreston, and Philip Rous, and says that 'they do not appear because their experiences and practices are typical of their times; each of them is interesting in part because they were unusual, and the evidence they have left is exceptional.'[33] I do not agree with that; the thing that is exceptional is survival of the evidence, but I do not believe their book-owning patterns are as unusual, for their time, as we can be led to believe. Adam Fox, following Peter Clark, wrote in *Oral and literate culture in England* that 'the ownership of books, and the consequent increases in literacy levels, were much more evident in towns and cities than in the countryside', but this chapter has selected several examples which suggest that we should not underestimate the extent of rural distribution; many more such examples can be found.[34] We should also not forget that although towns grew during the seventeenth century, over 80 per cent of the population lived in villages and hamlets spread around the country: 'at the beginning of the seventeenth century, most people were farmers'.[35] The thing that will always elude us is any kind of comprehensive evidence-based census to quantify exactly how extensive this kind of book ownership was. It would be good to be able to take a map of Bristol, or Hull, or any other town, in the seventeenth century and assess how many books there were in each house, street by street, but we will never be able to do that as so many of the books which were once there no longer exist, nor do we have archival sources to fill the gap. We have to operate in a qualitative rather than a quantitative world, recognizing that book ownership was very widespread, even if largely manifested in a few standard texts, but we are never likely to be able to put a precise percentage on it. What we can say is that ubiquitous is nearer the mark than unusual, when talking about the distribution of books, and we might be surprised by what we would have found if we went into every dwelling going down the average town or village street in 1630, or 1690.

---

[32] Williams, *Social life*, 5.

[33] Joad Raymond (ed.), *The Oxford history of popular print culture*, vol. 1 (Oxford: Oxford University Press, 2011), 2.

[34] Adam Fox, *Oral and literate culture in England, 1500–1700* (Oxford: Oxford University Press, 2000), 107.

[35] Mark Kishlansky, *A monarchy transformed: Britain 1603–1714* (London: Allen Lane, 1996), 6.

5

Physical spaces and book formats

Library rooms

Our knowledge of the seventeenth-century private library space is limited by a
lack of surviving primary evidence. There are hardly any surviving library rooms
from this time, in anything like their original state, because so much remodelling
took place in houses with libraries from the eighteenth century onwards; one of the
few extant examples (commonly said to be the earliest we have) is the much-
photographed library room at Ham House, created for the Duke of Lauderdale in
the 1670s, which retains its contemporary shelving and layout.[1] There are very few
earlier drawings or representations of libraries, and when Colin Tite was seeking to
visualize Sir Robert Cotton's famous library with its busts and bookcases he had to
resort to an artist's imagination, as no original images exist.[2] This has led to a
received wisdom that 'the idea of a separate library room for the display of books
on shelves took hold only gradually even among the wealthier gentry', and that books
were commonly being stored in chests and trunks well into the seventeenth century.[3]

More recently, the picture has been filled out, particularly by Mark Purcell and
Susie West, whose researches have brought to light plentiful evidence of shelved
library rooms or studies throughout the Stuart period. Purcell's overview of the
development of the country house library has uncovered numerous examples of
library spaces being established from at least the sixteenth century onwards,
including an intriguing moveable contraption in the Earl of Northumberland's
'Paradise' (confirming that those early depictions of moveable book-reading
devices are less fanciful than they look).[4] He has reproduced a surviving panelled
and shelved room at Holcombe Court, significantly earlier than Ham House, and
reminded us that the handsome painted book cupboards of the Kedermister

---

[1] Mark Purcell, *The country house library* (New Haven, CT: Yale University Press, 2017), pp. 97–8
and fig. 226.

[2] Colin Tite, *The manuscript library of Sir Robert Cotton* (London: The British Library, 1994),
pp. 96–7.

[3] P. Selwyn and D. Selwyn, '"The profession of a gentleman": books for the gentry and the nobility',
in E. Leedham-Green and T. Webber (eds), *The Cambridge history of libraries in Britain and Ireland*,
vol. 1 (Cambridge: Cambridge University Press, 2006), pp. 489–519, 505, 507 (following J. T. Cliffe, *The
world of the country house in seventeenth-century England* (New Haven, CT: Yale University Press,
1999), 163).

[4] Purcell, *The country house library*, 49–55.

Book Ownership in Stuart England: The Lyell Lectures, 2018. David Pearson, Oxford University Press (2021).
© David Pearson.
DOI: 10.1093/oso/9780198870128.003.0005

Library, although technically a parish not a private library, provide a model of 'what a Jacobean grandee's study may have looked like'.[5]

West, focusing on the latter half of the period, has used architectural drawings and other archival evidence to uncover numerous examples of East Anglian houses with library rooms, including a study made c.1670 at Ryston Hall for Sir Roger Pratt, a larger one built for Sir Roger North at Rougham Hall at the turn of the eighteenth century, and another large (three-windowed) late seventeenth-century one at Melton Constable Hall. The study of the Hobarts at Blickling (before the long library room which is now there was built) was 'richly furnished with gilt leather on the walls, damask upholstered seats, walnut book stands and a reading desk'.[6] Other works on particular houses have brought to light similar proof of the existence of purpose-designed library spaces, such as the Earl of Leicester's study at Penshurst in the 1660s, 'with its fireplace, its cupboards and wall shelving, and the rich hangings that attest to its owner's elite status'.[7] Earlier in the century, when Northumberland House in London was built for the Earl of Northampton around 1610, it included both an upper and lower library room, on different floors.[8] As West has said, we should recognize 'the ubiquity of country house library rooms after 1660', and for some time before that.[9] Larger library rooms were typically shelved with recessed book cases separated by panelling or windows, but dedicated spaces for books at this time would often have been what we commonly describe as closets, smaller rooms, or subdivisions of rooms, often associated with bedchambers, with a sense of privacy and opportunities for private study and reflection. Men and women, in larger houses, would often have their own places of this kind, though the man's might more often be termed a study than a closet. West has considered these distinctions in more detail, while recognizing fluidity or ambiguity across our sources; Purcell pointed out that 'terms like library, study and closet were used interchangeably'.[10] Many houses, particularly larger ones, would have had books in multiple places, and the existence of a library room would not preclude a separate closet for the lady of the household and possibly for her husband also.

Of course, this is all the territory of the wealthier echelons of society, of the aristocracy and the gentry: how were books stored by all the other kinds of book owners represented in the Appendix? Here, we are more reliant on inference and

---

[5] Ibid. 65–7 (and on the dust jacket of this book).

[6] Susie West, 'An architectural typology for the early modern country house library, 1660–1720', *The Library*, 7th ser. 14 (2013), pp. 441–64.

[7] Germaine Warkentin et al. (eds), *The library of the Sidneys of Penshurst Place, ca.1665* (Toronto: Toronto University Press, 2013), 30.

[8] M. Guerci, 'The construction of Northumberland House', *Antiquaries Journal* 90 (2010), pp. 341–400.

[9] West, 'An architectural typology', 463.

[10] Ibid. 458–63; Purcell, *The country house library*, 62. See also the discussion of the terminology in Patrick Collinson et al., 'Religious publishing in England, 1557–1640', in J. Barnard and D. F. McKenzie (eds), *The Cambridge history of the book in Britain*, vol. 4 (Cambridge: Cambridge University Press, 2002), pp. 29–66, 60.

assumption than on primary evidence, beyond a few surviving pictures. The well-known image of John Boys, Dean of Canterbury (1571–1625) in his study (Fig. 5.1), which began to appear on title pages to his works in the 1620s, shows him sitting at a table in a small room surrounded by walls of shelved books, and it seems plausible to imagine that kind of model being found in many clergy or academic settings throughout the century. The mid-century representation of John Selden (1584–1654; Fig. 5.2) against a backdrop of shelves no doubt reflects what many of the walls in his rooms at the Inner Temple would have looked like. Both Boys's and Selden's books are all shown with fore-edges outwards, as would be expected at that time, but from mid-century onwards these kinds of depictions increasingly show a mixture as the convention evolved for shelving with the spine outwards; this can be seen in the mid-1650s study of Alexander Ross (1591–1654, Fig. 5.3), where there is carved panelling adjacent to the desk and the shelves start halfway up the wall.[11] Curtains are also shown in this picture, and these appear so often in images like this that it seems safe to assume that they were commonly provided in reality, to protect the books from dust and light.

As an alternative to wall shelving, we know that free-standing bookcases were making an appearance by the end of the century, as Samuel Pepys commissioned a set around 1690, which were depicted *in situ* in his apartment in Westminster (Fig. 5.4).[12] Very similar bookcases were made around the same time for William Blathwayt, at Dyrham Park.[13] The 1647 will of Dorothy Cotton refers to books being kept 'in my new cupboard' and smaller assemblages of books were no doubt kept in boxes, trunks, or cupboards; Elizabeth Freke put 78 books into the deal box beside the fireside in her closet in 1711.[14] Pictures of English domestic interiors of this time, with books, are elusive, but a painting of a study made about 1710 by the Dutch artist Jan van der Heyden shows bookshelves—again, curtained—built against a wall behind a table with globes and a large open atlas (Fig. 5.5). Lady Heath's inventory of 1647 refers to half a dozen large books, including maps, lying in the parlour, and the use of large pictorial books or atlases on display, rather than closed on shelves, was no doubt a common practice.[15] Bibles, similarly, would be placed on tables or stands in central places of the household, as in the case of John Bruen of Chester who 'set upon a deske, both in his hall, and in his parlour, two goodly fair Bibles of the best edition, and largest volume'.[16] The

---

[11] On the shelving conventions, see David Pearson, *English bookbinding styles 1450–1800* (London: The British Library, 2005), pp. 105–7.

[12] Kate Loveman, *Samuel Pepys and his books* (Oxford: Oxford University Press, 2015), pp. 246–7.

[13] http://www.nationaltrustcollections.org.uk/object/452939 (accessed 28 Nov. 2018).

[14] Paul Pixton (ed.), *Wrenbury wills and inventories* (Chester: Lancashire and Cheshire Record Society, 2009), pp. 390–94, and see p. 42 above.

[15] M. Empey, 'Lady Margaret Heath', in *Private libraries in Renaissance England* 11 (forthcoming).

[16] Collinson et al., 'Religious publishing in England', 61. See also Raymond Irwin, *The origins of the English library* (London: Allen and Unwin, 1958), pp. 186–7, who comments on a fashion for country gentlemen to display open books in their hall windows.

Fig. 5.1 An image of John Boys (Dean of Canterbury, 1571–1625) in his study, surrounded by shelved books. Bodleian Library Douce B subt.203 (John Boys, *The workes*, 1622). By permission of the Bodleian Libraries, The University of Oxford.

Fig. 5.2 John Selden with his books, from the frontispiece to his edition of Eutychius, published shortly after his death. Bodleian Library Vet A3 e.383 (Eutychius, *Annales*, 1658). By permission of the Bodleian Libraries, The University of Oxford.

inventory of Helmingham Hall, Suffolk in 1626 notes 'nexte the parlour door... one peece of joyned worke like a deske, to sett a booke or a loookinge glasse against it'.[17] We should not assume that people stored their books all in one place;

[17] Moira Coleman (ed.), *Household inventories of Helmingham Hall, 1597–1741* (Woodbridge: Boydell Press, 2018), 46.

Fig. 5.3 An image of the Scottish writer Alexander Ross (*c*.1590–1654), with his books. Bodleian Library Montagu 534 (A. Ross, [*Pansebeia*], 1655). By permission of the Bodleian Libraries, The University of Oxford.

Fig. 5.4 Samuel Pepys's library, *c.*1690, in his rooms, with free-standing bookcases around the walls. By permission of the Pepys Library, Magdalene College, Cambridge.

Lucy Gwynn noted that Sir Thomas Browne (1605–82) kept them in various locations throughout the house.[18]

Contemporary images of men and their bookshelves often show books in a range of sizes; Boys is an example, with his larger books on low shelves and smaller ones higher up, much as we would commonly do today. Owners of all kinds typically had books in all formats, though there is a recurring theme in gifts to institutions that only larger books were sufficiently serious, or capable of being repositories of permanent knowledge, to merit preservation there. Lancelot Andrewes (1555–1626) bequeathed all his folio volumes to Pembroke College, Cambridge, with no instructions regarding his smaller books, just as William Butler (1535–1618) bequeathed his folios to Clare College.[19] At the other end of the century, Richard Drake (1609–81) gave first choice of his books in folio and quarto to Pembroke, with the ones left over to be offered to Salisbury Cathedral, and Sir Leoline Jenkins (1625–85) directed that 40 volumes in folio or quarto be selected from his books for Doctors' Commons, 'to begin their library'.[20] In between, Robert Pinck (1573–1647) left all his books in folio and quarto (not

---

[18] Lucy Gwynn, *The library of Sir Thomas Browne*, PhD thesis, Queen Mary College, University of London, 2016, https://qmro.qmul.ac.uk/xmlui/handle/123456789/25850 (accessed 1 Feb. 2019), 83.

[19] D. Chambers, 'A catalogue of the library of Bishop Lancelot Andrewes', *Transactions of the Cambridge Bibliographical Society* 5 (1970), pp. 99–121; Cambridge University Library, VCCt. Wills III.

[20] The National Archives PROB 11/368/361, PROB 11/381/217.

Fig. 5.5 Jan van der Heyden, *Corner of a library*, painted in 1711. Museo Nacional Thyssen-Bornemisza, Madrid.

already held) to New College, Oxford, the rest of his books being given to a nephew.[21] This kind of bibliographical sizeism can be seen in Sir Nathaniel Bacon's (1546?–1622) phrase in his will giving 'such great books as I have' to his grandson Roger Townshend (and it may be noted that the great majority of the 300 books in Townshend's library list of *c*.1625 are folios or quartos).[22] Humphrey

[21] TNA PROB 11/203/154.
[22] P. Reid, 'Proto-bibliophiles among the British aristocracy', *Library History* 18 (2002), pp. 25–38; R. J. Fehrenbach, 'Sir Roger Townshend's books', in R. J. Fehrenbach and E. S. Leedham-Green (eds), *Private libraries in Renaissance England*, vol. 1 (Binghamton, NY: Center for Medieval and Early Renaissance Studies, 1992), pp. 79–135.

Gower (1638–1711), leaving to St John's College, Cambridge 'such of my books that are of a sort or edition of which the College has none ... and shall be judged fit to have a place there', observed that 'little inconsiderable books' would not pass that test.[23]

Bound and unbound books

One point which has never been properly acknowledged, when considering early modern period private libraries, is the extent to which material was owned and used in what we would consider unbound form. When we think of historic libraries, either private or institutional, we envisage the neat rows of books typically bound in leather-covered boards that are represented in any of Figs 5.1–5.5 (in Fig. 5.5, they are mostly parchment; that proportion of parchment covers is more characteristic of a Dutch library than it would be of an English one). In doing so, we overlook the number of books which circulated and were used in much more temporary structures, stab-stitched in paper wrappers (or perhaps no wrappers at all)—books whose later trajectory would usually follow one of two paths, to be bound more solidly (and preserved), or to become waste paper. Either of these typical options leads to the loss of huge numbers of these books in their original condition.

This is, obviously, the territory of what are commonly called pamphlets, which do have a literature as a genre, defined by their contents: pamphlets 'were generally vernacular works of a topical nature, whether relating to the political, religious, social or economic debates with which they engaged ... [including] almanacs, news-pamphlets and newspapers ... [and] political and religious polemics'.[24] They 'contained anything between 8 and 96 pages', and 'were often not produced to very high standards'.[25] Other writers have acknowledged that 'no clear and stable lines can be drawn to distinguish between a pamphlet, a small book, and a book', but there is a common association of the idea of a pamphlet with the seditious, the controversial, and the ephemeral.[26] '"Pamphlet" became a perjorative word'; pamphleteers risked 'single combat, branding with irons, and slitting of the ears'.[27] Following on from this train of thought, items perceived as pamphlets may also be thought to have been placed lower in the intellectual or

[23] TNA PROB 11/520/273.

[24] Jason Peacey, 'Pamphlets', in J. Raymond (ed.), *The Oxford history of popular print culture*, vol. 1 (Oxford: Oxford University Press, 2011), ch. 33, 454.

[25] Ibid. 454, 455.

[26] Alexandra Halasz, *The marketplace of print: pamphlets and the public sphere in early modern England* (Cambridge: Cambridge University Press, 1997), 3.

[27] Brian Findlay, 'Pamphlet', in M. F. Suarez and H. Woudhuysen (eds), *The Oxford companion to the book* (Oxford: Oxford University Press, 2010), pp. 997–8.

cultural pecking order than proper books: their 'seemingly shabby physical form constitutes strong evidence of lower value in the eyes of their contemporaries'.[28] Hence the well-known strictures of Sir Thomas Bodley against 'many pamphlettes, not worth the custody in suche a Librarie'.[29]

Aaron Pratt has convincingly challenged this received wisdom, seeking particularly to overturn the view that stab-stitched plays were accounted "low status" and taken less seriously by early seventeenth-century readers.[30] He assembled an impressive body of evidence from many libraries, surveying pre-1640 publications, to show that many such books now in sturdy bindings must originally have circulated in some kind of stab-stitched form, probably with paper or parchment wrappers, because their gutter margins retain the needle holes going through the entire text block, through which the original thread passed. He found that 'of 335 books between ninety-seven and 304 leaves in length, just over thirty percent contain tell-tale holes'.[31] My own observations of many books over many years would support that broad finding: it is not at all unusual to find books in bindings perhaps 50 or 100 years later than their imprint dates, with stab-stitch holes in the inner margin testifying to their earlier lives. I published an illustration of one, a copy of Bacon's 1622 folio *Historie of . . . Henry the seventh*, some years ago; Fig. 5.6, one of Brian Twyne's books which was bound up not long after publication, shows what to look for.[32]

Another type of evidence for this mixed economy of formats in private libraries of this time is manifested in the many hundreds of printed sale catalogues which began to appear in the last quarter of the seventeenth century. Anyone who has spent any time looking at these will be familiar with a standard arrangement which most of them follow: books are subdivided into categories by format, subject, and language with varying degrees of sophistication, often starting with Latin folio theology and running through to small-format English books. At the end, it is very common to find final sections of pamphlets and 'stitched books', usually not listed in detail, running to hundreds of items which their owners had held in these thriftily bound states. Some would have been sermons, polemical tracts, and works of just a few pages, which we might expect to see under the pamphlet rubric, but there would be likely to be a wider mix. Examples are too numerous to list in detail; to select just a few, the sale of Kenelm Digby (scientist and philosopher, 1603–65) ended with 88 bundles of stitched pamphlets; Thomas

[28] Aaaron Pratt, 'Stab-stitching and the status of early English playbooks as literature', *The Library*, 7th ser. 16 (2015), pp. 304–28, 307.

[29] G. W. Wheeler (ed.), *Letters of Sir Thomas Bodkey to Thomas James* (Oxford: Clarendon Press, 1926), 40.

[30] Pratt, 'Stab-stitching' his findings are nicely summarized in his conclusion on 327–8.

[31] Ibid. 325.

[32] David Pearson, *Books as history*, rev. edn (London: The British Library, 2012), [188]; more examples of tract volumes with this kind of evidence, from Bryan Twyne's books, are mentioned below (p. 134).

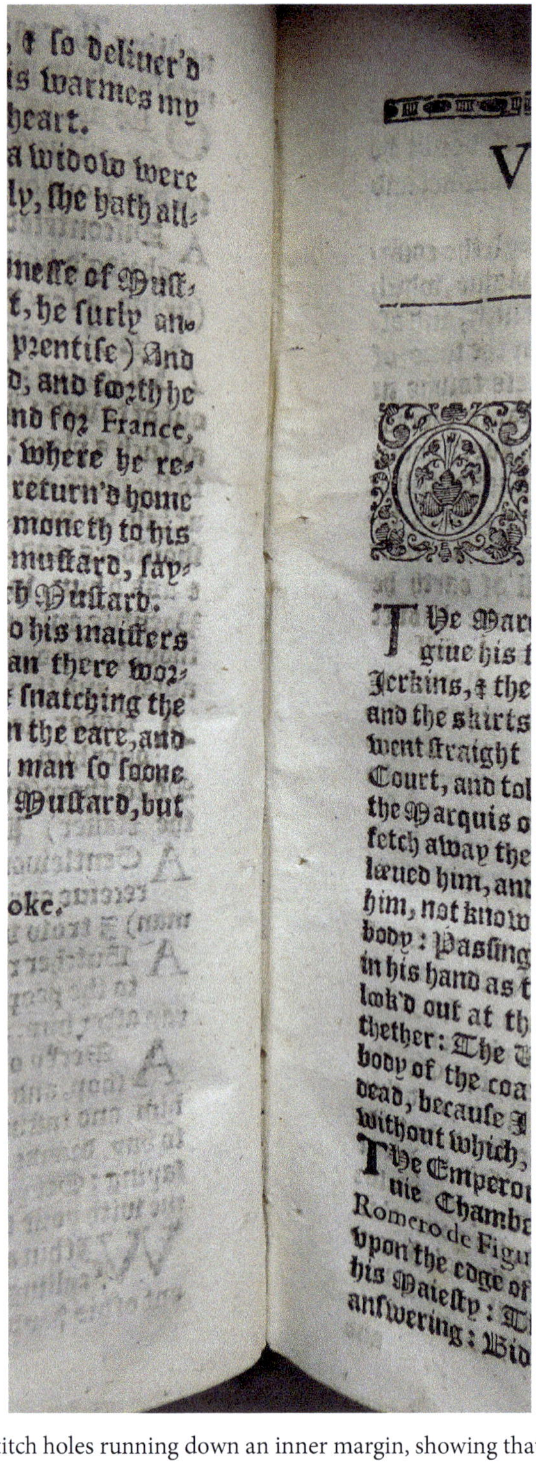

Fig. 5.6 Stab-stitch holes running down an inner margin, showing that the book was a stitched pamphlet before it was put into a more permanent binding. Corpus Christi College, Oxford Delta.16.18 (Anthony Copley, *Wits, fits and fancies*, 1614, and other works). By permission of the President and Fellows of Corpus Christi College, Oxford.

Manton (Presbyterian clergyman, 1620–77) had 37 bundles of unbound pamphlets; George Ashwell (Oxfordshire rector, 1612–94) had 54 lots of 'stitcht books'; John Collins (lawyer, d. 1682) had 228 items sold off in thirteen bundles.[33] The sale catalogue for Richard Lee's library (Hertfordshire rector, 1657?–83), which concluded with 50 'bundles of pamphlets', stated that 'there will also be exposed to sale the same way, in the close of the auction, a large collection of scarce and curious tracts and pamphlets, ancient and modern, of most subjects... in bundles'.[34] Many more such examples will be found by browsing late seventeenth- and early eighteenth-century printed sale catalogues.

What we find much less commonly is primary evidence manifested through libraries of this time whose stitched pamphlets survive in their contemporary state. This kind of material, if it has survived the accidents of time, has usually found its way into some kind of institutional custodianship, where it is rare indeed for it to have escaped the understandable drive to ensure both preservation and usability by having it more solidly bound. Owners as well as librarians have been doing this for a long time—two seventeenth-century Oxford owners who gathered up their tracts for binding, Nicholas Crouch and Bryan Twyne, are noted in the following chapter—and Pratt's survey shows how commonly stab-stitched material ended up between boards. One unusual survival, which shows us how seventeenth-century owners more usually left their books at the end of their lives, can be found in Maldon, Essex, in the library which Thomas Plume (1630–1704) built and bequeathed to his home town there. Plume's library of around 8,000 titles—large for its time—includes around 1,600 stitched pamphlets, most of which remain today in their original seventeenth-century form. Having been kept as Plume intended for the last three centuries, and relatively little used during that time, the library is a striking instance of the benefits of benign neglect in the heritage sphere.[35]

The Plume pamphlets embrace a diverse range of material, in subject, size, and format, and their coverings demonstrate pretty much every variation possible; Fig. 5.7 shows a representative sample. There are pamphlets of a few gatherings with the simplest stab-stitching at the spine edge, and ones with a little more protection provided with plain, coloured, or marbled paper, plain parchment, or waste parchment cut from an earlier manuscript. Many sixteenth- and earlier seventeenth-century imprints have the ownership markings and annotations of owners before Plume, showing that these books circulated and were traded like

[33] *Bibliotheca Digbeiana, sive, catalogus librorum in variis linguis editorum* (London, 1680); *Catalogus variorum et insigniorum librorum... Thomas Manton* (London, 1678); *Catalogus librorum tam antiquorum tam recentium in omne facultate* (Oxford, 1696); *A curious collection of law-books, ancient and modern... of John Collins... And of another fam'd practicer of the law* (London, 1683).
[34] *A catalogue of the library of choice books... of... Dr. Richard Lee* (Hatfield, 1685).
[35] David Pearson, 'Thomas Plume's Library in its contemporary context', in Christopher Thornton and Tony Doe (eds), *Dr Thomas Plume, 1630–1704: his life and legacies* (forthcoming).

Fig. 5.7 A representative sample of the many hundreds of stitched pamphlets, in various covering materials, found in the Plume Library, Maldon. By permission of the Trustees of Thomas Plume's Library.

this over multiple generations. There are items which appear to be disbound—to have been previously bound up in boards of some kind, with sewn gatherings stitched to sewing supports across the spine which would once have been laced in to covers—and others with a similar structure, but whose projecting lacing-in cords and untrimmed edges suggest a half-bound book, taken that far in preparation for binding in boards but never finished.[36] Many of the tracts are quite short, less than 100 pages, but there are plentiful examples of more substantial books, which we would more usually encounter today in solid bindings; Richard Baxter's 1681 *Second true defence of the meer nonconformists*, in quarto, stitched with no wrappers, does fall under the heading of controversial doctrinal writing, but is 195 pages long.[37] The 1677 English translation of Jean-Pierre Camus's *Alcime, A true tragical history of two Italian families*, has nearly 300 pages.[38]

Apart from the pamphlets, Plume's library is noteworthy for its size but otherwise largely fits patterns typical of many collections of his time, as regards its breadth of subject coverage, mixture of new and second-hand books, and primarily workaday bindings, commissioned for functionality rather than glamour. The pamphlet collection is however remarkable and precious as a snapshot of that mixture of the bound and the flimsy, which (as the auction catalogues demonstrate) was once a standard feature of seventeenth-century libraries. Another smaller but similar collection survives as part of the Forbes Library now in the Thomas Fisher Library at the University of Toronto, the books of James Forbes (1628/9–1712), a Congregationalist clergyman who left his books to be an ongoing resource for Nonconformist ministers in Gloucestershire.[39] Here there are about 300 pamphlets in a total library of *c.*1,600 items—the proportion, 19 per cent of the whole, is very similar to the ratio in Plume's Library—with a similar mixture of formats and structures. Outside these, there are probably some other survivals *en bloc* in country house libraries and lesser-known ecclesiastical ones, but stab-stitched books and pamphlets from the seventeenth century are more typically found as odd examples rather than in the concentrations in which they once existed.

Conclusions

Our knowledge of the ways in which books were stored in seventeenth-century domestic interiors is, and always will be, partial, because of the limitations of the evidence base. So many rooms in which books were once kept have been remodelled or lost over time, and the cases where we do have an archival or architectural record tend to be the grander houses. Certainly, such houses regularly had libraries, or at least spaces described as closets or studies, during this period,

---

[36] An example of the former is Plume pamphlet 122, H. Mason, *The tribunal of the conscience* (London, 1627); of the latter, Plume pamphlet 229, H. Horche, *Sacerdotium romanum*, [1690?]. On the phenomenon of part-bound books circulating, see Nicholas Pickwoad, 'Unfinished business: incomplete bindings made for the booktrade', *Quaerendo* 50 (2020), pp. 41–80.
[37] Plume pamphlet 295.   [38] Plume pamphlet 55.
[39] P. L. Heyworth, 'The Forbes Library', *The Book Collector* 19 (1970), pp. 317–27; it survived as a working Nonconformist library until the 19th c., and after a period of storage was sold to Toronto in 1966.

becoming bigger or more imposing as time went by. Books were likely to be stored or displayed in multiple locations, depending on their nature or perceived purpose. We should also remember, when thinking about libraries as tidy rows of bound books standing on shelves, that many physical formats made up the holdings of early modern owners, and that we may very easily overlook the likely proportion of the unbound, the stab-stitched, or the otherwise flimsy material which would have been found there. Contemporary images of people and their books, like those in Figs 5.1–5.3, usually include only the neatly bound volumes, but there is clearly an element of idealism there. Pamphlets and books without stiff covers may have been stored upright on shelves, but they may have lent themselves more readily to boxes or drawers; either way, they commonly constituted a greater proportion of the whole than their survival pattern might suggest.

6

Books for use and books for show

In 1693, the auctioneer Edward Millington commended the books of the recently deceased John Cropper to his prospective customers with the assurance that 'his learning rendred him capable of reading and thoroughly understanding what he had collected, designing his proper use not the show of them, and was more conversant in the insides, than delighted with the outsides of them'.[1] Cropper was however 'earnestly desirous of the fairest copies that were at any rate to be procured ... [with] many significant books of the large paper, and most of them extraordinary well bound'. Questions of motivation behind book ownership constitute an important theme throughout this book; as noted in the opening chapter, there are multiple possible reasons for possessing books and building private libraries, and we need to know why they did it, as well as what they owned. The final chapter focuses on ideas of collecting in the seventeenth century, and how they might differ from those of today, while other chapters have looked at the kinds of libraries formed by different types of owner, primarily for reading or reference. This chapter is concerned with the ownership of books beyond their textual utility: to what extent did people own books partly or solely as objects of display, as projections of their wealth and status?

The tradition of mocking those who own books more for show than for use is a very ancient one, pretty much as old as books themselves, which in turn reflects how long people have been doing that very thing. The image which most readily comes to mind is perhaps the much-reproduced one of the book-fool from the late fifteenth-century edition of Sebastian Brandt's *Ship of fools*, 'the first fool of all the whole navy / For this is my mind, this one pleasure have I / Of books to have great plenty, but what they mean I do not understand'.[2] But there are numerous similar criticisms in classical literature; Lucian of Samosata addressed a satire to an illiterate book-fancier, and Ausonius mocked an affluent friend who filled his house with books to persuade people of his gravitas.[3] In the 380s, St Jerome inveighed against the vanity of wealthy people who stained the leaves of their

---

[1] E. Millington, *Bibliotheca Cropperiana* (London, 1693) [2].
[2] Among many modern reproductions and facsimiles, see e.g. S. Brant, tr. William Gilles, *The ship of fools* (London: Folio Society, 1971), 8.
[3] Nicholas Basbanes, *A gentle madness* (New York: Henry Holt, 1995), pp. 60–61 (where other similar examples from classical writers are mentioned).

Book Ownership in Stuart England: The Lyell Lectures, 2018. David Pearson, Oxford University Press (2021).
© David Pearson.
DOI: 10.1093/oso/9780198870128.003.0006

books purple, and bejewelled their covers.[4] In the seventeenth century, the standard text is that of Gabriel Naudé, librarian to Cardinal Mazarin, with his much-quoted strictures about 'cutting off all the superfluous expenses, which many prodigally and to no purpose bestow upon the binding and ornaments of their books,... it becoming the ignorant only to esteem a book for its cover'.[5] Those words come from John Evelyn's 1661 translation of Naudé, and it will be readily evident to anyone who has seen books from Evelyn's own library, handsomely gilded with his monograms and armorial binding tools, that he is one person who clearly did not follow that advice.[6] Neither, for that matter, did the Earl of Clarendon, to whom Evelyn dedicated his translation, and whose surviving books are generally found in handsome gilt-tooled goatskin with the Hyde arms.[7] A more mature view is expressed by the much less well-known words in the introduction to the 1711 sale catalogue of the surgeon Charles Bernard, where it was observed that 'he always thought the best books deserved the best covering, and considered that many a good book happening to fall into ignorant hands, is thrown away and lost by the meanness of its dress, which would have been preserved, had its ornament been suitable to its worth'.[8] However, when the considerably larger library of his physician brother Francis had been auctioned thirteen years earlier, the catalogue noted that 'being a person who collected his books for use... he seem'd no more solicitous about his dress than his own... a gilt back or a large margin was very seldom any inducement for him to buy'.[9] There has always been a spectrum of attitudes and views around this theme.

The culture of luxury

Luxury in material culture is of course a topic which has been more widely explored within what the editor of the *Oxford handbook of the history of consumption* has described as 'a publishing boom, with a deluge of books and dedicated journals, conferences and research programmes' looking at the evolution of shopping, spending, desiring and consuming in Western society.[10] Late

---

[4] W. H. J. Weale, *Bookbindings and rubbings of bindings in the National Art Library*, vol. 1 (London: HMSO, 1898), viii.

[5] G. Naudé, tr. J. Evelyn, *Instructions concerning erecting a library* (London, 1661), 61.

[6] See the examples in the colour plates at the end of *The Evelyn Library*, Christie's sale catalogue, London, 22–3 June 1977; and Giles Mandelbrote, 'John Evelyn and his books', in F. Harris and M. Hunter (eds), *John Evelyn and his milieu* (London: The British Library, 2003), pp. 71–94 (p. 73: 'Evelyn clearly took pleasure in the aesthetic aspect of his library').

[7] E.g. the one reproduced in *The collection of Robert S. Pirie*, Sotheby's (New York) sale catalogue, 2 Dec. 2015, lot 56; and see https://armorial.library.utoronto.ca/stamp-owners/HYD003 (accessed 25 Oct. 2018).

[8] J. Hooke, *Bibliotheca Bernardiana* (London, 1711), 'To the reader'.

[9] *A catalogue of the library of the late learned Dr. Francis Bernard* (London, 1698), a2 verso.

[10] Frank Trentmann (ed.), *The Oxford handbook of the history of consumption* (Oxford: Oxford University Press, 2012), 1.

medieval books were the focus of an essay by Ryan Perry in one such compendium, where he reflected that 'perhaps some medieval books were viewed by their owners as objects to be used performatively, as material symbols of prestige rather than having been constructed to be actively, or easily read'.[11] The study which most readily comes to mind in the seventeenth-century context is probably Linda Levy Peck's *Consuming splendor*, in which she maps the burgeoning fashion for luxury goods in Stuart England, encouraged by royal and aristocratic patronage, and often depending on imported goods from Europe and Asia.[12] She talks of the reinvention of identities through new artefacts, and the potential of luxury goods to project political and economic power. Books do feature in her work, though less centrally than pictures, sculpture, silk, plate, and porcelain, and more in terms of their contents than their materiality, looking at the availability of romances or lavishly illustrated travel books.[13] Books become caught up here in the dilemma which is endemic to book history as a discipline, which Perry described as 'the strange capacity of books to exist coevally in a physical and semiotic state which separates them from so many everyday objects'.[14] It was expressed in plainer English by Leslie Howsam when she said that 'as artefacts of the past books suffer among historians from the familiarity that breeds contempt...relatively few historians have yet become convinced that books have a history in the sense that Canada has a history.'[15] Books can exist both for use and for show, but our academic and custodial traditions have focused perhaps disproportionately only on the former.

   Two ways of using ownership markings in books in ways that demonstrate personal status matured, or effectively began, in the seventeenth century: the use of armorial binding stamps, and the use of bookplates. Putting a coat of arms onto a binding is a practice with roots in the late fifteenth century, which spread across Europe and came to England in the 1530s, where the earliest examples were exclusively royal; the first recorded non-royal example is a binding of the mid-1550s for the Earl of Arundel.[16] The idea gradually took off, and during the succeeding centuries many hundreds of such stamps were used. Our knowledge of them is greatly enhanced by the database of British Armorial Bindings which is largely the work of Philip Oldfield, based on an extensive survey of many libraries both in Britain and North America; it has been online since 2012, but has yet to be quarried as a book-historical research tool beyond simple identification queries.[17]

[11] R. Perry, 'Objectification, identity, and the late medieval codex', in T. Hamling and C. Richardson (eds), *Everyday objects: medieval and early modern material culture and its meanings* (Farnham: Ashgate, 2010), pp. 309–20, 317.
[12] Linda Levy Peck, *Consuming splendor* (Cambridge: Cambridge University Press, 2005).
[13] Ibid. 124–8.   [14] Perry, 'Objectification', 318.
[15] Leslie Howsam, *Old books and new histories* (Toronto: University of Toronto Press, 2006), 46.
[16] David Pearson, *Provenance research in book history* (Oxford: Bodleian Library, 2019), 130.
[17] https://armorial.library.utoronto.ca/ (accessed 25 Oct. 2018).

Armorial bookbindings

This database shows that at the beginning of the seventeenth century, there were somewhere between 20 and 30 people in England actively using armorial stamps to mark their books. It is difficult to be exact, as a number of the stamps recorded reflect gifts rather than personal ownership, and the date that people began using armorials is not always easily established when there are not many surviving books.[18] About half of them are aristocrats, about a third knights (no baronets, of course, before 1611), but there is a handful of wealthy commoners, like the lawyer William Rich (b. 1567) and the merchant William Harborne (d. 1617). By the middle of the century there were at least 40 people using armorials, and in the last quarter I count nearly 60 people on the database who were having coats of arms put on their bindings. Again, about half of them are aristocrats, but knights and baronets constitute a smaller ratio of the whole, and there is a larger proportion of untitled people. They include well-known late seventeenth-century bibliophiles like John Evelyn (1620–1706) and Ralph Sheldon (1623–84), each of whom had multiple armorial stamps, and less well-known people like the Staffordshire MP and antiquary Walter Chetwynd (1633–93), who was also a serial commissioner of stamps.[19]

The importance of heraldry in the early modern period is well known; it was a signifier of status and a driver of much antiquarian research in the seventeenth century. Nearly 4,000 grants of arms were made between 1560 and 1640.[20] Linda Peck, in her 2005 book, observed that 'identity began with a coat of arms', and when Laurence Stone was chronicling the crisis of the aristocracy 50 years ago he noted that the late Tudor and early Stuart period was one where 'heraldry moved into a baroque phase, a lush profusion of improbable quarterings'.[21] Writing about the genealogical and antiquarian pursuits of Sir Thomas Shirley (*c*.1590–1654), who compiled a 'massive compendium of heraldry and family

---

[18]   My tally takes in: Arthur Agarde (1540–1615); Charles Blount, Earl of Devonshire (1563–1606); Henry Brooke, 11th Baron Cobham (1564–1619); George Carew, 1st Earl of Totnes (1555–1630); Robert Cecil, 1st Earl of Salisbury (1563–1612); William Crashawe (1572–1626); Edward de Vere, 17th Earl de Vere (1550–1604); Richard Eedes (1565–1604); Thomas Egerton, 1st Viscount Brackley (1540–1617); Sir Moyle Finch (1550–1614); Roger Goad (1538–1610); William Harborne (d. 1617); Sir Christopher Hatton (d. 1619); John Holles, 1st Earl of Clare (1564–1637); Charles Howard, 1st Earl of Nottingham (1536–1624); Henry Howard, Earl of Northampton (1540–1614); Sir Rowland Lytton (1562–1616); Sir Robert Naunton (1563–1635); Sir William Paddy (1554–1635); Sir Thomas Parry (d. 1616); Henry Percy, 9th Earl of Northumberland (1564–1632); William Rich (b. 1567); Edward Russell, 3rd Earl of Bedford (1572–1627); Thomas Sackville, 1st Earl of Dorset (1536–1608); Edward Seymour, 1st Earl of Hertford (1539?–1621); Richard Towneley (1566–1628); and Sir Thomas Tresham (1543–1605).
[19]   https://armorial.library.utoronto.ca/stamp-owners/EVE001; https://armorial.library.utoronto.ca/stamp-owners/SHE004; https://armorial.library.utoronto.ca/stamp-owners/CHE007 (all accessed 25 Oct. 2018).
[20]   Laurence Stone, *The crisis of the aristocracy, 1558–1641* (Oxford: Clarendon Press, 1965), 67.
[21]   Peck, *Consuming splendor*, 28; Stone, *Crisis*, 24.

history', Richard Cust commented on the 'vast amount of scholarly energy expended in tracing family trees' by people like him.[22] More recently, a collection of essays edited by Nigel Ramsay has illustrated numerous ways in which aristocratic and gentry families incorporated arms into paintings, domestic interiors, and various household objects, though bindings are not explicitly mentioned.[23] A number of the armorial book stamps used in the seventeenth century testify to the importance attached to multiply quartered arms to demonstrate lineage, and the more striking examples are not necessarily aristocratic ones; Walter Chetwynd is a case in point, as is the early seventeenth-century statesman Sir Robert Naunton (1563–1635), and his contemporary Sir Walter Covert (d. 1632; Fig. 6.1). The obvious question around all these armorial bindings, going back to that dichotomy expressed about medieval books, is whether they are acting performatively as objects of prestige, or as functional books to be read. Were these books for use, for show, or both?

Anthony Hobson observed that Jean Grolier's famous 'et amicorum' bindings began to appear after his release from prison and a period of court disfavour; the bindings were 'an announcement to the world that he had resumed his place in the world of letters'.[24] These armorial bindings were clearly making a statement about rank and lineage, and there are cases of multiple stamps being made to reflect career advancement. Toby Matthew (1546–1628) used an armorial stamp as Bishop of Durham and had a new one made when he became Archbishop of York in 1606.[25] The judge Sir James Ley (1550–1629) had an armorial stamp which reflects his status as a baronet from 1619, and found time in the last three years of his life to commission a new stamp showing his elevation to an earldom in 1626.[26] Sir John Holles (1564–1637), who became Baron Haughton in 1616 and Earl of Clare in 1624, first used a stamp stating his rank as a knight, and incorporating the date that he was knighted, 1593. Later, he had two stamps with an earl's coronet, one using his coat of arms and one the family crest.[27] I wonder whether there may have been a lost one in the sequence here, as we might expect him to have had a baronial one in between. We know that he cared about these bindings, as there is a reference in one of his letters to his son, in 1618, to having a book 'bound up according to the fashion that I use, with a place for my arms'.[28]

---

[22] R. P. Cust, 'Catholicism, antiquarianism, and gentry honour: the writings of Sir Thomas Shirley', *Midland History* 23 (1998), pp. 40–70, 42.

[23] Nigel Ramsay (ed.), *Heralds and heraldry in Shakespeare's England* (Donington: Shaun Tyas, 2014); see e.g. Richard Cust's essay, 'Heraldry and gentry communities in Shakespeare's England', pp. 190–203.

[24] A. R. A. Hobson, *Renaissance book collecting: Jean Grolier and Diego Hurtado de Mendoza* (Cambridge: Cambridge University Press, 1999), 59.

[25] https://armorial.library.utoronto.ca/stamp-owners/MAT001 (accessed 25 Oct. 2018).

[26] https://armorial.library.utoronto.ca/stamp-owners/LEY001 (accessed 25 Oct. 2018).

[27] https://armorial.library.utoronto.ca/stamp-owners/HOL006 (accessed 25 Oct. 2018).

[28] P. R. Seddon (ed.), *Letters of John Holles 1587–1637*, Thoroton Society Record Series 31, 35, 36 (Nottingham: 1975–86), vol. 1, 213.

Fig. 6.1 A binding made for Sir Walter Covert (d. 1632), with his multiply quartered arms. Bodleian Library Douce V 202 (G. J. Vossius, *Theses theologicae*, 1628). By permission of the Bodleian Libraries, The University of Oxford.

But we should not assume that these books are merely showpieces for family honour, as Holles is a man noted for his learning. His nephew Gervase Holles (1606–75), who also briefly used an armorial stamp before war and penury interrupted his career, described the earl's noble mind and the pleasures of dining with him, when, 'after he had reasonably well checked his appetite, he would ever start some discourse either in divinity, philosophy or history'.[29] His letters to his son between the 1610s and 1630s contain numerous references to seeking, obtaining, or reading books, and in 1618 he wrote how he had 'falln in deeply into Aristotles Rhetorick', comparing translations by Pierre de la Ramée and Francesco Porto, and preferring the latter as nearest the Greek.[30] His copy of the 1616 folio edition of Ben Jonson, with the first of his stamps and now in the National Art Library, is disappointingly clean and unannotated, but a copy of Daniel's 1617 *History of England* in the Bodleian, with the stamp of his arms beneath an earl's coronet, is covered with underlinings, marginal annotations, and pages of flyleaf notes drawing out or summarizing aspects of the text (Fig. 6.2).[31] The title page bears a note that 'the Author Sam. Daniel gaue me this book. 1618', and the slight cropping of some of the notes, together with the varying ink colours, suggests that the annotation took place over a period of time between 1618 and the making of this binding after his elevation to the earldom in 1626.

George Carew, Earl of Totnes (1555–1629) had a library which was both extensive and handsome. He was a professional soldier, courtier, and what we would today call a senior civil servant, who saw extensive military action in Ireland and the Caribbean in the 1570s and 1580s, was sheriff of County Carlow and master of the Irish Ordnance, went to Cadiz with the Earl of Essex and became Lord President of Munster around the time that he was ennobled as Baron Carew in 1605.[32] He had a life which was more obviously active than contemplative, but he was also a cultured man with historical interests, and a friend and patron of the Jacobean antiquaries. At least 50 printed books from his library can be traced today, spread across many libraries, though he is better known for his important collection of manuscripts on Irish history, now bound in 70 volumes split mostly between Oxford and Lambeth Palace Library.[33] In the words of the *ODNB*, 'in spite of his hatred of the Irish, he was very interested in Irish history and preserved contemporary documents relating to Ireland, as well as buying older ones'.

All Carew's surviving books, including the manuscripts, were originally bound in calf or vellum decorated with his arms. He had five armorial stamps, of differing sizes but all of the same design, and he was unusual in going to the trouble of having them painted as well as gilt-stamped, to represent the correct heraldic tinctures; most armorial binding stamps are just gilt on leather and do not try to show proper colours. On the vellum bindings, particularly, the three lions on the

---

[29] G. Holles, ed. A. C. Wood, *Memorials of the Holles family*, Camden Society 3rd ser. 55 (London, 1937), 111.

[30] Seddon, *Letters*, 216.   [31] The Jonson is National Art Library CLE L11.

[32] U. Lotz-Heumann (3 Jan. 2008), 'Carew, George, earl of Totnes (1555–1629), soldier and administrator', *Oxford Dictionary of National Biography*. Retrieved 25 Oct. 2018 from: http://www.oxforddnb.com/view/10.1093/ref:odnb/9780198614128.001.0001/odnb-9780198614128-e-4628.

[33] M. R. James, 'The Carew manuscripts', *English Historical Review* 42 (1927), pp. 261–7.

Fig. 6.2A The armorial stamp of John Holles, 1st Earl of Clare (1564–1637), on a copy of Samuel Daniel's *Collection of the historie of England*, given to him by the author. Bodleian Library D.2.16 Art. By permission of the Bodleian Libraries, The University of Oxford.

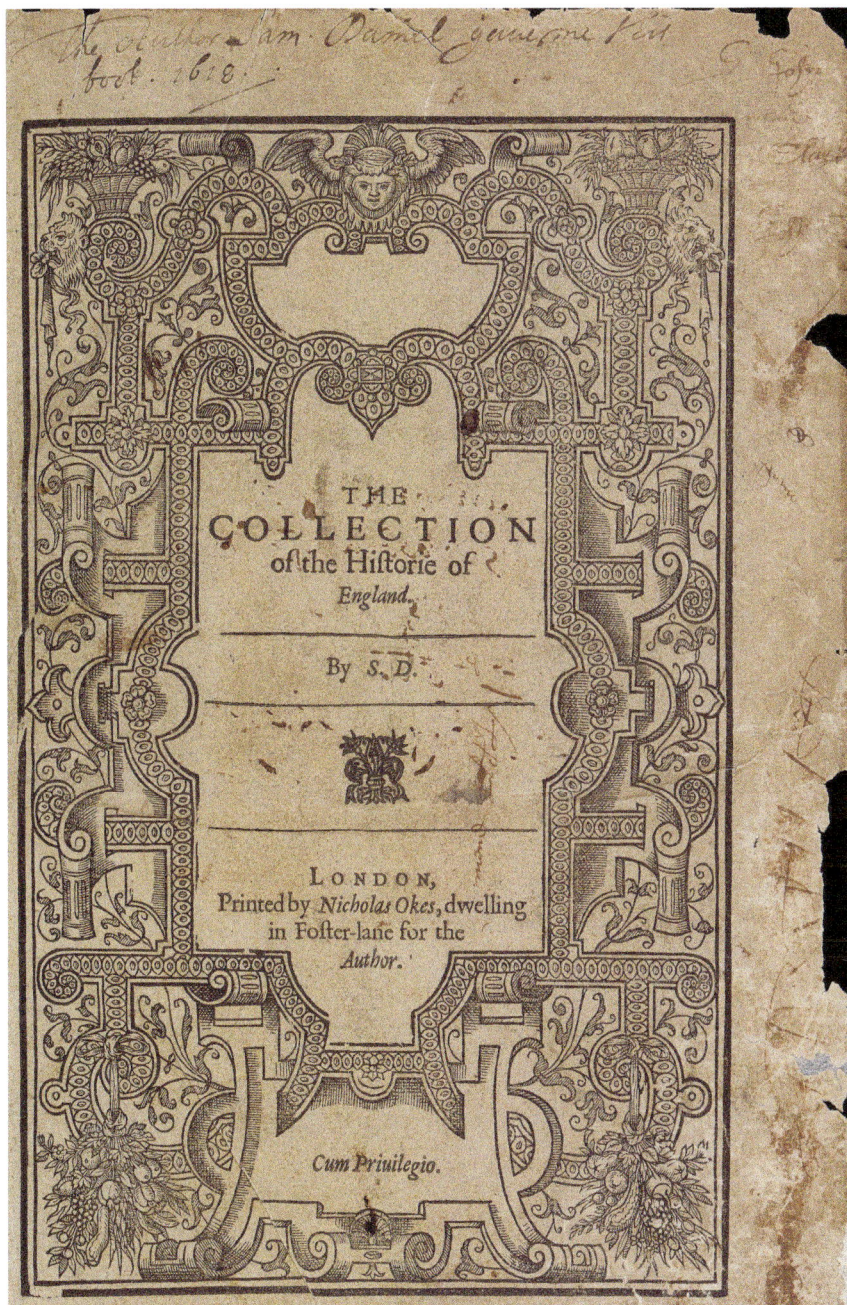

Fig. 6.2B Holles's inscription on the title page, noting the gift by Daniel. By permission of the Bodleian Libraries, The University of Oxford.

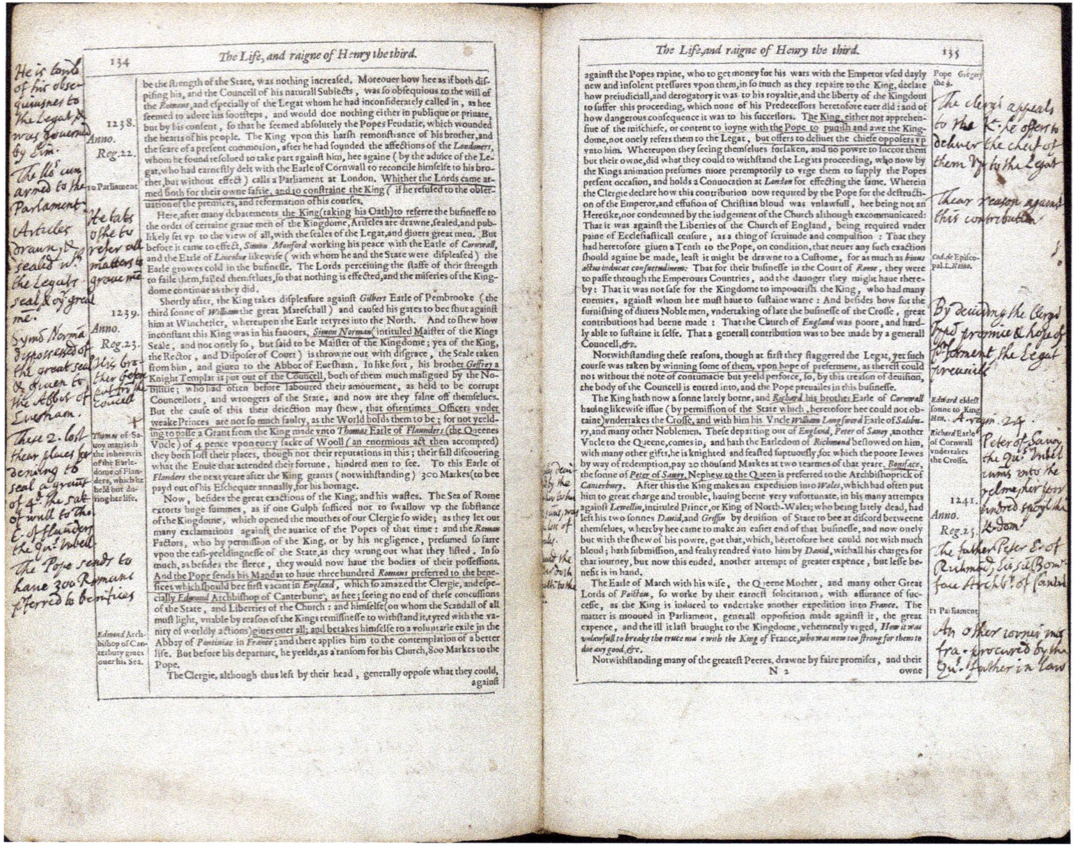
134 The Life, and raigne of Henry the third.

be the ſtrength of the State, was nothing increaſed. Moreouer how hee as if both diſpiſing his, and the Councell of his naturall Subiects, was ſo obſequious to the will of the *Romans*, and eſpecially of the Legat whom he had inconſiderately called in, as hee ſeemed to adore his footſteps, and would doe nothing either in publique or priuate, but by his conſent, ſo that he ſeemed abſolutely the Popes Feudatie, which wounded the hearts of his people. The King vpon this harſh remonſtrance of his brother, and the feare of a preſent commotion, after he had ſounded the affections of the *Londoners*, whom he found reſolued to take part againſt him, hee againe (by the aduice of the Legat, who had earneſtly delt with the Earle of Cornwall to reconcile himſelfe to his brother, but without effect) calls a Parliament at London. Whither the Lords came armed both for their owne ſaftie, and to conſtraine the King (if he refuſed to the obſeruation of the premices, and reformation of his courſes.

1238. *Anno.* Reg.22.

to Parliament

Here, after many debatements the King (taking his Oath) to referre the buſineſſe to the order of certaine graue men of the Kingdome, Articles are drawne, ſealed, and publikely ſet vp to the view of all, with the ſeales of the Legat, and diuers great men. But before it came to effect, *Simon Monford* working his peace with the Earle of *Cornwall*, and the Earle of *Lincolne* likewiſe (with whom he and the State were diſpleaſed) the Earle growes cold in the buſineſſe. The Lords perceiuing the ſtaffe of their ſtrength to faile them, failed themſelues, ſo that nothing is effected, and the miſeries of the Kingdome continue as they did.

1239. *Anno.* Reg.23.

Shortly after, the King takes diſpleaſure againſt *Gilbert* Earle of Pembrooke (the third ſonne of *William* the great Mareſchall) and cauſed his gates to bee ſhut againſt him at Wincheſter, whereupon the Earle retyres into the North. And to ſhew how inconſtant this King was in his fauours, *Simon Norman* (intituled Maiſter of the Kings Seale, and not onely ſo, but ſaid to be Maiſter of the Kingdome; yea of the King, the Rector, and Diſpoſer of Court) is throwne out with diſgrace, the Seale taken from him, and giuen to the Abbot of Eueſham. In like ſort, his brother *Geffrey* a Knight Templar is put out of the Councell, both of them much maligned by the Nobilitie; who had often before laboured their amouement, as held to be corrupt Councellors, and wrongers of the State, and now are they falne off themſelues. But the cauſe of this their deiection may ſhew, that oftentimes Officers vnder weake Princes are not ſo much faulty, as the World holds them to be; for not yeelding to paſſe a Grant from the King made vnto *Thomas* Earle of *Flaunders* (the Queenes Vncle) of 4 pence vpon euery ſacke of Wooll (an enormious act then accompted) they both loſt their places, though not their reputations in this; their fall diſcouering what the Enuie that attended their fortune, hindred men to ſee. To this Earle of *Flanders* the next yeare after the King grants (notwithſtanding) 300 Markes (to bee payd out of his Eſchequer annually, for his homage.

Thomas of Sauoy marrieth the inheretrix of the Earledome of Flanders, which he held but during her life.

Now, beſides the great exactions of the King, and his waſtes. The Sea of Rome extorts huge ſummes, as if one Gulph ſufficed not to ſwallow vp the ſubſtance of the Kingdome, which opened the mouthes of our Clergie ſo wide; as they let out many exclamations againſt the auarice of the Popes of that time: and the *Roman* Factors, who by permiſſion of the King, or by his negligence, preſumed ſo farre vpon the eaſi-yeeldingneſſe of the State, as they wrung out what they liſted. In ſo much, as beſides the fleece, they would now haue the bodies of their poſſeſſions. And the Pope ſends his Mandat to haue three hundred *Romans* preferred to the benefices which ſhould bee firſt vacant in *England*, which ſo amazed the Clergie, and eſpecially *Edmond* Archbiſhop of Canterburie, as hee; ſeeing no end of theſe concuſſions of the State, and Liberties of the Church: and himſelfe (on whom the Scandall of all muſt light, vnable by reaſon of the Kings remiſſneſſe to withſtand it, tyred with the vanity of worldly actions) giues ouer all; and betakes himſelfe to a voluntarie exile in the Abbay of *Pontiniac* in *France*; and there applies him to the contemplation of a better life. But before his departure, he yeelds, as a ranſom for his Church, 800 Markes to the Pope.

Edmond Archbiſhop of Canterbury giues ouer his Sea.

The Clergie, although thus left by their head, generally oppoſe what they could, againſt

The Life, and raigne of Henry the third. 135

againſt the Popes rapine, who to get money for his wars with the Emperor vſed dayly new and inſolent preſſures vpon them, in ſo much as they repaire to the King, declare how preiudiciall, and derogatory it was to his royaltie, and the liberty of the Kingdom to ſuffer this proceeding, which none of his Predeceſſors heretofore euer did: and of how dangerous conſequence it was to his ſucceſſors. The King, either not apprehenſiue of the miſchiefe, or content to ioyne with the Pope to puniſh and awe the Kingdome, not onely refers them to the Legat, but offers to deliuer the chiefe oppoſers vp vnto him. Whereupon they ſeeing themſelues forſaken, and no powre to ſuccor them but their owne, did what they could to withſtand the Legats proceeding, who now by the Kings animation preſumes more peremptorily to vrge them to ſupply the Popes preſent occaſion, and holds a Conuocation at *London* for effecting the ſame. Wherein the Clergie declare how this contribution now required by the Pope for the deſtruction of the Emperor, and effuſion of Chriſtian bloud was vnlawfull, hee being not an Heretike, nor condemned by the iudgement of the Church although excommunicated: That it was againſt the Liberties of the Church of England, being required vnder paine of Eccleſiaſticall cenſure, as a thing of ſeruitude and compulſion: That they had heretofore giuen a Tenth to the Pope, on condition, that neuer any ſuch exaction ſhould againe be made, leaſt it might be drawne to a Cuſtome, for as much as *binus actus inducat conſuetudinem:* That for their buſineſſe in the Court of *Rome*, they were to paſſe through the Emperours Countries, and the daunger they might haue thereby: That it was not ſafe for the Kingdome to impoueriſh the King, who had many enemies, againſt whom hee muſt haue to ſuſtaine warre: And beſides how for the furniſhing of diuers Noble men, vndertaking of late the buſineſſe of the Croſſe, great contributions had beene made: That the Church of *England* was poore, and hardly able to ſuſtaine it ſelfe. That a generall contribution was to bee made by a generall Councell, &c.

Pope Gregory the 9.

Cod. de Episcopal. L. Neino.

Notwithſtanding theſe reaſons, though at firſt they ſtaggered the Legat, yet ſuch courſe was taken by winning ſome of them, vpon hope of preferment, as the reſt could not without the note of contumacie but yeeld perforce, ſo, by this treaſon of deuiſion, the body of the Councell is entred into, and the Pope preuailes in this buſineſſe.

The King hath now a ſonne lately borne, and *Richard* his brother Earle of *Cornwall* hauing likewiſe iſſue (by permiſſion of the State which, heretofore hee could not obtaine) vndertakes the Croſſe, and with him his Vncle *William Longſword* Earle of *Salisbury*, and many other Noblemen. Theſe departing out of *England*, *Peter* of *Sauoy*, another Vncle to the Queene, comes in, and hath the Earledom of *Richmond* beſtowed on him, with many other gifts, he is knighted and feaſted ſuptuouſly, for which the poore Iewes by way of redemption, pay 20 thouſand Markes at two tearmes of that yeare. *Boniface*, the ſonne of *Peter* of *Sauoy*, Nephew to the Queen is preferred to the Archbiſhoprick of *Canterbury*. After this the King makes an expedition into *Wales*, which had often put him to great charge and trouble, hauing beene very vnfortunate, in his many attempts againſt *Lewellin*, intituled Prince, or King of North-Wales; who being lately dead, had left his two ſonnes *David*, and *Griffin* by deuiſion of State to bee at diſcord betweene themſelues, whereby hee came to make an eaſier end of that buſineſſe, and now onely but with the ſhew of his powre, got that, which, heretofore hee could not with much bloud; hath ſubmiſſion, and fealty rendred vnto him by *David*, withall his charges for that iourney, but now this ended, another attempt of greater expence, but leſſe benefit is in hand.

Edward eldeſt ſonne to King Hen.

Richard Earle of Cornwall vndertakes the Croſſe.

1241. *Anno.* Reg.25.

The Earle of March with his wife, the Queene Mother, and many other Great Lords of *Poicton*, ſo worke by their earneſt ſolicitation, with aſſurance of ſucceſſe, as the King is induced to vndertake another expedition into *France*. The matter is mooued in Parliament, generall oppoſition made againſt it, the great expence, and the ill it laſt brought to the Kingdome, vehemently vrged, *How it was vnlawfull to breake the truce ma e with the King of* France, *who was now too ſtrong for them to doe any good, &c.*

Parliament

Notwithſtanding many of the greateſt Peeres, drawne by faire promiſes, and their

N 2 owne

Fig. 6.2C An opening of the book, with Holles's extensive marginalia. By permission of the Bodleian Libraries, The University of Oxford.

Fig. 6.3 A binding made for George Carew, Earl of Totnes (1555–1629), with his armorial stamp gilt-tooled on parchment covers. Bodleian Library 4° M.63 Art.Seld (P. Mantuano, *Aduertencias a la historia de Iuan de Mariana*, 1611). By permission of the Bodleian Libraries, The University of Oxford.

gold background—which is heraldically correct—are painted black, with little red tongues. When new, these books would have been seriously handsome, as can still be seen today when well-preserved examples are found (Fig. 6.3). His books are mostly in English, Latin, French, or Italian and he had many which today we would regard as interesting and collectable. In the Royal College of Physicians in London there is a batch of a dozen, which include some very striking Italian books on warfare and fortifications, and he had numerous other books on military operations which clearly reflected and supported his professional activities.[34] He had books on duelling, seamanship, history, and politics, and his English books included a copy of Chaucer's works, Grafton's Chronicle, and Florio's Italian–English dictionary.[35] These are ones we know about because they survive today, but the original library must have been much larger; no lists exist, but he made explicit mention of his books and manuscripts in his will, directing that they go to Sir Thomas Stafford (d. 1655), who is generally believed to have been his illegitimate son.[36] There is almost nothing theological among the books that remain, which is unusual, and it seems likely that they would once have existed, but have disappeared. The books were dispersed by the London bookseller Cornelius Bee in the 1650s, and inscriptions show that they quickly found new homes.[37]

Carew did not add an aristocratic coronet to his binding arms, though he could have done so after 1605. He occasionally wrote his name on title pages, typically in the earlier part of his life, in the 1590s, but the continuation of his book buying throughout his career is demonstrated by imprint dates of the late 1620s among what survives. What we do not have, with his books, is internal evidence of use; examination of many of them, across different libraries, shows no regular patterns of annotation that can be associated with him with any confidence; there are occasional underlinings and marginal markings, which may be his, but equally possibly by previous or subsequent owners. The pages of his books are generally clean and even crisp; his copy of Florio's Italian dictionary, which we might expect him to have used to help with his Italian military books, is almost spotless. The volvelle in *The seaman's secrets* goes round as well as it did on the day it was put together, and the numerous fold-out plates in Lorini's book on fortifications, a large and attractive book which he acquired and signed in its year of publication, 1597, are in immaculate condition with no tears.[38] From all that we know of the man and his career, there is an obvious, indeed quite a striking, match between his books and his professional activities; their contents imply books for use, but their physical attributes suggest at least some element of books for show. Of course, it doesn't have to be either/or, and my guess would be a bit of both, but when he was a reader, he was a careful one.

---

[34] E.g. (in the RCP Library): B. Lorini, *Delle fortificationi* (Venice, 1597); B. Rocca, *De discorsi di guerra* (Venice, 1582); P. Sardi, *L'artiglieria* (Venice, 1621).

[35] G. Chaucer, *Workes* (London, 1602), Parham House, Sussex; R. Grafton, *A chronicle at large* (London, 1569), Bodleian Library fo. BS.162; G. Florio, *Queen Anna's new world of words* (London, 1611), Royal College of Physicians of London.

[36] TNA PROB 11/129/47.   [37] James, 'The Carew manuscripts', 264.

[38] J. Davis, *The seaman's secrets* (London, 1595), Royal College of Physicians of London; Lorini, see n. 34 above.

There are other cases where show rather than use is more demonstrably the motive. It is well known that around the beginning of the eighteenth century and thereafter bookbinders began to advertise their services in going around gentlemen's libraries to brighten them up, not only to add title labels but also to add gilt and sparkle to their rows of dark leather spines.[39] It is very common to find seventeenth-century bindings, and earlier, with eighteenth-century spine decoration. Mark Purcell, in his book on the country house library, notes the creation of a number of libraries by Restoration period statesmen and grandees like Lauderdale and Anglesey, who did indeed bring money as well as learning to the creation of handsomely housed libraries which impressed their viewers.[40] He mentions in that context Henry Bennet, Earl of Arlington (1618–85), whose library at the newly built Euston Hall in Suffolk was visited by John Evelyn in 1677, when he described it as being full of excellent books. Arlington, who was a close confidant of Charles II when in exile and between 1662 and 1674 his longest-serving secretary of state once Charles was restored as king, has also been studied by Helen Jacobsen in her book *Luxury and power*. She notes that his reputation has suffered from the pens of enemies like Clarendon and Burnet, but that he was certainly acutely aware of the importance of display, and that his carefully managed identity included voracious artistic patronage: 'it's not the fact that Arlington had Italian marble chimney pieces in his house that is important, but the fact that his came directly from Carrara while those in the Duke of Lauderdale's house came only from a merchant in London.'[41]

Arlington was a genuinely learned man, thoroughly versed in European culture, and Evelyn said: 'he reades much, having both the Latine, French & Spanish tongues in perfection'.[42] He sourced his Euston library from numerous places, with agents commissioned to buy books in France and Italy.[43] He knew what was being bought and specified his choices, but the tale which is told by surviving books from this library confirms rather than contradicts Jacobsen's view that he was buying books by the yard, that his library was designed to be seen and discussed by the court elite who stayed with him. Arlington used an armorial bookstamp in which we certainly cannot miss the earl's coronet and there are numerous surviving books, on a variety of subjects, with imprints from all over Europe and dates from the mid sixteenth to late seventeenth century.[44] All the ones I have seen are entirely uniform; they are all bound in English mottled calfskin, 1670s or thereabouts, with gilded spines and marbled edges, and

[39] M. M. Foot, *The history of bookbinding as a mirror of society* (London: The British Library, 1998), 108; David Pearson, *English bookbinding styles, 1450–1800* (London: The British Library, 2005), 167.
[40] Mark Purcell, *The country house library* (New Haven, CT: Yale University Press, 2017), pp. 96–100.
[41] Helen Jacobsen, *Luxury and power* (Oxford: Oxford University Press, 2012), 122.
[42] J. Evelyn, ed. J. S de Beer, *The diary* (Oxford: Clarendon Press, 1955), vol. 4, 118.
[43] Jacobsen, *Luxury and power*, 131.
[44] https://armorial.library.utoronto.ca/stamp-owners/BEN002 (accessed 25 Oct. 2018).

Arlington's armorial on the covers. They are internally clean and crisp, with no inscriptions or annotations, and no evidence of having been used (Fig. 6.4). Closely cropped margins of earlier books indicate that volumes which came to Euston with earlier bindings were routinely rebound to the house style to achieve uniformity and leave no doubt about their new ownership.[45] The evidence suggests that Arlington's books were definitely more for show than for use.

Bookplates

The other technique for marking book ownership which came to maturity in the seventeenth century was the use of bookplates. The idea of pasting some kind of label into a book to signify its provenance dates back to the gift labels which were placed in books given to the Carthusian monastery of Buxheim by Hildebrand Brandenberg in the late fifteenth century, and bookplates as personal ownership signifiers evolved initially in Germany over succeeding decades, gradually spreading across Europe.[46] They were used occasionally in Britain from the late sixteenth century onwards; the British proto-plate is commonly said to be an armorial gift label pasted into books given to Cambridge by Sir Nicholas Bacon in 1574, though there are earlier candidates.[47] Their use throughout the seventeenth century was sporadic until the end of the century, when there was a sudden explosion of interest. It is well known in the chronicles of bookplate literature that in the 1680s and 1690s there was a great flowering of the production of plates, when the first of the recognizable and datable ornamental styles was developed, and which continued to be popular until about 1720.[48] During those few decades, hundreds of personal plates looking like those in Fig. 6.5 were made, in what is commonly called Early Armorial style—to put it another way, anyone visiting an engraver around 1700 to commission one of these newly fashionable objects would come out with something looking like those.

There are some obvious questions arising from this phenomenon. Firstly, why the sudden development of popularity at this time? Should we interpret the rise of bookplates as another manifestation of the Arlington approach, an opportunity to use books as vehicles of display and status? The first question is a puzzle to which we do not have an answer. We know why book auctions began in England in 1676—a British Nonconformist minister who had spent time in Holland, and observed them there, suggested to a bookseller that they would be a good

[45] An example is Bodleian Library 50.d.20, L. Rusius, *La mareschalerie* (Paris, 1610).

[46] Pearson, *Provenance research*, 67.

[47] David Pearson, 'What is the earliest British bookplate?', *The Library*, 7th ser. 20 (2019), pp. 527–32.

[48] B. N. Lee, *British bookplates: a pictorial history* (Newton Abbot: David and Charles, 1979), 10.

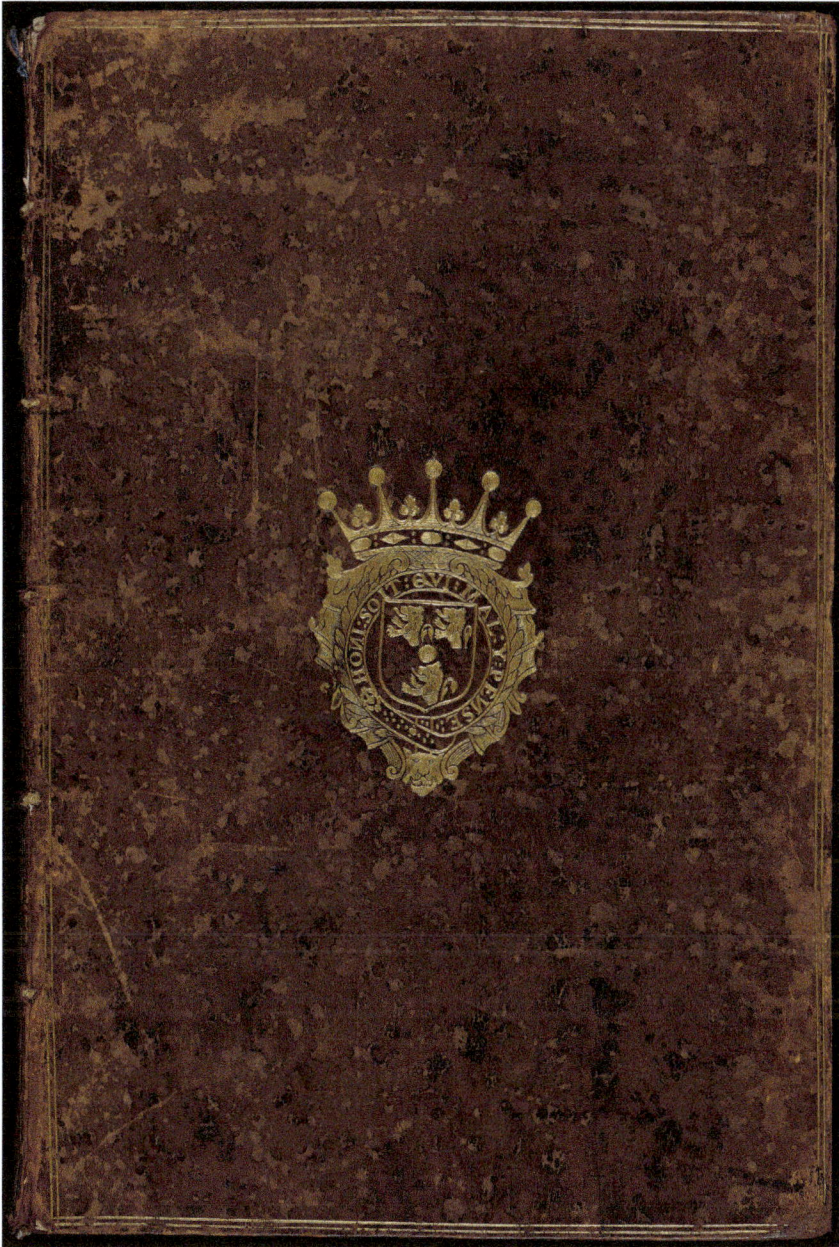

Fig. 6.4 A binding made for Henry Bennet, Earl of Arlington (1618–85), with his armorial stamp. Bodleian Library Douce B subt.293 (J. T. de Bry, *Kunstbuchlein*, 1619). By permission of the Bodleian Libraries, The University of Oxford.

idea—and it is logical to look for some similar catalyst behind the rise of book-plates.[49] There is a much-quoted letter from the engraver David Loggan to Sir Thomas Isham, written in 1676, noting that persons of quality are now pasting their arms into their books instead of writing their names, but no explanation there of the phenomenon.[50] But beyond the obvious explanations of the rise of non-essential consumerism in Restoration England, we do not know what the vital spark was, whose adoption or promotion of the idea led to the fashion taking off. What is observably the case is that it certainly did, and while the number of British bookplates in use in the middle of the seventeenth century can be counted in tens, in 1710 it was in hundreds.

These first-generation bookplates are handsome and pleasing things to a modern eye, and they would surely have evoked the same response in 1700. They invariably manifest heraldry, declaring the social status of the owner. They were created for gentlemen, baronets, and aristocrats, and for a few of their wives, and although they clearly have a function in marking ownership it is hard to avoid some sense of flamboyant display. They were made for doctors and lawyers, for a few deans, bishops, and senior academics, and for the town and country houses of the wealthy. They were made for people for whom otherwise we have no record of book ownership, for aldermen and civic dignitaries, like Sir John Shorter (1625–88; Fig. 6.5B) who was a goldsmith by trade, Lord Mayor of London in 1687, and died the following year.[51] John Evelyn mentioned him in his Diary as 'a very odd ignorant mechanic'.[52] I cannot point to any surviving volumes with this plate in them, and his will has no mention of books.[53] It does reveal extensive wealth and property holdings, and maybe his main residence had a library, of the kind such a house ought to have. Maybe someone was paid to paste these plates into the books, or maybe not, perhaps they were printed and never used: we do not know. But the rise of this fashion provides additional evidence of books being valued for show at least as much as for use.

Bookbindings more generally

Returning to bindings, we should think further about what they may be able to tell us about attitudes to books. Bindings, other than handsomely decorated ones,

---

[49] S. Wright (23 Sept. 2004), 'Hill, Joseph (1625–1707), nonconformist minister', *Oxford Dictionary of National Biography*. Retrieved 25 Oct. 2018 from: http://www.oxforddnb.com/view/10.1093/ref:odnb/9780198614128.001.0001/odnb-9780198614128-e-13283.

[50] Lee, *British bookplates*, 9; as Lee notes there, 1676 actually seems quite early to be commenting on the rise of bookplate popularity, which we would date a decade or so later based on the surviving evidence.

[51] E. R. J. Gambier Howe, *Franks bequest. Catalogue of the British and American book plates bequeathed by ... Sir Augustus Wollaston Franks*, vol. 3 (London: The British Museum, 1903), 34, where Shorter's plate is illustrated.

[52] Evelyn, *Diary*, vol. 4, 562.   [53] TNA PROB 11/392/393.

Fig. 6.5 Bookplates in the 'Early Armorial' style which is typical of British bookplates of the turn of the eighteenth century, when the use of bookplates became fashionable: (A) for James Bertie (1674–1735) (B, overleaf) for Sir John Shorter (1625–88). By permission of The British Museum.

have typically been woefully ignored in book-historical work, although binding historians are gradually turning that tide by pointing out how integral they are to any kind of whole-book material object approach.[54] Before the middle of the nineteenth century and the gradual introduction of mass-production techniques, every binding was an individually hand-crafted product which represented a

[54] E.g. M. M. Foot, *Bookbinders at work* (London: the British Library, 2006), ch. 1 ('Bibliography and bookbinding history', 3–32; Julia Miller, *Books will speak plain* (Ann Arbor, MI: Legacy Press, 2010), introduction (1–12); Nicholas Pickwoad, 'Coming to terms', in G. Boudalis et al. (eds), *Historical book binding techniques in conservation* (Horn: Berger, 2016), pp. 11–28; David Pearson, 'Bookbinding history and sacred cows', *The Library* (forthcoming).

Fig. 6.5 Continued.

choice made by an owner or a bookseller around how much to spend on it. The more they spent, the more handsomely decorated the end product was likely to be, as well as solidly constructed. We know that the latter feature was often important to people; primary archival evidence of the commissioning of bindings at this time is very thin on the ground, but where it exists it commonly talks about the structural functionality of the end product. Sir Robert Cotton, in the 1620s, told his binder to bind it strong, trim its edges and press it well; Sir William Boothby, half a century later, complained when he found defects in his binding work, and specified levels of edge trimming.[55] But we also know that people did or did not choose to spend money on making their books look nice, to please themselves or make an impression on others, and that the choices made are not necessarily a reflection of personal means. Thomas Plume, archdeacon of Rochester, whose large library is now in his home town, Maldon, could certainly have afforded some sparkle on his book covers, but the only gilt to be found among his 8,000 or so books is that which came by the accident of being second-hand, or a presentation copy.[56] His contemporary Samuel Pepys—they were born and died within a few years of one another—had a very different approach; it is well known that he cared very much about the look of his books, that he bought three books in 1660 'for the love of the binding', and that he spent considerable sums in having them bound to look pleasing on his shelves.[57] But we also know that he was just as interested in the contents as Plume was, and his was certainly not a library assembled only for show.

More debatable is the library of Edward Worth (1678–1733), which sits slightly outside my chronological and geographical limits, but which is too germane to this theme to exclude. Worth was born in Dublin, the son of the Dean of St Patrick's Cathedral, and after studying in Oxford and the Netherlands in the 1690s, returned in 1702 to Dublin, where he spent the rest of his life, establishing a successful practice as a physician.[58] He was buying books from his Oxford days onwards and bequeathed his library of a little over 4,000 volumes to Dr Steevens' Hospital in Dublin, of which he was a governor; the books have been there ever since, in the handsome glass-cased library room which his executors created.[59] Worth, like Pepys, wanted his books to look nice, and in the 1720s (when his financial circumstances improved) he spent a lot of money patronizing several high-end Dublin binders, who created many shelves' worth of books for him with fancily gilded spines.[60] He also bought books from London and abroad (many of his marked-up sale catalogues survive), developing a taste for Aldines and other

[55] Foot, *History of bookbinding*, 105; Peter Beal, 'My books are the great joy of my life', *The Book Collector* 46 (1997), pp. 350–78, 359.

[56] David Pearson, 'Thomas Plume's Library in its contemporary context', in Christopher Thornton and Tony Doe (eds), *Dr Thomas Plume, 1630–1704: his life and legacies* (forthcoming).

[57] H. M. Nixon, *Catalogue of the Pepys Library*, vol. 6 (Bindings) (Woodbridge: Brewer, 1984) (esp. the Introduction); see also Kate Loveman, *Samuel Pepys and his book* (Oxford: Oxford University Press, 2015), pp. 35–9.

[58] T. O'Riordan, 'Edward Worth', *Dictionary of Irish biography*: https://dib-cambridge-org.ezp.lib. cam.ac.uk/viewReadPage.do?articleId=a9128&searchClicked=clicked&quickadvsearch=yes (accessed 25 Nov. 2018).

[59] Davis Coakley, 'Edward Worth and his Library', in Danielle Westerhof (ed.), *The alchemy of medicine and print: the Edward Worth Library, Dublin* (Dublin: Four Courts Press, 2010), pp. 36–47; Elizabethanne Boran, 'Dr Edward Worth: a connoisseur book collector in early eighteenth-century Dublin', in E. Boran (ed.), *Book collecting in Ireland and Britain, 1650–1850* (Dublin: Four Courts Press, 2018), pp. 80–103.

[60] J. McDonnell and P. Healy, *Gold-tooled bookbindings commissioned by Trinity College Dublin in the eighteenth century* (Leixlip: Irish Georgian Society, 1987), 76 (though there is much more work to be done on Worth's Irish binders).

collectable early European imprints.[61] Subject-wise, the library is the wide-ranging mix of humanities and sciences which we would expect for the time, and has been described and appreciated for its contents, with particular attention paid to its medical books. But the really remarkable aspect of the Worth Library, its truly distinctive feature, is the condition of the books; almost without exception, they are crisp, clean, and seemingly unhandled. This is hard to describe in print, but there are so many examples on Worth's shelves of books in bindings of all kinds, the simple as well as the fancy, which provide that rare opportunity to experience an early eighteenth-century book pretty much in the condition it would have been in when first bought.[62] This applies not only to his early Aldines, where we might feel their acquisition is more about collecting than reading, but also to many of his medical books; whatever his purpose in owning them, it was not for poring over in search of professional knowledge. Worth's books must have looked handsome in his house and consulting rooms in fashionable Werburgh Street, near Dublin Castle, and one can imagine their showcase qualities impressing his visitors as well as pleasing their owner. This unread library suggests one whose use was primarily for show.

The college libraries of Oxford or Cambridge provide many opportunities to investigate these kinds of questions, to ask what the evidence can tell us about individual attitudes to books as artefacts as well as texts, what was important to people. Most colleges have at least one seventeenth-century collection which was bequeathed by an individual and which survives in more or less original condition, although the books may now be scattered around the library shelves. At Oxford, Brasenose has the books of Henry Mason (1575/6–1647), Merton those of Griffin Higgs (1589–1659), Oriel those of George Royse (1655–1708), Wadham those of Philip Bisse (d. 1613)—the list could go on.[63] At Balliol will be found the books of Nicholas Crouch (1641–89), bequeathed to the college after a career spent almost entirely in Oxford, as a fellow for 50 years and a practising physician. There are about 4,000 items in a little over 300 volumes, many but not all of them tracts bound up in fat composites; he also kept a register of book loans to his friends and colleagues.[64] His bindings were almost invariably made for him at his direction, and he was unusual for his time in regularly noting on the endleaves not only the

---

[61] Elizabethanne Boran, *Aldines at the Edward Worth Library* (Dublin: Edward Worth Library, 2015).

[62] An example of the stunning condition of Worth's more ordinary (as opposed to gilt-tooled goatskin) bindings is illustrated in ibid. Worth Aldine no. 71. This paragraph is based on a week spent working around the shelves of the Worth Library in Nov. 2018, and examples really are too numerous to mention. But anyone wishing to see the Cambridge 1713 edition of Newton's *Principia* in a simple but typical contemporary binding, as crisp, clean, and fresh as the day it was bought, should go to see the Worth copy.

[63] These and many more can be found summarily mentioned in Paul Morgan, *Oxford libraries outside the Bodleian*, 2nd edn (Oxford: Bodleian Library, 1980).

[64] https://balliollibrary.files.wordpress.com/2018/08/crouch_booklet_online.pdf, and see the numerous postings about the Crouch project on the Balliol Library website.

Fig. 6.6 A plain and simple binding, typical of the many made for Nicholas Crouch (1641–89). Balliol College, Oxford 910.f.12 (W.B., *A touch-stone for gold and silver wares*, 1677, and other works). By permission of The Master and Fellows of Balliol College, Oxford.

cost of each binding but also sometimes the name of the bookbinder. They are always of dark brown calfskin over boards, decorated in a variety of styles which are completely characteristic of their day, plain, simple, absolutely nothing fancy about them: the kinds of bindings that reflect a default option, basic, no frills, no unnecessary expense (Fig. 6.6). The one add-on feature of Crouch's bindings is the regular multicolouring of the leaf edges to distinguish individual tracts within the volumes—the crudity with which this was often done suggests that Crouch applied the colour himself, but it may have been applied by the binders.

Crouch's slightly younger contemporary, John Fitzwilliam (d. 1699), also bequeathed his books to his college, Magdalen, where around 500 survive today. He too was a regular noter of prices on his flyleaves, alongside his favoured

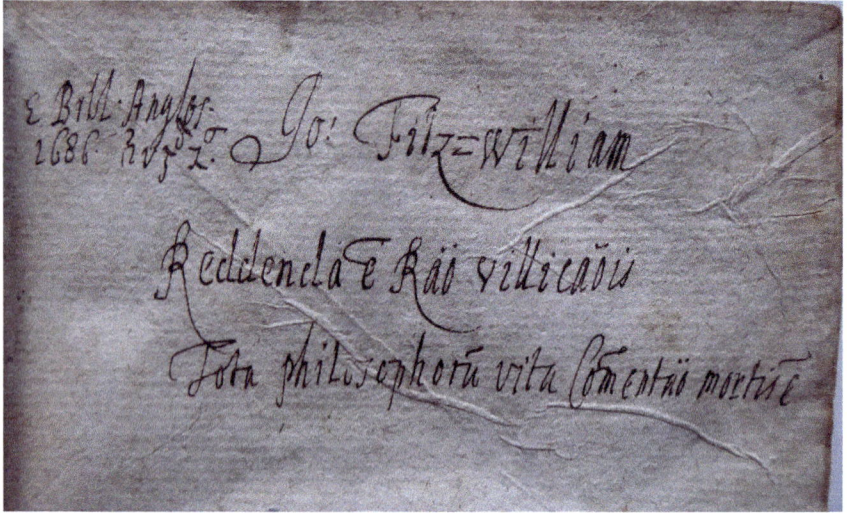

Fig. 6.7 The inscription and motto of John Fitzwilliam (d. 1699). Magdalen College, Oxford G.1.2 (*Institutiones Justiniani*, 1676). By permission of The Master and Fellows of Magdalen College, Oxford.

mottoes, taken from the Bible and Petrarch, that an account of one's stewardship must be given, and that the life of philosophers is the meditation of death (Fig. 6.7). His books have a distinctively different character from Crouch's; many of his bindings are plain and simple, but a noticeable proportion have what the sale catalogues of the period call gilt backs, elaborately decorated spines in a style that is typical of the last quarter of the seventeenth century (Fig. 6.8). His career was also perhaps more eventful; Oxford roots and contacts remained with him throughout, but he spent time as a chaplain in aristocratic and royal circles.[65] His taste for the finer things in life may have come from those influences, or from earlier reaction against austerity; he was not born with a silver spoon in his mouth, as he came from a Presbyterian background, but as a young student in Oxford he was noted for his zeal to restore Laudian practices around ceremonies and the beauty of holiness. He bought many of these more gilded books from London booksellers like Robert Scot and Henry Herringman in the 1670s, less commonly but still occasionally in his later years, even in his last decade when he had been deprived of his livings as a nonjuror. He did not own these books just for show, as his scholarly use of his library is evident from his manuscript writings which are now in the Bodleian via Thomas Smith and Richard Rawlinson, but his books evidently had a value and interest to him beyond the purely textually functional.

---

[65] D. Brunton (23 Sept. 2004), 'Fitzwilliam, John (d. 1699), nonjuring Church of England clergyman', *Oxford Dictionary of National Biography*. Retrieved 25 Oct. 2018 from: http://www.oxforddnb.com/view/10.1093/ref:odnb/9780198614128.001.0001/odnb-9780198614128-e-9658.

Fig. 6.8 Gilt-tooled spines of books from Fitzwilliam's library. Magdalen College, Oxford. By permission of The Master and Fellows of Magdalen College, Oxford.

His approach was different from Crouch's and there is surely more to the expressed choices we see here than simply a depth of purse.

Countless people, throughout the seventeenth century and in the centuries on either side, have spent more money than they needed to on bookbindings in order to have books that were aesthetically pleasing as well as workable, and we should want to explore their motives. One thing which book culture throughout the early modern period did not develop, despite its technical possibility, was the creation of personalized bindings based only on abstract decoration. This may be counter-intuitive, given the hand-crafted nature of it all, but customers did not specify their decorative designs; they got what they paid for, of an appropriate grade and quality, according to the prevailing ornamental fashions of the day. Unless a book has an armorial stamp or similar, it is not generally possible to look at the outside of a book that belonged to Robert Burton, or John Selden, or Samuel Pepys, or

John Moore, or any of the hundreds of documented book owners of the time, and know it was one of theirs. Exceptions to this rule are very uncommon, but there is one intriguing example in another of those seventeenth-century Oxford college collections, among the books of Brian Twyne at Corpus Christi. Twyne (1581–1644) spent most of his life in Oxford; he graduated from Corpus in 1599, became a fellow in 1607, was reader in Greek there from 1614, and was the first Keeper of the University Archives, the role for which he is best known, for the last ten years of his life. He inherited many books from his father, the physician Thomas Twyne (1543–1613), and was an avid book buyer throughout his life. He bequeathed his printed books to his college, where there are about 750 items in half as many volumes today; we don't know how much more there may once have been. His library, of which a simple catalogue was published in 1952, is understandably celebrated for its remarkable holdings of tracts on gardening, music, games, dogs, and what Ovenell called 'lighter contemporary literature', but his bindings also display some unusual and unique features.[66]

Many of Twyne's books are in completely standard blind-tooled leather bindings such as would be found on the shelves of scores of his contemporaries, including large numbers in Oxford centrepiece bindings of the kind that the binding trade there were turning out in great numbers on a daily basis. Among them is a batch of about 25 volumes covered in parchment over pasteboards which stand out because the tooling on them is applied in black ink rather than in blind or gold as was normal (Fig. 6.9).[67] Tooling in black on parchment is not in itself remarkable (though it is more commonly found on Continental European bindings than English ones), but in the context of early seventeenth-century Oxford binding, it is. Having looked at thousands of Oxford bindings of this period, working around the colleges chronicling them, I can say with confidence that Twyne was the only person among the extensive Oxford book-buying community of the time to be buying bindings like this.[68]

The books are almost all tract volumes, commonly containing four to seven tracts on a wide range of subjects, in octavo or quarto, dating from anywhere in the middle of the sixteenth century to the second decade of the seventeenth. The latest date found among them is 1614, from which year there are several spread across the volumes. They conform to standard Oxford binding practice of the time in many of their characteristics; they have the kind of hatching on their spines and edges that is typical of early seventeenth-century Oxford binding, they have yellow

---

[66] R. F. Ovenell, *Brian Twyne's library* (Oxford: Oxford Bibliographical Society, 1952).

[67] I illustrated and described another of these books in David Pearson, 'A binding made in Oxford for Brian Twyne, ca.1615', *The Book Collector* 49 (2000), pp. 248–51.

[68] My evidence base is the work undertaken for David Pearson, *Oxford bookbinding 1500–1640*, Oxford Bibliographical Society Publications 3rd ser. 3 (Oxford, 2000).

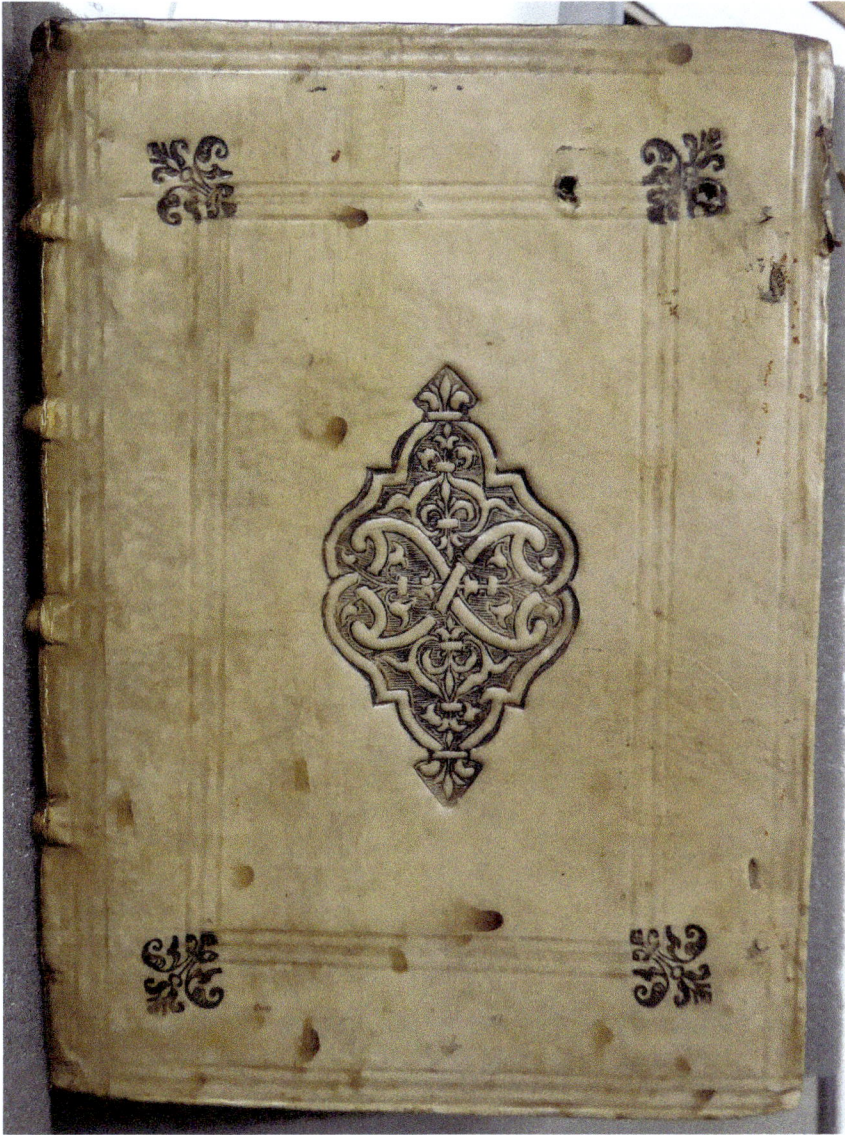

Fig. 6.9 A binding made in Oxford for Brian Twyne, *c.*1615, with black-stamped tooling on parchment covers. Corpus Christi College, Oxford Phi.A.1.8. (L. Gauricus, *Tractatus astrologiae*, 1540, and other works). By permission of the President and Fellows of Corpus Christi College, Oxford.

stained edges, and blue and pink headbands such as will be found on countless more conventionally books bound there.[69]

What is going on here? The evidence suggests that sometime in the mid-1610s Twyne decided to have a number of his small books bound up for tidiness and convenience of use, batched them up, and took them to a local binder. Many of them in their now-bound form have cropped inscriptions and headlines, and stab-stitch holes in their gutter margins, testifying to earlier existences as stitched pamphlets (see Fig. 5.6 above).[70] A few of them have discrete notes, '4 books', '6 books', which is either Twyne or the binder noting how many tracts are going in the volume.[71] So far so commonplace, but how did they come to have their distinctive decoration? The most obvious explanation seems to be that Twyne asked the binder for something different, for experimentation with black on white; perhaps he had seen a parchment binding like that and liked the look of it. Or the binder may have suggested it, based on some element of the conversation between the client and the customer. There is a little bit of further evidence of aesthetic motivation, because early seventeenth-century bindings most commonly have green cloth ties, and some of these Twyne ones were originally pink (now faded), and at least one of them had blue and white striped ones, which is distinctly unusual.[72] Many of the books today look a bit tired and grubby, but when they were new they would have been handsome and distinctive, Twyne's popinjay bindings. They manifest something very unusual.

Conclusions

This chapter has marshalled a number of case studies which demonstrate various points on a spectrum from utility to display, from simplicity to ostentation, inviting us to ask what motivation lay behind the choices made by the owners. At the extremities, the interpretation looks straightforward; Nicholas Crouch and Thomas Plume were interested in functionality and texts, Sir John Shorter and the Earl of Arlington wanted books primarily to impress. In between, we can see a matrix of motives at work; the Earls of Totnes and Clare were surely making a statement to the world with their books, but they were also readers. I doubt that

[69] The books are all catalogued on SOLO though they are not uniformly described so as to make picking them out straightforward. 'Twyne black ink' as a search term in copy-specific notes will return most of them (101 results, in Oct. 2018); as they are nearly all tract volumes, there are many more items than there are bound volumes.
[70] Examples are Corpus Christi Delta.8.12, Delta.17.18, Delta.16.18, Delta.18.17.
[71] E.g. Corpus Christi Delta.18.17, Delta.22.15.
[72] Pink ties were put on Corpus Christi Delta.8.12, Delta.22.15; Phi.A.1.8 had blue and white ones (in all these cases, only stubs of the originals remain). It is worth adding that the only instance of multicoloured rainbow ties that I have ever seen on a British binding (again, sadly, just remaining stubs) is on another Brian Twyne book, a standard Oxford centrepiece binding in tanned leather, Corpus Christi Delta.17.20.

Twyne was looking to impress his friends with his unusual bindings, and think the motivation there is more personal, around liking books in a physical way. I would also see that as a bigger driver for Pepys and Fitzwilliam, although they surely also liked their acquaintances to admire their shelves.

The key word is matrix; usually, the answers are not black and white, either/or, because a mixture of motives are at work. As Lisa Jardine put it in *Worldly goods*, 'the book as art-object and the book as treasured text (important to read and study) were curiously intertwined'.[73] Arlington was a learned man, and although much of his reading may have been done with other books at other times of his life, he certainly knew what was in his Euston Hall library. Methodologically, we might develop a set of attributes which pertain to all book owners to varying degrees: reading and reference use; display for influencing others; and personal delight in the aesthetics of books. The score of a particular individual against each attribute would create a profile to help us to compare and contrast, and better understand, the range of behaviours with and towards books which the historical record has left us to observe.

It may be argued that this is no more than common sense, and that no rocket science has been displayed here. The fact that books had multiple uses in a status- and display-conscious society, that sometimes they were not only not read, but never really intended to be, is perhaps a trivial observation. But this relates to questions which should be at the centre of our book-historical enquiries, about the purpose of books, about the place where their cultural value resides. We tend to be obsessed with texts, and reading: that's what books are for, that's what our libraries are geared to, that's where our research is focused. Compendia of book history, which flourish like mushrooms in the dark, focus on the history of reading as a great frontier: James Raven's enquiry *What is the history of the book?* has a whole chapter on it, and states that the understanding of reading is 'the most significant and challenging dimension of the history of books'.[74] Maybe sometimes we are missing the point about why the books were there, and we need to understand that interweaving of purpose, if we want to achieve a judicious understanding of the reasons why people owned books.

---

[73] Lisa Jardine, *Worldly goods* (London: Macmillan, 1996), 149.
[74] James Raven, *What is the history of the book?* (Cambridge: Polity Press, 2018), pp. 115–35.

7

Cultures of collecting

The c-word pervades the field of study around which this book is focused. People who amass private libraries are described, more often than not, as 'collectors', and their libraries as 'collections'. Is it an appropriate word, in a seventeenth-century context? Book collecting was defined by A. W. Pollard in the famous early twentieth-century edition of the *Encyclopaedia Britannica* as 'the bringing together of books which in their contents, their form, or the history of the individual copy possess some element of permanent interest, and either actually or prospectively are rare'.[1] That encapsulates a set of ideas around the accumulation of books (or coins, or stamps, or teddy bears, or pretty much any kind of artefact) which is readily recognizable, and which is manifested in the titles of many of the countless books written about book collecting during the last 100 years or so: *How to collect books, This book-collecting game, Fishers of books, The anatomy of bibliomania, A gentle madness*.[2] It can be analysed within the broader framework of the psychology of collecting, on which there is an even more extensive literature.[3] 'What do you collect?' is a familiar question among people who are interested in books, anticipating an answer which relates to a particular author or subject, and an aspiration to some kind of comprehensiveness within the defined boundaries. I collect books by and about Samuel Johnson, or books on beekeeping, or books printed in York, or 1930s crime novels. Is this kind of mindset one which is recognizable among, or which would be recognized by, many of the people listed in the Appendix?

Isaac Casaubon (1559–1614) and George John, 2nd Earl Spencer (1758–1834) are men a couple of hundred years apart who both assembled famous libraries which contained many early printed texts of classical authors.[4] The character and

---

[1] A. W. Pollard, 'Book-collecting', in *Encyclopaedia Britannica*, 11th edn, vol. 4 (Cambridge, 1910), 221.

[2] J. H. Slater, *How to collect books* (London: George Bell and Sons, 1905); A. E. Newton, *This book-collecting game* (Boston, MA: Little, Brown, 1926); Holbrook Jackson, *The anatomy of bibliomania* (London: Soncino Press, 1930); Barton Currie, *Fishers of books* (Boston, MA: Little, Brown, 1931); Nicholas Basbanes, *A gentle madness: bibliophiles, bibliomanes, and the eternal passion for books* (New York: Henry Holt, 1995).

[3] E.g. Werner Muensterberger, *Collecting: an unruly passion: psychological perspectives* (Princeton, NJ: Princeton University Press, 1994); Susan Pearce et al. (eds), *The collector's voice: critical readings in the practice of collecting*, 4 vols (London: Ashgate, 2000–2002); Michael Findlay, *The value of art: money, power, beauty* (Munich: Prestel, 2012).

[4] Among the numerous studies of these men and their libraries, obvious ones to mention are T. A. Birrell, 'The reconstruction of the library of Isaac Casaubon', in A. Groiset van Uchelen (ed.),

Book Ownership in Stuart England: The Lyell Lectures, 2018. David Pearson, Oxford University Press (2021).
© David Pearson.
DOI: 10.1093/oso/9780198870128.003.0007

purpose of those libraries was, however, very different. Casaubon was a textual scholar, Spencer was a Regency aristocratic connoisseur of the age of Roxburghe bibliomania. Casaubon acquired his books to read, study, and quarry in pursuit of his work, and was interested in their material qualities only so far as they were functional; he would not have an old book rebound unless it was falling apart, and he was not interested in gilded exteriors. Spencer did sometimes read his books, but he was buying them very much as collectable trophies of taste and fashion at a time when aristocrats demonstrated their cultured credentials through the rows of *editiones principes* and incunabula on their shelves. He routinely had his early books taken apart, washed to remove the markings of earlier owners, and rebound in gold-tooled goatskin so that today there is hardly a fifteenth-century binding to be found among the 3,000 or so incunables in the Spencer Collection in the John Rylands Library.

Spencer would have recognized the applicability of Pollard's definition of book collecting to his library-building activities, but I don't believe that Casaubon would have done, or his contemporary William Crashawe, the puritan clergyman who assembled one of the largest English private libraries of his generation. Or Richard Holdsworth, or John Selden, or Thomas Barlow, or Thomas Plume (to select some of the larger library-formers from the lists in the Appendix). They would have agreed that the contents of their books possessed elements of permanent interest, but they would have said that utility, not rarity, was the driving concept behind their book buying, and that Pollard's ideas were off-centre. They would have acknowledged the desirability of acquiring hard-to-obtain books, if their contents had knowledge value, but not that their actual or prospective rarity made them worth having. Reviewing Pollard's prose half a century after he wrote it, in another classic text on book collecting, John Carter recognized the distinction, saying that we need to be more discriminating in separating out the true collectors from 'mere accumulators of books'.[5] Pollard did recognize this, excluding Jean Grolier, Thomas Cranmer, John Lord Lumley, and Jacques de Thou from the annals of book-collecting because 'they brought their books together for use and study, to be read by themselves and the scholars who frequented their houses, and no evidence has been produced that they appreciated what a collector might now call the points of a book other than its fine condition and literary or informational merits'.[6] Carter produced a definition of a book collector as someone 'who has a reverence for, and a desire to possess,

Hellinga festschrift (Amsterdam: Nico Israel, 1980), pp. 59–68; and the extensive references to Spencer in Kristian Jensen, *Revolution and the antiquarian book* (Cambridge: Cambridge University Press, 2011), the exemplary study of the social and bibliographical evolution of attitudes to collectable books in the late 18th c.

[5] John Carter, *Taste and technique in book collecting* (London: Private Libraries Association, 1970), 2.
[6] Pollard, 'Book-collecting', 222.

the original or some other specifically admirable, curious or interesting edition of a book he loves or respects . . . and [it] must be either in its original state or in some contemporary, associative or otherwise appropriate condition.'[7]

Earl Spencer would have understood and identified with all of that, but would those seventeenth-century owners and their contemporaries? The purpose of this final chapter is to look more closely at the library-building behaviours of the seventeenth century in this context, using material and documentary evidence, to ask whether any or all of the kinds of values which we have come to associate with book collecting can be seen there, or whether the past is in fact another country. It is not an exercise merely of intellectual curiosity, as it clearly relates to key questions of motivation in acquiring and keeping books, and of understanding where their value was seen to lie.

Interest in old and collectable books

We have a broadly understood framework of the development of values around books and libraries in the early modern period which might be summarized as follows. Book collecting underwent an evolution, a transformation, during the eighteenth century, when notions of age and rarity increasingly overtook textual value as reasons for owning books. Taste and fashion drove up prices for old books which would previously not have been thus regarded. The early nineteenth century saw a high-water mark of bibliomania, but ever since then, book collecting in the Carter sense has flourished, with libraries large and small formed around ideas of rarity, beauty, author, or subject with a rationale that earlier centuries would not have recognized. The changes were partly catalysed, in a symbiotic kind of way, by bibliographical scholarship which opened up awareness of printing history, and by political upheavals across Europe which led to thousands of antiquarian books leaving institutional homes for the open market. The new wave of owners, from the eighteenth century onwards, were great interferers, who regularly wanted their books to be cleaned up and rebound according to the taste of the day, another significant change from the behaviours which were typical of earlier generations.

This story has been chronicled many times, with broad agreement on the chronology. Giles Mandelbrote, in the *Cambridge History of Libraries*, says that 'the first decades of the eighteenth century were a formative period in the development of book collecting in England', agreeing with de Ricci, who put it more memorably but perhaps with a shade too much drama when he said that 'it was about the year 1700 that several members of the British nobility became

---

[7] Carter, *Taste and technique*, 9.

simultaneously seized by a violent desire to collect incunabula'.[8] Arnold Hunt, also in the *Cambridge History*, observes that 'the period 1750–1850 can be regarded as the beginning of the modern era in book-collecting'.[9] Kristian Jensen suggested that it was the decade 1715–25 when 'something unprecedented happened to the collecting of old printed books'; he presents a variety of evidence to show that Caxtons were not being valued at a premium in late seventeenth-century sales, and that the value of early editions of the Church Fathers was still being expressed then in textual rather than typographical terms.[10] He looked in some detail at John Selden's incunabula, less than 2 per cent of his total library, and it is clear that there is no evidence to suggest that Selden acquired them for any reason other than their textual utility.

Most recently, this territory has been explored by David McKitterick, looking to describe *The invention of rare books*.[11] His tale is another one of stirrings in the seventeenth century, but of the early to mid-eighteenth as the time when things really changed: 'by the 1720s there was an identifiable shift in priorities and in taste.'[12] He draws extensively on the evidence of early sale catalogues, and the ways in which books are described there, to see the evolution and change taking place: 'it was some years after the earliest English sales before auction and book catalogues habitually used such terms as "rare".'[13] Discussing Robert Scott's 1674 book catalogue, he senses that 'the notion of annotations concerning condition … and rarity was for a future generation'; 'in these early catalogues of secondhand books … it is difficult to distinguish any kind of bibliophilic preferences.'[14] He notes an interesting distinction between the values applied by John Moore (1646–1714) and Edward Harley (1689–1741), two of the most noted private library owners of their succeeding generations. Moore belonged to the world of Selden, who, like him but 50 years previously, had assembled one of the largest personal libraries of his time; he did own many incunables, but they were acquired primarily for textual and knowledge-quarrying reasons, with no discernible interest in condition: 'content was more important than visual display.'[15] When Harley came to consider buying Moore's books after his death, he was advised by his librarian Wanley that there were too many 'old books of small or no value … such as vulgar Latin Bibles, psalters, primers … old scholemen, postils, sermons, and such trash … notes of divinity, law, physic, chirurgery, heraldry'.[16] This speaks not only to the breadth of Moore's library, in the best seventeenth-century traditions, but also

---

[8] Giles Mandelbrote, 'Personal owners of books', in G. Mandelbrote and K. Manley (eds), *The Cambridge history of libraries in Great Britain and Ireland*, vol. 2 (Cambridge: Cambridge University Press, 2006), pp. 173–89, 186; Seymour de Ricci, *English collectors of books and manuscripts* (Cambridge: Cambridge University Press, 1930), 33.

[9] Arnold Hunt, 'Private libraries in the age of bibliomania', in Mandelbrote and Manley, *Cambridge history*, pp. 438–58, 438.

[10] Jensen, *Revolution and the antiquarian book*, 69, 76–81.

[11] David McKitterick, *The invention of rare books* (Cambridge: Cambridge University Press, 2018).

[12] Ibid. 139.   [13] Ibid. 125.   [14] Ibid. 114, 116.   [15] Ibid. 98.   [16] Ibid. 103.

to the emergence of a connoisseurship and set of judgements around taste and fashion which belong to that succeeding generation.

Another way of interrogating sale catalogues is to analyse the proportion and nature of the incunabula that turn up in the seventeenth-century libraries which were dispersed that way. I have looked at some of the larger ones, choosing examples where books are listed at title level with what seems to be a fair level of accuracy over imprints and dates, and fifteenth-century books are only occasionally to be seen. The earliest auction sale in London with a printed catalogue was that of Lazarus Seaman (d. 1675), in 1676; of the 5,610 books in that listing, only 15 are noted as pre-1500 imprints, a mixture of classical, patristic, and medieval theologico-philosophical texts. When the books of Arthur Annesley, Earl of Anglesey (1614–86) were sold in 1686 there were four incunables listed in a catalogue of 6,500 items, and Annesley's library was noted as one of the great aristocratic collections of its day. The library of the nonjuring scholar George Hickes (1642–1715), sold in 1715, had eight fifteenth-century books in a catalogue of 2,100. I cannot point to an English private library of this time in which there is evidence that printed books were being systematically acquired or valued for their age in that later bibliophilic sense, despite occasional exceptions which may be thought to break the mould.[17] David McKitterick noted that a volume of four Caxton books bound together, 'having roused no interest at auction, was given by the bookseller Moses Pitt to the Bodleian in 1680'.[18] Sir Peter Leycester, whose 1670 book list features in Chapter 2, did own an edition of Aesop's Fables printed in 1482, but it was kept as part of the group called 'school-books for boys', alongside dictionaries, grammars, and textbook editions of the classics, for practical daily use.[19]

Evidence from bookbindings

Do we find evidence of incunabula being specially bound in the seventeenth century, in the way that they certainly were in the eighteenth and nineteenth, as signifiers of their bibliographical importance? The recataloguing of the Bodleian

[17] Perhaps the earliest, though we know little about him, is the mysterious Robert Hedrington, who is noteworthy not only because he used an unusually early ink ownership stamp dated 1577, but also because many of the small handful of surviving books on which it is found are English incunables or 15th-c. manuscripts: Richard Foster, 'Robert Hedrington and Wynkyn de Worde at Winchester College', https://www.new.ox.ac.uk/sites/default/files/7NCN4%20%282016%29%20Foster%20on%20Hedrington.pdf (accessed 7 Dec. 2018).

[18] McKitterick, *The invention*, 121. See also Leah Orr, 'The prices of English books at auction, c.1680', *The Library*, 7th ser. 20 (2019), pp. 501–26, 524, where she observes that 'older books, including incunabula and books produced by famous early printers … are not marked out in [the analysed sale catalogue] as special nor did they bring unusually high prices'.

[19] E. M. Halcrow (ed.), *Charges to the grand jury … by Sir Peter Leicester*, Chetham Society 3rd ser. 5 (Manchester, 1953), 149.

Library's holdings mean that it is now possible to explore the 7,000 or so fifteenth-century printed books held there from a variety of angles, including their bindings.[20] There are about 240 seventeenth-century English calfskin bindings across the whole, but apparently none from that century in the goatskin that was the material of choice for more upmarket work. There are however 900 in eighteenth-century calf or goat, and 2,000 in nineteenth-century calf or goat. Those figures clearly reflect that evolution of collecting fashions, and enthusiasm for rebinding, already described. Of the 240, the kind of catalogue description which comes up over and over again is that of simple, functional blind-tooled work of a very workaday nature; many relate to bindings put onto Selden books on behalf of the Bodleian after they were acquired in the 1650s. Many were bound up in tract volumes with sixteenth- and seventeenth-century books, and there was clearly no perception that they were in any way special for their age, or even that attributes like a late fifteenth-century decorated border with the arms of Archbishop Rotherham should be spared the binder's shears (Fig. 7.1). There is plentiful evidence in these kinds of books of having been used as working texts by sixteenth- and seventeenth-century owners, through inscriptions and marginalia, but certainly no sense that seventeenth-century custodians were giving them any special treatment in their bindings.

The same methodology can be applied to other kinds of books which we know came to be valued as collectable in the eighteenth century, with similar results. Lord Spencer's books in the John Rylands Library are notable not only for incunabula but also for the collection of many hundreds of books from the Venetian press of Aldus Manutius and his successors.[21] Aldine books belonged to the pantheon of desirable and fashionable books during the high-water years of bibliomania, and were noticeably beginning to receive special treatment by the second quarter of the eighteenth century. They were one of a number of European presses whose books had long been recognized for the quality of their scholarship and the reliability of their editions; books which had textual utility, irrespective of any values of historical significance or aesthetics which might be overlaid later.[22] In Seaman's 1676 sale catalogue, books from the presses of Henri or Robert Estienne are often identified as such; in the catalogue of Richard Smith's large and learned library six years later, although (as McKitterick notes) 'few distinctions were made...about the interest of one book rather than another', Estienne,

---

[20] http://incunables.bodleian.ox.ac.uk/ (accessed 7 Dec. 2018).

[21] Karen Attar (ed.), *Directory of rare book and special collections*, 3rd edn (London: Facet, 2016), 285.

[22] 'Very early on in the days of the Aldine press, its books became noted for their scholarship and ground-breaking design': Paolo Sachet, 'Selling Aldus in the UK (c.1630–2015)', in J. Kraye and P. Sachet (eds), *The afterlife of Aldus* (London: Warburg Institute, 2018), pp. 145–56, 151; see also Nicholas Poole-Wilson, 'The Aldine in British book trade history', in the same book, pp. 157–69; Jensen, *Revolution and the antiquarian book*, 71; Elizabethanne Boran, *Aldines at the Edward Worth Library* (Dublin: Edward Worth Library, 2015).

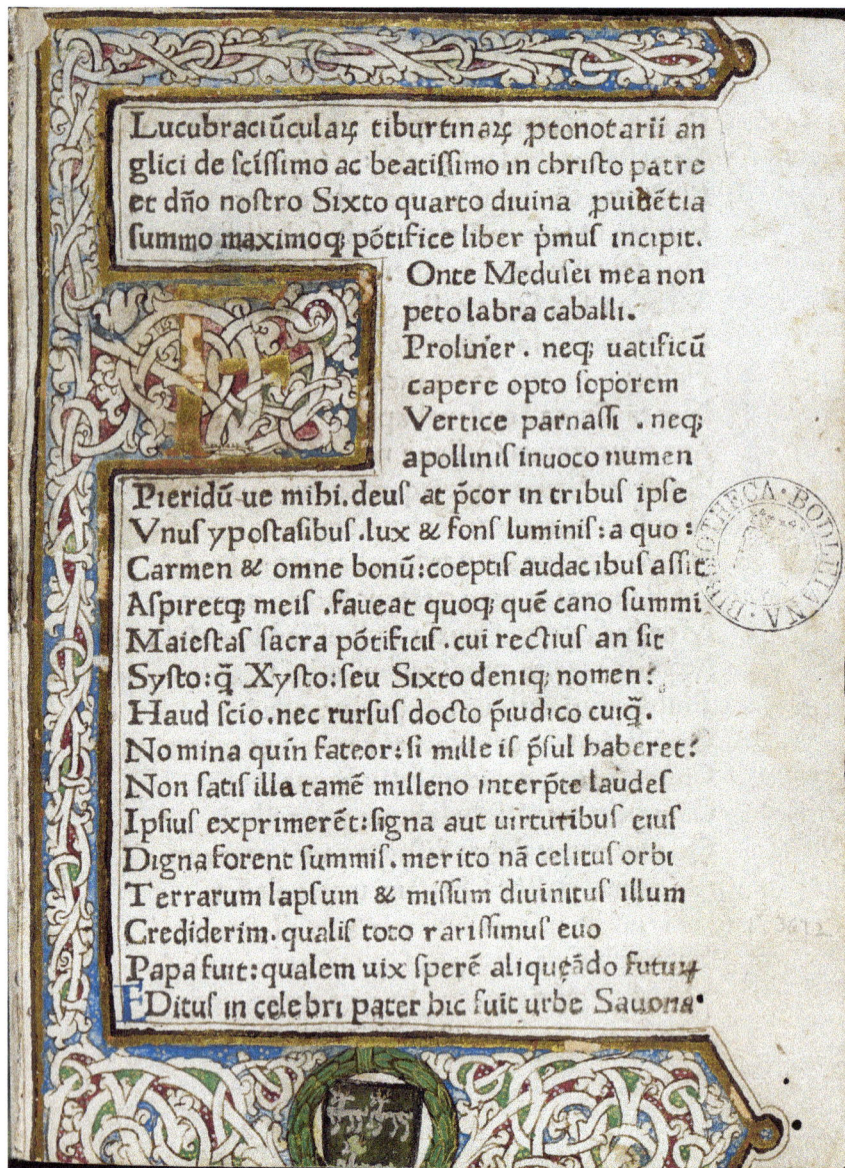

Lucubraciūculaȝ tiburtinaȝ ptonotarii an
glici de scissimo ac beatissimo in christo patre
et dño nostro Sixto quarto diuina puidētia
summo maximoq̃ pótifice liber p̄mus incipit.

Once Medusei mea non
peto labra caballi.
Proluier . neq̃ uatificū
capere opto soporem
Vertice parnassi . neq̃
apollinis inuoco numen
Pieridū-ue mibi. deus at p̄cor in tribus ipse
Vnus ypostasibus .lux & fons luminis: a quo :
Carmen & omne bonū: coeptis audacibus assiē
Aspiretq̃ meis .faueat quoq̃ qué cano summi
Maiestas sacra pótificis. cui rectius an sit
Systo: q̃ Xysto: seu Sixto deniq̃ nomen?
Haud scio.nec rursus docto p̄udico cuiq̃.
Nomina quin fateor: si mille is p̄sul baberet?
Non satis illa tamē milleno interp̄te laudes
Ipsius exprimerēt: signa aut uirtutibus eius
Digna forent summis. merito nā celitus orbi
Terrarum lapsum & missum diuinitus illum
Crediderim. qualis toto rarissimus euo
Papa fuit: qualem uix spere aliquēado futuȝ
Dituf in celebri pater bic fuit urbe Sauona·

Fig. 7.1 An illuminated border cut through by a binder's plough in the seventeenth century, when the book was bound up with others. Bodleian Library BB 19(3) Art.Seld (R. Flemming, *Lucubratiunculae Tiburtinae*, 1477). By permission of the Bodleian Libraries, The University of Oxford.

Froben, and Plantin imprints are regularly noted.[23] A few decades later, sale catalogues began to feature small separate sections of books from noteworthy presses, such as the 1719 sale of the Duke of Newcastle's library, which has a dedicated listing of Elzevir books.[24]

If we call up early sixteenth-century Aldine books from library stacks they will more often than not be found to be in much later bindings, like the Bodleian's incunabula. Fig. 7.2 shows an example from the Bodleian Library, an English binding of *c.*1725 on a 1513 octavo Aldine Cicero; as an early eighteenth-century binding it is simple and straightforward, but it is noteworthy that its spine label (also contemporary with the rest of the binding) reads 'Tullii Epistolae Aldi'. Unfortunately, it has no provenance to identify the owner who was sufficiently interested in its Aldine nature to have it thus labelled, but printers are not normally signalled like this on early spine labels.[25] Looking to undertake a more systematic investigation of the extent to which this might be have been a common practice (or of how early we might find it happening), I worked through a little over 100 Aldine editions printed between 1500 and 1530 now in Cambridge University Library. Only sixteen had bindings which could be dated between 1600 and 1720; apart from a small handful of sixteenth-century bindings, the rest were in eighteenth- or nineteenth-century ones (or later).[26] Many of the seventeenth-century bindings carry later, nineteenth-century stamping to mark them as Aldines, but nothing earlier. A few have spine labels of that period which follow the more usual convention of author and title; only one, which is definitely of the right date, has Aldus mentioned on the spine.[27] A typical trajectory for an Aldine book through, and beyond, the seventeenth century is well illustrated by Fig. 7.3, a Greek and Latin edition of the Renaissance grammarian Constantine Lascaris. It was bound around 1640 in a very plain but sturdy English calfskin binding, with a spine title noting its Aldine credentials added in the nineteenth century; cropped manuscript foliation speaks to an earlier, replaced binding. Around the time it was bound it belonged to William Dugard (1606–62), school-master, textbook author, and royalist printer, who added contents and index

---

[23] McKitterick, *The invention*, 121.

[24] *Bibliotheca nobilissimi principis Johannis Ducis de Novo-castro* (London, 1719), 83–4.

[25] Another more upmarket English binding of more or less the same date, with spine lettering referring to Aldus, is illustrated in Boran, *Aldines*, Worth Aldine no. 13.

[26] The sixteen examples with bindings in that date range are: Cambridge University Library 3.6.15 (Lactantius, 1515); Aa*.3.39(D) (Constantine Lascaris, [1501?]); Adv.a.25.1 (Hesychius, 1514); Adv. b.19.1–2 (*Rhetores*, 1508); C*.5.31(D) (Sedulius, [1502?]); Cc.9.45 (Alexander Aphrodaeus, 1513); F150.d.4.13 (Valerius Maximus, ca.1504); Q.6.4 (Livy, 1521); Q.8.42 (Livy, 1521); Q.12.45 (Nerva, 1519); R*.2.35 (Joannes Grammaticus, 1504); Sel.3.150 (Bessarion, 1503); Sel.6.29 (Homer, 1517); Sel.6.48 (Juvenal, 1501); Sel.6.63 (Catullus, 1515); X.5.71 (Ovid, 1502).

[27] Cambridge University Library Q.8.42, Livy, 1521; this binding resists easy localization, but was entirely in English ownership from at least the third quarter of the 17th c., and its clumsy lettering looks more likely to be pre- than post-1700.

Fig. 7.2A An early eighteenth-century English binding on an early sixteenth-century book printed by Aldus Manutius. Bodleian Library Vet F1.f.240 (M. T. Cicero, *Epistolarum ad Atticum*, 1513). By permission of the Bodleian Libraries, The University of Oxford.

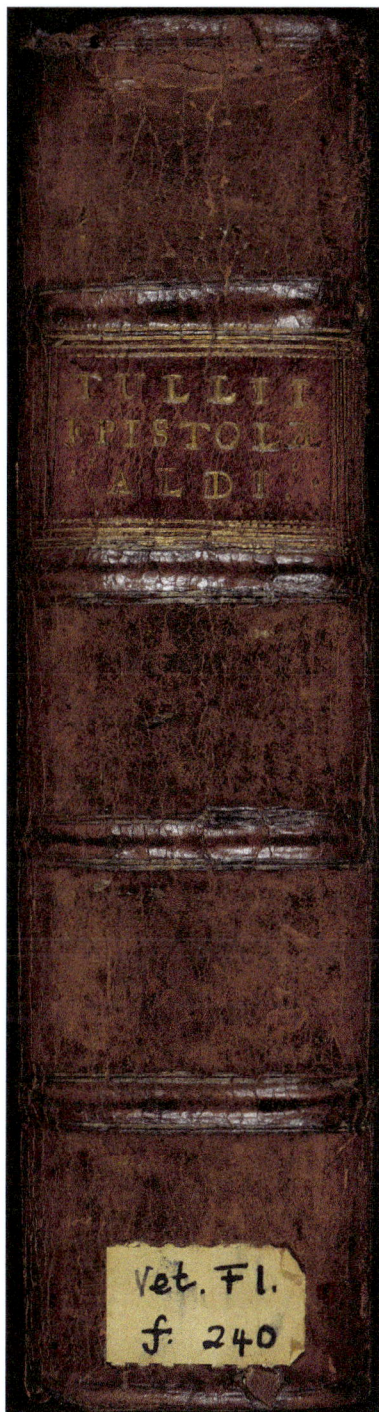

Fig. 7.2B The spine label, noting that the book comes from the Aldine Press.
By permission of the Bodleian Libraries, The University of Oxford.

Fig. 7.3A A simple mid-seventeenth-century English binding on a copy of
Constantine Lascaris, *De octo partibus orationis*, 1501. Cambridge University Library
Aa*.3.39(D). Reproduced by permission of the Syndics of Cambridge University
Library.

notes, and extensive marginalia; for him, this was no collector's trophy, but a
useful working book.[28]

---

[28] W. Meyer (8 Oct. 2009), 'Dugard, William (1606–1662), schoolmaster and printer', *Oxford Dictionary of National Biography*. Retrieved 7 Dec. 2018 from: http://www.oxforddnb.com/view/10. 1093/ref:odnb/9780198614128.001.0001/odnb-9780198614128-e-8182.

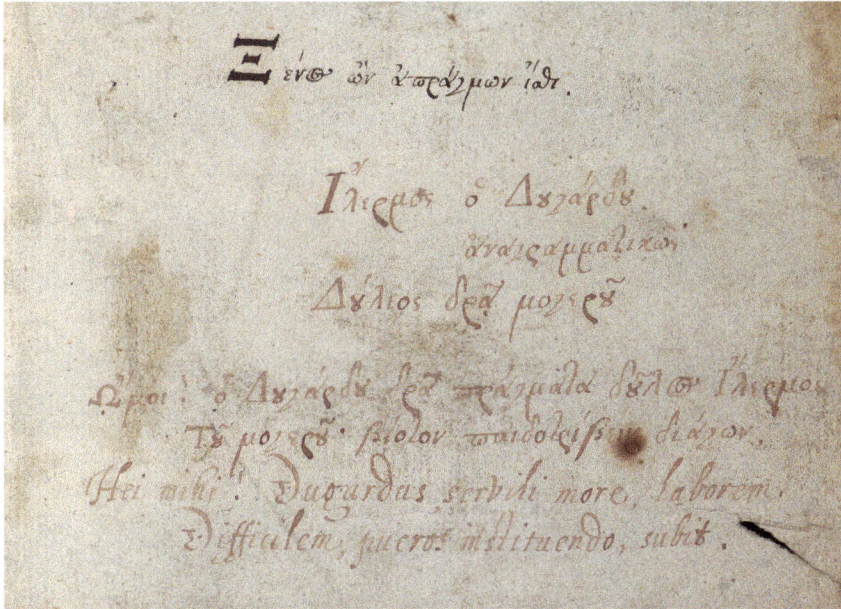

Fig. 7.3B Inscriptions on the flyleaf recording the ownership by William Dugard (1606–62). Reproduced by permission of the Syndics of Cambridge University Library.

I undertook a similar exercise in the Elzevir collection at Senate House Library, where there are over 700 mostly seventeenth-century Elzevir editions assembled during the nineteenth century, and helpfully shelved together.[29] The results were similar: a lot of later rebinding, when their special status would commonly be recognized in external labelling, but no such spine labels from my period of interest, and when seventeenth-century bindings survive they tend to be functional and workaday. There are a number of parchment bindings where the spine labelling includes an Elzevir identification, whose precise dating is slippery but at least some of which may be relatively early.[30] Overall, the conclusions of this Aldine and Elzevir research confirm that during the seventeenth century, the typical material treatment of these books does not suggest anything special, in the way that became much commoner one or two centuries later, though there are one or two exceptions to stop and make us think. Books from these presses were recognized for their editorial and textual standards, and their perceived value was still very focused on utility, not in collectability in some kind of modern sense. Nicholas Poole-Wilson saw 'the cult of the Aldine among English collectors'

[29] https://www.senatehouselibrary.ac.uk/our-collections/special-collections/printed-special-collections/elzevier-collection (accessed 7 Dec. 2018).
[30] Examples where the lettering may be quite early are Senate House Library W225 [New Testament, Greek], 1624; W808, de Saumaise, 1657.

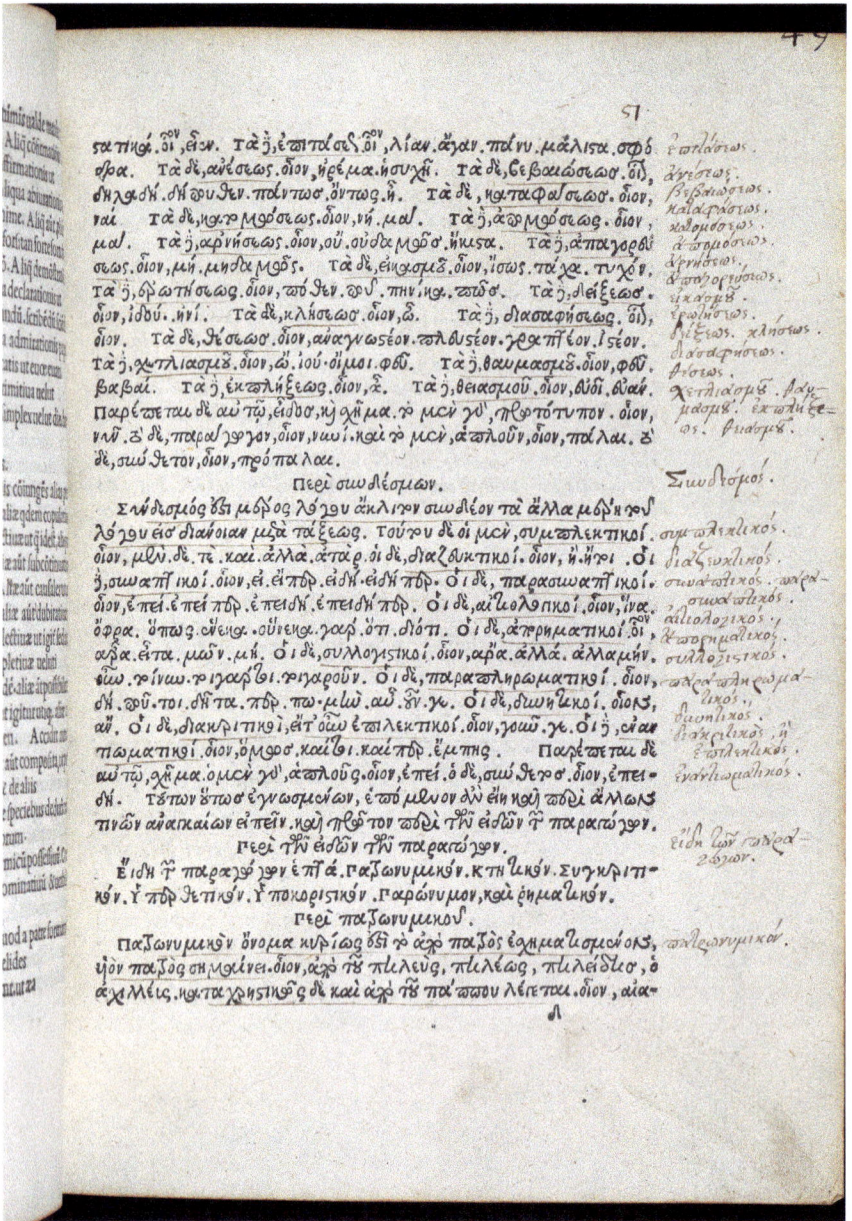

Fig. 7.3C One of the many pages of the book extensively annotated by Dugard, with underlining and marginalia in Greek. Reproduced by permission of the Syndics of Cambridge University Library.

evolving from the beginning of the eighteenth century, and in 1713 the library of the MP and author Arthur Maynwaring (1668–1712) included a set of 23 volumes of Elzevir classical texts, nicely bound in gilt-tooled goatskin, flagged as such: 'authores classici, in coreo Turcico & foliis deauratis nitidissime compacti edit. Elzivir, 12mo'.[31] This is the cusp of the change.

The idea of collecting bindings, in the way that Henry Clements or J. R. Abbey did in the twentieth century, was wholly alien to the seventeenth-century mind. Plenty of bindings were made and bought throughout the period that were more decorative, luxurious, and therefore expensive than they needed to be for the purposes of holding the books together to be read; some of the reasons behind that are explored in Chapter 6, and in other studies of bookbinding history.[32] Sale catalogues can again be used to track evidence of a growing attention paid to better-than-average bindings as time passed. Jacquie Glomski, in her article on notions of rarity and identification of value in seventeenth-century books, pointed out that descriptions of bindings and other physical characteristics that might make books desirable, like large paper, began to appear in French booksellers' catalogues in mid-century, though not in English ones until the 1680s, and David McKitterick has similarly tracked these developments.[33] The first English book auction catalogue, Lazarus Seaman's sale of 1676, is devoid of such details, but once into the 1680s it is not uncommon to find mentions both in introductory blurbs and in individual catalogue entries of turkey leather, and gilt or labelled spines. The introduction to the 1689 sale catalogue of Edward Carter, archdeacon of St Albans, noted that he had the most beautiful copies of the most valuable books, with plentiful references to gilt backs.[34] Such things clearly made books more desirable but was not a sign that people had started to collect books for their bindings. 'Lettered' as well as 'gilt' is often a feature of such descriptions, reminding us that spine labelling began to be commonly added to English bindings around the end of the seventeenth century; the usefulness of a title label may account for the appeal of such books as well as any pleasure derived from ornamental gilding.

Evidence from wills

What might wills tell us in the context of these questions about collecting? I have already explored, in Chapter 3, their value in elucidating some patterns of women's book ownership. The pattern which is most commonly found throughout the

[31] *A catalogue of the library of Arthur Mainwaring* (London, 1713).
[32] E.g. M. M. Foot, *The history of bookbinding as a mirror of society* (London: The British Library, 1998).
[33] Jacqueline Glomski, 'Book collecting and bookselling in the seventeenth century: notions of rarity and identification of value', *Publishing History* 1 (1996), pp. 5–21, 13; McKitterick, *The invention*, 94–7.
[34] *Bibliotheca Carteriana* (London, 1689).

seventeenth century is one where specified books left to relatives or friends are clearly chosen for their textual merit, of either an academic or spiritual kind. Books are not left to people because they are fellow bibliophiles but because the books will help their work, or their salvation. It was surely in that spirit that Valentine Carey, Bishop of Exeter, bequeathed the works of St Augustine to his chaplain in 1626, or William Burkitt left Lightfoot's works to Nathaniel Parkhurst, a neighbouring clergyman, in 1703; there are many other examples which could be cited.[35] Books which are noted in wills as being in some way remarkable are often Bibles, like the one in green velvet with silver clasps which Arthur Lake left to his godson in 1626, or the Bible stamped with his name, that he used in the pulpit, that John Bowle bequeathed to his brother-in-law in 1637.[36] In 1634 Sir William Paddy marked out his 'rich and extraordinary Ortelius' as a book to go to St John's College, Oxford, having already given them many hundreds of books during his lifetime, and more less specifically identified ones after his death; it is not hard to see why this was thought special, as it is a particularly finely hand-coloured copy, with capitals as well as the maps coloured in.[37]

Something else which is also occasionally, but only occasionally, found in wills is evidence of a library being treasured in its entirety as an heirloom, to be kept together and descend down succeeding generations; both Sir Matthew Hale and Sir Roger Twysden incorporated this in their wills in the 1670s, and 30 years later Thomas Brotherton, of a Lancashire gentry family, directed that his books should be and remain as heirlooms within his manor house.[38] In the 1630s Sir Walter Covert used the memorable wording: 'all my books in my study shall remain as standards in my house to be and inure to the sole use and benefit of my next heirs'.[39] In 1692 Charles Blount expressed in his will the hope that his son and grandson, 'if they have any value for my memory they will never sell or dispose of that study and choice collection which I have with so much charge and trouble gathered together'.[40] We can see here a sense of a family library being seen as an integral part of the total estate, that helps to define identity and status, as well as something which will have permanent usefulness for succeeding generations.

The idea of subject collecting

As noted earlier, we are used to the idea that book collectors focus on particular subjects, or authors. That kind of topic-focused collecting has been familiar to,

---

[35] The National Archives, PROB 11/149/376; PROB 11/473/499.
[36] TNA PROB 11/152/531; PROB 11/175/149.
[37] TNA PROB 11/166/448; A. Ortelius, *Theatrum orbis terrarum* (Antwerp, 1603), St John's College, Oxford Cpbd c 2 lower shelf 4.
[38] TNA PROB 11/353/141; PROB 11/343/478; PROB 11/481/113.   [39] TNA WARD 7/83/147.
[40] TNA PROB 11/438/177.

indeed closely associated with the whole concept of book collecting since at least the nineteenth century, and many important institutional concentrations of books rely on having ingested such collections. Eric Holzenberg, writing about the bibliophile as bibliographer, looked at scholarly collections like this which became subject bibliographies; he cites some early Continental European examples, his oldest being the sixteenth-century library of Suffridus Petri, as the basis of his 1593 bibliography of Friesian writers.[41] His earliest English example is White Kennett, the Bishop of Peterborough who died in 1728, and whose *Bibliothecae Americanae primordia*, published in 1713, is a catalogue of a collection of books and pamphlets relating to 'the particular affairs of America'.[42] This is indeed a subject collection deliberately formed, as Kennett explains, so as to create a library which would be useful to missionaries and others associated with the evangelizing mission of the Society for the Propagation of the Gospel, and he described the efforts involved in deliberately gathering it, and the challenges of finding 'the lesser tracts and single papers'.

I cannot point to an earlier British example which unequivocally fits this mould. Thomas Gore's *Catalogus . . . de re heraldica*, published in 1666, is an international bibliography of books on heraldry which may well be based largely or entirely on the contents of his own shelves, but it is not presented in those terms, and although he undoubtedly had a sizeable library, hardly any of its contents can be traced today.[43] The 'Catalogue of chymical books which have been written originally, or translated into English', which the bookseller William Cooper appended to his *Philosophicall epitaph* (1673)—a list of *c*.180 alchemical and related scientific books published in England between the early sixteenth and late seventeenth centuries—may reflect a personal collection, or a wider pool of titles known to Cooper.[44] There are numerous early published bibliographies and book lists, from Conrad Gesner's 1545 *Bibliotheca universalis* onwards, just as there are lists of recommended books for particular purposes of study or salvation, but there is a clear difference between these and a catalogue whose authority in a

---

[41] Eric Holzenberg, 'The bibliophile as bibliographer', *Papers of the Bibliographical Society of America* 104 (2010), pp. 421–31, 425.

[42] White Kennett, *Bibliothecae Americanae primordia* (London, 1713), ii (which can be usefully accessed via the modern edited facsimile, F. R. Goff (ed.), *The* Primordia *of Bishop White Kennett, the first English bibliography of America* (Washington, DC: Pan American Union, 1959).

[43] T. Gore, *Catalogus alphabetice digestus, plerumque omnium authorum . . . de re heraldica* (London, 1666). A noted antiquary but described by Aubrey as 'a fidling peevish fellow', Gore's lengthy will includes detailed directions for the disposal amongst his family of what was clearly an extensive library, although only one book from it can be identified today, a manuscript geneaology (National Art Library CLE S7). I am grateful to Will Poole for pointing out the possible relevance of his *Catalogus* in this context.

[44] S. Linden (5 Jan. 2006), 'Cooper, William (bap. 1639, d. 1689), bookseller and writer on the occult sciences', *Oxford Dictionary of National Biography*. Retrieved 12 Apr. 2019 from: http://www.oxforddnb.com/view/10.1093/ref:odnb/9780198614128.001.0001/odnb-9780198614128-e-53668. I am grateful to Scott Mandelbrote for pointing out Cooper's relevance here.

subject field reflects the dedicated collecting by an individual in that field.[45] That kind of collecting mentality, so familiar to modern minds, is one which was alien to seventeenth-century book-owning culture, and is not an approach which is typically found with library formers large or small. Breadth of coverage, rather than concentration of focus, tends to be the defining feature of libraries of this time of any size, and we can recognize that the gathering of books of professional relevance is not the same as collecting because of historical or antiquarian interest in a subject. Both Francis Bernard (1628–98), the physician whose library was one of the largest of its time, and William Osler (1849–1919), whose famous medical historical collection was bequeathed to McGill University, had extensive holdings of sixteenth-century medical books, but they owned them for different reasons. The numerous books on artillery and military practice which George Carew owned at the turn of the seventeenth century are mentioned in Chapter 3; he must have acquired them by deliberate design, not accident, but I would not describe him as a collector of military books.

There is a long tradition of valuing books for their annotations, if they are those of learned owners whose observations have scholarly or editorial use.[46] Isaac Casaubon's books were appreciated for their adversaria, and keenly acquired by succeeding generations of learned book buyers like John Moore and Edward Stillingfleet.[47] Books with these kinds of annotations or interleavings can be found flagged up in late seventeenth-century sale catalogues; in the 1711 sale of the library of the surgeon Charles Bernard, the introduction noted the added value of his annotations, 'by writing now and again in the blank leaves . . . particular remarks upon the author, or that edition'.[48] The cataloguer of the 1698 sale of his physician brother Francis Bernard, by contrast, observed how useful it would have been if he had done the same: 'if he had but taken the trouble . . . of setting down in the vacant leaf of many of his books the reasons which he had to buy them . . . it had become . . . a singular piece of service to the future possessors.'[49] What is much less usual is finding any kind of interest in previous ownership by way of association, or for most of the reasons for which we now value provenance. Fig. 7.4 shows an unusual exception; this copy of *Archaio-ploutos* (1619), translated from various sources by Thomas Milles, has a nice contemporary plain red velvet binding boldly gilt-stamped RED. Inside, in a later seventeenth-century hand, is an inscription noting that the letters stand for Richard Sackville, 3rd Earl of Dorset (1589–1624), and that the book had been bequeathed, together with seven other books similarly bound, by his daughter Margaret Tufton, Countess of Thanet (1614–76). The author of the inscription is her son-in-law Christopher, 1st

---

[45] For a mapping of the development of early published bibliographies, internationally, see Luigi Balsamo, tr. W. Pettas, *Bibliography* (Berkeley, CA: Bernard M. Rosenthal, 1990).

[46] McKitterick, *The invention*, 104–8.   [47] Birrell, 'The reconstruction', 65.

[48] *Bibliotheca Bernardiana: or, a catalogue of the library of the late Charles Bernard* (London, 1711).

[49] *A catalogue of the library of the late learned Dr. Francis Bernard* (London, 1698).

Fig. 7.4A A red velvet binding on a copy of Thomas Milles, *Archaio-ploutos*,
1619, gilt-stamped 'RED' (Richard [Sackville], Earl of Dorset). Folger Shakespeare
Library STC 17936.5 copy 3.

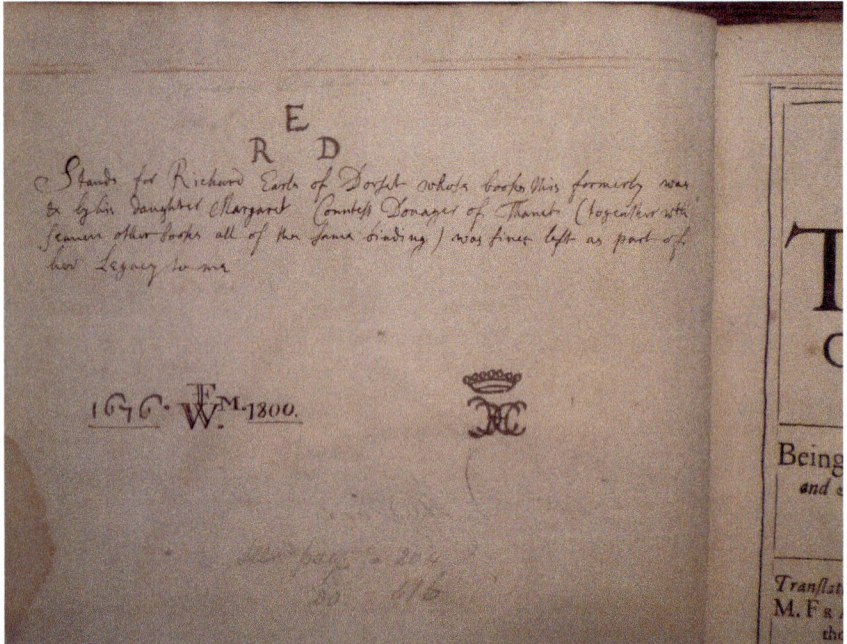

Fig. 7.4B The inscription on the pastedown, by Christopher, 1st Viscount Hatton, noting the book's pedigree.

Viscount Hatton (1632–1706), and the bequest is noted in Lady Margaret's will, where the distinctive bindings are described.[50] They were clearly a handsome group of books, and the inscription perhaps reflects an element of fond memory or family piety, but it is unusual at this time to find this level of interest expressed in personal association. Provenance researchers are much more used to finding seventeenth-century owners obliterating or removing former marks of ownership than paying them any kind of reverential heed.[51]

Manuscripts

The focus thus far has been on printed books; we should also consider manuscripts, where a number of broad facts are well known. Gathering up of the huge numbers of medieval books which were dispersed in the middle of the sixteenth century began not long afterwards, and the preservation of that documentary heritage today relies significantly on the activities of many seventeenth-century owners. The dividing lines between manuscript and print culture were more

---

[50] The National Archives PROB 11/351/509.
[51] David Pearson, *Provenance research in book history* (Oxford: Bodleian Library, 2019), pp. 7–9.

blurred in the early modern period than we perceive them today, both in the circulation of texts and in the storage of books in libraries.[52] In the context of manuscripts and private libraries at that time some well-known names come most immediately to mind, most obviously Sir Robert Cotton (1571–1631) and celebrated antiquaries like Sir Edward Dering (1598–1644), Sir Simonds d'Ewes (1602–50), and Scipio Le Squyer (1579–1659), not forgetting the industry that went into amassing oriental manuscripts by the likes of Edmund Castell (1606–85), Edward Pococke (1604–91), John Selden (1584–1654), James Ussher (1580–1656), and numerous others.[53] But there was also a host of less well-known names who were active in acquiring manuscripts throughout the seventeenth century; there are nearly 50 individuals listed in Bernard's union catalogue of manuscripts in the British Isles, published just after his death in 1697.[54]

A number of these relate to the collections of essentially professional working material built up by lawyers, doctors, heralds, and antiquaries, manuscript sets of law reports and accounts of national and local history, ranging in date from the Middle Ages to their own time. The 26 manuscripts recorded by Bernard as belonging to Edward Tyson, physician to Bethlem Hospital, are almost entirely medical and mostly but not entirely post-medieval. Beyond those kinds of obviously practical collections, there were many accumulations of manuscripts of monastic origin in the hands of people who are not household names in the annals of manuscript studies. Sir Henry Langley of Shrewsbury (d. 1688) owned 50 medieval manuscripts; Sir John Hoby, of Bisham in Berkshire (1635–1702), owned 23; the 111 mostly medieval manuscripts of Robert Burscough, archdeacon of Barnstaple (1651–1709) subsequently went into the Harleian Library.[55] In 1682 the sale of the library of John Humphrey (d. 1679), vicar of Rothwell in Northamptonshire, about whom we know very little, included about 70 medieval manuscripts in Latin and English.[56]

A number of seventeenth-century academics and clergymen formed small but significant collections of manuscripts which they gave to academic or institutional libraries. Around 1670 George Davenport (d. 1677), rector of Houghton-le-Spring, gave 71 medieval manuscripts to the newly opened diocesan library for Durham founded by John Cosin, which had been assembled by him from a variety of sources, some northern and some further afield, over the preceding two

[52] Harold Love, *Scribal publication in seventeenth-century England* (Oxford: Clarendon Press, 1993); H. R. Woudhuysen, *Sir Philip Sidney and the circulation of manuscripts, 1558–1640* (Oxford: Clarendon Press, 1996); Angus Vine, *Miscellaneous order: manuscript culture and the early modern organization of knowledge* (Oxford: Oxford University Press, 2019).
[53] On the gathering of oriental manuscripts in the 17th c., G. J. Toomer, *Eastern wisedome and learning* (Oxford: Clarendon Press, 1996) is the standard and authoritative reference.
[54] Edward Bernard, *Catalogi librorum manuscriptorum Angliae et Hiberniae* (Oxford, 1697).
[55] On Burscough's manuscripts, see C. E. Wright and R. C. Wright (eds), *The diary of Humfrey Wanley*, vol. 1 (London: Bibliographical Society, 1966), 2, 11.
[56] *Catalogus librorum bibliothecae Joannis Humphry nuper de Rowell* (London, 1682).

decades; he started acquiring them soon after he graduated from Cambridge and began his clerical career.[57] In 1685 Thomas Man, then a 30-year old fellow of Jesus College, Cambridge, gave about 80 manuscripts to the college; they mostly came from northern monastic houses, including Durham, Hexham, and Rievaulx.[58] They were acquired not by him but by his father, another Thomas Man, who was rector of Northallerton in the 1650s and 1660s.[59] Documentation on Man is elusive, but William Moore (1590–1659), who bequeathed around 150 manuscripts to Gonville and Caius College in Cambridge, was eulogized in his own day as Cambridge University Librarian and for his diligence for the public good.[60] Moore was, according to his contemporary biographer, 'through his whole life a diligent collectour and transcriber of the choicest manuscripts which he could possibly purchase by love or money'; they came from a range of southern monastic houses large and small, including Canterbury, Reading, and Peterborough, and were noted by M. R. James as adding to Caius's library such of its manuscripts as could be especially distinguished by age or beauty.[61]

How and why were these kinds of collections formed? Sometimes, books of monastic origin clearly remained associated with their localities when estates passed into the hands of new post-Reformation owners, and stayed there for some generations thereafter, perhaps valued as relics, particularly in recusant circles, or curiosities, or (in the case of cartularies) as documents of potential legal value. But inertia was only sometimes the significant factor: there was plenty of active buying and seeking out of this kind of material. Were people motivated by an appreciation of the value of preserving the past, by a recognition of the potential of historic texts to fight the battles of the present, or was it about advancing pedigrees, property rights, and social status? The answer is a mixture of these things, depending on individual circumstances. The collecting habits of Sir Edward Dering, who had significant holdings of medieval manuscripts, were motivated in no small part by the wish to strengthen the foundations of the Dering pedigree, leading him not only to plunder the muniments of Canterbury Cathedral but also to embellish the stolen documents with forged additions to bolster his family credentials.[62] He asked rhetorically in his pocket book 'what is

[57] A. I. Doyle, 'The Cosin manuscripts and George Davenport', *The Book Collector* 53 (2004), pp. 32–45.
[58] M. R. James, *A descriptive catalogue of the manuscripts in the library of Jesus College, Cambridge* (London: C. J. Clay and Sons, 1895), vii; Ralph Hanna, 'The Thomas Mans, their books, and Jesus College librarianship', *The Library* 7th ser 21 (2020), pp. 46–73.
[59] A. G. Matthews, *Walker revised* (Oxford: Clarendon Press, 1948), 389: http://db.theclergydatabase.org.uk/jsp/persons/CreatePersonFrames.jsp?PersonID=159094 (accessed 10 Dec. 2018).
[60] J. C. T. Oates, *Cambridge University Library: a history from the beginnings to the Copyright Act of Queen Anne* (Cambridge: Cambridge University Press, 1986), pp. 268–70.
[61] Ibid. 270; M. R. James, *A descriptive catalogue of the manuscripts in the library of Gonville and Caius College*, vol. 1 (Cambridge: Cambridge University Press, 1907–14), viii.
[62] Nigel Ramsay, 'The Cathedral Archives and Library', in P. Collinson et al. (eds), *A history of Canterbury Cathedral* (Oxford: Oxford University Press, 1995), pp. 341–407, 379–80.

history but the pedigree of the world...and succession of the eminent persons therein mentioned', noting that 'God hath made me heade of a tribe, and master of a family'.[63]

John Evelyn, in his posthumously published essay on manuscripts, saw their utility in the possibility of discovering lost works by classical writers.[64] Kevin Sharpe, who wrote extensively about Cotton, stressed that 'the new interest in libraries was utilitarian'; Cotton and his fellow Jacobean antiquaries studied history primarily for its use and application in contemporary affairs rather than for the advancement of historical understanding in a more abstract sense, and the library was extensively quarried in that way both in his own day and by subsequent seventeenth-century writers.[65] Sharpe's description of the library as 'an arsenal for the continuing war against Antichrist' brings to mind the nationalist ecclesiastical agenda behind Matthew Parker's collecting of Anglo-Saxon manuscripts 50 years earlier, and in the 1620s Laud had a plan to write an ecclesiastical history of England based on Cotton's manuscripts.[66] Richard Ovenden has written about the manuscript collection of Lord William Howard of Naworth (1563–1640), who was not only a friend of Cotton but regarded in his day as one of the leading aristocratic antiquaries, if less of a household name today.[67] Commenting on Howard's extensive holdings of medieval chronicles, monastic cartularies, and illuminated manuscripts, Ovenden too saw a mixture, 'a collector with multiple motives', including an interest in history, the wish to look after sacred objects of a banished faith (to which Howard, as a Roman Catholic, still belonged), and possibly an appreciation of the artistic qualities of the manuscripts.

All these men—the Davenports and the Humphreys as well as the Cottons and Derings—clearly saw value in this material and the desirability of its safe preservation for posterity. They may have perceived its utility differently from the way we do today but they sought it out, or were known as people to whom it could be offered—men who would pay good money for old monkish books whose contents would have been impenetrable to many post-Reformation eyes. Justifying the sale of the Pirckheimer Library to the Earl of Arundel in the 1630s, Hans Imhoff commented that the library 'was very old, many of the books, especially the manuscripts, illegible, that such books were available in new and better editions, much easier to read than the uncomfortable old books and of far greater

---

[63] N. Krivatsky and L. Yeandle, 'Sir Edward Dering', in R. J. Fehrenbach and E. S. Leedham-Green (eds), *Private libraries in Renaissance England*, vol. 1 (Binghamton, NY: Center for Medieval and Early Renaissance Studies, 1992), pp. 136–269, 149.

[64] John Evelyn, *The miscellaneous writings*, ed. W. Upcott (London: Henry Colburn, 1825), pp. 323–36.

[65] Kevin Sharpe, *Sir Robert Cotton 1586–1641: history and politics in early modern England* (Oxford: Oxford University Press, 1979), 49ff.

[66] Ibid. 54, 49.

[67] Richard Ovenden, 'The manuscript library of Lord William Howard of Naworth', in J. Willoughby and J. Catto (eds), *Books and bookmen in early modern Britain* (Toronto: Pontifical Institute of Mediaeval Studies, 2018), pp. 278–318.

contemporary use'—sentiments with which many seventeenth-century book buyers would have concurred.[68]

Alongside that mainstream view, evidenced by the ongoing dismemberment of medieval manuscripts during the seventeenth century for the purposes of book-binders, upholsterers, and grocers, there was a steady and sometimes competitive culture for acquiring those uncomfortable old books, for various reasons, in a spirit that is closer to collecting as we understand it, and as defined by Pollard. Although I would not call the Earl of Totnes a collector of military books, there is more of a case for saying he was a collector of manuscripts on Irish history, which he made an effort to acquire and which he did not need in the same way that he might have needed books on artillery. Sometimes, there is evidence of special treatment given to books, because they are manuscripts; James Ley, Earl of Marlborough (1552–1629) is noted in Chapter 6 as an example of someone who used more than one armorial binding stamp during his progression through ranks of the peerage. His first stamp, which reflects his status as a baronet (which he became in 1619), is known only from half a dozen medieval manuscripts now dispersed among as many libraries; it is not recorded on any printed books.[69]

Libraries and museums

If we are looking into collecting cultures, we should consider the connections between libraries and museums, both conceptually and physically. They both depend on gathering, preserving, organizing, and interpreting materials in pursuit of knowledge and understanding, although they are usually perceived today as belonging to different branches within the family of cultural institutions, with their own professional standards and practices. The study of museum evolution is an area which has burgeoned during recent decades, with an extensive literature and dedicated journals. As with the story of British book collecting in the eighteenth and nineteenth centuries, there is a broadly understood narrative around the history of museums which in a few simple and high-level sentences may be set out as follows. A fashion for assembling cabinets of curiosities, bringing together all kinds of objects from ancient or other civilizations and the natural world, spread across European aristocratic households in the sixteenth century as one manifestation of the Renaissance. The earliest publication describing a museum, with recommendations for its organization and contents, was published

---

[68] Linda Peck, 'Uncovering the Arundel Library at the Royal Society', *Notes and Records of the Royal Society of London* 52 (1998), pp. 3–24, 6.
[69] https://armorial.library.utoronto.ca/stamps/ILEY001_s1 (accessed 12 Dec. 2018).

by Samuel Quiccheberg in 1565.[70] The idea came a little later to Britain, but during the seventeenth century a growing number of such collections were assembled and began to be documented and opened to the public. Tradescant's Ark, which began receiving visitors in the 1630s and whose collections ultimately became one of the building blocks of the Ashmolean Museum, is perhaps the best known but by no means the only one. The shift of primacy of museum collections from the private to the public and institutional sphere, which as with libraries was mainly a nineteenth- and twentieth-century development, was boosted by the creation of the British Museum in 1753, founded on the collections of Hans Sloane.[71]

How did seventeenth-century owners perceive the relationships between libraries and museums? Were they one seamless continuum of knowledge quarries to be garnered and organized, or did they live in different spaces, physically and intellectually? Mark Purcell, in his book on the country house library, is rather dismissive of cabinets in association with libraries—'museums of this kind were clearly uncommon, and have perhaps received disproportionate attention from those reluctant to accept that libraries in Restoration Britain were primarily about books rather than ostrich eggs and coral'—but I would challenge that.[72] Quiccheberg, in his 1565 *Institutiones*, specifies a library as an essential adjunct to a museum of objects, and Francis Bacon at the end of the sixteenth century specified the four essential accoutrements of a learned gentleman as a library, a garden, a cabinet, and a laboratory.[73] The interconnection and mutually entwined evolution of early libraries and museums in Munich has been explored by Franz Kaltwasser.[74] Numerous library owners of the seventeenth century were also collectors of coins, specimens, and artefacts, including Cotton, Sir Walter Cope, Sir Thomas Browne, Ralph Sheldon, and Elias Ashmole.[75] John Laughton, the Cambridge University Librarian who died in 1712, was noted by Hearne as having left behind a good collection not only of books but also of coins, and Ann Sadleir,

[70] Samuel Quiccheberg, *Inscriptiones vel tituli theatri amplissimi* (Munich, 1565); see the modern translation/edn by M. Meadow and B. Robertson, *The first treatise on museums* (Los Angeles, CA: Getty Research Institute, 2013).

[71] Among the many useful writings of Arthur MacGregor in this field, his essay on 'The cabinet of curiosities in seventeenth-century Britain', in A. MacGregor and O. Impey (eds), *The origins of museums* (Oxford: Clarendon Press, 1985), pp. 147–58, is a good place to start for an overview of early museum developments in Britain. See also, on the wider Continental context, E. Schulz, 'Notes on the history of collecting and museums', *Journal of the History of Collections* 2 (1990), pp. 205–18.

[72] Mark Purcell, *The country house library* (New Haven, CT: Yale University Press, 2017), 100.

[73] Meadow and Robertson, *The first treatise*, 71; Arthur MacGregor, 'Introduction', in MacGregor and Impey, *The origins of museums*, pp. 1–4, 1. Bacon's original text, in his *Gesta Grayorum*, can be found in Francis Bacon, *Early writings, 1584–1596*, ed. A. Stewart (Oxford: Clarendon Press, 2012), 598–9.

[74] F. G. Kaltwasser, 'The common roots of library and museum in the sixteenth century: the example of Munich', *Library and Information History* 20 (2004), pp. 163–82.

[75] Sharpe, *Sir Robert Cotton*, 66–7; Linda Levy Peck, *Consuming splendor* (Cambridge: Cambridge University Press, 2005), 156–7; J. Evelyn, *The diary*, ed. E. S. de Beer (Oxford: Clarendon Press, 1955), vol. 3, 594; J. T. Cliffe, *The world of the country house in seventeenth-century England* (New Haven, CT: Yale University Press, 1999), pp. 163–4; MacGregor, 'The cabinet of curiosities', 152.

Fig. 7.5 The museum of Jacob de Wilde, *c*.1700, with artefacts on top of the bookcases. Bodleian Library Douce WW 120 (J. de Wilde, *Signa antiqua*, 1700). By permission of the Bodleian Libraries, The University of Oxford.

one of the daughters of Chief Justice Coke, gave coins as well as illuminated manuscripts to Trinity College, Cambridge in the 1660s.[76]

Depictions of early museum spaces sometimes imply co-located storage arrangements for both books and objects; there are no early English examples, but the well-known engraving of the museum of the Neapolitan apothecary Ferrante Imperato at the end of the sixteenth century, albeit dominated by the crocodile to which our eyes are most immediately drawn, shows that his books were in cases on one side of the room with objects on the other.[77] A portrait of the French physician and coin collector Charles Patin (1633–93), found in some copies of his 1672 *Thesaurus numismatum*, shows him in a space where his books and coin cabinet are clearly coexisting.[78] The visit of Peter the Great to the museum of the Dutchman Jacob de Wilde (1645–1721) around 1700 was captured in an engraving which shows an integral organization of books and artefacts, with the latter almost secondary decoration at the top and sides of the bookcases (Fig. 7.5). The will of John Batteley (1646–1708), archdeacon of

---

[76] David McKitterick, *Cambridge University Library: a history, the eighteenth and nineteenth centuries* (Cambridge: Cambridge University Press, 1986), 46; Philip Gaskell, *Trinity College Library: the first 150 years* (Cambridge: Cambridge University Press, 1980), 121.

[77] This image seems too well-known to need to be reproduced here; a good online copy of it can be seen at https://en.wikipedia.org/wiki/Ferrante_Imperato (accessed 13 Dec. 2018).

[78] C. E. Dekesel, *Charles Patin: a man without a country* (Ghent: Bibliotheca Numismatica Siciliana, 1990), 354.

Canterbury whose manuscripts were on Harley's shopping list, refers to his medals and antiquities 'in my gallery or below in my study', suggesting a two-tier space with objects above and books below.[79]

Books do not feature in Tradescant's museum, as catalogued in 1656, but the *Musaeum Thoresbyianum*, the collections of the Yorkshire antiquary Ralph Thoresby (1658–1725), as set out in a published catalogue of 1715, included sections on editions of the Bible, manuscripts, and 'ancient printed books', which were largely but not wholly incunabula.[80] Thoresby, like Maynwaring and his gilt-tooled Elzevirs catalogued around the same time, stands at the cusp, the evolution, of historic books passing from the seventeenth-century world of books as useful objects to the eighteenth-century one of books as collectables, where they do indeed fit alongside historical artefacts of all kinds to help us understand the past, the way that museums do. Writing in the middle of the last century about the concept of the seventeenth-century virtuoso, Walter Houghton, citing Bacon, saw a distinction between their approach to books, and to their cabinets of curiosities: 'Coins or pictures, shells or insects, none are valued for use, neither for the advancement of learning, but for individual gain; they are valued themselves because they arouse curiosity and stimulate delight.'[81] This may be too sweeping a generalization, but its hinge around the word use is the vital point; 'use' or 'utility' are the words which reverberate through the world of the seventeenth-century private library, the justification or motivation behind the ownership. The library was an essential adjunct to Quiccheberg's museum, but the books were not integral with the shells and specimens in the way they were beginning to be perceived in that way by Thoresby. Of course, Spencer and Osler used their books, but not so much in the ways their makers intended as did Casaubon and Bernard.

Conclusions

The key conclusion of this review is that we should be much more careful with the c-word in the seventeenth-century context, and should avoid describing someone of this time as a collector, unless there is evidence that they were doing something which we would recognize as going beyond the building of a private library, however big or important it may be. 'Owners', which I use throughout this book, is much to be preferred; all book collectors are book owners, but not all owners are collectors, and the word 'collector' creates an association of ideas

[79] The National Archives PROB 11/504/208.
[80] R. Thoresby, *Ducatus Leodiensis...to which is added...a catalogue of his museum* (London, 1715), pp. 501–14.
[81] W. E. Houghton, 'The English virtuoso in the seventeenth century', *Journal of the History of Ideas* 3 (1942), pp. 51–73, 190–219, 56.

which we cannot avoid with our twenty-first century mindset. Book history is burdened with received wisdom which has created sloppy terminology, which may create distorted understanding. It may be protested that the word was used in my period, by people describing contemporary libraries: John Aubrey said of Sir Henry Blount (1602–82) that 'when he was young, he was a great collector of books, as his son [Sir Thomas] is now', and his other son Charles (1654–92) referred in his will to 'that study and choice collection which I have … gathered together'.[82] Thomas Rawlinson noted that Humfrey Dyson (1582–1633) 'was a great collector of books'.[83] Of course, the word had currency in the seventeenth century, but that does not signify that it created the same set of ideas in seventeenth-century minds, which would be more tuned to ideas of gathering or guardianship than connoisseurship, Nathan Bailey's dictionary, first published in 1721, does include 'a collection of books' as an exemplar of the word collection ('a gathering together, or picking up'), though for Edward Phillips in his *New world of English words* (1658) a collection is 'a gathering or levie', the latter being itself defined in terms of the gathering in of taxation.[84] Neither dictionary features the word 'collector'.

We should, similarly, reconsider our use of the r-word as a synonym for what people do with books. As noted at the end of Chapter 6, the history and under-standing of reading has become a major facet of book history; and while the ability to read was undoubtedly a major driver behind much library formation and ownership, other motives and purposes have surfaced throughout this book. Jason Scott-Warren, in an article about the books of the mid-seventeenth century clergyman Francis Meres, is one of several recent writers who call for an expansion of horizons, recognizing that there are many ways in which texts are read (not all of which would count as conventional reading), and many other ways in which the utility and value of books is manifested.[85] I would join that growing chorus and suggest that we replace the r-word with the u-word, that we consider book use as the central concept in unpicking and understanding their historical impact. Books may have a variety of purposes and may fulfil more than one role in their owners' lives, in a simultaneous and polychrome kind of way. To appreciate the matrix, we need to look at the books in their totality and physicality, at more than lists of titles in a catalogue or words on a page.

---

[82]   Kate Bennett (ed.), *Brief lives, with an apparatus* (Oxford: Oxford University Press, 2014), 338; TNA PROB 11/438/177.

[83]   Bodleian Library, Oxford, MS Rawl.D.138/207.

[84]   N. Bailey, *An universal etymological English dictionary* (London, 1721); E. Phillips, *The new world of English words* (London, 1658).

[85]   Jason Scott-Warren, 'Commonplacing and originality: reading Francis Meres', *Review of English Studies* 68 (2017), pp. 902–23, 902.

A classified list of book owners, 1610–1715

This list brings together summary information about English people who died between 1610 and 1715 for whom we have documented evidence of book ownership and the existence of a private library. It draws on evidence of many kinds, but cannot pretend to be a comprehensive list of everyone who owned books in the seventeenth century, which would be a huge and never-ending aspiration. Rather, it presents a critical mass of data which both constitutes the foundation upon which this book is built, and a reference source for ongoing use.

The list comprises the backbone of a fuller directory, *Book Owners Online*, which is being developed online and is freely available there: http://bookowners.online. There, each name is accompanied not only by fuller biographical information but also by a summary of what we know about their libraries, as regards size, contents, evidence of use or value, etc. Entries also include images of the characteristic book markings of the owners (where traceable), and of the locations of surviving examples of their books. The list in its brief form here is intended only to give basic information, and the bibliographical references are not comprehensive; they are limited to key places to turn both for more narrative and for signposts to other references. Fuller references will often be found in *Book Owners Online*, and links to websites (the list printed here is deliberately not overburdened with urls). As a general rule, only one standard biographical source is cited; if someone has an *ODNB* entry, there is not also a reference to the *History of Parliament* or the university lists, but those sources will be cited, in a descending order of preference, if nothing else is available. Other references are ones which focus primarily on their books/libraries, rather than other aspects of their careers or activities. The key questions which the list is intended to answer are: 'Do we know whether this person had a library, and where do I look for more information?'

Contents and criteria for inclusion

The list is arranged in sections according to the background of the people (academics, clergy, etc.), and chronologically by date of death within the sections. Knowing where best to classify some individuals is debatable, so all the names are covered by the Index. I have tried to include everyone who died within the timeframe who used a bookplate, or an armorial binding stamp, or whose books were dispersed in a documented sale. Beyond that, the list relies extensively on probate inventories (mostly where these have been published), donations and surviving books, and a wide range of secondary literature. Within its defined criteria, it cannot pretend to be comprehensive, and anyone who works in this field will probably be able to identify names which could be added; there are, for example, countless unpublished probate inventories and wills mentioning books which could be candidates for inclusion. Nor does it aspire to be a kind of provenance index for all the seventeenth-century names found in the books in the world's libraries; that would be a different (and very large) undertaking, and the list is not a one-stop shop for cataloguers looking to identify all their seventeenth-century inscriptions. The endless number and range of those testifies, rather, to my point about the ubiquity and spread of book ownership in Stuart England.

For sale catalogues, I have preferred to cite Robin Alston's *Inventory* rather than Munby and Coral's *Union list*, because there is generally fuller information in the former (as well as more names). In the case of single-library sales, I have always sought to add the number of lots which they comprised, as that gives a rough indication of size, but for combined sales (which were very common) I have not, as it is rarely possible to untangle which books came from which owner.

Abbreviations used in the list

Alston, *Inventory*: R. C. Alston, *Inventory of sale catalogues of named and attributed owners of books sold by retail or auction 1676–1800* (St Philip: privately printed for the author, 2010).

Armorials database: *British armorial bindings*: https://armorial.library.utoronto.ca/.

Aubrey, *Brief lives*: John Aubrey, *Brief lives*, ed. Kate Bennett (Oxford: Oxford University Press, 2015).

BC: *The Book Collector*.

BCI: E. S. Leedham-Green, *Books in Cambridge inventories* (Cambridge: Cambridge University Press, 1986).

Birrell, 'Books and buyers': T. A. Birrell, 'Books and buyers in seventeenth-century English auction sales', in R. Myers et al. (eds), *Under the hammer* (London: The British Library, 2001), 51–64.

BL: British Library.

Blatchly: John Blatchly, *Some Suffolk and Norfolk ex-libris* (London: Bookplate Society, 2000).

BLR: *Bodleian Library Record*.

BQR: *Bodleian Quarterly Record*.

Burden: Mark Burden, *A biographical dictionary of tutors at the Dissenters' private academies*: http://www.qmulreligionandliterature.co.uk/online-publications/a-biographical-dictionary/.

Calamy revised: A. G. Matthews, *Calamy revised* (Oxford: Clarendon Press, 1934).

Cambers: Andrew Cambers, *Godly reading* (Cambridge: Cambridge University Press, 2011).

CELM: *Catalogue of English Literary Manuscripts, 1450–1700*: http://www.celm-ms.org.uk/. See, in each case, the page under the heading 'Introductions' for the relevant person.

CHL: Peter Hoare (gen. ed.), *The Cambridge history of libraries in Britain and Ireland*, 3 vols (Cambridge: Cambridge University Press, 2006).

Complete baronetage: G. E. Cokayne, *Complete baronetage* (Exeter: Pollard, 1900–09).

Complete peerage: G. E. Cokayne, *The complete peerage of England, Scotland, Ireland*, new edn (London: St Catherine Press, 1910–59).

eBLJ: *Electronic British Library Journal*.

Fontes Harleianae: C. E. Wright, *Fontes Harleianae* (London: The British Library, 1972).

Foster: J. Foster, *Alumni Oxonienses* (Oxford: Parker & Co., 1891).

Franks: E. R. J. Gambier Howe, *Franks bequest: catalogue of British and American book plates bequeathed to the . . . British Museum* (London: The British Museum, 1903).

Gaskell/TCC: Philip Gaskell, *Trinity College Library: the first 150 years* (Cambridge: Cambridge University Press, 1980).

Hackel: Heidi Brayman Hackel, *Reading material in early modern England* (Cambridge: Cambridge University Press, 2005).

Herefordshire bookplates: Paul Latcham, *Herefordshire bookplates* (Hereford: Herefordshire City Museum, 1988).

HoP: The History of Parliament: www.historyofparliamentonline.org.

Lee, *British*: B. N. Lee, *British bookplates: a pictorial history* (Newton Abbot: David & Charles, 1979).

Lee, *Labels*: B. N. Lee, *Early printed book labels* (Pinner: Private Libraries Association, 1976).

Lee, *London*: B. N. Lee, *London bookplates* (London: Bookplate Society, 1985).

Macray: W. D. Macray, *Annals of the Bodleian Library*, 2nd edn (Oxford: Clarendon Press, 1890).

Maggs: catalogues of the London booksellers Maggs Bros.

Mandelbrote, 'Auctions': Giles Mandelbrote, 'The organisation of book auctions in late seventeenth-century London', in R. Myers (ed.), *Under the hammer* (London: The British Library, 2001), 15–36.

Morgan: Paul Morgan, *Oxford libraries outside the Bodleian*, 2nd edn (Oxford: Bodliean Library, 1980).

Munby: A. N. L. Munby, *Cambridge college libraries* (Cambridge: Heffer, 1960).

Munk: W. Munk, *The roll of the Royal College of Physicians of London*, 2nd edn (London: Royal College of Physicians, 1878).

Oates: J. C. T. Oates, *Cambridge University Library: a history* (Cambridge: Cambridge University Press, 1986).

OBS: Oxford Bibliographical Society.

ODNB: The Oxford Dictionary of National Biography: www.oxforddnb.com.

PBSA: Papers of the Bibliographical Society of America.

Pearson, 'Bishops': David Pearson, 'The libraries of English bishops 1600–40', *The Library*, 6th ser. 14 (1992), 221–57.

Pearson, *Provenance research*: David Pearson, *Provenance research in book history*, new edn (Oxford: Bodleian Library, 2019).

Perkin: Michael Perkin, *A directory of the parochial libraries of the Church of England* (London: Bibliographical Society, 2004).

Philip: Ian Philip, *The Bodleian Library in the seventeenth and eighteenth centuries* (Oxford: Clarendon Press, 1983).

PLRE: Private Libraries in Renaissance England (ongoing series, ed. R. L. Fehrenbach & J. L. Black).

Purcell: Mark Purcell, *The country house library* (New Haven, CT: Yale University Press, 2017).

Roy: I. Roy, 'The libraries of Edward, 2nd Viscount Conway, and others', *Bulletin of the Institute of Historical Research* 43 (1968), 35–46.

Sears Jayne: Sears Jayne, *Library catalogues of the English Renaissance*, new edn (Godalming: St Paul's Bibliographies, 1983).

TCBS: Transactions of the Cambridge Bibliographical Society.

Thornton: J. Thornton, *Thornton's medical books, libraries and collectors*, 3rd edn, ed. A. Besson (Aldershot: Gower, 1990).

Thornton & Tully: J. Thornton & R. Tully, *Thornton and Tully's scientific books, libraries and collectors*, 4th edn, ed. A. Hunter (Aldershot: Ashgate, 2000).

Toomer: G. J. Toomer, *Eastern religion and learning* (Oxford: Clarendon Press, 1996).

V&A: Victoria & Albert Museum London.

Venn: J. Venn & J. A. Venn, *Alumni Cantabrigienses* (Cambridge: Cambridge University Press, 1922).
Walker revised: A. G. Matthews, *Walker revised* (Oxford: Clarendon Press, 1948).
Wanley, *Diary*: C. E. Wright & R. Wright (eds), *The diary of Humfrey Wanley* (London: Bibliographical Society, 1966).
West: Susie West, *The development of libraries in Norfolk country houses* (University of East Anglia PhD thesis, 2000).
Woodhead: J. Woodhead, *The rulers of London 1660-1689* (London: London and Middlesex Archaeological Society, 1965).
Young: Thomas Young, *Some Yorkshire bookplates* (Edgbaston: Bookplate Society, 1991).

Academics

This section lists men whose careers were primarily spent in the universities, as teachers, scholars, and/or administrators. They were usually ordained clergymen and many of them held ecclesiastical livings at some point; they are included here, rather than in the lists of clergy, when their primary focus and/or place of residence was more evidently academic than pastoral. The first section lists those who held senior academic positions (masters, wardens, presidents, provosts, etc.), the second those who held fellowships, teaching posts, or similar.

Senior Academics

Roger Goad 1538–1610
    Provost of King's College, Cambridge. Instrumental in re-establishing King's Library; bequeathed his books among his family. Books with his armorial stamp survive.
    ODNB. W. Cargill Thompson, 'Notes on King's College Library, 1500–1570', *TCBS* 2 (1954): 38–54. Armorials database.

John Cowell 1554–1611
    Master of Trinity Hall, Cambridge; lawyer. Bequeathed 48 books to King's College, Cambridge, and his legal books to Trinity Hall.
    ODNB. Sears Jayne, 142.

George Ryves 1561–1613
    Warden of New College, Oxford. Gave books to the college during his lifetime and bequeathed it all his folio volumes.
    W. Poole, 'An early-modern New College dynasty', http://www.new.ox.ac.uk/sites/default/files/4NCN1%20Ryves%27%20notes.pdf.

John Spencer 1558/9–1614
    President of Corpus Christi College, Oxford. Bequeathed *c.*50 volumes to Corpus Christi.
    ODNB. Sears Jayne, 145.

Humphrey Tyndall 1549–1614
    Master of Queens' College, Cambridge. Probate inventory includes 190 volumes, valued at £47 2*s.* 4*d.*
    Venn. *BCI*, 191.

William Smith 1556?–1615
> Provost of King's College, Cambridge. Gave *c*.90 books to King's, *c*.1615.
> Venn. Sears Jayne, 146.

John Fleming 1574/5–1617
> Warden of Wadham College, Oxford. His books were valued on decease at £6 8*s*. 6*d*.
> Foster. W. Poole, *Wadham College books in the age of John Wilkins* (2014), 38.

Anthony Blencowe *c*.1542–1618
> Provost of Oriel College, Oxford. Bequeathed 67 books, mainly canon law, to Oriel; also
> gave 16 books to the Bodleian Library in 1601.
> Foster. Sears Jayne, 146. G. Richards & H. Salter, *The Dean's register of Oriel* (1926), 166.

William Branthwaite 1563–1619
> Master of Gonville & Caius College, Cambridge. Bequeathed *c*.1,750 books/MSS to
> Caius, and *c*.20 books to Emmanuel College.
> *ODNB*. Sears Jayne, 147–8. C. Brooke, *A history of Gonville and Caius College* (1985),
> 104–6. F. Stubbings, *Forty-nine lives* (1983), no. 4.

Griffith Powell 1560/1–1620
> Principal of Jesus College, Oxford. Bequeathed *c*.100 volumes to the college, largely law.
> *ODNB*. Morgan. C. Fordyce & T. Knox, *The library of Jesus College, Oxford* (1937),
> 59–60.

Sir Henry Savile 1549–1622
> Warden of Merton College, Oxford, Provost of Eton. Books with his armorial stamp
> survive. Part of his library, and that of his elder brother, Sir John Savile, was sold at
> Sotheby's in 1860–61. Established the Savilian Library at Oxford, drawn originally from
> his own books, to support the lectureships he established in mathematics, astronomy,
> and geometry.
> *ODNB*. J. Hirshfield, 'An autograph manuscript commonplace book of Sir Henry Savile',
> *BLR* 7 (1963): 73–83. Armorials database.

John Richardson d. 1625
> Master of Trinity College, Cambridge. Bequeathed £120 to Emmanuel College,
> Cambridge to buy books; a printed gift label was added to those bought.
> *ODNB*. Lee, *Labels*, 32. S. Bush & C. Rasmussen, *The Library of Emmanuel College,
> Cambridge 1584–1637* (1986), 24–5.

Henry Alvey d. 1627
> President of St John's College, Cambridge; Provost of Trinity College, Dublin 1601–9.
> Bequeathed books, and 100 marks for the purchase of books, to St John's.
> Venn. P. Fox, *Trinity College Library Dublin: a history* (2014), 10–11.

Walter Travers 1548?–1635
> Provost of Trinity College, Dublin 1594–8, later unsuccessfully sought ecclesiastical
> preferment in England. Bequeathed *c*.150 books to Sion College.
> *ODNB*. Sears Jayne, 168. *CHL* I 393. E. Pearce, *Sion College and Library* (Cambridge,
> 1913), 243–4.

Sir Henry Wotton 1568–1639
> Provost of Eton College, after a diplomatic career. Bequeathed his MSS to Eton, Italian
> books to Isaac Bargrave; the fate of the rest of his library is unknown.
> *ODNB*. *CELM*. R. Birley, *The history of Eton College Library* (1970), 26–7.

Ralph Kettell 1563–1643
President of Trinity College, Oxford. Probate inventory lists books valued at £80, from a total estate valued at £724. Gave books to Trinity, and bequeathed books to Edward, George, and Ralph Bathurst, fellows of Trinity.
ODNB. Morgan. Oxford University Archives Hyp.B.15.

Samuel Ward 1572–1643
Master of Sidney Sussex College, Cambridge. Ward's notebooks and papers, at Sidney Sussex, noted for including the earliest known draft of the King James Bible, also include some book lists.
ODNB. M. Todd, 'The Samuel Ward papers at Sidney Sussex College', *TCBS* 8 (1985): 582–92.

John Tolson 1576?–1644
Provost of Oriel College, Oxford. Gave 21 books to Oriel, *c*.1640.
Foster. Sears Jayne, 172.

Robert Pinke 1573–1647
Warden of New College, Oxford. Bequeathed *c*.170 books to New College.
Foster. Morgan.

Degory Wheare 1573–1647
Principal of Gloucester Hall, Oxford, and first Camden Professor of History at Oxford. Some of his books were bought by the Bodleian after his death.
ODNB. Macray, 107.

Samuel Radcliffe d. 1648
Principal of Brasenose College, Oxford. Bequeathed his books to the college, and money to build a new library.
Foster. A. J. Butler, 'An account of benefaction', monograph IV in *Brasenose College quatercentenary monographs* (Oxford, 1909), vol. 1, 23–4. J. Mordaunt Crook, *Brasenose: the biography of an Oxford college* (2008), 75–7.

Richard Holdsworth 1590–1649
Master of Emmanuel College, Cambridge. His library of *c*.10,000 volumes was possibly the largest private English one of its generation. It was bequeathed to the University of Cambridge under complex conditions which eventually meant that the books went to the University Library, once the Lambeth Palace books were returned from there to Lambeth. He also gave some books to St John's, Cambridge.
ODNB. Oates, 314–48. *CHL* I 313–15.

William Bagge *c*.1623–57
President of Gonville & Caius College, Cambridge. Bequeathed books, largely medical, to Caius; many have pastedowns made from cut-up letters to Bagge.
Venn. C. Brooke, *A history of Gonville and Caius College* (1985), 131–2.

Gerard Langbaine 1609–58
Provost of Queen's College, Oxford. Gave books to Queen's; some of his MSS were bought by the Bodleian.
ODNB. Morgan. Macray, 126.

George Marshall d. 1658
Warden of New College, Oxford. Probate inventory notes his library valued at *c*.£50, including 65 folios, 124 bound quartos, and various smaller formats and stitched books.
Foster. W. Poole, 'Book economy in New College, Oxford in the later 17th century', *History of Universities* 25 (2010): 56–127, 84–5.

Francis Rous 1580/81–1659
Provost of Eton College. A collection of *c.*800 pamphlets and broadsheets of the early Civil War period, in Eton College Library, is thought to have been his.
ODNB. R. Birley, *The history of Eton College Library* (1970), 30–31.

Mark Frank 1613–64
Master of Pembroke College, Cambridge. Bequeathed 360 volumes to Pembroke.
ODNB. See p. 24 above.

Francis Mansell 1579–1665
Principal of Jesus College, Oxford. Gave his library, *c.*600 volumes, to the college.
ODNB. Morgan. C. J. Fordyce & T. M. Knox, 'The Library of Jesus College, Oxford', *Oxford Bibliographical Society Proceedings & Papers* 5 (1937): 53–115, 62–3.

Thomas Walker d. 1665
Master of University College, Oxford. Gave 13 MSS and 52 printed books to University College 1640.
Foster. Sears Jayne, 172.

Richard Baylie 1585/6–1667
President of St John's College, Oxford. Compounded for delinquency in 1647 when his books (with other goods) were valued at £100.
ODNB. Walker revised.

Anthony Tuckney 1599–1670
Master of Emmanuel College, later of St John's College, Cambridge during the Interregnum (forced to resign, 1661). Gave books to the parish library of Boston, Lincolnshire (of which he was vicar), and to Emmanuel.
ODNB. Perkin, 144–6.

Michael Woodward 1602–75
Warden of New College, Oxford. Bequeathed *c.*600 books to the college.
Foster. Morgan.

John Breton d. 1676
Master of Emmanuel College, Cambridge. Bequeathed books valued at £200 to Emmanuel.
Venn. S. Bendall et al., *History of Emmanuel College Cambridge* (1999).

Isaac Barrow 1630–77
Master of Trinity College, Cambridge. Gave *c.*60 volumes to Trinity during his lifetime, 10 more were bought after his death. A catalogue of his library, *c.*1,100 volumes, is in Bodleian Library MS Rawl.D.878, fos 39–59.
ODNB. Gaskell/TCC 131.

Robert Mapletoft 1609–77
Master of Pembroke College, Cambridge; Dean of Ely. Lost books during the Civil War period; bequeathed his library, and £100 for book purchase and library furnishing, to Ely Cathedral.
ODNB. D. Owen, *The library and muniments of Ely Cathedral* (1973).

Theophilus Dillingham 1612–78
Master of Clare College, Cambridge. Bequeathed books, and money for the purchase of books, to Clare.
ODNB. Clare College 1326–1926 (1928), 316.

James Duport 1606–79
> Master of Magdalene College, Cambridge. Maintained three libraries, at different places of residence, at Magdalene, Peterborough, and Boxworth; he left his Magdalene library (over 2,100 volumes) to Trinity College, Cambridge, his Peterborough library to Magdalene, and his Boxworth library to two nephews.
> *ODNB*. Oates, 428–9.

Thomas Holbech 1603?–80
> Master of Emmanuel College, Cambridge. Bequeathed books to the college, along with bequests of other parts of his library to relatives.
> Venn. *Walker revised*.

Sir Leoline Jenkins 1625–85
> Principal of Jesus College, Oxford. Bequeathed his library to the college.
> *ODNB*. C. Fordyce & T. Knox, 'The library of Jesus College, Oxford', *OBS Proceedings* (1937): 65.

Thomas Marshall 1621–85
> Rector of Lincoln College, Oxford, noted oriental scholar. Bequeathed his library mostly to the Bodleian (*c*.600 books/MSS), and Lincoln College (*c*.1,100 books).
> *ODNB*. Morgan. Philip, 58. Toomer, 279–81.

William Stone 1615–85
> Principal of New Inn Hall, Oxford, minister at Wimborne, Dorset. Bequeathed *c*.90 books from his collection in Oxford to refound Wimborne Minster Library.
> Foster. Perkin, 392–4. *Walker revised*.

Ralph Cudworth 1617–88
> Master of Christ's College, Cambridge. Library auctioned in London, 2 Feb. 1691 (1,960 lots).
> *ODNB*. Alston, *Inventory*.

Henry Wilkinson 1616–90
> Principal of Magdalen Hall, Oxford, ejected 1662; licensed to preach at Gosfield, 1672. Library auctioned in London, 15 Nov. 1694 (1,161 lots). An earlier collection of his was given to Magdalen Hall.
> *ODNB*. W. Poole, *Wadham College books in the age of John Wilkins* (2014), 27–8. Alston, *Inventory*.

Sir Thomas Clayton *c*.1612–93
> Warden of Merton College, Oxford, Regius Professor of Medicine. Bequeathed his books to Merton.
> *HoP*. Morgan.

Nathaniel Coga 1637?–93
> Master of Pembroke College, Cambridge. Library auctioned in Cambridge, 27 Nov. 1694 (1,554 lots).
> Venn. D. Pearson, 'Patterns of book ownership in late seventeenth-century England', *The Library*, 7th ser. 11 (2010): 139–67. Alston, *Inventory*.

William Levinz 1625–98
> President of St John's College, Oxford. Library auctioned in Oxford, 29 June 1698 (3,678 lots).
> *ODNB*. D. McKitterick, *Cambridge University Library: a history*, vol. 2 (Cambridge, 1986), 62–3. Alston, *Inventory*.

Obadiah Walker 1616–99
Master of University College, Oxford. Gave books to University College, and to the Bodleian. Library sold by retail sale in London, 13 July 1699 (no catalogue survives).
ODNB. Morgan. Alston, *Inventory*.

Timothy Halton 1632?–1704
Provost of Queen's College, Oxford. Part-funded, and oversaw, the building of a new library for Queen's in the 1690s; bequeathed 300 books in folio, and 200 in quarto, to the college. Remainder of library auctioned in Oxford, 13 Feb. 1706 (no catalogue survives).
ODNB. Alston, *Inventory*.

Roger Mander d. 1704
Master of Balliol College, Oxford. Bequeathed his books to the college.
Foster. Morgan.

Thomas Bayley d. 1706
President of Magdalen College, Oxford. Library auctioned in Oxford, 29 Oct. 1706 (joint sale, with one other).
Foster. Alston, *Inventory*.

Richard Duckworth 1631?–1706
Principal of St Alban Hall, Oxford. Library auctioned in Oxford 24 Mar. 1707 (joint sale, with one other; no catalogue survives).
ODNB. Alston, *Inventory*.

John Mill 1644/5–1707
Principal of St Edmund Hall, Oxford. His library was sold, after his death, to Henry Penton of New College for 200 guineas.
ODNB. C. Doble, *Remarks and collections of Thomas Hearne*, vol. 2 (1886), 74.

William Thornton 1641?–1707
Principal of Hart Hall, Oxford. Library auctioned in Oxford, 10 Nov. 1707 (1864 lots)
Foster. Alston, *Inventory*.

George Royse d. 1708
Provost of Oriel College, Oxford. Bequeathed books to Oriel; other books from his library were auctioned in Oxford, 13 Mar. 1710 (no catalogue survives).
Foster. Morgan. Alston, *Inventory*.

Edmund Marten 1659?–1709
Warden of Merton College, Oxford. Library auctioned in Oxford, 20 Oct. 1709 (joint sale, with one other).
Foster. Alston, *Inventory*.

Henry Aldrich 1647–1710
Dean of Christ Church, Oxford. Bequeathed his library, including 3,000 books, 8,000 pieces of music, and 2,000 engravings, to Christ Church.
ODNB. W. Hiscock, *Henry Aldrich of Christ Church* (1960). W. Hiscock, 'Henry Aldrich, book-collector, musician, architect' in *A Christ Church miscellany* (1946).

Humphrey Gower 1638–1711
Master of St John's College, Cambridge. Bequeathed his library to St John's; over 1,400 books can be identified there today.
ODNB. P. Linehan (ed.), *St John's College Cambridge: a history* (2011), 168–71.

Benjamin Woodroffe 1638–1711
  Principal of Gloucester Hall, Oxford. Library sold by retail sale in London, 9 July 1718
  (joint sale, with one other).
  ODNB. Alston, *Inventory*.

Jonathan Edwards 1638/9–1712
  Principal of Jesus College, Oxford. Bequeathed his library to the college.
  ODNB. Morgan.

Thomas Thurlin d. 1714
  President of St John's College, Cambridge. Bequeathed *c*.440 books to the parish of
  King's Lynn, and £300 to the library of St John's, for the purchase of books (a printed gift
  label was placed in the books bought).
  Venn. Perkin, 254. T. Maw, 'The church libraries of King's Lynn', *The Antiquary* 40
  (1904): 235–40.

Thomas Turner 1645–1714
  President of Corpus Christi College, Oxford. Bequeathed books to the college.
  ODNB. Morgan.

Other academics

Abel Trefry 1577–1610
  Fellow of All Souls, Oxford. Probate inventory (transcribed and edited as PLRE 158) lists
  45 books.
  Foster. J. Black and J. Cunico, 'Abel Trefry', in R. Fehrenbach and J. Black (eds), PLRE 7
  (2009): 103–112.

John English d. 1613
  Fellow of St John's College, Oxford. Probate inventory lists 518 books/MSS.
  Foster. W. Costin, 'The inventory of John English', *Oxoniensia* 11–12 (1946–7): 106–16.

William Gibson d. 1613
  Fellow of Peterhouse, Cambridge. Inventory lists 85 volumes, valued at £2 13*s*.
  Venn. *BCI*, 190.

Edward Homer 1581?–1614
  Of St John's College, Oxford (MA 1606). Probate inventory (transcribed and edited as
  PLRE 160) lists *c*.60 books.
  Foster. S. Gillespie, 'Edward Homer', in R. Fehrenbach and J. Black (eds), PLRE 7 (2009):
  211–20.

John Reynolds 1581/2–1614
  Fellow of New College, Oxford. Probate inventory notes his books valued at 58*s*.
  Foster. W. Poole, 'Book economy in New College, Oxford in the later 17th century',
  History of Universities 25 (2010): 56–127.

Henry Banister d. 1617
  Vice-Provost of King's College, Cambridge. Bequeathed books and maps to the college.
  Venn. *A list of the incunabula in the Library of King's College, Cambridge* (1908).

John Blythe d. 1617
  Fellow of Peterhouse, Cambridge. Bequeathed money to Peterhouse to buy books, and
  also to his 'little god-daughter' to buy a specified list of devotional titles.
  T. A. Walker, *A biographical list of Peterhouse men* (1930), 49.

Richard Fletcher d. 1617

Fellow of Jesus College, Cambridge. Probate inventory lists *c.*60 books valued at *c.*£20. Venn. *BCI*, 192. W. Griffith, 'Richard Fletcher of Bangor: an early seventeenth century Welsh student at Cambridge', *Caernarvonshire Historical Society Transactions* 39 (1978): 44–73.

Richard Kilbye d. 1620

Regius Professor Hebrew at Oxford. Bequeathed *c.*40 books, largely relating to Hebrew scholarship, to Lincoln College, Oxford (list of these transcribed and edited as PLRE 162); his total library would have been larger.
ODNB. J. Black and R. Fehrenbach, 'Richard Kilby', PLRE 7 (2009): 225–35.

Alexander Clugh d. 1621

Graduate of Emmanuel College, Cambridge. Probate inventory lists 61 volumes, valued at £1 19*s.* 3*d.*
Venn. *BCI*, 193.

George Ruggle 1575–1622

Fellow of Clare Hall; author of the controversial Latin comedy *Ignoramus*. Gave 284 books to Clare in 1620, including a noteworthy collection of Italian plays.
ODNB. M. Forbes (ed.), *Clare College 1326–1926* (1930).

Gilbert Drake d. 1629

Fellow of Wadham College, Oxford. Bequeathed books to Wadham.
Foster. Morgan. W. Poole, *Wadham College books in the age of John Wilkins* (2014), 40.

Thomas James 1572/3–1629

Bodley's librarian, and theological author. His books were valued at his death at £40. Books survive with his inscription and motto 'Non quaero mihi utile est sed quod utilis'.
ODNB. Pearson, *Provenance research.*

Henry Briggs 1561–1630

Savile Professor of geometry at Oxford, mathematician. Books of his are found in the Bodleian, and in Halifax Parish Library.
ODNB. M. Feingold, *The mathematicians' apprenticeship* (1984).

John Collins *c.*1576–1634

Regius Professor of Physick at Cambridge. Gave *c.*300 books to St John's College, and £100 to purchase more; a printed gift label was made for the books.
Venn. Sears Jayne, 163. *CHL* I 468.

Sylvius Elwes 1576–1638

Chaplain of Trinity College, Cambridge. Gave 184 books and 4 MSS to Trinity, *c.*1630. Two armorial stamps are attributed to him in the Armorials database.
Venn. Gaskell/TCC. Armorials database.

Paul Micklethwaite 1588/9–1639

Master of the Temple Church, London; previously fellow of Sidney Sussex College, Cambridge. Bequeathed 73 Hebrew books to Sidney Sussex; the rest of his library, whose extent is unknown, passed to his nephew.
ODNB.

Robert Burton 1577–1640

Student and librarian of Christ Church, Oxford; author of *The anatomy of melancholy*. Bequeathed his books to the Bodleian Library, on condition that any duplicates should be given to Christ Church. His total library comprised *c.*1,740 books, of which 750 are in the Bodleian, 780 in Christ Church, 42 elsewhere, and the remainder currently unlocated. They include a small number with the inscription of his father, Ralfe Burton (d. 1620), and of his brother William Burton (d. 1645).

ODNB. CELM. N. Kiessling, *The library of Robert Burton* (1988). N. Kiessling, 'The library of Robert Burton: new discoveries', *BC* 45 (1996): 172–79. N. Kiessling, 'The library of Robert Burton: addenda and corrigenda', *Notes & Queries* 258 (2013): 523–6. Macray, 90–93. L. Erne, *Shakespeare and the book trade* (2013), 210.

Edmund Leigh d. 1641?

Fellow of Brasenose College, Oxford. Gave books to the college.

Foster. Morgan.

John Barkham 1571/2–1642

Prebendary of St Paul's. Gave 1 MS and 60 printed books to the Bodleian Library in 1602; books from his library can be found at Corpus Christi College, Oxford, and elsewhere. He also had coin collections, now at the Ashmolean Museum and Corpus Christi.

ODNB. Sears Jayne, 136.

Dudley Digges 1613–43

Fellow of All Souls College, Oxford, political writer. Bequeathed his library (*c.*1,300 volumes) to All Souls.

ODNB. E. Craster, *The history of All Souls College library* (1971), 60–63.

Brian Twyne *c.*1580–1644

Reader in Greek at Corpus Christi College, Oxford; Keeper of the University Archives. Bequeathed his library to Corpus Christi; *c.*750 books/tracts survive today, from what was probably once a larger collection, noteworthy for many unusual and ephemeral items. Includes books inherited from his father and grandfather.

ODNB. R. Ovenell, *Brian Twyne's library* (1952). D. Pearson, 'A binding made in Oxford for Brian Twyne', *BC* 49 (2000): 248–51. See above, p. 134.

John Alsop d. 1647

Fellow of Christ's College, Cambridge; chaplain to Archbishop Laud. Died in exile in France. Bequeathed 60 books to Christ's, valued at £30.

Venn. Sears Jayne, 170. *Walker revised.*

William Hutchings d. 1647

Vice-Principal of Brasenose College, Oxford. Bequeathed books to the college.

Foster. Morgan.

John Morris 1595–1648

Regius Professor of Hebrew at Oxford. Bequeathed money to Christ Church, Oxford, for the purchase of oriental books; his own books, with his inscription and Greek motto, are now dispersed across many libraries.

Foster.

John Goodrich d. 1651

Fellow of Wadham College, Oxford; warden of Trinity Hospital, Greenwich. Gave the bulk of his library of books to Wadham.

Foster. Morgan. W. Poole, *Wadham College books in the age of John Wilkins* (2014), 55–6.

John Greaves 1602–52

Savilian Professor of Astronomy at Oxford, orientalist. A library of more than 375 volumes, valued at £59 11s. 4d., was seized from his London house by the London Committee for Sequestration in 1643.

ODNB. Roy. Toomer, 127ff.

John Hutton 1627/8–52
Fellow of New College Oxford. Probate inventory lists *c.*150 books valued at £2 18*s.* 7*d.*
Foster. W. Poole, 'Book economy in New College, Oxford in the later 17th century',
History of Universities 25 (2010): 56–127, 85–102. J. Butler, 'John Hutton', PLRE 7
(2009), 253–79.

Henry Jacob *c.*1608–52
Lecturer in Philology at Oxford; amanuensis to John Selden. A brief inventory of his
goods made in 1653 (transcribed and edited as PLRE 166) shows he had a library of *c.*370
books, though these are not listed by title.
ODNB. R. Nicholson, 'Henry Jacob', in R. Fehrenbach and J. Black (eds), PLRE 7 (2009):
281–5.

John Smith 1618–52
Fellow of Queens' College, Cambridge; mathematician, and philosopher. Bequeathed his
library of *c.*600 volumes to Queens', where a contemporary inventory survives.
ODNB. J. Saveson, 'The library of John Smith, the Cambridge Platonist', *Notes & Queries*
203 (1958), 215–16. M. Feingold, *The mathematicians' apprenticeship* (1984), 53.

Peter Turner 1586–1652
Savilian Professor of Mathematics at Oxford. Bequeathed Greek MSS to the Bodleian.
ODNB. Macray, 108.

John Tolly d. 1655
Fellow of Peterhouse, Cambridge; Rector of Little Gransden, Cambridgeshire 1643
(ejected 1645). Will refers to books held at Peterhouse and at Haddon, Derbyshire.
Venn. *Walker revised.*

John Hales 1584–1656
Fellow of Eton 1613–50 (ejected); subsequently sold his library for *c.*£600, though it was
said to have cost him £2500.
ODNB. Walker revised. Aubrey, *Brief lives.* W. Poole, 'Analysing a private library, with a
shelflist attributable to John Hales', in E. Jones (ed.), *A concise companion to the study of
manuscripts, printed books, and the production of early modern texts* (2015), 41–65.

Nicholas Hobart d. 1657
Fellow of King's College, Cambridge; agent for the Levant Company. Bequeathed money
to several libraries, and gave books, collected in Constantinople, to Cambridge
University Library.
Venn. Oates, 289–92.

Gilbert Watts 1590?–1657
Fellow of Lincoln College, Oxford. Bequeathed £60 worth of books to the college, and
one book to each fellow.
ODNB. Morgan. *Walker revised.* Armorials database.

Robert Waring 1614?–58
Camden Professor of Ancient History at Oxford 1647, ejected the same year and forced
to release his books to the parliamentary visitors. His will refers to books at Tew, Apley,
and Oldbury.
ODNB. Walker revised.

William Moore 1590–1659
Fellow of Gonville & Caius College, Cambridge; Cambridge University Librarian. Bequeathed
his collection of *c.*150 MSS, including many of English monastic provenance, to Caius.
ODNB. Oates, 268–70.

John Nidd d. 1659
> Fellow of Trinity College, Cambridge. Bequeathed 125 volumes to Trinity (largely medical), with other books left to friends and family. Nidd's probate inventory lists c.300 volumes; many of the books not left to Trinity were bequeathed to William Lynnet (also a fellow of Trinity), who in turn bequeathed then to the College.
> Venn. BCI, 195. Gaskell/TCC, 131.

John Sterne d. 1661
> Chaplain of New College, Oxford. Probate inventory notes his books valued at £1 10s.
> Foster. W. Poole, 'Book economy in New College, Oxford in the later 17th century', History of Universities 25 (2010): 56–127, 84.

Philip Bacon d. 1665
> Fellow of Pembroke College, Cambridge. Bequeathed 273 volumes to Pembroke.
> Venn. Pembroke College Donors' Book (MS LC.II.77).

Edmund Fauchin d. 1668
> Fellow of New College Oxford. Probate inventory notes his books valued at £7.
> Foster. W. Poole, 'Book economy in New College, Oxford in the later 17th century', History of Universities 25 (2010): 56–127, 84.

Richard Samwayes 1625?-69
> Fellow of Corpus Christi College, Oxford. Bequeathed his library to the college.
> Foster. Morgan.

Samuel Howlett d. 1671?
> Fellow of St John's College, Cambridge. Bequeathed c.80 volumes to St John's, mostly in European languages.
> Venn.

Henry Gostling 1646?–75
> Fellow of Corpus Christi College, Cambridge. Bequeathed his books (120 volumes) to Corpus Christi.
> Venn. B. Dickins, 'Henry Gostling's library', TCBS 3 (1961): 216–24.

Francis Junius 1589–1677
> Philological scholar, librarian and tutor for the Earl of Arundel. Bequeathed important collections of books and MSS, to the Bodleian.
> ODNB. Philip, 57–8.

Henry Oldenburg c.1619–77
> Secretary of the Royal Society. Lists of his books, c.1670, in BL Add. Ms.4255, run to c.330 titles. Many of his books were sold, after his death, to Arthur Annesley, Earl of Anglesey.
> ODNB. N. Malcolm, 'The library of Henry Oldenburg', eBLJ 2005 article 7: http://www.bl.uk/eblj/2005articles/pdf/article7.pdf.

William Pindar d. 1678
> Fellow of University College, Oxford; bequeathed books to the college.
> Foster. Morgan.

Roger Stanley 1642/3–78
> Fellow of New College Oxford. Probate inventory notes his books valued at £80.
> Foster. W. Poole, 'Book economy in New College, Oxford in the later 17th century', History of Universities 25 (2010): 56–127, 84.

John Prestwich d. 1679
Fellow of All Souls, Oxford. Gave books to the town of Manchester during his lifetime, and bequeathed 'all my folios quartos and larger octavos bound up either in leather or parchment' to Manchester.
Foster. Perkin, 245. R. Christie, *The old church and school libraries of Lancashire* (1885), 9–19.

Nicholas Lloyd 1630?–80
Sub-warden of Wadham College, Oxford. Library auctioned in London, 4 July 1681 (1,088 lots).
ODNB. Alston, *Inventory*.

Richard Allestree 1619–81
Regius Professor of Divinity at Oxford. Bequeathed his library of *c*.3,500 books to the care of Christ Church, Oxford, for the use of the Regius Professor.
ODNB. W. Hiscock, *A Christ Church miscellany* (1946), 14–15. M. Purcell, '"Useful weapons for the defence of that cause": Richard Allestree, John Fell and the foundation of the Allestree Library', *The Library*, 6th ser. 21 (1999): 124–47.

Samuel Brooke d. *c*.1681?
Described as a fellow of St Catharine's, Cambridge, but not traced in Venn. Library auctioned in London, 21 Mar. 1681 (1,662 lots).
Alston, *Inventory*.

Richard Drake 1609–81
Prebendary of Salisbury. Gave books to Pembroke College, Cambridge in the 1630s; bequeathed his folios and quartos jointly between Pembroke and Salisbury Cathedral.
ODNB. *Walker revised*. Armorials database.

John Ledgard d. 1683
Fellow of University College, Oxford. Left books to University College.
Foster. Morgan.

James Chamberlaine 1635?–84
Fellow of St John's College, Cambridge. Library auctioned at Stourbridge Fair, 8 Sept. 1686 (1,350 lots).
Venn. Alston, *Inventory*.

Edmund Castell 1606–85
Professor of Arabic at Cambridge. Bequeathed Hebrew books to Emmanuel College, and oriental MSS to Cambridge University Library. Bequeathed Bibles and lexicons to Henry Compton, who subsequently gave them to Sion College. Residue of his library auctioned in Cambridge, 30 June 1686 (1,051 lots). A list of books given, or intended to be given, by Castell to Henry Compton in 1684 is in BL Add. MS 22905, fo. 99.
ODNB. Munby. Toomer, 255–65. E. Pearce, *Sion College and Library* (1913), 264–5. F. Stubbings, *Forty-nine lives* (Cambridge, 1983). Birrell, 'Books and buyers', 59–60. Oates, 448–50. Mandelbrote, 'Auctions', 24. Alston, *Inventory*.

John Bennet 1657–86
Of Christ Church, Oxford (MA 1683). Several books with his armorial stamp survive in Christ Church Library.
ODNB. Armorials database.

Samuel Desmaitres d. 1686
Fellow of Oriel College, Oxford. Bequeathed his books (including many medical ones) to Oriel.
Foster. Morgan.

Ralph Widdrington 1614/5-88
Regius professor of divinity at Cambridge. Directed that his library be sold after his death and the proceeds added to an endowment for Christ's College, after the death of his nephews. His books are now widely dispersed, including a group at Eton College Library, received as part of the bequest of Henry Godolphin; his library is likely to have included over 1,000 volumes.
ODNB. H. Rackham (ed.), *Christ's College in former days* (1939), 182-91, 280. R. Birley, *The history of Eton College Library* (1970), 36.

Nicholas Crouch 1641-89
Fellow of Balliol College, Oxford, physician. Bequeathed to Balliol such books as the college selected; *c.*4,000 items, mostly bound in *c.*320 tract volumes, survive, together with records of purchase, binding and borrowing.
Foster. Morgan. See above, p. 130.

Thomas Man 1655?-90
Fellow of Jesus College, Cambridge. Gave *c.*80 MSS, many from northern English monasteries, to Jesus, earlier owned by his father Thomas Man, rector of Northallerton (d. 1669?).
Venn. R. Hanna, The Thomas Mans, their books, and Jesus College librarianship, *The Library* 7th ser.21 (2020), 46-73. See above, p. 158.

Christopher Wase 1627-90
Classical scholar, supervisor of the University Press at Oxford. Many of his books were subsequently acquired by Francis Yarborough, Principal of Brasenose (d. 1770), who bequeathed his books to that college. His MSS went to Corpus Christi, Oxford. Bodleian Library MS Rawl.poet.117 contains an inventory of some of his books.
ODNB. Morgan.

Humfrey Babington 1615-91
Vice-Master of Trinity College, Cambridge. Library auctioned in Cambridge, 12 July 1692 (865 lots); also bequeathed books and maps to Trinity College, and Leicester Town Library.
ODNB. D. Pearson, 'Patterns of book ownership in late seventeenth-century England', *The Library*, 7th ser. 11 (2010): 139-67. Alston, *Inventory.*

Edward Pococke 1604-91
Regius Professor of Hebrew at Oxford. 420 oriental MSS from his collection were bought by the Bodleian after his death. Remainder of his library ('the theological part') auctioned in London, 11 Apr. 1692 (joint sale, with part of the stock of the bookseller Richard Davis).
ODNB. Philip, 59-60. Toomer, 116ff. Alston, *Inventory.*

Henry Paman *c.*1623-95
Professor of physic at Gresham College, Master of the Faculties at Cambridge University. Bequeathed his library (with an additional £50 to buy books) to St John's College, Cambridge. *ODNB.*

Anthony Wood 1632-95
Oxford historian. Bequeathed his library to the Ashmolean Museum (transferred to the Bodleian, 1860); over 6,500 vols are in the Bodleian today. Some books and MSS were also sold by him during his lifetime.
ODNB. N. Kiessling, *The library of Anthony Wood* (2002). S. Baron, 'Anthony Wood', in W. Baker (ed.), *Pre-nineteenth-century British book collectors and bibliographers* (1999), 401-6. *CHL* II 40-41. N. Kiessling, *The life of Anthony Wood in his own words* (2009).

Robert Plot 1640–96
  Professor of chemistry at Oxford, Keeper of the Ashmolean Museum, naturalist. Edward
  Bernard's *Catalogi manuscriptorum* (1697), lists him as owning 26 manuscripts.
  ODNB.

Edward Bernard 1638–97
  Savilian professor of astronomy at Oxford. A significant proportion of his library
  was purchased from his widow, after his death, by the Bodleian Library (£140
  for printed books, £200 for MSS); the remainder were sold by auction in Oxford
  (25 Oct. 1697, 1,462 lots). His *Catalogi manuscriptorum* (1697) lists 218 manuscripts
  owned by him.
  ODNB. Thornton & Tully. Philip, 61. Toomer, 299–305. P. Heyworth, 'Humfrey Wanley
  and "Friends of the Bodleian"', *BLR* 9 (1976), 219–30, 228–9. Alston, *Inventory.*

Alexander Green 1639/40–97
  Fellow of Pembroke College, Cambridge 1650–62 (ejected). Bequeathed £10 or £10
  worth of his books to Pembroke.
  Venn. *Calamy revised.*

Michael Harding 1649?–97
  Fellow of Trinity College, Oxford. Library auctioned in Oxford, 8 Nov. 1697 (1,748 lots).
  Foster. Alston, *Inventory.*

John Fitzwilliam d. 1699
  Fellow of Magdalen College, Oxford, nonjuror. Bequeathed most of his books to
  Magdalen (*c*.840 volumes, of which over half survive there today).
  ODNB. Morgan. See above, p. 131.

Timothy Nourse *c*.1636–99
  Fellow of University College, Oxford (deprived 1673, on conversion to Roman
  Catholicism). Bequeathed books to University College, and his coins to the Bodleian.
  ODNB. Morgan.

Robert Whitehall 1664/5–99
  Vice-principal of St Mary Hall, Oxford. Library auctioned in Oxford, 11 Mar. 1700
  (1,707 lots).
  Foster. Alston, *Inventory.*

Thomas Creech 1659–1700
  Fellow of All Souls, Oxford. Library auctioned in Oxford, 20 Nov. 1700 (1,967 lots)
  ODNB. Alston, *Inventory.*

William Corker d. 1702
  Fellow of Trinity College, Cambridge. Bequeathed his books to Trinity.
  Venn. D. McKitterick, *The making of the Wren Library* (1995), 56.

Henry Parkhurst d. 1706?
  Fellow of Corpus Christi College, Oxford. Library auctioned in Oxford, 29 Oct. 1706
  (joint sale, with one other).
  Foster. Alston, *Inventory.*

Humphrey Hody 1659–1707
  Regius professor of Greek at Oxford. Bequeathed his library to the University of Oxford
  to have first choice, and after that to Wadham College.
  ODNB.

William Ford d. 1708
Fellow of New College, Oxford. Library auctioned in Oxford, 21 Mar. 1709 (2,169 lots).
Foster. Alston, *Inventory*.

Edward Lhuyd 1660–1709
Keeper of the Ashmolean Museum. Assembled an important collection of Welsh MSS,
sold to Sir Thomas Sebright 1715; his printed books, of uncertain extent, seem to have
been divided between Oxford and Wales.
ODNB. E. Rees & G. Walters, 'The dispersion of the manuscripts of Edward Lhuyd',
Welsh History Review 7 (1974): 148–78. B. Roberts, Edward Lhuyd's collection of printed
books, *BLR* 10 (1979): 112–27.

Daniel Osborne 1669/70–1710
Fellow of Exeter College, Oxford. Library auctioned in Oxford, 7 July 1710 (joint sale,
with one other).
Foster. Alston, *Inventory*.

Thomas Smith 1638–1710
Fellow of Magdalen College, Oxford, deprived as a nonjuror 1692, librarian of the
Cotton Library. Gave oriental MSS to the Bodleian, bequeathed MSS to Thomas
Hearne, on condition that they subsequently passed to the Bodleian.
ODNB. Macray, 208–9.

Edward Thwaites 1667–1711
Regius professor of Greek at Oxford. Library auctioned in Oxford, 27 May 1712 (joint
sale, with one other).
ODNB. Alston, *Inventory*.

Joshua Barnes 1654–1712
Professor of Greek at Cambridge. Used an engraved armorial bookplate dated 1700.
ODNB. Franks 1537/*533.

John Laughton d. 1712
Cambridge University Librarian. Gave *c*.2,000 books to Trinity College, Cambridge
during his lifetime; most of his library was dispersed at his death. Also noted as a coin
collector. The English part of his library was sold by auction in Sheffield, 9 Dec. 1713 (no
catalogue survives).
Oates. D. McKitterick, *The making of the Wren Library* (1995), 59–60. Alston, *Inventory*.

Roger Farbrother 1688/9–1715
Scholar of Corpus Christi College, Oxford. Library auctioned in Oxford 6 Mar. 1716
(joint sale, with one other).
Foster. Alston, *Inventory*.

Charles King 1663/4–1715
Fellow of Merton College, Oxford. Library auctioned in Oxford 6 Mar. 1716 (joint sale,
with one other)
Foster. Alston, *Inventory*.

Architects

Inigo Jones 1573–1652
Architect and designer, surveyor to James I and Charles I. Forty-six books from his
library have been identified, though there must have been more; his marginalia extend
the known range of his reading.

ODNB. C. Anderson, *Inigo Jones's library and the language of architectural classicism in England* (PhD, MIT, 1993). R. Handa, 'Authorship of *The most notable antiquity* (1655); Inigo Jones and early printed books', *PBSA* 100 (2006): 357-78.

Aristocracy

Robert Cecil, 1st Earl of Salisbury 1563-1612
William Cecil, 2nd Earl of Salisbury 1591-1668
James Cecil, 3rd Earl of Salisbury d. 1683
James Cecil, 4th Earl of Salisbury 1666-94

> The library now at Hatfield House (moved there from London in the early 18th c.) was largely formed initially by William Cecil, Baron Burghley (1520-98) and his son the 1st Earl, and added to by successive generations of the family. A catalogue of 1637 shows ca.1900 books at Salisbury House, in London, then; books were also held in other family houses. A number of MSS originally owned by Burghley, which descended to Robert Bruce, 1st Earl of Ailesbury (1626-85), were auctioned in London, 21 Nov. 1687.
> *ODNB*. Sears Jayne, 168. The Marquis of Salisbury, 'The library at Hatfield House', *The Library*, 5th ser. 18 (1963): 83-7. D. Cecil, *The Cecils of Hatfield House* (London, 1973). R. Beadle, 'Medieval English manuscripts at auction, 1676-*c*.1700', *BC* 53 (2004): 46-63. *CHL* I 501, 510-13. Alston, *Inventory*. Armorials database.

Sir Moyle Finch *c*.1550-1614
Sir Heneage Finch 1580-1631
Heneage Finch, 1st Earl of Nottingham 1621-82
Heneage Finch, 3rd Earl of Winchilsea 1610-89
Heneage Finch, 4th Earl of Winchilsea 1672-1712

> This successful and prominent family of statesmen, lawyers, and landowners included numerous book owners although the history of the various family libraries is not currently clear. A few books survive with an armorial stamp attributed to Sir Moyle. Other armorial stamps can be attributed to later family members. The 4th Earl used an engraved armorial bookplate; he was succeeded by his uncle Heneage Finch, 5th Earl, for whom family books were sold by Thomas Osborne in 1758.
> *ODNB*. Franks 10492/*60. Armorials database.

John Harington, 2nd Baron Harington 1592-1614

> In 1616 Anne (*c*.1554-1620), widow of John, 1st Baron Harington (1539/40-1613) gave *c*.120 books to found a parish library for Oakham, Rutland; in 1626 her daughter Lucy, Countess of Bedford (1581-1627), gave books to Sidney Sussex College, Cambridge. Both sets are likely to have belonged originally to John, the 2nd Baron, and/or other members of the family.
> *ODNB*. Perkin, 309-10. *CHL* I 417. J. Scott-Warren, *Sir John Harington and the book as gift* (2001). L. Erne, *Shakespeare and the book trade* (2013), 198. Armorials database.

Henry Howard, Earl of Northampton 1540-1614

> Books with his armorial stamp survive and it is clear that he had an extensive library. Most, possibly all, of his books passed to his nephew Thomas, 2nd Earl of Arundel (1586-1646) and thence to Henry Howard, 6th Duke of Norfolk, and on to the Royal Society via his gift of 1667.

ODNB. N. Barker, 'The books of Henry Howard, Earl of Northampton', *BLR* 13 (1990): 375–81. M. Guerci, 'The construction of Northumberland House', *Antiquaries Journal* 90 (2010): 341–400. Armorials database.

Thomas Egerton, 1st Viscount Brackley 1540–1617
John Egerton, 1st Earl of Bridgewater 1579–1649
Frances Egerton, Countess of Bridgewater 1585–1636
John Egerton, 2nd Earl of Bridgewater 1623–86
John Egerton, 3rd Earl of Bridgewater 1646–1701

A dynasty of statemen and landowners who established what became known as the Bridgewater Library, begun by Thomas Egerton and added to significantly by his son John. John's wife, Frances, had her own collections of books; an inventory of 241 of 'my Ladies bookes at London', made in 1627, survives and is edited by Hackel. The Library began to be dispersed in the 19th c. and a significant portion of it was purchased by Henry Huntington in 1917, and is now in the Huntington Library.

ODNB. S. Pargeter, *A catalogue of the library at Tatton Park* (1977). S. Tabor, 'The Bridgewater Library', in W. Baker (ed.), *Pre-nineteenth-century British book collectors and bibliographers* (1999), 40–50. *Fine bindings 1500–1700 from Oxford libraries* (Bodleian Library, 1968), 146. Hackel, 240–81. M. Mendle, 'Preserving the ephemeral', in J. Andersen (ed.), *Books and readers in early modern England* (2002), 201–16 (on pamphlets in the collection). S. West, 'An architectural typology for the early modern country house library, 1660–1720', *The Library*, 7th ser. 14 (2013): 441–64, 460. L. Erne, *Shakespeare and the book trade* (2013), 202–6. Armorials database.

Henry Brooke, 11th Baron Cobham 1564–1619

Warden of the Cinque ports, imprisoned in his later years for plotting. Records show he had a personal library of over 700 volumes during his imprisonment in the Tower.

ODNB. P. Reid, 'Proto-bibliophiles amongst the English aristocracy, 1500–1700', *Library History* 18 (2002): 25–38.

Sir Edward Seymour, 1st Earl of Hertford 1539?–1621

Courtier. Books with his armorial stamp and inscription survive.

ODNB. Armorials database.

Charles Howard, 1st Earl of Nottingham 1536–1624

Lord Admiral under Elizabeth I. Books with his armorial stamp survive. Presented books/MSS to the Bodleian Library.

ODNB. Macray, 421. Armorials database.

Henry Wriothesley, 3rd Earl of Southampton 1573–1624

Courtier, literary patron. Gave £100 to the Bodleian in 1605; at the end of his life, he bought *c*.1,000 books and *c*.200 MSS of William Crashaw's to give to St John's College, Cambridge.

ODNB. Sears Jayne, 152.

Edward la Zouche, 11th Baron Zouche 1556–1625
Sir Edward Zouche d. 1634

Of Harringworth, Northamptonshire; diplomat. Bought the estate of Bramshill, Hampshire in 1605 where he built a new mansion, including a library. This was inherited by Sir Edward, whose probate inventory identifies a library room in the recently completed house, containing *c*.250 volumes.

ODNB. *CHL* I 507. J. Cliffe, *The world of the country house in seventeenth-century England* (1999), 163. Purcell, 63.

Robert Sidney, 1st Earl of Leicester 1563–1626
Robert Sidney, 2nd Earl of Leicester 1595–1677
Philip Sidney, 3rd Earl of Leicester 1619–98
Robert Sidney, 4th Earl of Leicester 1649–1702
Philip Sidney 5th Earl of Leicester 1676–1705
  The Sidney family library at Penshurst began to be developed in the 16th c. but was substantially built up by the 1st and 2nd Earls; a catalogue compiled by Gilbert Spencer in the 1650s/60s lists *c.*4,800 vols. After the death of the 2nd Earl it was less augmented by later family members, and the whole collection was sold at auction in 1743. A book with the 1st Earl's armorial stamp survives in the Clements Collection, V&A; the 5th Earl had a bookplate made dated 1704.
  ODNB. G. Warkentin & P. Hoare, 'Sophisticated Shakespeare', *PBSA* 100 (2006): 313–56. G. Warkentin et al., *The library of the Sidneys of Penshurst Place* (2013). Franks 28696–7, *41, *56. Armorials database.

Francis Bacon, Viscount St Alban 1561–1626
  Statesman, Lord Chancellor, philosopher. Numerous books survive with his armorial stamp.
  ODNB. CELM. D. Rogers, *The Bodleian Library and its treasures* (1991), 124–5. Armorials database.

Edward Russell, 3rd Earl of Bedford 1572–1627
Lucy Russell, Countess of Bedford 1581–1627
  A number of surviving books with variant forms of the Russell armorial crest indicate the existence of a library which has been suggested to be 'a joint interest' (Armorials database). Lucy bequeathed books from her own (Harington) family to Sidney Sussex College, Cambridge.
  ODNB. Armorials database.

George Villiers, 1st Duke of Buckingham 1592–1628
  Courtier and statesman. Books with his armorial stamp survive. Purchased the oriental MSS of Thomas Erpenius (d. 1624), which were then given to Cambridge University Library.
  ODNB. Oates, 164–7. Armorials database.

William Cavendish, 2nd Earl of Devonshire 1590–1628
  Archival evidence of book buying and binding, and surviving books (now at Chatsworth), show that he developed an extensive library at Hardwick Hall, partly with the help of his tutor, Thomas Hobbes. A catalogue of the late 1620s, made by Hobbes, lists *c.*1,400 books, probably then at Hardwick.
  ODNB. L. Peck, *Consuming splendor* (2005), 125–6. M. Purcell & N. Thwaite, 'Libraries at Hardwick, 1597–1957', in D. Adshead & D. Taylor (eds), *Hardwick Hall* (2016), 177–91. Armorials database.

George Carew, 1st Earl of Totnes 1555–1629
  Soldier and administrator, particularly involved in Irish affairs. Assembled an important collection of MSS on Irish history, now mostly divided between the Bodleian and Lambeth Palace Library. Numerous books with his armorial stamp survive; bequeathed his books to Sir Thomas Stafford (d. 1655), after whose death they were dispersed. Used several armorial stamps.
  ODNB. M. R. James, 'The Carew manuscripts', *English Historical Review* 42 (1927): 261–7. Armorials database. See above, p. 117.

Francis Fane, 1st Earl of Westmorland 1580–1629

Mildmay Fane, 2nd Earl of Westmorland 1602–66
   Landowners and politicians, of Apethorpe Hall, Northamptonshire; Francis was created Earl of Westmorland in 1624. His library above the gateway in the north range contained 210 books in 1629. Numerous books survive with the second Earl's inscription and motto, 'Solus Deus protector meus'.
   G. Morton, *A biography of Mildmay Fane* (1990). Pearson, *Provenance research*. Purcell, 63. Maggs 1121 (1990)/16; 1324 (2002)/26. Armorials database.

Sir James Ley, 1st Earl of Marlborough 1552–1629
   Lawyer and judge with antiquarian interests; his books, manuscripts, and works of art remained in the family for several generations. Books with his armorial stamps survive.
   ODNB. Armorials database.

William Paget, 4th Baron Paget 1572–1629
   Courtier and politician. Catalogue of *c*.1,550 books/MSS from his library, *c*.1617, in BL MS Harl.3267.
   ODNB. Sears Jayne, 147. T. Birrell, 'Reading as pastime: the place of light literature in some 17th-century gentlemen's libraries,' in R. Myers (ed.), *Property of a gentleman* (Winchester, 1991), 113–31, 118–19. P. Reid, 'Proto-bibliophiles amongst the English aristocracy, 1500–1700', *Library History* 18 (2002): 25–38.

Robert Ratcliffe, 5th Earl of Sussex 1573–1629
   Soldier and courtier. A book with his armorial stamp is in the British Library.
   ODNB. Armorials database.

William Herbert, 3rd Earl of Pembroke 1580–1630
   Courtier, politician, Chancellor of Oxford University, noted for his patronage of the arts. Books with his armorial stamps survive. Bought the Barocci collection of Greek MSS in 1629, most of which he gave to the Bodleian.
   ODNB. Macray, 68–72. Armorials database.

Edward Conway, 1st Viscount Conway *c*.1564–1631
   Soldier, diplomat, Secretary of State. Owned at least 500 books, documented in two catalogues, made *c*.1610 and at the time of his death. The first list (*c*.225 books) is edited as PLRE 266.
   ODNB. D. Smith, 'Sir Edward Conway', PLRE 9 (2017): 103–147.

Francis Manners, 6th Earl of Rutland 1578–1632
   Courtier and landowner. Books with his armorial stamp survive.
   ODNB. Armorials database.

Henry Percy, 9th Earl of Northumberland 1564–1632
   Estimated to have owned a library of over 1,250 books, of which several hundred survive today at Petworth and Alnwick. Gave £100 to the Bodleian in 1603. Books from his ownership sold at Sotheby's, 23–4 Apr. 1928.
   ODNB. Sears Jayne, 161. G. Batho, 'The library of the Wizard Earl', *The Library*, 5th ser. 15 (1960): 246–61. P. Reid, 'Proto-bibliophiles amongst the English aristocracy, 1500–1700', *Library History* 18 (2002): 25–38. L. Erne, *Shakespeare and the book trade* (2013), 211–12. Purcell, 86–89.

Richard Lovelace, 1st Baron Lovelace 1564–1634
   Soldier and politician. Gave 27 books to create a parish library at Hurley, Berkshire (all now lost).
   Foster. Perkin, 248.

Richard Robartes, 1st Baron Robartes *c.*1580–1634
John Robartes, 1st Earl of Radnor 1606–85
  Landowners, politicians, administrators. Developed the library at Lanhydrock House, Cornwall.
  ODNB. D. Keep, 'Works by Zurich reformers in the library at Lanhydrock', *National Trust Yearbook* (1976–7), 73–80. N. Barker, *Treasures from the libraries of National T rust country houses* (New York, 1999), no. 45. M. Purcell, 'The library at Lanhydrock', *BC* 54 (2005): 195–230.

Anne Southwell, Lady Southwell 1574–1636
  Author and poet. Daughter of Sir Thomas Harris, married Sir Thomas Southwell and, after his death in 1626, Captain Henry Sibthorpe. Her commonplace book, which includes original writings of hers, is now Folger MS V.b.198. In 1631, she moved three trunkfuls of books to her new household.
  ODNB. J. Cavanaugh, 'The library of Lady Southwell and Captain Sibthorpe', *Studies in Bibliography* 20 (1967): 243–54. H. Hackel, 'The Countess of Bridgewater's London library', in J. Andersen & E. Sauer (eds), *Books and readers* (2002), 138–59, 139.

John Holles, 1st Earl of Clare 1564–1637
John Holles, 2nd Earl of Clare 1595–1666
  Landowners, politicians, courtiers. The letters of the elder Holles include references to his book buying and reading; books with his armorial stamps survive. The Portland MSS (University of Nottingham) include a 1654 'Note of my books at Haughton in my upper closet and in an ould trunk', listing 200 books, and a 1658 'ancient note of my books', listing 403 books, belonging to the 2nd Earl.
  ODNB. P. R. Seddon (ed.), *Letters of John Holles, 1587–1637*, Thoroton Society Record Series 31, 35–6 (1975, 1983, 1986). University of Nottingham, Portland MSS Pw V 4 pp. 195–200, 185–92. Armorials database. See above, p. 32.

William Petre, 2nd Baron Petre 1575–1637
  Of Thorndon Hall, Essex; money was spent on decorating a study in the late 16th c. The Petre family accounts in Folger Library MS 1772 include a note of 35 books purchased. 'My Lords library' was estimated to be worth £35 in 1639.
  Sears Jayne, 141. G. Dawson, 'A gentleman's purse', *Yale Review* 39 (1950): 645. Purcell, 63.

Anne Carleton, Viscountess Dorchester d. 1639
  Daughter of Sir Henry Glenham; married firstly Paul Bayning, Viscount Bayning, and after his death in 1629, Dudley Carleton, Viscount Dorchester (1574–1632). On her death, she left books valued at *c.*£77.
  F. Steer, 'The inventory of Anne, Viscountess Dorchester', *Notes & Queries* 198 (1953). H. Hackel, 'The Countess of Bridgewater's London library', in J. Andersen & E. Sauer (eds), *Books and readers* (2002), 138–59, 139.

Lord William Howard 1563–1640
  Of Naworth Castle; antiquary. Assembled a significant library of medieval MSS and printed books; the MSS were dispersed after his death but *c.*250 books remained at Naworth until sold at Sotheby's, 15 Dec. 1992; these were bought en bloc by Durham University Library. Gave £100 worth of books to St John's College, Cambridge, in 1629.
  ODNB. E. Rainey, 'The library of Lord William Howard', *Friends of the National Libraries, Annual Report for 1992*, 20–23. R. Ovenden, 'The manuscript library of Lord William Howard of Naworth', in J. Willoughby and J. Catto (eds), *Books and bookmen in early modern Britain* (Toronto, 2018), 278–318. Armorials database.

Nicholas Sanderson, 2nd Viscount Castleton 1593-1640
Lincolnshire landowner. Books with his armorial stamp survive.
Foster. Armorials database.

Thomas Wentworth, 1st Earl of Strafford 1593-1641
William Wentworth, 2nd Earl of Strafford 1626-90
The 1st Earl was a prominent statesman, Lord Lieutenant of Ireland; his son led a less
public life. Books with both their armorial stamps survive; many of their books seem to
have stayed in the family over succeeding generations.
ODNB. Armorials database. Maggs 1075 (1987)/20, 1075 (1987)/22.

Thomas Windsor, 6th Baron Windsor 1591-1641
Courtier, rear admiral of the Navy. Numerous books with his armorial stamps survive.
Armorials database.

Henry Hastings, 5th Earl of Huntingdon 1586-1643
Ferdinando Hastings, 6th Earl of Huntingdon 1609-56
Theophilus Hastings, 7th Earl of Huntingdon 1650-1701
Rutland landowners. Books with their various armorial stamps survive. The Hastings MSS in
the Huntington Library include a list of 17 books purchased by the 5th Earl, 1638-40.
ODNB. Armorials database.

Robert Devereux, 3rd Earl of Essex 1591-1646
Courtier, parliamentary soldier. An inventory of his books and MSS, made in 1646
(ca.150 volumes), is in BL Add. MS 46189, fos 155-8.
ODNB. V. Snow, 'An inventory of the Lord General's library, 1646', *The Library*, 5th ser.
21 (1966): 115-123.

Thomas Howard, 14th Earl of Arundel 1586-1646
Politician and art collector. Collections partly dispersed after his death. His printed
books were given to the Royal Society in 1666 by his grandson Henry Howard, 6th Duke
of Norfolk.
ODNB. R. Ovenden, 'Thomas Howard', in W. Baker (ed.), *Pre-nineteenth-century British
book collectors and bibliographers* (1999), 155-63. L. Peck, *Consuming splendour* (2005),
126-9. *CHL* I 518-19, 544. Armorials database.

Henry Somerset, 1st Marquess of Worcester 1577-1646
Of Raglan Castle, Monmouthshire, Royalist in the Civil War. He 'read devotional books
in his Closet, weeping over them as he said his prayers and inviting his gentlemen to join
him after dinner and share them'.
Dictionary of Welsh biography. Purcell, 63.

Oliver St John, 1st Earl of Bolingbroke *c.*1584-1646
Politician, parliamentarian. Books with his armorial stamps survive.
ODNB. Armorials database.

John Brudenell 1584-1647
Thomas Brudenell, 1st Earl of Cardigan 1578-1663
Of Deene, Northamptonshire. Thomas married the daughter of Sir Thomas Tresham
(1547-1605) and thereby inherited his library (*c.*1,700 vols), to which he steadily added.
Many of his books survive today at Deene Park, Northamptonshire (despite the temporary sequestration of the library during the Civil War). Books also survive, at Deene
and elsewhere, with the armorial stamp associated with Thomas's younger brother John.
J. Wake, *The Brudenells of Deene* (London, 1954). N. Barker and D. Quentin, *The library
of Thomas Tresham and Thomas Brudenell* (2006). Armorials database.

Sir William Paston 1610–63
Robert Paston, 1st Earl of Yarmouth 1631–83
   Of Oxnead Hall, Norfolk. Sir William began the development of the family library (and
   other collections), continued by his son Robert; the books were auctioned in London, 10
   Apr. 1734 (1,513 lots).
   ODNB. West. A. Moore et al. (eds), *The Paston treasure: microcosm of the known world* (2018).

Ferdinando Fairfax, 2nd Baron Fairfax 1584–1648
   Parliamentarian army officer, governor of York in the 1640s. As well as being noted for saving
   York Minster Library at this time, he gave over 400 volumes from his personal library.
   ODNB. C. Barr, 'The Minster Library', in G. Aylmer & R. Cant (eds), *A history of York
   Minster* (1977), 487–539. Cambers, 149.

Edward Herbert, Baron Herbert of Cherbury 1582?–1648
   Bequeathed his Latin and Greek books to Jesus College, Oxford, *c*.900 volumes. Also
   established a library at Montgomery Castle, Wales; numerous books survive today in
   Powis Castle and elsewhere.
   ODNB. CELM. C. Fordyce & T. Knox, 'The library of Jesus College, Oxford', *OBS
   Proceedings & Papers* (1937): 62–3. Sotheby's 16–18 Jan. 1956, portion of the library
   of Powis Castle, 'in part derived from the libraries of Edward First Lord Herbert of
   Cherbury'. D. Roberts, '"Abundantly replenisht with books of his own purchasing and
   choyce": Lord Herbert of Cherbury's library at Montgomery Castle', *Library &
   Information History* 31 (2015): 117–36. D. Roberts, 'The chained parish library of
   Chirbury', *The Library* 19 (2018): 469–83. D. Roberts, *The library of Edward Lord
   Herbert of Chirbury* (forthcoming). Armorials database.

William Percy 1574–1648
   Poet and playwright, 3rd son of Henry Percy, 8th Earl of Northumberland (*c*.1532–85).
   A group of *c*.150 Elizabethan and Jacobean plays, now at Petworth House, was probably
   assembled by him.
   ODNB. E. Miller, 'A collection of Elizabethan and Jacobean plays at Petworth', *National
   Trust Yearbook* (1975–6), 62–4.

Elizabeth Talbot Grey, Countess of Kent 1581–1651
   Daughter and co-heir of Gilbert Talbot, 7th Earl of Shrewsbury. First married Henry
   Grey, Earl of Kent (d. 1639), then apparently married John Selden, to whom much of her
   property passed, including books. Some but not all of these went to the Bodleian. Books
   with her armorial stamp survive.
   ODNB. CHL I 321. Armorials database.

Anne Stanhope, dowager Countess of Clare d. 1651
   The Portland MSS in the University of Nottingham include 'A note of my mothers
   book[s] writ with her own hand', dated 1649, listing 164 books.
   University of Nottingham, Portland MSS Pw V 4 pp. 192–4.

James Stanley, 7th Earl of Derby 1607–51
Charles Stanley, 8th Earl of Derby 1628–72
William Stanley, 9th Earl of Derby 1655–1702
   Politicians, administrators, landowners. Books with their armorial stamps are known.
   William, 9th Earl is listed in Edward Bernard's *Catalogi manuscriptorum* (1697) as
   owning a small number of manuscripts. His library was auctioned in Liverpool, 9 June
   1707 (2,035 lots).
   ODNB. Maggs 1075 (1987)/73, 82. Alston, *Inventory*. Armorials database.

Edward Sackville, 4th Earl of Dorset 1590–1652
> Soldier and courtier. Books with his armorial stamp survive.
> *ODNB.* Armorials database.

Henry Bourchier, 5th Earl of Bath *c.*1587–1654
> Royalist soldier, Keeper of the Privy Seal. Known to have been a 'lover of learning', whose library was sold soon after his death.
> *ODNB.*

Edward Conway, 2nd Viscount Conway 1594–1655
> Politician and soldier. Numerous books survive with his armorial stamp; 50 books, together with a MS catalogue of his library listing *c.*9,900 titles, are in the Robinson Library, Armagh. His library was sequestered by the Long Parliament, but bought back by him in 1647; it descended through his daughter to the Marquis of Hastings and was eventually sold at auction in 1868.
> *ODNB.* H. R. Plomer, 'A cavalier's library', *The Library*, 2nd ser. 5 (1904): 158–72. Roy. D. Smith, '"La conquest du sang real": Edward, second Viscount Conway's quest for books', in J. Hinks and M. Day (eds), *From compositors to collectors* (2012), 199–216. L. Erne, *Shakespeare and the book trade* (2013), 207–9. Purcell, 93. Armorials database.

Philip Stanhope, 1st Earl of Chesterfield 1584–1656
> Gave 55 books to Sidney Sussex College, Cambridge, *c.*1630. Books with his armorial stamp survive.
> *ODNB.* Sears Jayne, 156. Armorials database.

Walter Devereux, 5th Viscount Hereford 1578–1657
> Landowner, politician, administrator. Books survive with his coronetted monogram stamp.
> *HoP.* Armorials database.

Robert Rich, 2nd Earl of Warwick 1587–1658
> Colonial developer, admiral of the parliamentary fleet. Books with his armorial stamp survive.
> *ODNB.* Armorials database.

William Seymour, 2nd Duke of Somerset 1587–1660
> Statesman, royalist army officer. Books with his armorial stamp survive. His library was given to Lichfield Cathedral by his widow, Frances, in 1673.
> *ODNB. CHL* II 125. Armorials database.

Christopher Hatton, 1st Baron Hatton 1605–70
> Politician, antiquary. 112 MSS from his celebrated library were bought by the Bodleian Library after his death. Numerous monastic cartularies owned by him are now among the Cotton MSS in the British Library. Books with his armorial stamp survive.
> *ODNB.* Philip, 56–8. D. Pinto, 'The music of the Hattons', *Royal Musical Assoc. Research Chronicle* 23 (1990): 79–108. J. P. Wainwright, *Musical patronage in seventeenth-century England* (1997). D. Pinto, 'Placing Hatton's great set', *Chelys* 32 (2004): 1–20. M. Foot, *The Henry Davis gift*, vol. 2 (1983), no. 97. N. Stacey, 'Antiquarian patronage in the 17th century: Sir Christopher Hatton's library at Kirby Hall', *English Heritage Historical review* 9 (2014), 66–81. Maggs 1075 (1987)/33, 39. Armorials database.

Sir John Scudamore, 1st Viscount Scudamore 1601–71
> Politician, diplomat, courtier. Noted by Hartlib as 'a great scholar' in the 1640s; books with his armorial stamp survive. Gave books to Hereford Cathedral.
> *ODNB.* Armorials database.

Thomas Fairfax, 3rd Baron Fairfax 1612–71
Parliamentary general. An active reader and writer, and collector of coins and engravings. Noted for having protected the Bodleian from looting when Oxford was captured; bequeathed 129 medieval MSS to the Bodleian, and the MSS collections which were left to him by Roger Dodsworth.
ODNB. Philip, 57. Armorials database.

Anne Hyde, Duchess of York 1637–71
Daughter of Edward Hyde, Earl of Clarendon, and wife of James Duke of York (later James II). Books with her armorial stamps survive.
ODNB. Armorials database.

Thomas Leigh, 1st Baron Leigh 1596–1672
Lanowner, politician. Books with his armorial stamps survive.
ODNB. Armorials database.

Edward Hyde, 1st Earl of Clarendon 1609–74
Henry Hyde, 2nd Earl of Clarendon 1638–1709
The 1st Earl was Charles II's Lord Chancellor until forced into exile in 1667; his son also had a career as a statesman, was Lord Lieutenant of Ireland under James II, and became a nonjuror. The 1st Earl established a significant library, augmented by his son; the combined library was estimated to contain 6350 volumes. The 2nd Earl was listed in Edward Bernard's *Catalogi manuscriptorum* (1697) as owning 140 MSS. A London retail sale of 'the library of a person of honour', identified as the 2nd Earl, has been variously dated 1701, 1703, and 1709, but it is possible this sale did not take place. At least some of the Hyde library was sold to James Brydges, Duke of Chandos (1674–1744), whose library was auctioned in London, 12 Mar. 1747. An auction of the manuscripts of the first 3 Earls of Clarendon was held in London, 9 Apr. 1764.
ODNB. *CELM.* Franks *59. P. Hardacre, 'Portrait of a bibliophile: I: Edward Hyde', *BC* 7 (1958): 361–8. 'The Ware–Clarendon manuscripts', *BLR* 6 (1960): 586–7. L. Gwynn, 'The architecture of the English domestic library, 1600–1700', *Library & Information History* 26 (2010): 56–69. Alston, *Inventory.* Armorials database.

John Mordaunt, 1st Viscount Mordaunt 1626–75
Courtier, governor of Windsor Castle. A few books with his armorial stamp survive.
ODNB. Armorials database.

Robert Greville, 4th Baron Brooke 1638?–76
Diplomat, Recorder of Warwick. Library auctioned in London, 2 Dec. 1678 (joint sale, with one other).
Foster. Alston, *Inventory.*

Margaret Cavendish, Duchess of Newcastle 1623?–73
William Cavendish, 1st Duke of Newcastle 1592–1676
Henry Cavendish, 2nd Duke of Newcastle 1630–91
John Holles, 3rd Duke of Newcastle 1662–1711
Statesmen and landowners. The libraries of the three dukes were sold at fixed price in London, 2 Mar. 1719 (3,244 lots). The 3rd Duke used several engraved armorial bookplates. Margaret, wife of the 1st Duke, is best remembered for her writings; no particular personal library of hers has been identified, but some of her reading has been deduced from the contents of the sale catalogue.
ODNB. Franks 15108–9/*20. J. Crawford, 'Margaret Cavendish's books', in L. Knight (ed.), *Women's bookscapes in early modern Britain* (Ann Arbor, MI, 2018), 94–114. Armorials database.

Anne Clifford, Countess of Pembroke 1590–1676
Noblewoman who acquired significant wealth through inheritance and marriage. Several books with her armorial stamps survive, together with other evidence of her extensive ownership and reading of books. Her library is famously pictorially represented in a painting of 1646; an attempt has been made to reconstruct her library, based on that (PLRE 277).
ODNB. CELM. D. Clifford (ed.), *The diaries of Lady Anne Clifford* (1990). R. Spence, *Lady Anne Clifford* (1997). Hackel 222–40. Richard Kuhta, '"I beegane, to ovrloke this booke…": Lady Anne Clifford's copy of *Titles of honor*', in G. T. Tanselle (ed.), *Other people's books* (2011), 42–5. Leah Price, 'Lady Anne Clifford', PLRE 9 (2017): 346–63. L. Knight, 'Reading proof: or, problems and possibilities in the text life of Anne Clifford', in L. Knight et al. (eds), *Women's bookscapes in early modern Britain* (Ann Arbor, MI, 2018), 253–73. R. Harding, '"Scraps of insignificant scribbling": the Rev. Dr. Thomas Raffles and a lost book from the library of Lady Anne Clifford', *Poetica* 89, 90 (2018): 123–38. Purcell, 63. Armorials database.

George Digby, 2nd Earl of Bristol 1612–77
Politician, soldier, 'one of the foremost English examples of irresponsible brilliance' (*ODNB*). Bought much of Sir Kenelm Digby's Paris library after his death in 1665, and returned it to England. Library auctioned in London, 19 Apr. 1680 (joint sale, with one other).
ODNB. Alston, *Inventory.*

Anne Bayning, Viscountess Bayning 1619–78
Wife of Sir John Baber, physician to Charles II. Created Viscountess Bayning 1673. Books with her armorial monogram stamps survive.
Complete peerage. Armorials database.

Mary Rich, Countess of Warwick 1624–78
Wife of Charles Rich, 4th Earl of Warwick. Her MS diaries (BL Add MS 27351–5) contain extensive references to her reading in her closet.
ODNB. Cambers, 48–50.

William Ducie, 1st Viscount Downe 1615?–79
Of Tortworth, Gloucestershire. Library auctioned in London, 1680 (1,720 lots).
Alston, *Inventory.*

Nicholas Tufton, 3rd Earl of Thanet 1631–79
High sheriff of Westmorland. An inventory taken in 1664 shows him to have had a library of *c.*100 vols.
P. Reid, 'Proto-bibliophiles amongst the English aristocracy, 1500–1700', *Library History* 18 (2002): 25–38.

William Brereton, 3rd Baron Brereton 1631–80
Politician, musician, founder member of the Royal Society. Library auctioned in London, 8 June 1697 (1,051 lots).
ODNB. Alston, *Inventory.*

Anne Fanshawe, Lady Fanshawe 1625–80
Elder daughter of John Harrison of Balls, Herts; married Sir Richard Fanshawe (1608–66). Several books survive with her armorial stamp; noted for her autobiographical journal (BL Add MS 41161).
ODNB. Armorials database.

Henry Pierrepont, Marquis of Dorchester 1606–80
Statesman and courtier, with scientific and botanical interests. His library of *c.*2,000 books was bequeathed to the Royal College of Physicians, where much of it remains today.

ODNB. J. Fulton, 'The library of Henry Pierrepont', *Journal of the History of Medicine* 14 (1959): 89–90. L. Payne & C. Newman, 'The Dorchester Library', *Journal of the Royal College of Physicians* 4 (1970): 234–45. Purcell, 95.

James Compton, 3rd Earl of Northampton 1622–81
Landowner, administrator, playwright. About 250 books were seized from his home by the London Committee for Sequestration in 1643, and sold for £57 3s. 6d. His MS plays and translations, long held at Castle Ashby, are now in the British Library.
ODNB. Roy. W. P. Williams, 'The Castle Ashby manuscripts', *The Library*, 6th ser. 2 (1980), 391–412.

John Maitland, 1st Duke of Lauderdale 1616–82
Statesman and politician. Acquired books throughout his career, and had a sizeable library at Ham House, where he incorporated the handsome library room in the mid-1670s which still survives. Library auctioned in London, in a series of sales between 1687 and 1692. Books with his armorial stamp survive.
ODNB. P. Thornton & M. Tomlin, *The furnishing and decoration of Ham House* (London, 1980). R. Beadle, 'Medieval English manuscripts at auction, 1676–c.1700', *BC* 53 (2004): 46–63. M. Purcell, 'The library at Ham House', *BC* 55 (2006): 509–24. G. Mandelbrote, 'The library of the Duke of Lauderdale', in C. Rowell (ed.), *Ham House* (2013), 222–31. S. West, 'An architectural typology for the early modern country house library, 1660–1720', *The Library*, 7th ser, 14 (2013), 441–64. Armorials database. Alston, *Inventory.*

Arthur Capell, 1st Earl of Essex 1631–83
Algernon Capell, 2nd Earl of Essex 1670–1710
Politicians and landowners. The 1st Earl formed a large library at his house at Cashiobury, described by John Evelyn as 'very nobly furnished, and all the books richly bound'. A MS catalogue of the library, made by William Stanley 1681–3, is now in the Grolier Club Library. His son the 2nd Earl, who inherited the Cashiobury estate, used an armorial stamp and an engraved armorial bookplate dated 1701.
ODNB. Lasting impressions: the Grolier Club Library (2004), 66. Franks 5079–80/*54/ *57. Armorials database.

Anthony Ashley Cooper, 1st Earl of Shaftesbury 1621–83
Anthony Ashley Cooper, 2nd Earl of Shaftesbury 1652–99
Anthony Ashley Cooper, 3rd Earl of Shaftesbury 1671–1713
Politicians, statesmen, landowners; the 3rd Earl's *Characteristicks of men* was published in 1710. The 1st Earl inherited a house and estate at St Giles, Wimborne, from his mother, Anne Ashley; an inventory of the estate made in 1639 lists 'the books that were in the study next to the white room most of them now being removed by Sir Anthony', valued at £10. The probate inventory of the 2nd Earl, made in 1699, lists 'Books in several volumes bought by my late Lord (the great Library being the present Earl's)'.
ODNB. L. Cooper (ed.), *Two 17th century Dorset inventories* (Dorset Record Society, 1974).

Henry Bennet, 1st Earl of Arlington 1620?–85
Politician, Secretary of State. Books with his armorial stamp survive. John Evelyn described his library at Euston Hall as 'full of excellent books'; his correspondence includes instructions on the choice and purchase of books.
ODNB. H. Jacobsen, *Luxury and power* (2012), ch. 5. Armorials database. See above, p. 123.

Robert Bruce, 1st Earl of Ailesbury 1626–85
  Lord Chamberlain. Noted as a collector of manuscripts and antiquities. Library auctioned in London, 19 May 1690 (1,275 lots).
  ODNB. Alston, *Inventory*.

Arthur Annesley, 1st Earl of Anglesey 1614–86
  Politician, Lord Privy Seal. Amassed one of the larger libraries of his time, auctioned in London 25 Oct. 1686 (6,564 lots). Known to have bought other libraries en bloc.
  ODNB. D. McKitterick, *Cambridge University Library: a history*, vol. 2 (1986), 118. R. Beadle, 'Medieval English manuscripts at auction, 1676–c.1700', *BC* 53 (2004): 46–63. Birrell, 'Books and buyers', 60–62. Mandelbrote, 'Auctions', 24. Cambers, 133. N. Malcolm, 'The library of Henry Oldenburg', *eBLJ* (2005): article 7. Alston, *Inventory*.

Horatio Townshend, 1st Viscount Townshend 1630–87
  Politician and landowner. Surviving book bills and correspondence testify to the existence of a substantial library at his house at Raynham, Norfolk, developed during his lifetime.
  ODNB. J. Rosenheim, *The Townshends of Raynham* (1989). West.

Christopher Monck, 2nd Duke of Albemarle 1650–88
  Governor of Jamaica. Books with his armorial stamp, probably also used by his father, George Monck, 1st Duke (1608–70), survive. The library passed, through his wife's second marriage, to the Dukes of Montague.
  ODNB. Armorials database.

William Wentworth, 2nd Earl of Strafford 1626–90
  Son of the first Earl, restored to the title after the execution of his father. Books with his armorial stamps survive.
  Armorials database.

Francis Holles, 2nd Baron Holles 1627–90
  Son of the parliamentarian Denzil Holles (1599–1680), MP. A few books with his armorial stamp survive.
  HoP. Armorials database.

John Stawell, 2nd Baron Stawell 1669?–92
  Landowner, of Somerton, Somerset. Library auctioned in London, 3 Dec. 1695 (1,905 lots), 4 Feb. 1696 (1,792 lots).
  Foster. Alston, *Inventory*.

Robert Spencer, Viscount Teviot 1629–94
  Politician and administrator. Books with his armorial stamp survive.
  HoP. Armorials database. Maggs 1495 (2017)/90.

Henry Booth, 1st Earl of Warrington 1652–94
  Statesman, *custos rotulorum* for the county of Chester. Although the family house and library at Dunham Massey were substantially enhanced by his son George, the 2nd Earl (1675–1758), it is clear that many of the 17th-c. books there were acquired by Henry, whose posthumously published works make it clear that he had a substantial private library.
  ODNB. E. Potten, '"A great number of usefull books": the hidden library of Henry Booth', *Library & Information History* 25 (2009): 33–49.

Anthony Cary, 5th Viscount Falkland 1656–94
  Politician, First Lord of the Admiralty. Library sold by retail sale in London (presumably prompted by the death of his widow in 1709), 20 July 1710 (no catalogue survives).
  ODNB. Alston, *Inventory*.

Richard Graham, 1st Viscount Preston 1648–95
   Politician, disgraced as a Jacobite, translator of Boethius. Library auctioned in London, 9 Nov. 1696, 24 Nov. 1697 (pt 1, 1,482 lots; pt 2, 1,142).
   ODNB. Alston, *Inventory.*

George Savile, 1st Marquis of Halifax 1633–95
William Savile, 2nd Marquis of Halifax 1664/5–1701
   Landowners and politicians. Catalogues of the early 1690s, now in Cambridge UL, indicate a library of *c.*2,000 volumes. Library auctioned in London, beginning sometime in 1701, and continuing 2 Aug. 1701, 25 Nov. 1701 (no catalogues survive).
   ODNB. CELM. Alston, *Inventory.*

William Craven, Earl of Craven 1608–97
   Lanowner, soldier, administrator. Library sold in London by retail sale, 16 Oct. 1697 (no catalogue survives). His books apparently included the library of Prince Rupert of the Rhone, inherited on his death in 1682.
   ODNB. Alston, *Inventory.*

Henry Mordaunt, 2nd Earl of Peterborough 1624?–97
   Courtier, politician. Bought books at the Richard Smith sale of 1682. Listed in Edward Bernard's *Catalogi manuscriptorum* (1697) as owning 42 manuscripts.
   ODNB.

George Berkeley, 1st Earl Berkeley 1628–98
   Landowner, politician, governor of the Levant Company. Inherited a library of books made by Sir Robert Coke (1587–1653, who married his aunt); gave 555 volumes to Sion College in 1681, and bequeathed the remainder to the College.
   ODNB. E. Pearce, *Sion College and Library* (1913), 258–60. Armorials database.

James Bertie, 1st Earl of Abingdon 1653–99
   Landowner, Lord Lieutenant of Oxfordshire. Used an engraved armorial bookplate.
   Complete peerage. Franks 2370/*43.

William Maynard, 2nd Baron Maynard 1623–99
   Landowner, administrator. His house at Westoe Manor, Cambridgeshire included a library of *c.*220 books in 1660.
   Complete peerage. A. Wright (ed), *A history of the county of Cambridge and the Isle of Ely*, vol. 6 (1978), 36–48.

Robert Bertie, 3rd Earl of Lindsey 1630–1701
   Landowner, administrator. Books with his armorial stamp survive.
   HoP. Armorials database.

Anthony Grey, 11th Earl of Kent 1645–1702
   Landowner and courtier. Used two engraved bookplates, dated 1702; amended versions of the plate were used by later members of the family.
   Complete peerage. Lee, *British*, 30. Franks 12827/*35. Maggs 1212 (1996)/41.

Bridget Bennet, Lady Ossulston 1650–1703
   Wife of John Bennet, politician, 1st Baron Ossulston (1616–95). Two separate library lists of hers, dated 1680 and 1699, show that she had over 200 books.
   ODNB. M.-L. Coolahan and M. Empey, 'Women's book ownership and the reception of early modern women's texts', in L. Knight et al. (eds), *Women's bookscapes in early modern Britain* (Ann Arbor, MI, 2018), 231–52.

Lionel Boyle, 3rd Earl of Orrery 1670–1703
Landowner, MP for East Grinstead. Library sold by retail sale in London, 5 Oct. 1703 (no catalogue survives).
HoP. Alston, *Inventory.*

Robert Russell *c.*1644–1703
Younger son of the 1st Duke of Bedford; MP for Tavistock 1689. Library sold in London by retail sale, 14 Oct. 1703 (no catalogue survives).
HoP. Alston, *Inventory.*

Henry Yelverton, 1st Viscount de Longueville 1664–1704
Landowner. Inherited many books from his father and grandfather; the library of his father, Sir Henry (d. 1670), was valued at £1,500. Many books with his 'HL' stamp survive. The Yelverton family books were said by Carew Hazlitt to have been sold in London in 1784. A catalogue of his library, made in 1694, is in BL Hargrave MS 107. Used engraved armorial bookplates dated 1702. Listed in Edward Bernard's *Catalogi manuscriptorum* (1697) as owning 187 manuscripts.
Complete peerage. J. Cliffe, *The world of the country house in seventeenth-century England* (1999), 168. Franks *100/*103. Armorials database.

Edward Radcliffe, 2nd Earl of Derwentwater 1655–1705
Landowner. Used an engraved armorial bookplate dated 1702.
Complete peerage. Franks 24441/*45.

Charles Sackville, 6th Earl of Dorset 1643–1706
Politician, poet, and literary patron. Used engraved armorial bookplates made *c.*1700.
ODNB. Lee, *British*, 28. Franks 25914–5/*30–1.

Henry Hare, 2nd Baron Coleraine 1636–1708
MP for Old Sarum; antiquary. Numerous books with his armorial stamp are known. After his grandson, the 3rd Earl, died without heirs in 1749, the family books were sold in London in 1754.
ODNB. Armorials database.

Hans Willem Bentinck, 5th Earl of Portland 1649–1709
Soldier and statesman, of Bulstrode Park, Buckinghamshire. Used an engraved armorial bookplate dated 1704.
ODNB. Franks 2257/*113.

Mary Dormer, Countess of Carnarvon 1655–1709
Second wife of Charles Dormer, 2nd Earl of Carnarvon. Books survive with her coronetted binding stamps.
Armorials database.

John Leveson-Gower, 1st Baron Gower 1675–1709
MP for Newcastle under Lyme 1692, Chancellor of the Duchy of Lancaster 1702. Used engraved armorial bookplates.
ODNB. Franks 12390/*119/*137.

John Lovelace, 4th Baron Lovelace d. 1709
Soldier, governor of New York; of Hurley, Buckinghamshire. Used an engraved armorial bookplate dated 1704.
ODNB. Franks *87.

Ralph Montagu, 1st Duke of Montagu 1638–1709
Politician and diplomat. Used an engraved armorial bookplate dated 1705; books with his armorial stamp survive.
ODNB. Franks *11. Armorials database.

Charles Fanshawe, 4th Viscount Fanshawe 1643–1710
Diplomat, soldier, administrator. Library sold by retail sale in London, 12 June 1710 (no catalogue survives).
HoP. Alston, *Inventory*.

John Thompson, 1st Baron Haversham 1647–1710
Politician. Library sold in London by retail sale, 13 Mar. 1711 (293 lots, perhaps not his entire library?).
ODNB. Alston, *Inventory*.

Fulke Greville, 5th Baron Brooke 1643–1710
MP and Recorder for Warwick. Used an engraved armorial bookplate dated 1705.
HoP. Franks *76.

Laurence Hyde, 1st Earl of Rochester 1642–1711
Politician and diplomat. Used an engraved armorial bookplate.
ODNB. Franks *106.

Thomas Coventry, 2nd Earl of Coventry d. 1711
Recorder of Coventry. Used an engraved armorial bookplate dated 1705.
Complete peerage. Franks *108.

William Craven, 2nd Baron Craven 1668–1711
Of Coombe Abbey, Warwickshire; Lord Lieutenant of Berkshire. Used an engraved armorial bookplate.
Complete peerage. Franks 7271-2/*74.

John Manners, 1st Duke of Rutland 1638–1711
Politician and landowner. Used an engraved armorial bookplate.
ODNB. Franks 19636-7.

Edward Villiers, 1st Earl of Jersey 1655?–1711
Politician and diplomat. Used an engraved armorial bookplate. Library sold by retail sale in London, 25 Nov. 1712 (joint sale; no catalogue survives).
ODNB. Alston, *Inventory*. Franks *69.

Thomas Osborne, Duke of Leeds 1632–1712
Politician and courtier. Used engraved armorial bookplates dated 1701. A catalogue of his library, made in 1686, is in British Library Egerton MS 3394.
ODNB. Franks 22435/*14/*21. Maggs 1272 (1999)/134.

William Paget, 6th Baron Paget 1637–1713
Politician and diplomat. Used engraved armorial bookplates.
ODNB. Franks *90/*117.

Philip Stanhope, 2nd Earl of Chesterfield 1634–1713
Politician and courtier. Books with his armorial stamp survive.
ODNB. Armorials database.

James Brydges, 8th Baron Chandos 1642–1714
Ambassador of the Turkey Company at Constantinople. Used an engraved armorial bookplate.
Complete peerage. Franks *75.

Baptist Noel, 3rd Earl of Gainsborough 1684–1714
Landowner and courtier. Both he and his wife, Dorothy, used a series of engraved armorial bookplates.
Complete peerage. Franks 21939–42/*39.

Henry Somerset, 2nd Duke of Beaufort 1684–1714
Politician and landowner. Used armorial book stamps, and engraved armorial bookplates dated 1705, 1706; a bookplate dated 1706 was also made for his wife, Rachel (d. 1709).
ODNB. Franks 27572–3/*4. Armorials database.

Thomas Thynne, Viscount Weymouth 1640–1714
Politician and landowner, of Longleat, Wiltshire. Used an engraved armorial bookplate dated 1704, as did his son Henry, who predeceased him (1675–1708).
ODNB. J. Collins, *A short account of the library at Longleat House* (Sotheby's, 1980). *CHL* I 501. Franks 29448/*217.

Philippa Mohun, Baroness Mohun d. 1715
Daughter of Arthur Annesley, Earl of Anglesey; married firstly Charles Mohun, 4th Baron Mohun (d. 1677), and secondly (sometime after 1683) William Coward. In 1679 she placed a newspaper advertisement, as Lady Mohun, offering a reward for a number of books stolen from her closet.
Complete peerage. H. Hackel, 'The Countess of Bridgewater's London library', in J. Andersen & E. Sauer (eds), *Books and readers* (2002), 138–59, 139.

Charles Montagu, 1st Earl of Halifax 1661–1715
Politician and landowner. Books with his armorial stamp survive. Used engraved armorial bookplates dated 1702. Library auctioned in London, 11 Apr. 1740, along with that of his nephew George Montagu (d. 1739, also 1st Earl, of the 3rd creation).
ODNB. Franks 20877–8/*68/*71. Armorials database.

Astrologers

John Booker 1602–67
Astrologer, almanac compiler. His books were bought from his widow by Elias Ashmole in 1667, for £140.
ODNB. H. A. Feisenberger, *Sale catalogues of libraries of eminent persons*, 11: *Scientists* (London, 1975), 3.

William Lilly 1602–81
Astrologer. His books were bought after his death for £50 by Elias Ashmole; 146 books in the Ashmolean collection can be identified as being Lilly's.
ODNB. R. T. Gunther, 'The Ashmole printed books', *BQR* 6 (1930), 193–5. H. A. Feisenberger, *Sale catalogues of libraries of eminent persons*, 11: *Scientists* (London, 1975), 3.

John Gadbury 1627–1704
Astrologer, almanac compiler. Library sold by retail sale in London, 29 Nov. 1704 (joint sale, with several others). Listed in Edward Bernard's *Catalogi manuscriptorum* (1697) as owning 4 astrological manuscripts.
ODNB. Alston, *Inventory.*

John Partridge 1644–1715
Astrologer, almanac compiler. Library auctioned in London, 13 Jan. 1718 (606 lots).
ODNB. Alston, *Inventory.*

Authors, poets, dramatists

People are listed here if their main occupation was a literary one, and/or they do not fit better under another heading (e.g. gentry, or civil servants; there are people on those lists who are also remembered as writers).

John Florio 1553–1625
> Lexicographer, author, language tutor at the court of James I. Florio's will refers to *c.*340 Italian, French, and Spanish books, bequeathed to the Earl of Pembroke, and to an unknown number of English books, left to his wife.
> *ODNB.*

Edward Alleyn 1566–1626
> Actor and theatre owner, founder of Dulwich College. Bequeathed his books to the college; 26 are listed in a contemporary MS.
> *ODNB.*

Gabriel Harvey 1552/3–1631
> Writer, scholar, and (briefly) barrister in the Court of Arches. About 180 volumes from his library survive today, in numerous collections, often distinguished by their extensive annotations.
> *ODNB. CELM.* V. Stern, *Gabriel Harvey: his life, marginalia and library* (1979). L. Jardine & A. Grafton, ' "Studied for action": how Gabriel Harvey read his Livy', *Past & Present* 129 (1990): 30–78. R. Shaddy, 'Gabriel Harvey', in W. Baker (ed.), *Pre-nineteenth-century British book collectors and bibliographers* (1999), 131–46.

John Marston 1576–1634
Mary Marston d. 1657
> Poet and playwright; later an ordained clergyman. In his will, he bequeathed all his goods to his wife, Mary. When she died, she left to her kinsman Matthew Poore 'a trunk full of books, with lock and key and a book of martyrs in 3 volumes not in the trunk'.
> *ODNB.* J. Marston, ed. A. B. Grosart, *The poems* (1879).

Ben Jonson 1574–1637
> Poet and playwright. About 300 books with his inscriptions are now known to survive, widely dispersed. He regularly wrote the motto 'Tanquam explorator' on his title pages.
> *ODNB. CELM.* D. McPherson, 'Ben Jonson's library and marginalia: an annotated catalogue', *Studies in Philology* 71 (1974): 1–106. R. Evans, 'Ben Jonson's library and marginalia: new evidence from the Folger collection', *Philological Quarterly* 66 (1987): 521–8. R. Evans, 'Ben Jonson's Chaucer', *English Literary Renaissance* 19 (1989): 324–45. A. Smyth, 'Burning to read: Ben Jonson's library fire of 1623', in G. Partington et al (eds), *Book destruction from the medieval to the contemporary* (2014), 34–54.

George Sandys 1578–1644
> Traveller and poet, treasurer of Virginia, youngest son of Edwin Sandys, Archbishop of York (1519?–88). Books with his armorial stamp survive.
> M. Rogers, 'Books from the library of George Sandys', *BC* 23 (1974): 361–70. R. Davis, 'Volumes from George Sandys's library now in America', *Virginia Magazine of History and Biography* 65 (1957): 450–57. Armorials database.

William Browne 1590/1–1643/5?
> Poet and antiquary. Acquired various medieval and literary MSS.
> *ODNB.* A. Edwards, 'Medieval manuscripts owned by William Browne of Tavistock', in J. Carley and C. Tite (eds), *Books and collectors 1200–1700* (London, 1997), 441–9.

Roger Dodsworth 1585–1654

Antiquary, who assembled extensive collections underpinning the *Monasticon Anglicanum*. Bequeathed his MSS to his patron Thomas, 3rd Baron Fairfax (1612–71), who left them to the Bodleian (161 volumes).

ODNB. Macray, 137–9. N. Denholm-Young & H. Craster, 'Roger Dodsworth (1585–1654) and his circle', *Yorkshire Archaeological Journal* 32 (1936), 5–32.

John Milton 1608–74

Poet and political writer. Although an attempt has been made to deduce the contents of his library from his writings, and there are various pieces of documentary evidence testifying to his owning or buying books, only a small number of books survive today which were demonstrably his. His Bible, with typical family events inscribed in his hand, is BL Add MS 32310; his annotated Shakespeare First Folio in the Free Library of Philadelphia was identified in 2019.

ODNB. *CELM*. J. C. Boswell, *Milton's library* (Garland, 1975). W. Poole, *Milton and the making of* Paradise Lost (2017).

Thomas Stanley 1625–78

Poet and classical/philosophical scholar. Books with his armorial stamp survive; his MSS were bought by John Moore and passed to Cambridge University Library.

ODNB. M. Flower, 'Thomas Stanley (1625–1676): a bibliography', *TCBS* 1 (1950): 139–72. D. McKitterick, *Cambridge University Library: a history* (1986), 129. Armorials database.

Thomas Killigrew 1612–83

Dramatist, theatre manager. Books with his armorial stamp survive.

ODNB. Armorials database.

Izaak Walton 1593–1683

Author of biographical works, and *The compleat angler*; steward to George Morley, Bishop of Winchester (1598?–1684). Numerous books of his survive in Salisbury Cathedral Library, and elsewhere; the list of 65 books from his library, published in 1980, is likely to represent only a minority of the original whole.

ODNB. *CELM*. J. Bevan, 'Some books from Izaak Walton's library', *The Library*, 6th ser. 2 (1980): 259–63. S. Naiman, 'Izaak Walton', in W. Baker (ed.), *Pre-nineteenth-century British book collectors and bibliographers* (1999), 386–93.

William Cartwright 1606–86

Actor and theatre manager. Bequeathed his library (along with a large picture collection, and other goods) to Dulwich College; the collection was never received in its entirety and the size of his library is unknown, but he had a substantial estate.

ODNB. G. Waterfield (ed.), *Mr. Cartwright's pictures* (Dulwich Picture Gallery, 1987).

John Aubrey 1626–97

Biographer, scientist, antiquary. Bequeathed many of his books to the Ashmolean Museum (hence now in the Bodleian), but also gave books to Gloucester Hall (there are now *c*.40 of Aubrey's books at Worcester College).

ODNB. M. Hunter, *John Aubrey and the realm of learning* (London, 1975). J. Buchanan-Brown, 'The books presented to the Royal Society by John Aubrey', *Notes and Records of the Royal Society of London*, 28 (1974): 167–93. C. H. Wilkinson, 'Worcester College Library', *Oxford Bibliographical Society Proceedings & Papers* 1 (1927): 263–320, 266. R. Gunther, 'The library of John Aubrey', *BQR* 6 (1931): 230–36. K. Bennett, 'John Aubrey's collections and the early modern museum', *BLR* 17 (2001): 185–212. Lee, *British*, 4.

John Dryden 1631–1700
Poet and playwright. A tentative list of books thought to have been owned by him was compiled in 1940. Known to have bought books at the 1682 sale of Richard Smith's library. *ODNB. CELM.* J. M. Osborn, *John Dryden* (1940), 229–33. T. Birrell, 'John Dryden's purchases at two book auctions', *English Studies* 42 (1961): 1–25. Birrell, 'Books and buyers'. P. Hammond, 'Dryden's library', *Notes & Queries* 229 (1984): 344–5.

Edward Chamberlayne 1616–1703
Author of *Angliae notitia* and other works. His library was sold, together with that of his son, in London, 11 Mar. 1724; 33 MSS were purchased by Harley. Reputedly had some of his books buried with him, encased in wax. *ODNB. Fontes Harleianae.* Alston, *Inventory.*

John Locke 1632–1704
Philosopher, administrator. Acquired books throughout his life; left *c.*2,600 volumes when he died. His library was largely divided, after his death, between the King and Masham families, and was variously dispersed thereafter; some parts were kept together and *c.*800 volumes are now in the Bodleian. *ODNB.* J. Harrison and P. Laslett, *The library of John Locke*, 2nd edn (1971). J. Lough, 'John Locke's reading during his stay in France (1675–79)', *The Library*, 5th ser. 8 (1953): 229–58. G. Keynes, 'A note on Locke's library', *TCBS* 4 (1967): 312–13. R. Ashcraft, 'John Locke's library: portrait of an intellectual', *TCBS* 5 (1969): 47–60. P. Kelly, 'A note on Locke's pamphlets on money', *TCBS* 5 (1969): 61–73. S. Rosenblum, 'John Locke', in W. Baker (ed.), *Pre-nineteenth-century British book collectors and bibliographers* (1999), 221–34. Notes in *BLR* 11(2) (1983): 120–21, and 11(3): 191–2.

Thomas Betterton 1635–1710
Actor and theatre manager. Library auctioned in London, 24 Aug. 1710 (546 lots, plus prints and paintings; edited by David Roberts, see below). *ODNB.* D. Roberts (ed.), *Pinacotheca Bettertoneana: the library of a seventeenth-century actor* (2013). Alston, *Inventory.*

Philip Ayres 1638–1712
Poet and miscellaneous writer; tutor to the Drake family, of Agmondesham, Buckinghamshire. Library sold by retail sale in London, 10 Nov. 1713. *ODNB.* Alston, *Inventory.* Christie's 23 June 1977 (Evelyn sale)/262.

Businessmen, merchants, tradesmen, citizens of unknown profession

This section covers a range of people whose activities seem best described under this heading, or are likely to have been. They include rich people, who made their fortune primarily through trade or merchant activity (rather than inheritance), and those much more of the middling sort, from around the country. There are numerous book sales recorded from the late 17th and early 18th c. (often with no surviving catalogue) where all we have is a name, not readily identifiable from standard sources, which have generally been classified here by default.

Christopher Harrison d. 1612
Of Kendal, possibly a clothier; apparently 'a comfortable landowner with livestock and ample property'. Probate inventory (edited as PLRE 267) includes about 40 books. J. L. Black & R. Fehrenbach, 'Christopher Harrison, merchant', PLRE 9 (2017): 149–55.

William Harborne *c.*1542–1617
Merchant, ambassador to Turkey, author. Books with his armorial stamps survive. *ODNB*. Armorials database.

Nicholas Wanton 1544?–1618
Member of the Grocers' Company in London, lived and died in York in the late 16th/early 17th c. A number of surviving books in American libraries with Wanton's inscription, motto, and numbering system suggest that he had a library of at least 900 volumes.
F. B. Williams, 'John Bodenham', *Studies in Philology* 31 (1934): 198–214, 213–14.

Edward Pearson 1563–1619
Churchwarden of Howden, Yorkshire; his main occupation is unknown. His list of 'the naymes of all my bookes 1604' which he noted on the flyleaf of one of them (a little over 50 titles) has been edited as PLRE 265.
R. J. Fehrenbach, 'Edward Pearson, churchwarden', PLRE 9 (2017): 89–102.

John Tayer fl.1627
Shoemaker and glover, of Gloucestershire. A list of the books he owned in 1627 (at least 20 titles) is preserved in his account book.
CHL I 523.

Samuel Rowlands 1565–1627
Of East Smithfield, London, cooper and poet/satirist. A list of 34 books owned at the time of his death is edited as PLRE 271.
J. L. Black, 'Samuel Rowlands. Craftsman', PLRE 9 (2017): 191–9.

Frances Jodrell d. 1631
Of Stockport, spinster. Probate inventory lists 'in the presse' two boxes containing 57 books, 'most of them old historie bookes', valued at 4*s.* 8*d.*, together with a few other books elsewhere.
C. Phillips (ed.), *Stockport probate records 1620–1650* (1992), 315.

Edward Lightfoot d. 1635?
Of London; graduate of St John's College, Cambridge. Bequeathed over 30 books to St John's.
Venn. Lee, *Labels*, 115.

Anthony Abdy d. 1640
Alderman and sheriff of London. Probate inventory includes books 'in the little parlour' in his house at Lime Street, valued at £12; he also had a house at Leytonstone, Essex, with a small number of books including Pliny and 'ye Turkish historie', valued at 12*s.*
London Metropolitan Archives CLC/521/MS03760.

Nathaniel Brading d. 1645
Merchant adventurer, of Godshill, Isle of Wight. A list of *c.*30 books which he took with him on a voyage to Madagascar and the East Indies (where he died) is edited as PLRE 275.
R. J. Fehrenbach, 'Nathaniel Brading: merchant adventurer', PLRE 9 (2017): 309–17.

Sir John Gayer 1584–1649
East India merchant, Lord Mayor of London. Books with his armorial stamp survive. *ODNB*. Armorials database.

Sir Paul Pindar 1565/6–1650
Merchant and diplomat. Gave 19 oriental MSS to the Bodleian Library in 1611, and 15 MSS to Sion College in 1629.
ODNB. Sears Jayne 142, 155. Macray, 42.

John Morris d. 1658
> Wealthy London citizen, who inherited watermills from his father, and described his library of c.1,500 volumes as 'the cheife pleasure and imployment of my life'; many of his books were purchased by the Royal Library and c.1,300 remain in the BL today.
> ODNB. T. Birrell, *The library of John Morris* (1976).

Nehemiah Wallington 1598–1658
> Turner, resident of the parish of St Leonard Eastcheap, London, whose diary includes references to his buying and reading of books, showing that he owned over 200 titles.
> ODNB. P. Seaver, *Wallington's world: a puritan artisan in seventeenth-century London* (1985).

Peter Cardonnel 1614–67
> Born at Caen, moved to Southampton in the 1630s where he developed a career as a merchant; reputedly lent money to Charles II during the Civil War. Undertook various literary works and translations; a number of his surviving books have been documented. Library auctioned in London, 6 June 1681 (1,336 lots).
> N. Malcolm, *Aspects of Hobbes* (2002), 259–316 ('Pierre de Cardonnel's library', 311–16). R. Beadle, 'Medieval English manuscripts at auction, 1676–c.1700', *BC* 53 (2004): 46–63, 54. Alston, *Inventory*.

Sir Henry Creswicke d. 1668
> Master of the Merchant Venturers in Bristol, Mayor of Bristol 1660. Probate inventory records 'books of all sorts' in the little new parlour, valued at £10.
> N. Glaisyer, *The culture of commerce in England, 1660–1720* (2006), 134.

Marmaduke Rawdon 1609–68
> Wine merchant, traveller, antiquary, who spent the last part of his life living with his cousin of the same name at Hoddesdon, Hertfordshire, where he compiled various MSS collections, and spent time 'in his closet reading or writing, being naturally inclined to study'.
> ODNB. Armorials database.

Daniel Rawlinson 1614–79
> Vintner, of London, keeper of the Mitre tavern, but a native of Hawkshead, Cumbria. Gave a number of books to Hawkshead Grammar School, c.1670–80.
> R. Christie, *The old church and school libraries of Lancashire* (1885), 143.

Edward Palmer d. c.1681?
> 'A worthy gentleman, of great learning and eminency'. Library auctioned in London, 14 Feb. 1681 (357 lots).
> Alston, *Inventory*.

Walter Rea d. c.1682?
> Library auctioned in London, 19 June 1682 (2,732 lots).
> Alston, *Inventory*.

Richard Chace d. c.1684?
> Library auctioned in London, 24 Mar. 1684 (joint sale, with two others).
> Alston, *Inventory*.

Thomas Craddock d. 1684
> Merchant, or Port Royal, Jamaica. Probate inventory lists c.90 books, apparently a mixture of stock for sale and a personal library.
> R. Cave, 'Thomas Craddock's books: a West India merchant's stock', *BC* 25 (1976): 481–90.

Thomas Jennings d. *c.*1684?
'Civis Londonensis ingeniosissimi'. Library auctioned in London, 17 Nov. 1684 (joint sale, with one other).
Alston, *Inventory.*

Peter Hushar d. 1685
Merchant, of London. Library auctioned in London, 18 Nov. 1685 (897 lots).
N. Glaisyer, *The culture of commerce in England, 1660–1720* (2006), 134. Alston, *Inventory.*

Francis Bacon d. 1686?
'Lately deceased'. Library auctioned in London, 19 May 1686 (183 lots, all English, 'chiefly history').
Alston, *Inventory.*

Elizabeth Sleigh, later Elizabeth Ireton d. 1686
Wife of Edmund Sleigh, London mercer (d. 1657), later of John Ireton (1615–90), also a mercer. An inventory of her books, in Wellcome Library MS 751, dated 1647, lists 53 books, edited as PLRE 255.
H. Hackel, 'The Countess of Bridgewater's London library', in J. Andersen & E. Sauer (eds), *Books and readers* (2002), 138–59, 139. R. J. Fehrenbach, 'Lady Elizabeth Ireton', PLRE 8 (2014): 281–92. See above, p. 39.

Jeremiah Copping d. 1687
Fishmonger, resident of (and benefactor to) Sion College. Library auctioned in London, 21 Mar. 1687 (joint sale, with one other).
Alston, *Inventory.*

Sir John Shorter 1625–88
Goldsmith and merchant; Lord Mayor of London 1687–8. Used an engraved armorial bookplate dated 1687.
Woodhead. Franks *469. See above, p. 126.

Sir Robert Viner 1631–88
Goldsmith and banker. Books with his armorial stamp survive.
ODNB. Armorials database.

Christopher Thomas d. *c.*1689?
Library auctioned in London, 1 Apr. 1689 (1,319 lots).
Alston, *Inventory.*

Humphrey Oldfield d. 1690
Woollen draper, of Salford. Bequeathed his theological books to Salford, to found a parish library.
Perkin, 337. R. Christie, *The old church and school libraries of Lancashire* (Manchester, 1885), 107.

Philip Mason d. *c.*1691?
Described as MA, but not found in the university lists. Library auctioned in London, 8 June 1691.
Alston, *Inventory.*

John Cropper d. 1693?
Unidentified, of London, described by the auctioneer (Millington) as a learned man but not traced in the university lists. Library auctioned in London, 19 June 1693 (420 lots).
Alston, *Inventory.*

Nicholas Fuller d. 1693?
> The library of the 'late learned Nichol. Fuller', including common law books, history, voyages, and plays, was auctioned in London 14 Dec. 1693, although no catalogue survives.
> Alston, *Inventory*.

John Lister fl.1693
> John Lister, who 'lodges at Mrs Unwin in Great St Ann's Lane…Westminster', advertised 'to sell all his books' beginning 18 Dec. 1693; no catalogue survives.
> Alston, *Inventory*.

Isaac Row d. *c*.1693?
> Library auctioned in London, 27 July 1693, including mathematical and architectural books, and prints.
> Alston, *Inventory*.

Francis Lodwick 1619–94
> London merchant, linguistic scholar. Shelf-lists of his two library collections, each containing *c*.2,500 volumes, are in BL MSS Sloane 855, 859. These were apparently dispersed after his death; many books are now in the Bodleian, where they can be identified from their distinctive numbering.
> *ODNB*. W. Poole, 'Francis Lodwick, Hans Sloane, and the Bodleian Library', *The Library*, 7th ser. 7 (2006): 377–418. F. Henderson & W. Poole, 'The library lists of Francis Lodwick', *eBLJ* 2009, article 1.

Palmer d. *c*.1694?
> Of Bristol. Library auctioned in London, 5 Apr. 1694 (844 lots).
> Alston, *Inventory*.

James Partridge d. 1695
> Haberdasher, of London. Library auctioned in London, 25 Nov. 1695 (1,468 lots), 16 Dec. 1695 (434 lots).
> Alston, *Inventory*.

Sir Josiah Child 1630–99
> Brewer, merchant, governor of the East India Company. Founded the library at Wanstead House (estate purchased 1673), which was developed by succeeding generations until being sold in 1822.
> *ODNB*. D. Keeling, *Wanstead House: the owners and their books* (1994).

Skinner d. *c*.1699?
> Library auctioned in London, 13 Feb. 1699 (joint sale, with one other).
> Mandelbrote, 'Auctions'. Alston, *Inventory*.

Brian Jarson d. 1700?
> Library sold by retail sale in London, 25 July 1700 (no catalogue survives).
> Alston, *Inventory*.

William Bucknell d. *c*.1707?
> Library sold by retail sale in London, 27 Oct. 1707 (joint sale, with one other; no catalogue survives).
> Alston, *Inventory*.

Sir Robert Clayton 1629–1707
> Banker, Lord Mayor of London, noted for his wealth. Used an engraved armorial bookplate, dated 1679.
> *ODNB*. Lee, *London*, 88. Franks 6024/6025.

John Davis d. *c.*1707?
Library auctioned in London, 24 Nov. 1707 (no catalogue survives).
Alston, *Inventory.*

Robert Evelyn d. *c.*1707?
Library sold by retail sale in London, 27 Oct. 1707 (joint sale, with one other; no catalogue survives).
Alston, *Inventory.*

Richard Ford d. *c.*1707?
Library auctioned in London, 10 Dec. 1707 (1,323 lots).
Alston, *Inventory.*

William Hayworth d. *c.*1707?
Library auctioned in London, 17 Mar. 1707 (no catalogue survives).
Alston, *Inventory.*

John Rawlins d. *c.*1707?
Of Sheen, Surrey. Library sold by retail sale in London, 1707; the continuation of the sale was advertised to begin 19 June 1707 (no catalogue survives).
Alston, *Inventory.*

William Roebey d. *c.*1707?
Library auctioned in London, 3 Dec. 1707 (only a title page of the catalogue survives).
Alston, *Inventory.*

Richard Fitzgerald d. *c.*1708?
Library sold by retail sale in London, 28 Apr. 1708 (no catalogue survives).
Alston, *Inventory.*

William Popple 1638–1708
London merchant, secretary of the Board of Trade. Library sold by retail sale in London, 2 Mar. 1711 (no catalogue survives).
ODNB. Alston, *Inventory.*

Seth Ratcliff d. *c.*1708
Resident of Bull Wharf, Queenhithe; household goods, including 'a fine library of books', auctioned in London, 12 Mar. 1708 (no catalogue survives).
Alston, *Inventory.*

Thomas Ravenscroft d. 1708
Of St Giles in the Fields, London, a member of a Roman Catholic family of merchants. Library auctioned in London, 7 Nov. 1709 (1,729 lots).
ODNB (see 'George Ravenscroft'). Alston, *Inventory.*

Nathaniel Shepheard d. *c.*1708?
Merchant, of London. Library auctioned in London, 7 Jan. 1709 (no catalogue survives).
Alston, *Inventory.*

John Burgess d. *c.*1709
Merchant, of London. Library auctioned in London, 21 Feb. 1709 (no catalogue survives).
Alston, *Inventory.*

Sir Charles Duncombe 1648–1711
Goldsmith and banker, Lord Mayor of London 1708. Used an engraved armorial bookplate dated 1702.
ODNB. Franks *266/*329.

Sir Henry Ashurst 1645–1711
London merchant, MP, commissioner of Hackney coaches. Used an engraved armorial bookplate.
ODNB. Franks 811/*141.

Daniel Thomas d. *c.*1711
'An eminent citizen of London, deceased'. Library sold by retail sale in London, 3 Oct. 1711 (no catalogue survives).
Alston, *Inventory*.

Thomas Brady d. 1713
?The man of this name buried at St Paul's, Covent Garden, 1713? Library sold by retail sale in London, 19 Aug. 1715 (1,123 lots).
Alston, *Inventory*.

Sir Owen Buckingham 1650–1713
London businessman (variously described as a butcher, salter, flaxman); MP, Lord Mayor 1704. Used an engraved armorial bookplate dated 1705.
HoP. Franks *431.

Sir John Chardin 1643–1713
Jeweller and traveller, born in Paris, moved to England 1681. Library auctioned in London, 23 July 1713, 23 Nov. 1713.
ODNB. Alston, *Inventory*.

Thomas Britton 1654–1714
Coal merchant, musician, and amateur chemist, also noted as a book collector. Books sold in two auction sales, 1 Nov. 1694 (1,500 lots), 24 Jan. 1715 (1,108 lots).
ODNB. W. A. Campbell, 'The chemical library of Thomas Britton', *Ambix* 24 (1977): 143–8. Alston, *Inventory*.

Harry Mullins d. *c.*1714?
Library auctioned in London, 15 Nov. 1714 (1124 lots).
Alston, *Inventory*.

Jenkins Dugdale d. *c.*1715?
Library sold by retail sale in London, together with that of 'another gentleman lately deceas'd', 2 May 1715 (no catalogue survives).
Alston, *Inventory*.

Arthur Henley d. *c.*1715?
Library sold by retail sale in London, 7 Apr. 1715 (no catalogue survives).
Alston, *Inventory*.

William Lindwood d. *c.*1715?
Library auctioned in London, 7 Feb. 1715 (992 lots).
Alston, *Inventory*.

Thomas Pakeman d. *c.*1715?
Of Bethnal Green. Library auctioned in London, 30 Mar. 1715 (342 lots).
Alston, *Inventory* (the identification with the Nonconformist minister, d. 1691, seems questionable).

Percival Serjeant d. *c.*1715?
'Of the East-India-House'. Library auctioned in London, 9 Nov. 1715 (no catalogue survives).
Alston, *Inventory*.

Sir Peter Seaman 1662–1715
> Of Norwich, brewer and alderman. Used an engraved bookplate, probably made at the end of the 17th c.
> Blatchly.

Civil servants and administrators

'Civil servant' is not an occupational classification we tend to associate with the 17th c., but the people here seem best thus described; they are all men who were employed in government, municipal or ecclesiastical administration, although some of them could arguably fit under other headings (e.g. Gentry).

Arthur Agarde 1540–1615
> Deputy chamberlain of the Exchequer, and antiquary. Many of his MSS collections passed to Sir Robert Cotton, and are now in the British Library; the extent of his printed book holdings is not known.
> ODNB. E. Hallam, 'Arthur Agarde and Domesday Book', in C. Wright (ed.), Sir Robert Cotton as a collector (1997), 253–61. Armorials database.

George Wilmer 1582–1626
> Collector of the Petty Customs. Books with his armorial stamp survive. Gave 38 MSS to Trinity College, Cambridge; the bulk of his library seems to have descended through his family for several generations.
> Venn. Gaskell/TCC, 82–3. Armorials database.

Rowland Woodward 1573–1636
> Secretary to Sir Henry Wotton, poet, friend of John Donne. His books, which initially entered the Fane family library at Apethorpe, are now dispersed; his inscriptions regularly include the Spanish motto 'De juegos el mejor es con la hoja'.
> ODNB. Maggs 1121 (1990)/16.

Henry Marston d. 1643
> Parish clerk of St Stephen, Bristol. Probate inventory lists several bibles and dictionaries, and 'one old cradle full of books', valued together at £1 5s. 10d.
> E. George (ed.), Bristol probate inventories 1542–1650 (2002), 135.

Sir Francis Windebank 1582–1646
> Politician, clerk of the signet, Secretary of State. 425 books were seized from his London house by the London Committee for Sequestration in 1643, and sold.
> ODNB. Roy.

Sir John Heydon 1588–1653
> Lieutenant general of the ordnance. More than 63 books were seized from him by the London Committee for Sequestration in 1643, and sold.
> ODNB. Roy.

Scipio Le Squyer 1579–1659
> Deputy chamberlain of the Exchequer, antiquary. A catalogue of his library made in 1632 lists c.500 printed books and over 200 MSS.
> ODNB. F. Taylor, 'The books and manuscripts of Scipio Le Squyer', Bulletin of the John Rylands Library 25 (1941): 146–64. T. Birrell, 'Reading as pastime: the place of light literature in some gentlemen's libraries of the 17th century', in R. Myers (ed.), Property of a gentleman (Winchester, 1991), 113–31, 119–21. R. Ovenden, 'Scipio le Squyer and the fate of monastic cartularies', The Library, 6th ser. 13 (1991), 323–37.

Henry Lucas 1587–1663
Secretary and agent for estates and politicians, MP. Bequeathed his library of c.4,000 volumes to Cambridge University Library.
ODNB. Oates, 349–367.

Sir William Clarke 1623?–66
Civil servant, Secretary at War after the Restoration. His extensive collection of Civil War pamphlets was bequeathed, with other books, to Worcester College, Oxford, by his son George (1661–1736).
ODNB. M. Mendle, 'Preserving the ephemeral', in J. Andersen (ed.), *Books and readers in early modern England* (2002), 201–16, 209–10. *CHL* II 40.

William Dowsing 1596–1668
Parliamentary agent, iconoclast, farmer. Owned an extensive library, which was dispersed by his son in 1704; a number of books survive, with distinctive cypher-like inscriptions.
ODNB. J. Morrill, 'William Dowsing, the bureacratic Puritan', in his *Public duty and private conscience in seventeenth-century England* (1993). D. Roberts, 'Additions to the library of William Dowsing', *eBLJ* (2013): art. 10. Maggs 1272 (1999)/64; 1324 (2002)/37.

William Somner 1598–1669
Registrar of the Diocese of Canterbury, antiquary, author. A catalogue of c.275 books of his, dated 1639, survives in BL Burney MS 368. He and his brother John gave books to Canterbury Cathedral Library c.1665, and books/MSS from his library were acquired by the Cathedral after his death.
ODNB. Sears Jayne, 170. N. Ramsay, 'The Cathedral Archives and Library', in P. Collinson (ed.), *A history of Canterbury Cathedral* (1995)2, 381.

Richard Smith 1590–1675
Secondary of the Poultry Counter. Amassed a library of over 8,000 books, auctioned in London, 15 May 1682.
ODNB. E. G. Duff, 'The library of Richard Smith', *The Library*, n.s. 8 (1907): 113–33. R. Beadle, 'Medieval English manuscripts at auction, 1676–c.1700', *BC* 53 (2004): 46–63. T. Birrell, 'Books and buyers', 55–8. Mandelbrote, 'Auctions', 24. Alston, *Inventory*.

Benjamin Worsley 1617/18–77
Government administrator in Ireland and London, businessman, physician. Library auctioned in London, 13 May 1678 (5,282 lots).
ODNB. Alston, *Inventory*.

Sir John Birkenhead 1615–79
Royalist polemicist (compiler of the newsbook *Mercurius Aulicus* during the Civil War), poet, MP. Had a noteworthy collection of Civil War tracts; his library was reputedly sold for £200 after his death, and his MSS for £900.
ODNB. Aubrey, *Brief lives*.

Sir Jonas Moore 1617–79
Surveyor, mathematician. Intended to bequeath his books to the Royal Society, but died intestate and his library was auctioned in London, 3 Nov. 1684 (1,560 lots).
ODNB. Mandelbrote, 'Auctions', 20. Alston, *Inventory*.

Sir George Carteret 1610?–80
Vice-chamberlain of the royal household, treasurer of the Navy, MP. Books with his armorial stamp survive.
ODNB. Armorials database.

Sir George Wharton, 1st Baronet 1617–81
Treasurer of the ordnance, astrologer, almanac writer. Library auctioned in London, 20 Oct. 1713 (joint sale, with one other).
ODNB. Alston, *Inventory*.

Henry Coventry 1619–86
Sir William Coventry 1628?–86
Brothers, younger sons of Thomas Coventry, 1st Baron Coventry (1578–1640), who each became successful government administrators and politicians. Their libraries were auctioned together in London, 9 May 1687 (Henry, 859 lots; Sir William, 1,231).
ODNB. D. McKitterick, *Cambridge University Library: a history*, vol. 2 (1986), 116. Alston, *Inventory*.

John Rushworth *c.*1612–90
Parliamentary clerk and historian, lawyer, MP. Library partly auctioned in London, 8 Dec. 1690, 5 Jan. 1691, with a further part sold by the London bookseller J. Woodman in 1722. Amassed major collections of Civil War pamphlets and newsbooks.
ODNB. R. Beadle, 'Medieval English manuscripts at auction, 1676–*c.*1700', *BC* 53 (2004), 46–63. F. Henderson, '"Posterity to judge": John Rushworth and his "historicall collections"', *BLR* 15 (1996): 247–59. *CHL* II 39–40. Alston, *Inventory*.

John Browne 1608–91
Clerk of the Parliaments. Noted for his collection of music MSS.
ODNB. A. Ashbee, 'Instrumental music from the library of John Browne', *Music and letters* 58 (1977): 43–59. D. Pinto, 'Pious pleasures in early Stuart London', *Royal Musical Association Research Chronicle* 41 (2008): 1–24.

Sir George Etherege 1636–91
Diplomat and dramatist. A list of *c.*65 books owned by him while British resident at Ratisbon in the 1680s is now British Library Add MS 11513; many of the books themselves survive in Ratisbon.
ODNB. *CELM*. P. Beal, '"The most constant and best entertainment": Sir George Etherege's reading in Ratisbon', *The Library* 10 (1988): 122–44. P. Beal, 'Sir George Etheridge's library at Ratisbon', *The Library*, 7th ser. 3 (2002): 315–16.

Sir Edward Sherburne 1616–1702
Chief Clerk of the Ordnance, poet, translator. Two MS catalogues of his library survive, one *c.*1670, listing *c.*1,000 titles (BL MS Sloane 857), and a later one dated 1681, listing *c.*2,000 titles (Bodleian MS Rawl.Q.b.3). He claimed to have lost an earlier library of 2,000 volumes during the Civil War.
ODNB. T. Birrell, 'The library of Sir Edward Sherburne', in A. Hunt et al (eds.), *The book trade and its customers* (1997), 189–204. W. Poole, 'Loans from the library of Sir Edward Sherburne', *The Library* 7th ser 14 (2013): 80–87.

Sir Joseph Williamson 1633–1702
Diplomat, Secretary of State, Keeper of the Royal Library. Bequeathed his library (*c.*6,000 volumes) to Queen's College, Oxford, where many of the books, and MS inventories, survive.
ODNB. T. Birrell, 'Reading as pastime: the place of light literature in some 17th-century gentlemen's libraries', in R. Myers (ed.), *Property of a gentleman* (Winchester, 1991), 113–131, 126–7. Armorials database.

William Griffith d. 1703?
Secretary to the Earl of Coventry. Library sold by retail sale in London, 28 June 1703 (joint sale, with one other; no catalogue survives).
Alston, *Inventory*.

Samuel Pepys 1633–1703
 Secretary to the Admiralty. His entire library (c.2,750 books, 250 MSS) is preserved intact in its original bookcases (designed and built for him in the 1690s) at Magdalene College, Cambridge, where they were received under the terms of his will.
 ODNB. CELM. Lee, *British*, 11/12. J. Rosenblum, 'Samuel Pepys', in W. Baker (ed.), *Prenineteenth-century British book collectors and bibliographers* (1999), 258–73. R. Latham (ed.), *Catalogue of the Pepys Library* (1978–). K. Loveman, 'Books and sociability: the case of Samuel Pepys's library', *Review of English Studies* 61 (2010): 214–33. K. Loveman, *Samuel Pepys and his books* (2015). Franks 23258–60. Armorials database.

Peter Hume d. 1707
 Of the Wardrobe. Library sold by retail sale in London, 22 Mar. 1708 (no catalogue survives).
 Alston, *Inventory.*

Sir Henry Sheres d. 1710
 Military engineer, author. Bequeathed his library to Henry Overton, the son of a former servant; it was sold by retail sale in London, 14 June 1713 (joint sale, with one other).
 ODNB. Alston, *Inventory.*

William Hewer 1642–1715
 Commissioner of the Navy, MP. Friend of Samuel Pepys, who lived in his house (and housed his own library there) towards the end of his life. Used a bookpile monogram bookplate dated 1699.
 ODNB. B. N. Lee, *Bookpile bookplates* (1992), no. 73. Franks 14623.

Clergy

As noted above, there can be some ambiguity between classifying people as 'clergy' or 'academics', as many people supported primarily academic careers from the income of ecclesiastical livings, often in the patronage of university colleges. This section is intended to comprise men whose primary occupation in the latter part of their life, and at their death, was based in the Church, as a parish incumbent or holder of a more senior office; it is arranged by those offices, in descending order of seniority.

Archbishops

Richard Bancroft 1544–1610
 Archbishop of Canterbury. Bequeathed his library of over 6,000 volumes for the use of his successors at Lambeth Palace; probably the largest English private library of his generation. Most are still at Lambeth, though examples will be found elsewhere.
 ODNB. M. R. James, 'The history of Lambeth Palace Library', *TCBS* 3 (1959): 1–31. A Cox-Johnson, 'Lambeth Palace Library', *TCBS* 2 (1955): 105–26. James Carley, 'The libraries of Archbishops Whitgift and Bancroft', *BC* 62 (2013): 209–228. Pearson, 'Bishops'. *CHL* I 390–91. Armorials database.

Toby Matthew 1546–1628
 Archbishop of York. Library given to York Minster by his widow (c.3,000 volumes); he also gave books to other institutions.

ODNB. J. Raine, *A catalogue of the... Library of the Dean and Chapter of York* (1896).
C. Barr, 'The Minster Library', in G. Alymer & R. Cant (eds), *A history of York Minster*
(1977), 500–02. Pearson, 'Bishops'. *CHL* I 396. Maggs 1272 (1999)/106; 1324 (2002)/66.
Armorials database.

Samuel Harsnett 1561–1631
Archbishop of York. Bequeathed his library (*c.*900 volumes) to Colchester, to be a town
library; the books are now in Essex University Library.
ODNB. G. Goodwin, *A catalogue of the Harsnett Library* (1888). F. Galligan, *The library
of Archbishop Samuel Harsnett: a report* (2012). Pearson, 'Bishops'. *CHL* I 383–4.

George Abbot 1562–1633
Archbishop of Canterbury. Bequeathed the bulk of his library (*c.*2,700 volumes) to
Lambeth Palace; gave books, or money to buy books, to several other institutions.
ODNB. M. R. James, 'The history of Lambeth Palace Library', *TCBS* 3 (1959): 1–31.
A Cox-Johnson, 'Lambeth Palace Library', *TCBS* 2 (1955): 105–26. Pearson, 'Bishops'.
CHL I 392. Armorials database.

Richard Neile 1562–1640
Archbishop of York. At least 20 books of his survive in York Minster Library; others are
found elsewhere.
ODNB. Pearson, 'Bishops'. A. Cambers, *Print, manuscript and godly cultures in the north
of England c.1600–1650* (DPhil. thesis, University of York, 2003).

William Laud 1573–1645
Archbishop of Canterbury. Gave major donations of MSS to the Bodleian Library
between 1635 and 1640; gave books/MSS to St John's, Oxford. His library was dispersed
following his arrest and execution.
ODNB. Morgan. H. O. Coxe, *Laudian manuscripts*, ed. R. W. Hunt (Oxford, 1973).
Macray 83–8. Toomer, 108–11. J. Gallagher, 'William Laud', in W. Baker (ed.), *Pre-
nineteenth-century British book collectors and bibliographers* (1999), 207–14. J. Fuggles,
'William Laud and the library of St John's College, Oxford', *BC* 309 (1981): 19–38.
Armorials database.

John Williams 1582–1650
Archbishop of York. Purchased a library of *c.*1,700 books to give to Westminster Abbey,
1623; funded the rebuilding of the Library at St John's in the 1620s, and gave money and
books there. Various MS lists of his books and donations at St John's.
ODNB. Sears Jayne. P. Linehan (ed.), *St. John's College, Cambridge: a history*
(Woodbridge, 2011), 103–6. *CHL* I 395. Armorials database.

James Ussher 1580–1656
Archbishop of Armagh. His extensive library (c.10,000 volumes) was purchased after his
death and given to Trinity College Dublin. Listed in Edward Bernard's *Catalogi manuscriptorum* (1697) as owning 340 manuscripts.
ODNB. Toomer, 78–85. P. Fox, *Treasures of the library, Trinity College Dublin* (1986).
S. Towers, 'James Ussher', in W. Baker (ed.), *Pre-nineteenth-century British book
collectors and bibliographers* (1999), 357–64. P. Fox, *Trinity College Library Dublin: a
history* (2014), 25–33. Armorials database.

William Juxon 1582–1663
Archbishop of Canterbury. His books were given to St John's College, Oxford after his
death (over 100 survive there today).
ODNB. Morgan. Armorials database.

Gilbert Sheldon 1598–1677
Archbishop of Canterbury. Instrumental in re-establishing Lambeth Palace Library after the Restoration. Divided his books, in his will, between Lambeth Palace Library and his nephew Gilbert Dolben (though the will was later contested).
ODNB. R. Palmer, 'Sancroft versus Sheldon: a case of books', *The Library*, 7th ser. 18 (2017): 271–91. Armorials database.

Richard Sterne 1596?–1683
Archbishop of York. His son Simon (d. 1703) gave books to Halifax parish church, including a number which had belonged to his father, and uncle William (these books are now in York UL).
ODNB. A. Cambers, 'Pastoral Laudianism? Religious politics in the 1630s: a Leicestershire rector's annotations', *Midland History* 27 (2002): 38–51. Cambers, 146.

Thomas Lamplugh 1615–91
Archbishop of York. Library auctioned in London (at least the Greek and Latin books), 8 Feb. 1704 (the only recorded copy, at the National Library of Ireland, cannot be found today).
ODNB. A. R. Jabez-Smith, 'Joseph Williamson and Thomas Lamplugh', *Transactions of the Cumberland and Westmorland Antiquarian and Archaeological Society* 86 (1986): 145–163. Alston, *Inventory*.

William Sancroft 1617–93
Archbishop of Canterbury. Gave his library of *c.*5,000 volumes to Emmanuel College, Cambridge, and gave other books elsewhere. Two MS catalogues of his collection, made by him, are in the Bodleian Library (MSS Sancroft 122, Sancroft 146).
ODNB. H. Carron, 'William Sancroft (1617–93): a seventeenth-century collector and his library', *The Library*, 7th ser. 1 (2000): 290–307. Armorials database.

John Tillotson 1630–94
Archbishop of Canterbury. Library sold in London, 9 Apr. 1695, 23 Apr. 1695 (a joint sale, with one other).
ODNB. Alston, *Inventory*.

John Sharp 1644–1714
Archbishop of York. Began the Sharp family collection which became the Bamburgh Castle Library, now in Durham University Library.
ODNB. A. I. Doyle, 'Unfamiliar libraries IV: the Bamburgh Library', *BC* 8 (1959): 14–24.

Thomas Tenison 1636–1715
Archbishop of Canterbury. Deposited a sizeable part of his library (*c.*3–4000 volumes) in St Martin in the Fields in 1684, to found a parish library there (dispersed 1861), but withdrew some on appointment as archbishop, and kept them at Lambeth. The 1,500 volumes in his study at his death were bequeathed to Lambeth Palace; other books were bequeathed to Edmund Gibson, from whom they subsequently passed to Lambeth Palace.
ODNB. Perkin, 271–3. P. Hoare, 'Archbishop Tenison's library at St Martin-in-the-Fields', *London Topographical Record* 29 (2006): 127–50. Armorials database.

Bishops

Gervase Babington 1550–1610
Bishop of Worcester. Many of his books, with his armorial stamp, are in Worcester Cathedral Library, given by his son John after his death.
ODNB. J. Wilson, 'The library of printed books in Worcester Cathedral', *The Library*, 3rd ser. 2 (1911): 1–33. Pearson, 'Bishops'. Armorials database.

William Barlow d. 1613
Bishop of Lincoln. Bequeathed some books to Trinity Hall, Cambridge, and the rest to his nephew.
ODNB. Pearson, 'Bishops'.

James Montagu 1568–1618
Bishop of Winchester. Bequeathed his books to Sidney Sussex College, Cambridge.
ODNB. Pearson, 'Bishops'. N. Rogers, 'The early history of Sidney Sussex College Library', in D. Beales & H. Nisbet (eds), *Sidney Sussex College: historical essays* (Woodbridge, 1996), 75–88, 81–3. Armorials database.

John Overall 1561–1619
Bishop of Norwich. A few of his books can today be identified in various locations but he is likely to have had an appreciable library.
ODNB. Pearson, 'Bishops'.

John King 1559?–1621, Bishop of London
Henry King 1592–1669, Bishop of Chichester
John King d. 1671
Henry King inherited books from his father John and developed a sizeable library, much of which was lost when Chichester Cathedral was seized in 1642; what remained passed to his son John who in turn bequeathed many to the diocese of Chichester.
ODNB. CELM. Pearson, 'Bishops'. Morgan. P. Simpson, 'The Bodleian manuscripts of Henry King', *BLQ* 5 (1928): 324–40. M. Hobbs, 'Henry King, John Donne and the refounding of Chichester Cathedral Library', *BC* 33 (1984): 189–205.

Arthur Lake 1569–1626
Bishop of Bath & Wells. Bequeathed a large portion of his library to New College, Oxford (over 400 volumes); also left books to Wells Cathedral, and to family members. Founded the church library at Bath, *c*.1619.
ODNB. Pearson, 'Bishops'. Perkin, 132–3.

Lancelot Andrewes 1555–1626
Bishop of Winchester. Bequeathed to Pembroke College, Cambridge, all his books in folio not already possessed by the College (*c*.400 volumes); the fate of the rest of his library is not known.
ODNB. CELM. D. Chambers, 'A catalogue of the library of Bishop Lancelot Andrewes', *TCBS* 5 (1970): 99–121. Pearson, 'Bishops'.

Valentine Carey d. 1626
Bishop of Exeter. Bequeathed his books to members of his family, and left £50 to St John's College, Cambridge, for the purchase of books.
ODNB. Pearson, 'Bishops'.

John Buckeridge 1562?–1631
Bishop of Ely. Bequeathed 20 volumes to St John's College, Oxford.
ODNB. Sears Jayne. Pearson, 'Bishops'.

Augustine Lindsell d. 1634
Bishop of Hereford. His library, said after his death to have been worth £800, was bequeathed among various colleagues and Clare College, Cambridge.
ODNB. Pearson, 'Bishops'.

Francis Dee d. 1638
> Bishop of Peterborough. Bequeathed choice of his books to St John's College, Cambridge (over 150 volumes were selected).
> *ODNB*. Pearson, 'Bishops'.

John Bancroft 1574–1640
> Bishop of Oxford. Gave 4 MSS and 31 printed books to University College, Oxford in 1632. Directed in his will that his books should be sold, with half the proceeds given to aid repair work at St Paul's Cathedral.
> *ODNB*. Pearson, 'Bishops'.

Richard Montagu 1577–1641
> Bishop of Norwich. A few scattered books with his inscription survive; his letters to John Cosin include numerous references to the obtaining of books.
> *ODNB*. Pearson, 'Bishops'.

John Prideaux 1578–1650
> Bishop of Worcester. Many of his books survive today in Worcester Cathedral Library.
> *ODNB*.

Thomas Morton 1564–1659
> Bishop of Durham. Gave many books to St John's College, Cambridge, *c.*1620–40.
> *ODNB*. Sears Jayne 149, 169. Armorials database.

Brian Walton 1600–61
> Bishop of Chester, and editor of the 1654–57 Polyglot Bible. Library auctioned in London, 30 Apr. 1683 (1,840 lots).
> *ODNB*. R. Beadle, 'Medieval English manuscripts at auction, 1676–*c.*1700', *BC* 53 (2004): 46–63. M. Mendle, 'Preserving the ephemeral', in J. Andersen (ed.), *Books and readers in early modern England* (2002), 201–16, 206. Alston, *Inventory*.

Robert Sanderson 1587–1663
> Bishop of Lincoln. Few of his books can be traced today, but he had a sizeable library and left extensive directions for its disposal in his will.
> *ODNB*. Armorials database.

John Warner 1581–1666
> Bishop of Rochester. Gave money for books to Magdalen College, Oxford, and Rochester Cathedral; bequeathed his books and papers to his nephew John Lee. Library auctioned in London, 16 Feb. 1685 (2,481 lots, 'principally' Warner's).
> *ODNB*. R. Beadle, 'Medieval English manuscripts at auction, 1676–*c.*1700', *BC* 53 (2004), 46–63. Alston, *Inventory*.

Matthew Wren 1585–1667
> Bishop of Ely. Gave books to Pembroke College, Cambridge over many years, and redeveloped the college library. Bequeathed his library around his family; numerous books with his motto 'Moriendo ViVam' survive today.
> *ODNB*. A. Attwater, *A short history of Pembroke College, Cambridge* (Cambridge, 1936), 66–7.

John Hacket 1592–1670
> Bishop of Lichfield. Bequeathed his books (over 1,000 volumes, some sold) to Cambridge University Library; also gave money for books to St John's, and Trinity College, Cambridge.
> *ODNB*. Lee, *British*, no. 14. Oates, 397–415. Armorials database.

John Cosin 1594–1672

Bishop of Durham. Built a diocesan library for Durham, to which he gave his books (*c*.5,500 volumes); also gave books to Peterhouse, Cambridge.

ODNB. A. I. Doyle, 'John Cosin (1595–1672) as a library maker', *BC* 24 (1975): 25–32. A. I. Doyle, 'John Cosin', in W. Baker (ed.), *Pre-nineteenth-century British book collectors and bibliographers* (1999), 51–6. Oates, 169–70. Armorials database.

Robert Creighton 1593–1672

Bishop of Bath & Wells. Gave books to Wells Cathedral Library; bequeathed his study of books to his son.

ODNB. *Wells Cathedral Library* (Wells, 1982). G. Clingham, 'Johnson's copy of The Iliad at Felbrigg Hall', *BC* 37 (1988) 503–21. Armorials database.

Humphrey Henchman 1592–1675

Bishop of London. Library sold by retail sale in London, 1677 (1,347 lots).

ODNB. Alston, *Inventory*.

Edward Reynolds 1599–1676

Bishop of Norwich. Bequeathed his library mostly around his family.

ODNB. Armorials database.

Peter Gunning 1614–84

Bishop of Ely. Bequeathed most of his books to St John's College, Cambridge, where several thousand survive today; left £100 to Canterbury Cathedral, with which books were purchased.

ODNB. N. Ramsay, 'The Cathedral Archives and Library', in P. Collinson (ed.), *A history of Canterbury Cathedral* (1995), 341–407, 386. Armorials database.

George Morley 1598?–1684

Bishop of Winchester. Bequeathed his books (*c*.2,000 volumes) to Winchester Cathedral Library.

ODNB. F. Bussby, *Winchester Cathedral Library*, 2nd edn (Winchester, 1975).

William Gulston 1636–84

Bishop of Bristol. Library auctioned in London, 3 Apr. 1689 (*c*.2,400 lots).

R. Beadle, 'Medieval English manuscripts at auction, 1676–*c*.1700', *BC* 53 (2004): 46–63.

John Fell 1625–86

Bishop of Oxford. Bequeathed all his property to his nephew Henry Jones, who gave many of his books/MSS to the Bodleian Library.

ODNB. M. Purcell, ' "Useful weapons for the defence of that cause": Richard Allestree, John Fell and the foundation of the Allestree Library', *The Library*, 6th ser. 21 (1999): 124–47. W. Poole, *John Fell's new year books* (2018).

Laurence Womock 1612–86

Bishop of St David's. Library auctioned in Cambridge, 23 May 1687 (joint sale, with the stock of a Cambridge bookseller).

ODNB. Alston, *Inventory*.

John Lloyd 1638–87

Bishop of St David's. Library auctioned in London, 6 Feb. 1699 (2,558 lots, though the sale includes later books which were not his).

ODNB. Alston, *Inventory*.

John Lake 1624–89

Bishop of Chichester. Library auctioned in London, 27 Apr. 1691, with a later second sale for which no catalogue survives.

ODNB. Alston, *Inventory*.

Seth Ward 1617–89
Bishop of Salisbury, and astronomer. Bequeathed 300 volumes to Salisbury Cathedral
Library.
ODNB. CHL II 125.

Thomas Barlow 1607–91
Bishop of Lincoln. Bequeathed his large collections to the Bodleian, with the proviso that
books already in that library should go to Queen's, Oxford.
ODNB. Philip 65. Macray 157–8. W. Poole, 'Thomas Barlow's books at Queen's', *Insight*
(Michaelmas 2013): 3–7.

Robert Grove *c.*1634–96
Bishop of Chichester. Library auctioned in London, 27 Apr. 1697 (1,949 lots).
ODNB. Alston, *Inventory.*

Thomas White 1628–98
Bishop of Peterborough. Bequeathed *c.*1,300 volumes to found a town library for
Newark-on-Trent.
ODNB. Perkin, 294–6.

Edward Stillingfleet 1635–99
Bishop of Worcester. His library (*c.*10,000 volumes) was divided mainly between
Narcissus Marsh, who bought the printed books for £2,500 in 1705 (thus creating one
of the major components of Marsh's Library in Dublin), and Robert Harley, who bought
the manuscripts for £175 in 1707 (these, therefore, are now among the Harleian
Manuscripts in the BL).
ODNB. Fontes Harleianae. M. McCarthy, *All graduates and gentlemen* (Dublin, 1980).

Robert Huntington 1637–1701
Bishop of Raphoe, previously chaplain to the English Factory at Aleppo, gathered
extensive oriental collections during his travels; gave oriental books to Merton,
Oriental MSS purchased by Bodleian after his death. Remainder of library sold at auction
in London, 27 Jan. 1702, 16 May 1702 (1,443 lots).
ODNB. Philip, 60–61. Alston, *Inventory.*

Thomas Smith 1615–1702
Bishop of Carlisle. Bequeathed his library to Carlisle Cathedral.
ODNB. C. Holtby, 'Carlisle Cathedral Library and records', *Transactions of the
Cumberland and Westmorland Archaeological and Antiquarian Society*, n.s. 66 (1966):
201–19, 214–19. D. Weston, *Carlisle Cathedral history* (2000), 124.

Richard Kidder 1633–1703
Bishop of Bath & Wells. Described as a man of many books; none were left to
Wells Cathedral, but the library there has a MS catalogue of *c.*500 volumes
owned by him. The collection appears to have passed to Nathaniel Brydges,
Chancellor of Wells.
ODNB. C. Church, 'Notes on the…Library of the Dean and Chapter…of Wells',
Archaeologia 57 (1901): 201–28.

Simon Patrick 1626–1707
Bishop of Ely. His extensive library was augmented by the bequest of his brother John's
books. Bequeathed books to Ely Cathedral Library; other books of his were sold by retail
sale in London, 13 Apr. 1713 (no catalogue survives).
ODNB. D. Owen, *The library and muniments of Ely Cathedral* (1973). Alston,
Inventory.

John Hall 1633–1710
Bishop of Bristol. Bequeathed his books to Pembroke College, Oxford (where he was
Master).
ODNB. Morgan.

Thomas Ken 1637–1711
Bishop of Bath & Wells (deprived). Bequeathed his books firstly to Viscount Weymouth
of Longleat, with duplicates to go to Wells Cathedral (*c*.450 volumes); and all his French,
Italian, and Spanish books to Bath Abbey Library.
ODNB. Wells Cathedral Library (Wells, 1982). S. West, An architectural typology for the
early modern country house library, 1660–1720, *The Library*, 7th ser. 14 (2013): 441–64, 445.

Thomas Wagstaffe 1645–1712
Nonjuring bishop of Ipswich. Library sold by retail sale in London, 13 Apr. 1713 (no
catalogue survives). Edward Bernard's *Catalogi manuscriptorum* (1697) lists him as
owning 48 manuscripts.
ODNB. Alston, *Inventory*.

Henry Compton 1632–1713
Bishop of London. Used an engraved armorial bookplate, dated 1701 (Franks 6576/
*599). Bequeathed *c*.1,900 volumes to St Paul's Cathedral Library; also bequeathed books
to Sion College. In 1707, gave to Sion College a collection of Bibles and lexicons,
bequeathed to him by Edmund Castell (1606–85).
ODNB. E. Pearce, *Sion College and Library* (1913), 264–5, 276. Lee, *British*, 31.

Edward Fowler 1632–1714
Bishop of Gloucester. Used an engraved armorial bookplate dated 1703 (Franks *596).
ODNB.

John Moore 1646–1714
Bishop of Ely. His collection of *c*.30,000 books, the largest private library of his
generation, was bought by George I for presentation to Cambridge University. His
household goods were sold by auction in London, 16 Mar. 1715. Listed in Edward
Bernard's *Catalogi manuscriptorum* (1697) as owning many hundreds of manuscripts.
ODNB. D. McKitterick, *Cambridge University Library: a history*, vol. 2 (1986): 47–152.
J. Baker, *A catalogue of legal manuscripts in Cambridge University Library* (1996), xlv–
xlvii. J. Ringrose, 'The Royal Library: John Moore and his books', in P. Fox (ed.),
Cambridge University Library: the great collections (1998). Alston, *Inventory*.

Gilbert Burnet 1643–1715
Bishop of Salisbury. Library auctioned in London, 19 Mar. 1716 (2,815 lots). Some books
of his are now in the Library Company of Philadelphia. Used an engraved armorial
bookplate (Franks 4460/*597).
DNB. E. Wolf, 'Some books of English provenance in the Library Company of
Philadelphia', *BC* 9 (1960): 275–84, 281. Alston, *Inventory*.

Deans

Thomas Neville *c*.1548–1615
Dean of Canterbury. Bequeathed 125 MSS and 75 printed books to Trinity College,
Cambridge.
ODNB. Gaskell/TCC.

Anthony Higgin d. 1623
Dean of Ripon. Gave over 700 books to Ripon Minster between 1615 and 1623.
J. Mortimer, 'The library catalogue of Anthony Higgin, Dean of Ripon', *Proceedings of the Leeds Philological and Literary Society*, Literature and History Section, 10(1) (1962).

John Boys 1571–1625
Dean of Canterbury. Depicted in his study of books in the frontispiece to his *Works*, 1622, although we do not know the size or fate of his library.
ODNB.

Henry Beaumont d. 1627
Dean of Windsor. Bequeathed *c.*80 volumes to St George's Windsor.
J. Callard, *A catalogue of printed books (pre-1751) in the Library of St George's Chapel Windsor* (Windsor, 1976), xvii.

Matthew Sutcliffe 1549/50–1629
Dean of Exeter; first provost of Chelsea College. Bequeathed his books to the College.
ODNB. CHL I 390.

John Donne 1572–1631
Dean of St Paul's, and poet. Over 200 volumes from his library survive.
ODNB. CELM. Appx IV ('Books from Donne's library') in G. Keynes, *A bibliography of Dr. John Donne*, 4th edn (1973). M. Hobbs, 'More books from the library of John Donne', *BC* 29 (1980), 590–92. G. Keynes, 'More books from the library of John Donne', *BC* 26 (1977): 29–35, and *BC* 27 (1978): 570–72. K. Whitlock, 'The Robert Ashley founding bequest to the Middle Temple Library and John Donne's library', *Sederi* 14 (2004): 153–75. H. Adlington, 'More books from the library of John Donne', *BC* 61 (2012): 55–64. H. Adlington, 'Close reader: John Donne's Horace', *TLS* (20 Jan. 2015): 14–15. H. Adlington, 'Seven more books from the library of John Donne', *BC* 67 (2018): 528–33.

Anthony Maxey d. 1648
Dean of Windsor. Bequeathed *c.*80 volumes to the Chapter Library of St George's, Windsor.
ODNB. J. Callard, *A catalogue of printed books (pre-1751) in the Library of St George's Chapel Windsor* (Windsor, 1976), xvii.

Richard Steward 1595–1651
Dean of Chichester, Provost of Eton (ejected), subsequently went to the Continent with the exiled English court. More than 370 books were seized from him by the London Committee for Sequestration in 1643, when they were valued at £110.
ODNB. Walker revised. Roy.

Christopher Wren 1591–1658
Dean of Windsor; father of the architect. Some annotated books of his are described in R. Colie, 'Dean Wren's marginalia and early science at Oxford', *BLR* 6 (1960): 541–51.
ODNB.

Griffin Higgs 1589–1659
Dean of Lichfield. Bequeathed his books to Merton College, Oxford; left £50 for the purchase of books to St John's, Oxford.
ODNB. P. S. Morrish, *Bibliotheca Higgsiana: a catalogue of the books of Dr Griffin Higgs* (1990).

Bruno Ryves c.1596–1677
Dean of Windsor. More than 110 books were seized from his London house by the London Committee for Sequestration in 1643, and partly sold.
ODNB. Roy.

Michael Honywood 1597–1681
Dean of Lincoln. Organized and paid for the building of Lincoln Cathedral Library, and bequeathed his books (c.5,000 volumes).
ODNB. D. Griffiths, 'Lincoln Cathedral Library', *BC* 19 (1970). J. Srawley, *Michael Honywood* (Lincoln, 1981). C. Hurst, *Catalogue of the Wren Library of Lincoln Cathedral* (Cambridge, 1982). N. Linnell, 'Michael Honywood and Lincoln Cathedral Library', *The Library*, 6th ser. 5 (1983): 126–39. I. Fenlon, 'Michael Honywood's music books', in C. Banks et al. (eds), *Sundry sorts of music books* (London, 1993), 183–200.

Matthew Smallwood 1615?–83
Dean of Lichfield. Library auctioned in London, 2 May 1684 (1,644 lots).
Foster. Alston, *Inventory*.

Thomas Pierce 1621/2–91
Dean of Salisbury, formerly President of Magdalen College, Oxford. Library auctioned in Oxford, 22 June 1709 (joint sale, with that of his son Robert Pierce, prebendary of Salisbury, d. 1707).
ODNB. Alston, *Inventory*.

Richard Meggott d. 1692
Dean of Winchester. Library auctioned in London, 6 Nov. 1693 (1,030 lots).
ODNB. Alston, *Inventory*.

George Bright d. 1696
Dean of St Asaph. Library sold by retail sale in London, July 1697 (no catalogue survives).
Venn. Alston, *Inventory*.

Thomas Comber 1645–99
Dean of Durham. His *Autobiographies and letters* contain numerous references to the acquiring and reading of books. Bequeathed his library around his family.
ODNB. C. Whiting (ed.), *The autobiographies and letters of Thomas Comber*, Surtees Society 156–7, 1946–7. C. B. L. Barr, 'The Minster Library', in G. E. Aylmer & R. Cant (eds), *A history of York Minster* (Oxford, 1977), 487–539, 506–9.

Thomas Gale 1635?–1702
Dean of York, and antiquary. A list of books belonging to him, dated c.1700, is in BL Sloane MS 203, fos 266–8. Gave oriental MSS to Trinity College, Cambridge. The bulk of his large library passed to his eldest son Roger (d. 1744), who gave their joint MSS collections to Trinity. Listed in Edward Bernard's *Catalogi manuscriptorum* (1697) as owning 491 manuscripts.
ODNB. D. McKitterick, *The making of the Wren Library* (Cambridge, 1995), 61–4.

Robert Woodward 1653?–1702
Dean of Salisbury. Library auctioned in London, 30 Nov. 1702 (1,203 lots).
Foster. Alston, *Inventory*.

Denis Granville 1637–1703
Dean of Durham, deprived as a nonjuror 1691. His library was then purchased by Sir George Wheler for £221.
ODNB.

Daniel Price d. 1706
Dean of St Asaph. Library auctioned in London, 24 Jan. 1709 (no catalogue survives).
Venn. Alston, *Inventory.*

George Hickes 1642–1715
Dean of Worcester, deprived as a nonjuror 1690; Anglo-Saxon and philological scholar.
Library auctioned in London, 15 Mar. 1716 (2,108 lots); gave coins and books to the
Bodleian Library.
ODNB. Macray. D. Douglas, *English scholars* (1939), ch. 4. Alston, *Inventory.*

Canons and Prebendaries

Richard Colfe d. 1613
Prebendary of Canterbury. Collected MSS from Canterbury Cathedral Priory and other
sources, some of which were given by his sons to the Bodleian Library in 1616.
Foster. Macray. N. Ramsay, 'The Cathedral Archives and Library', in P. Collinson (ed.),
A history of Canterbury Cathedral (Oxford, 1995), 341–407, 378.

Isaac Casaubon 1559–1614
Prebendary of Canterbury, classical scholar. Edward Bernard's *Catalogi manuscriptorum*
(1697), lists 110 MSS which belonged to him. Many of his books were bought for the Royal
Library; 61 volumes of his adversaria were bequeathed to the Bodleian by his son Meric in
1671. At the time of his death, he owned *c.*1,200 books in England and *c.*850 in Paris.
ODNB. Macray, 136. T. Birrell, 'The reconstruction of the library of Isaac Casaubon',
Hellinga festschrift (Amsterdam, 1980): 59–68. H. Craster, 'Casaubon's Greek MSS', *BLQ*
5 (1926): 97–100. A. Grafton and J. Weinberg, 'Isaac Casaubon's library of Hebrew
books', in G. Mandelbrote and B. Taylor (eds), *Libraries within the library* (2009), 24–42.

Richard Gerard d. 1614
Prebendary of Southwell, rector of Stockport, Cheshire. The will of his widow, Ursula
(d. 1624), bequeathed all her books and 'whole library' (apart from a couple of specified
titles) to their son Thomas.
Foster. C. Phillips, *Stockport probate records 1620–1650* (1992), 182.

William St Barbe d. 1619
Canon of Hereford Cathedral. Gave 22 books there *c.*1619.
Foster. Sears Jayne, 149.

Thomas White 1550–1624
Canon of St George's, Windsor. Founded Sion College, London, through a bequest of
£3,000; left his own folio and Latin books to St George's, and various Oxford benefac-
tions including money for books to Christ Church.
ODNB. E. H. Pearce, *Sion College and Library* (1913). Armorials database.

John Favour *c.*1557–1624
Canon of Southwell and York, vicar of Halifax. His personal library ('evidently a large
one'—*CHL*) was bequeathed to his son John and other family members.
ODNB. CHL I 400–01.

William Crashawe 1572–1626
Prebendary of Ripon and of York, vicar of St Mary Whitechapel. Assembled one of the
largest private libraries of his time, estimated at 4,000 books and 200 MSS in 1613, that
cost him £2,000. A proportion was bought by the Earl of Southampton in 1614 to give to
St John's College, Cambridge.

ODNB. P. J. Wallis, 'The library of William Crashawe', *TCBS* 2 (1956): 213–28. P. J. Wallis, 'William Crashawe, the Sheffield Puritan', *Transactions of the Hunter Archaeological Society* 8 (1960–63): ii–v. R. M. Fisher, 'William Crashawe's library at the Temple', *The Library*, 5th ser. 30 (1975): 116–24. Armorials database.

Thomas Thornton *c.*1541–1629
Canon of Christ Church, Oxford; canon of Hereford Cathedral and *custos* of the Cathedral Library 1595–7, 1610–17. Reformed and remodelled the library, partly at his own expense; bequeathed books to Hereford.
Foster. *CHL* I 394–5.

William Yemans 1553/4–1633
Prebendary of Bristol, vicar of St Philip & St Jacob, Bristol. Probate inventory lists 'the remainder of the books which were not given in the deceased's lifetime', valued at £20.
Foster. E. George (ed.), *Bristol probate inventories 1542–1650* (2002), 81.

Thomas Goad 1576–1638
Precentor of St Paul's, rector of Hadleigh, Suffolk. Inherited books from his father, Thomas, to which he added. Established a parish library at Hadleigh, and left an endowment to King's College, Cambridge, for the purchase of books.
ODNB. Perkin, 224–5. Armorials database.

Henry Mason 1575/6–1647
Prebendary of St Paul's. Gave books to Brasenose College, Oxford valued at £1,000; also gave a library to Wigan Grammar School, during his lifetime.
ODNB. Morgan. R. Christie, *Old church and school libraries of Lancashire* (1885), 192.

William Watts *c.*1590–1649
Prebendary of Wells, vicar of Barwick, Norfolk (ejected 1648). His goods, including 350 books, were ordered to be seized in 1643, when his books were valued at £94.
ODNB. *Walker revised*. Roy.

John Montfort d. 1651
Prebendary of Ely, rector of Anstey and Therfield, Hertfordshire 1640 (sequestrated 1643). His library was valued in 1643 at £1,000.
Venn. *Walker revised*.

Gilbert Wimberly d. 1653
Prebendary of Wells and Westminster, rector of Englefield, Berkshire. Goods seized in 1643, when he was said to have lost a library valued at £1,000.
Venn. *Walker revised*.

Henry Hutton *c.*1609–55
Canon of Carlisle, rector of Long Marton. His library of *c.*240 volumes was bequeathed to Arthur Savage, also a canon of Carlisle, who gave them to Carlisle Cathedral in 1691.
Venn. D. Weston, *Carlisle Cathedral history* (Carlisle, 2000), 123.

Barnaby Barlow d. 1657
Prebendary of York and Southwell, rector of Barton in Fabis, Nottinghamshire (ejected 1646). Will refers to the sale of his books for the benefit of the poor at Barton.
Venn. *Walker revised*.

John Cooth 1593/4–1661
Prebendary of Salisbury and of Wells, rector of Shepton Mallet, Somerset (ejected 1645). Library auctioned in London, 25 May 1685 (joint sale, with one other).
Foster. *Walker revised*. Alston, *Inventory*.

Peter Heylyn 1599–1662
Prebendary of Westminster, rector of Alresford (ejected 1644), historian. The goods seized from him in 1643 included his library, valued at £1,000, which was sent to Portsmouth and never recovered by him.
ODNB. Walker revised.

David Stokes 1590/92–1669
Canon of Windsor; held various ecclesiastical livings. Library auctioned in London, 1 Dec. 1685 (joint sale).
ODNB. Gaskell/TCC, 234. Alston, *Inventory.*

Meric Casaubon 1599–1671
Prebendary of Canterbury. Edward Stillingfleet bought many of his books, which are now in Archbishop Marsh's Library, Dublin. Some other volumes from his library came into Canterbury Cathedral Library through gifts to William Somner.
ODNB.

Edward Cotton 1616/7–75
Canon and Treasurer of Exeter. Bequeathed 1,200 volumes to the Cathedral.
Foster. *CHL* II 125.

Richard Wrench d. 1675
Prebendary of Durham, rector of Boldon. Gave 126 volumes to St John's College, Cambridge *c.*1640.
Venn. Sears Jayne, 172.

Thomas Greaves 1612–76
Prebendary of Peterborough, previously deputy professor of Arabic at Oxford. Inherited oriental MSS from his brother John (q.v.); 55 books and MSS from his collection were purchased by the Bodleian after his death.
ODNB. Macray, 147.

Richard Harrison 1611–76
Chancellor of Lichfield, vicar of St Mary's, Lichfield. Probate inventory lists 'a Bible a stand and Book of Martyrs' in the hall, valued at 14s. 0d., and 'books' in the study, valued at £50.
Venn. D. Vaisey (ed.), *Probate inventories of Lichfield and district 1568–1680* (1969), 252.

Edward Davenant d. 1680
Treasurer of Salisbury, vicar of Gillingham, Dorset. Said to have had a noble library, made up of his own books, those of his father, and those of his uncle John Davenant, Bishop of Salisbury (1572–1641).
Venn. Pearson, 'Bishops'.

William Hawkins d. 1683
Prebendary of Norwich. Library sold by retail sale in London, 13 Apr. 1685 (2,521 lots, but not clear that these were all his books).
Foster. Alston, *Inventory.*

Robert Sharrock 1630–84
Prebendary and archdeacon of Winchester. The joint libraries of Sharrock and his son (also Robert), over 2,000 volumes, were auctioned in London, 26 Feb. 1711.
ODNB. Alston, *Inventory.*

Ambrose Atfield d. 1684
Prebendary of St Pauls, vicar of St Mary Somerset, London. Library auctioned in London, 25 May 1686 (joint sale, with one other).
Venn. Alston, *Inventory.*

John Bradford d. 1685
Prebendary of Canterbury, vicar of Bexhill, Surrey. Library auctioned in London, 14 June 1686 (joint sale, with one other).
Venn. Alston, *Inventory*.

Edward Carter d. 1687
Prebendary of St Paul's, rector of St Albans. Library auctioned in St Albans, 5 Aug. 1689 (761 lots).
Venn. Alston, *Inventory*.

Anthony Scattergood 1611–87
Canon of Lincoln and Lichfield. Library auctioned in London, 26 July 1697, after the death of his son (1,960 lots).
ODNB. Alston, *Inventory*.

William Sill d. 1687
Prebendary of Carlisle, and of St Paul's; Rector of St Augustine's, Watling Street, London. Library auctioned in London, 21, 29 Nov. 1687 (joint sale, with one other).
Venn. Alston, *Inventory*.

Peter Scott d. 1689
Prebendary of Windsor. Library auctioned in London, 28 Apr. 1690 (1,209 lots).
Venn. R. Beadle, 'Medieval English manuscripts at auction, 1676–*c*.1700', *BC* 53 (2004), 46–63. Alston, *Inventory*.

James Jeffreys 1649/50–89
Prebendary of Canterbury, vicar of Chartham, Kent. Bequeathed £20 worth of books to Canterbury Cathedral Library.
N. Ramsay, 'The Cathedral Archives and Library', in P. Collinson (ed.), *A history of Canterbury Cathedral* (Oxford, 1995), 341–407, 386.

Thomas Spark 1655–92
Prebendary of Rochester. Library auctioned in London, 3 July 1693 (1,468 lots).
ODNB. Alston, *Inventory*.

Peter Samways 1615–93
Prebendary of York, rector of Bedale, Yorkshire. Several books with an armorial stamp attributed to him survive.
ODNB. Armorials database.

Adam Littleton 1627–94
Canon of Westminster, rector of Chelsea. Library auctioned in London, 15 Apr. 1695 (1,186 lots).
ODNB. Alston, *Inventory*.

John Hinckley 1618–95
Prebendary of Lichfield, rector of Northfield, Worcestershire. Bequeathed 'half my books or £40 at his choice' to his son Walter.
ODNB. W. Carter (ed.), *The records of King Edward's School, Birmingham*, vol. 3 (London, 1933), 194.

John Patrick 1632–95
Precentor of Chichester; brother of Simon Patrick, Bishop of Ely, to whom he left 'a noble library, which cost him above £1000'.
ODNB.

John Scott 1638/9–95
Canon of St Paul's, rector of St Giles in the Fields, London. Library auctioned in London, 23 May 1695 (the surviving copy of the catalogue is partial and defective).
ODNB. Alston, *Inventory*.

George Tullie 1654–95
Canon of York, rector of Gateshead. Library sold by retail sale in London, 21 Nov. 1695 (392 lots, 'with many others not here mentioned').
ODNB. Alston, *Inventory*.

Anthony Horneck 1641–97
Prebendary of Westminster, and Bath & Wells. Library auctioned in London, 15 Apr. 1697 (1,577 lots).
ODNB. Alston, *Inventory*.

William Hopkins 1647–1700
Prebendary of Worcester. Library auctioned in Oxford, 10 Feb. 1701 (2,041 lots).
ODNB. Alston, *Inventory*.

William Wigan d. 1700
Canon of St Paul's, rector of St Mary Abbots, Kensington. Library sold by retail sale in London, 31 Jan. 1701 (no catalogue survives).
Venn. Alston, *Inventory*.

John Milner 1628–1703
Prebendary of Ripon, deprived as a nonjuror, retired to St John's College, Cambridge. Library auctioned in London, 4 Apr. 1715 (joint sale, with one other).
ODNB. Alston, *Inventory*.

John Skelton d. 1704
Canon of Lincoln, archdeacon of Bedford. Library auctioned in London, 13 Nov. 1704 (2,342 lots).
Venn. Alston, *Inventory*.

Francis Durant de Brevall d. 1707
Prebendary of Westminster, minister of the French Church in the Savoy. Library sold by retail sale in London, 10 May 1708 (no catalogue survives).
ODNB (see entry for his son, John Durant Breval). Alston, *Inventory*.

Clement Sankey 1633?–1707
Canon of York, rector of Whitchurch, Shropshire. His books were bought by Jane, Dowager Countess of Bridgewater in 1707, for £305, and given to the parish of Whitchurch.
Venn. Perkin, 388–9.

Robert Pierce 1657/8–1707
Prebendary of Salisbury. Library auctioned in Oxford, 22 June 1709 (joint sale, with that of his father, Thomas Pierce, Dean of Salisbury, d. 1691).
Foster. Alston, *Inventory*.

Gilbert Atkinson d. 1709
Canon of York, rector of Methley, Yorkshire. Library auction in London, 31 Oct. 1710 (joint sale, with one other).
Venn. Alston, *Inventory*.

Robert Burscough 1650/1–1709
Prebendary of Exeter, rector of Cheriton Bishop, Devon. Bequeathed several hundred volumes to Exeter Cathedral Library. His collection of MSS was purchased for the Harleian Library in 1715. Listed in Edward Bernard's *Catalogi manuscriptorum* (1697) as owning 111 manuscripts.
ODNB. P. Thomas, *Medicine and science at Exeter Cathedral Library*, 2003. Wanley, *Diary* vol. 1, pp. 2, 11.

Humfrey Smith 1655?–1709
Prebendary of Exeter, vicar of Townstall, Devon. Bequeathed several hundred volumes to Exeter Cathedral Library.
Foster. P. Thomas, *Medicine and science at Exeter Cathedral Library* (2003).

Peter Birch 1651/2–1710
Prebendary of Westminster, vicar of St Bride's, Fleet Street. Library auctioned in London, 16 Oct. 1710 (joint sale, no catalogue survives).
ODNB. Alston, *Inventory*.

Joseph Kelsey d. 1710
Prebendary of Salisbury, archdeacon of Sarum. Library auctioned in Oxford, 17 Mar. 1712 (no catalogue survives).
Venn. Alston, *Inventory*.

William Nichols 1665/6–1711
Canon of Chichester, rector of Selsey, Sussex. Library auctioned in London, 1 Dec. 1712.
Foster. Alston, *Inventory*.

William Cave 1637–1713
Canon of Windsor, vicar of Isleworth. His library was purchased after his death by St George's Chapel, Windsor, for £645. Some of his books came from the library of his father, John Cave (d. 1657). A sale of duplicates from St George's Chapel Library, 'some of which were the late Dr Cave's', was held in London, 10 Jan. 1715 (no catalogue survives).
ODNB. Alston, *Inventory*.

Robert Middleton d. 1713
Prebendary of Ely; vicar of Cuckfield, Sussex. Bequeathed his library of *c*.700 books to the son of Symon Patrick, on condition that he become a clergyman not a lawyer; in fact the books were given to the SPCK.
Venn. Cambers, 125.

William Higden 1663/4–1715
Prebendary of Canterbury, rector of St Paul's, Shadwell. Library auctioned in London, 17 Oct. 1715 (no catalogue survives).
ODNB. Alston, *Inventory*.

Archdeacons

Richard Butler d. 1612
Archdeacon of Northampton. Gave 19 MSS and 2 printed books to St John's College, Oxford in 1613, bequeathing the rest of his books to John Buckeridge.
ODNB.

Philip Bisse 1541?–1613
Archdeacon of Taunton. Gave his library (c.2,000 volumes) to Wadham College, Oxford.
Foster. Morgan. J. Simpson, *The collection of Philip Bisse* (MPhil. thesis, Oxford, 1997).
W. Poole, *Wadham College books in the age of John Wilkins* (2014), 31–7.

Richard Buckenham c.1565–1628
Archdeacon of Lewes, prebendary of Chichester. Instrumental in organizing William
Smarte's gift of MSS to Pembroke College, Cambridge. Bequeathed his books to his son
Richard, on condition that he could sell them if necessary to fund his studies at
Cambridge.
Venn. J. Blattchly, *The town library of Ipswich* (1989), 3.

Henry Hammond 1605–60
Archdeacon of Chichester, canon of Christ Church, Oxford (ejected c.1646). 138
volumes from his collection passed to Richard Allestree, and hence into his
library left to Oxford (held at Christ Church) for the use of the Regius professor
of divinity.
ODNB. Morgan. M. Purcell, '"Useful weapons for the defence of that cause": Richard
Allestree, John Fell and the foundation of the Allestree Library', *The Library*, 6th ser. 21
(1999), 124–47.

Timothy Thurscross d. 1671
Archdeacon of Cleveland. Directed in his will that his study of books should be
distributed to three Yorkshire churches.
Foster. Perkin, 303.

John Riland d. 1673
Archdeacon of Stafford and of Coventry, rector of Exhall, Warwickshire (ejected).
During the Civil War he complained that his study in Oxford was broken up, with the
loss of all his books and papers, which were allegedly sold.
Foster. *Walker revised.*

Isaac Basire 1607–76
Archdeacon of Northumberland. Library auctioned in London, 5 Feb. 1710 (1,659 lots).
ODNB. Alston, *Inventory.*

William Outram 1626–79
Archdeacon of Leicester. Library auctioned in London, 12 Dec. 1681 (joint sale, with two
others).
ODNB. Alston, *Inventory.*

Edward Lake 1641–1704
Archdeacon of Exeter. Library auctioned in London, 15 and 25 May 1704 (1,267 lots).
ODNB. Alston, *Inventory.*

Thomas Plume 1630–1704
Archdeacon of Rochester. Bequeathed c.8,000 volumes to found a town library for
Maldon, Essex, in a redundant church which he paid to have repurposed.
ODNB. W. J. Petchey, *The intentions of Thomas Plume* (Maldon, 1985). K. Manley,
'Thomas Plume', in W. Baker (ed.), *Pre-nineteenth-century British book collectors and
bibliographers* (1999), 274–8. D. Pearson, 'Thomas Plume's Library in its contemporary
context', in C. Thornton & T. Doe (eds), *Dr Thomas Plume, 1630–1704: his life and
legacies* (2020).

John Batteley 1647–1708
Archdeacon of Canterbury. Bequeathed books to Canterbury Cathedral Library. Humphrey Wanley, on behalf of Robert Harley, conducted negotiations for the purchase of his library, 1715–25; 72 MSS were subsequently acquired by Harley.
ODNB. Wanley, *Diary*, vol. 1, pp. 15ff.

John Cawley 1632?–1709
Archdeacon of Lincoln, rector of Henley on Thames, Oxfordshire. Library auctioned in Oxford, 27 May 1712 (joint sale, with one other).
Foster. Alston, *Inventory*.

Edward Waple 1647–1712
Archdeacon of Taunton. Bequeathed his library (*c*.1,860 volumes, plus *c*.300 duplicates sold) to Sion College.
Foster. E. Pearce, *Sion College and Library* (Cambridge, 1913), 274–5.

Vicars, rectors and others of similar status

Walter Browne d. 1613
Rector of Cuddington, Oxfordshire. Probate inventory (transcribed and edited as PLRE 159) lists *c*.535 books.
Foster. I. G. Philip and P. Morgan, 'Libraries, books and printing', in N. Tyacke (ed.), *The history of the University of Oxford*, vol. 4 (Oxford, 1997), 659–85, 684. J. Black, 'Walter Brown', in R. Fehrenbach and J. Black (eds), PLRE 7 (2009): 113–209.

Jasper Gryffyth d. 1614
Vicar of Hinckley, Leicestershire. Owned a number of significant early Welsh MSS.
ODNB. R. Ovenden, 'Jaspar Gryffyth and his books', *BLJ* 20 (1994): 107–34.

William Charke d. 1617
Lecturer at Lincoln's Inn, suspended for his Puritanism in 1593. Books with his inscription are now found in many libraries, indicating a sizeable collection, dispersed soon after his death.
ODNB.

William Shorte d. 1617
Minister, of Banbury. Probate inventory lists 'his bookes in his study' valued at £5.
Foster. J. Gibson (ed.), *Banbury wills and inventories 1591–1620* (1985), 261–2.

Thomas Peter d. 1618
Rector of St Mawgan, Cornwall. Numerous books at Lanhydrock previously belonged to him; his library may have passed to Hannibal Gamon, his successor in the rectory.
M. Purcell, 'The library at Lanhydrock', *BC* 54 (2005): 195–230.

Richard Crakanthorpe 1568–1624
Rector of Paglesham, Essex; Calvinist author. His library, valued at £230, was left in his will to his son John.
ODNB. Cambers, 124–5.

William Neile 1560–1624
Rector of Sutton in the Marsh, Lincolnshire; steward to his brother Richard, Archbishop of York. A number of books survive with his inscription; his will refers to over 800 books, bequeathed among members of his family: www.english.cam.ac.uk/cmt/?s=neile.

Richard Pernham 1583?–1628
Vicar of Stowmarket, fellow of Corpus Christi College, Cambridge, Pastor Anglicus at Elbing, near Gdansk, 1618–24. Either he or his widow, Mary, donated c.40 MSS from the Brigettine convent at of Elbing to Corpus Christi.
Venn. Munby.

Richard Amadas d. 1629
Rector of Hallingbury Magna, Essex. A number of his distinctively annotated MSS/ printed books are now in Cambridge University Library.
Oates, 344–7.

Richard Harvey 1560–1630
Rector of Chislehurst, Kent; brother of Gabriel. Books with his inscription survive in numerous libraries, often annotated, suggesting that he had an appreciable library.
ODNB. V. Stern, Gabriel Harvey: his life, marginalia and library (1979).

Richard Rainsford d. 1631
Of Ipswich, clerk. Probate inventory lists 'the lybrarye of bookes' in the study, valued at £10.
M. Reed (ed.), The Ipswich probate inventories 1583–1631 (1981), 110.

Alexander Cooke 1564–1632
Vicar of Leeds. His will contains instructions about the division of his library, valued at over £100, around his family.
ODNB. J. Barnard, 'A Puritan controversialist and his books: the will of Alexander Cooke', PBSA 86 (1992): 82–6. Cambers, 172–8.

Abdias Ashton 1563–1633
Rector of Middleton, Lancashire. Bequeathed 100 marks to St John's, Cambridge to buy books 'of the fathers or the new writers as they see fit'.
Venn. Lee, Labels, 83.

Thomas Pierson c.1573–1633
Rector of Bampton Bryan, Herefordshire. Bequeathed a collection of c.450 volumes to 13 named local ministers.
ODNB. Perkin, 287–9. J. Eales, 'Thomas Pierson and the transmission of the moderate puritan tradition', Midland History 20 (1995): 73–102. Cambers, 125.

Henry Bury d. 1636
'Clerk'; founder of the school at Bury, Lancashire; during his lifetime, gave c.600 books to found a parish library for Bury, and bequeathed other books, globes, maps, and papers to members of his family.
Perkin, 163. R. Christie, The old church and school libraries of Lancashire (1885), 139–40. Oates, 243.

Roger Beare d. 1637
Rector of Morchard Bishop, Devon. Probate inventory lists 'his bookes' valued at £20.
M. Cash (ed.), Devon inventories of the sixteenth and seventeenth centuries (1966), 53.

Richard Knight d. 1639
Vicar of Temple, Bristol. Probate inventory lists 'his books' valued at '20 nobles or thereabouts'.
E. George (ed.), Bristol probate inventories 1542–1650 (2002), 110.

William Alabaster 1567–1640
Rector of Therfield, Hertfordshire; poet and dramatist. Books with his inscription are found in several libraries.
ODNB. CELM. J. Sparrow, 'The earlier owners of books in John Selden's library', BLQ 6 (1931).

William Milbourne d. 1640?

Graduated BA at Christ's College, Cambridge 1620; possibly rector of Brancepeth, Co. Durham; noted as a mathematician. His collection of books and mathematical instruments was bought by Elias Ashmole in 1650.

J. Peile, *Biographical register of Christ's College 1505–1905* (1910), vol. 1, p. 302. H. A. Feisenberger, *Sale catalogues of libraries of eminent persons*, 11: *Scientists* (1975), 3. M. Feingold, *The mathematicians' apprenticeship* (1984), 111.

Thomas Palmer d. 1640

Vicar of St Mary Redcliffe, Bristol. Probate inventory lists his study of books, valued at £60.

Venn. E. George (ed.), *Bristol probate inventories 1542–1650* (2002), 117.

Thomas Burdsell d. 1642

Minister of Stockport, Cheshire. Probate inventory lists books valued at £40 17s. 10d. In his will, he left his library to the ministers of Stockport in perpetuity, giving directions for their housing.

C. Phillips (ed.), *Stockport probate records 1620–1650* (1992), 231.

Thomas Pierce d. 1643

Rector of St Martin Outwich, London. His goods were seized in 1643, when his books were valued at £14 17s.

Foster. *Walker revised.*

Thomas Pilgrim d. 1644

Vicar of Wormingford, Essex. His library was purchased by Ralph Josselin after his death for £16 18s.

Venn. Cambers, 126–7.

Hugh Collins 1566/7–c.1646

Rector of Compton Pauncefoot, Somerset; ejected 1646, when his library was valued at £16 10s. 8d.

Foster. *Walker revised.*

Francis Meres 1565/6–1647

Rector of Wing, Rutland; author. A number of his books, often annotated, survive in Peterborough Cathedral Library and elsewhere.

ODNB. J. Scott-Warren, 'Commonplacing and originality: Reading Francis Meres', *Review of English Studies* 68 (2017): 902–23.

John Potter d. 1648

Of Newton St Petroc, Devon, Clerk. Probate inventory lists books valued at £10.

M. Cash (ed.), *Devon inventories of the sixteenth and seventeenth centuries* (1966), 103.

Richard Day d. 1650

Rector of Prescot, Lancashire. His will refers to a 'good store of books' at King's College, Cambridge, where he had been a fellow.

Venn. T. Steel (ed.), *Prescot churchwardens' accounts 1635–1663* (2002), xiv–xv.

Hannibal Gamon 1582?–1651

Rector of St Mawgan, Cornwall. About 350 books in the library at Lanhydrock, Cornwall, bear evidence of Gamon's previous ownership.

ODNB. M. Purcell, 'The library at Lanhydrock', *BC* 54 (2005): 195–230.

Daniel Berry d. 1653
Vicar of Knowstone and Molland, Devon (ejected 1646); reported that when seques-
trated, all his books (9 horse-loads) were seized.
Venn. *Walker revised.*

John Squire *c.*1587–1653
Vicar of St Leonard, Shoreditch (ejected 1643); confined in Newgate Prison 1643–6
during which time he built up a collection of *c.*260 pamphlets, many of which subse-
quently passed to Edward Waddington (*c.*1670–1732), who bequeathed his library to
Eton College.
ODNB. T. Connor, 'Malignant reading: John Squier's prison library', 1642–6, *The
Library,* 7th ser. 7 (2006): 154–184.

Abraham Colfe 1580–1657
Vicar of Lewisham. Founded Colfe's Grammar School, Lewisham, in 1652 and
bequeathed his library to it (the surviving books are now housed in Leathersellers' Hall).
ODNB.

Robert Levet d. 1658
Vicar of Wood Ditton, Cambridgeshire (ejected 1644). Will refers to books at Exning.
Venn. *Walker revised.*

Edward Burton 1596–1661
Rector of Seddlescombe, Sussex. Two books with an armorial stamp attributed to him
are recorded.
Foster. Armorials database.

Robert Hitchcock d. 1663
Vicar of Aston Abbots, Buckinghamshire. Probate inventory lists books in his study and
elsewhere, valued at £30.
M. Reed (ed.), *Buckinghamshire probate inventories 1661–1714* (1988), 46.

Anthony Richardson d. 1665
Rector of West Camel, Somerset (ejected 1646, restored 1660). At the time of his
sequestration, books worth £10 were alleged to be taken from him but subsequently
restored.
Foster. *Walker revised.*

Richard Samwayes 1615/16–69
Rector of Meysey Hampton, Gloucestershire. Bequeathed first choice of his
books to Corpus Christi College, Oxford, with the remainder distributed around
his family.
Foster. Morgan. *Walker revised.*

John Dunton 1628–76
Rector of Aston Clinton, Buckinghamshire, father of the bookseller of the same name.
Library auctioned in London, 29 Nov. 1680 (joint sale, with 4 others).
Venn. Alston, *Inventory.*

George Davenport d. 1677
Rector of Houghton-le-Spring, Durham. Gave MSS and books to Cosin's Library,
Durham.
Venn. A. I. Doyle, 'The Cosin manuscripts and George Davenport', *BC* 53 (2004): 32–45.
B. Pask and M. Harvey (eds), *The letters of George Davenport 1651–1677* (2011).

John Knightbridge 1619/20–77
Rector of Spofforth, Yorkshire. About 400 volumes from his collection were given by his brother after his death to found a parish library at Chelmsford.
ODNB. Perkin, 173.

Edward Lewis d. 1677
Vicar of Chirbury, Shropshire. Bequeathed his books (*c.*200 volumes) to form a parish library for Chirbury.
Foster. Perkin, 175. D. Roberts, 'The chained parish library of Chirbury', *The Library*, 7th ser. 19 (2018): 469–83.

Walter Snell d. 1677
Chaplain to the Robartes family at Lanhydrock, Cornwall. Books at Lanhydrock previously belonged to him; it is possible that Hannibal Gamon's books passed to him before coming to the house.
M. Purcell, 'The library at Lanhydrock', *BC* 54 (2005): 195–230.

Charles Walmisley d. 1677
Vicar of Chesham Magna, Buckinghamshire. Probate inventory lists 'a great trunk full of books', valued at £20.
Foster. M. Reed (ed.), *Buckinghamshire probate inventories 1661–1714* (1988), 131.

Richard Boss d. 1678
Vicar of Sevenoaks, Kent. Probate inventory lists in the study 'the library of bookes', valued at £73 13*s.* 4*d.*, bequeathed to his two eldest sons. Part of the library was inherited from his father, Richard (d. 1665), also vicar of Sevenoaks.
Venn. H. Lansberry, *Sevenoaks wills and inventories in the reign of Charles II* (1988), 148–52.

William Boswell 1581/2–1678
Vicar of St Lawrence Jewry, London. Gave books to Balliol College, and to Sion College, 1633; books of his are found in several Oxford colleges.
Foster. Sears Jayne, 162.

George Lawson 1598?–1678
Rector of More, Shropshire. Library auctioned in London, 30 May 1681 (joint sale, with one other).
ODNB. C. Condren, 'More parish library', *Library History* 7 (1987): 141–61. C. Condren, 'George Lawson', in W. Baker (ed.), *Pre-nineteenth-century British book collectors and bibliographers* (1999), 215–20. Perkin, 287–9. Alston, *Inventory.*

Richard Newte 1612–78
Rector of Tiverton, Devon. Bequeathed his books to his son John (1656–1716), who succeeded him as rector of Tiverton, and who left their combined libraries of *c.*250 volumes to found a parish library for Tiverton; at least half originally belonged to Richard.
ODNB. Perkin, 371–2. A. Welsford, 'Mr. Newte's library in St Peter's Church, Tiverton', *Report and Transactions of the Devonshire Association for the Advancement of Science* 106 (1974): 17–31; 107 (1974): 11–20. Cambers, 141–2.

William White 1604–78
Rector of Pusey, Berkshire. Bequeathed *c.*600 volumes to found a parish library for Marlborough, Wiltshire.
ODNB. Perkin, 281.

Benjamin Dillingham 1635/6–79
Vicar of Oundle, Northamptonshire. Library auctioned in London, 29 Nov. 1680 (joint sale, with four others).
Venn. Alston, *Inventory.*

John Humphrey d. 1679
Vicar of Rothwell, Northamptonshire. Library auctioned in London, 4 Dec. 1682, 'cum aliis eruditorum virorum libris'; included 70 medieval MSS.
Venn. R. Beadle, 'Medieval English manuscripts at auction, 1676–c.1700', *BC* 53 (2004): 46–63. Alston, *Inventory*.

Thomas Jessop 1629/30–79
Vicar of Coggeshall, Essex. Library auctioned in London, 1 Feb. 1681 (joint sale, with one other).
Venn. Alston, *Inventory*.

Giles Moore 1617–79
Rector of Stanmer, Sussex. Kept a detailed day book/account book, which includes long lists of books bought in London, 1656–79. Bequeathed his books to his son-in-law John Citizen, rector of Street.
Venn. R. Bird (ed.), *The journal of Giles Moore* (1971), 116–19, 180–92, and *passim. CHL* II 182.

Thomas Castell d. 1680
Possibly the man of this name who was rector of Ilketshall St John, Suffolk. Library auctioned in London, 1 Feb. 1681 (joint sale, with one other).
Venn. Alston, *Inventory*.

Charles Gataker 1613–80
Thomas Gataker 1574–1634
Father and son. Thomas was rector of Rotherhithe, Surrey, and Charles (who inherited his father's books) was rector of Hoggeston, Buckinghamshire. Their combined library auctioned in London, 12 Dec. 1681 (joint sale, with one other).
ODNB. Alston, *Inventory*.

Daniel Rogers 1610?–80
Rector of Haversham, Buckinghamshire. Library auctioned in London, 21 June 1683 (joint sale, with one other).
Venn. Alston, *Inventory*.

John Ward d. 1681
Vicar of Stratford-upon-Avon, Warwickshire. Probate inventory lists 'the bookes in the studye', valued at £25.
J. Jones (ed.), *Stratford-upon-Avon inventories*, vol. 2: *1626–99* (2002), 185.

John Lloyd d. c.1682?
Priest at North Mymms, Hertfordshire. Library auctioned in London, 3 Dec. 1683 (joint sale, with one other).
Alston, *Inventory*.

Josiah Simcox 1645–82
Vicar of Stratford-upon-Avon. Probate inventory lists, in his study, 'a desk and his bookes', valued at £20.
Foster. J. Jones (ed.), *Stratford-upon-Avon inventories*, vol. 2: *1626–99* (2002), 189.

Creswell Whateley d. 1682
Rector of Tadmarton, Oxfordshire. Library auctioned in London, 23 Apr. 1683 (joint sale, with one other).
Venn. Alston, *Inventory*.

Charles Adams 1638/9–83
Vicar of Great Baddow, Essex. Library auctioned at Chelmsford, 16 Nov. 1683 (581 lots).
Foster. Alston, *Inventory*.

Richard Lee 1611–84
> Rector of Bishop Hatfield, Hertfordshire. Library auctioned in Hatfield, 28 Apr. 1685 (1,192 lots).
> Venn. Alston, *Inventory*.

John Randolph d. 1684
> Vicar of Chicheley, Buckinghamshire. Probate inventory lists 'a cabinet and books' in the closet, valued at £2, and 'a table a chest and books' in the study, valued at £50.
> M. Reed (ed.), *Buckinghamshire probate inventories 1661–1714* (1988), 183.

Obadiah Sedgwicke d. 1685
> Rector of Rampton, Cambridgeshire. Library auctioned in Trumpington, 29 Mar. 1686 (625 lots).
> Venn. Alston, *Inventory*.

Thomas Hill 1646/7–86
> Rector of North Crawley, Buckinghamshire. Probate inventory lists 'his study of books', valued at £20.
> Venn. M. Reed (ed.), *Buckinghamshire probate inventories 1661–1714* (1988), 194.

Thomas Leigh 1634/5–86
> Vicar of Bishops Stortford, Essex, and master of the grammar school there. Books of his were acquired by Ralph Freman (d. 1774), fellow of All Souls, Oxford, who bequeathed them (with his other books) to All Souls.
> Venn. E. Craster, *The history of All Souls College Library* (1971), 91.

Clement Barksdale 1609–87
> Rector of Naunton and Stow on the Wold, Gloucestershire, author. Gave books to Hereford Vicars Choral Library, and gave/sold books to Gloucester Cathedral Library in the 1670s.
> *ODNB*. S. Eward, *No fine but a glass of wine* (1985), 263–4.

Robert Wallis d. 1686
> Rector of Ellesborough, Buckinghamshire. Library auctioned in London, 2 Apr. 1688 (1,221 lots).
> Venn. Alston, *Inventory*.

Thomas Chambers d. 1689?
> Described as 'reverend and learned'. Library auctioned in London, 28 May 1689 (1,400 lots).
> Alston, *Inventory*.

Robert Wenseley 1647?–89
> Vicar of Cheshunt, Hertfordshire. Library sold at auction in Cheshunt, 17 June 1689 (550 lots).
> Venn. Alston, *Inventory*.

Thomas Alston d. 1690
> Vicar of Assington, Suffolk. Bequeathed his library of just under 300 vols to Assington, to create a parish library; *c*.190 survive today.
> Foster. Perkin, 124. *Suffolk parochial libraries: a catalogue* (London, 1977), xiv.

Thomas Thackham 1619/20–90?
> Rector of Nuffield, Oxfordshire. Library sold in London by retail sale, 2 Feb. 1704 (no catalogue survives).
> Venn. Alston, *Inventory*.

Robert Peade d. 1691
Rector of Horton, Buckinghamshire. Library auctioned in London, 20 Feb. 1693 (884 lots).
Venn. Alston, *Inventory*.

Thomas Grey d. 1692
Vicar of Dedham, Essex. Library auctioned in London, 8 Feb. 1694 (1,561 lots).
Venn. Alston, *Inventory*.

Richard Squibb 1639/40–92
Rector of West Coker, Somerset. Library auctioned in London 14 Dec. 1696 (no catalogue survives).
Venn. Alston, *Inventory*.

Peter Brown d. 1692
Edward Brown d. 1711
Successively rectors of Langley, Kent. Library auctioned in London, 10 May 1714.
Venn. Alston, *Inventory*.

Matthew Blewett 1652?–93
Rector of Ickborough, Norfolk. Library auctioned in London, 31 Jan. 1693 (871 lots, but probably only part of the whole).
Venn. Alston, *Inventory*.

Timothy Puller 1638–93
Rector of St Mary-le-Bow, London. Library auctioned in London, 10 Dec. 1695 (2,241 lots, though probably not all Puller's).
ODNB. Alston, *Inventory*.

George Ashwell 1612–94
Rector of Hanwell, Oxfordshire, 1658–94. Library auctioned in Oxford, 5 May 1696 (2,801 lots, but not all his).
ODNB. Alston, *Inventory*.

Richard Lumley d. 1694
Vicar of Stainton, Yorkshire. Bequeathed *c*.300 volumes to found a parish library for Stainton.
Venn. Perkin, 252–3.

William Bassett 1645?–96
Rector of St Swithin, London. Library auctioned in London, 4 Feb. 1697 (1,651 lots).
ODNB. D. Pearson, 'Patterns of book ownership in late seventeenth-century England', *The Library*, 7th ser. 11 (2010): 139–67. Alston, *Inventory*.

Norton d. *c*.1696?
Library auctioned in London, 14 Dec. 1696 (187 lots).
Alston, *Inventory*.

William Payne 1649/50–97
Rector of St Mary, Whitechapel. Library auctioned in London, 24 Feb. 1698, 21 Feb. 1699 (not, apparently, his entire library, at least one further part may be lost).
ODNB. Alston, *Inventory*.

Daniel Chamier 1661–98
Minister of the French Church in Leicester Fields, London. Library auctioned in London, 19 Sept. 1698 (no catalogue survives).
Alston, *Inventory*.

Shaw d. 1698?
Unidentified; described as 'the reverend Mr Shaw, late of Hornchurch in Essex'. Library auctioned in London, 4 May 1698 (1,428 lots).
Alston, *Inventory.*

Nathaniel Sterry d. 1698
Dean of Bicking, Essex. Library sold by retail sale in London, 13 Mar. 1701.
ODNB. Alston, *Inventory.*

Henry Cornwall d. 1700
Rector of Clapton, Northamptonshire. Library auctioned in London, 22 Apr. 1700 (1,119 lots).
Alston, *Inventory.*

John Cock *c.*1639–1701
Vicar of St. Oswald's, Durham. Bequeathed his books (over 1,500 volumes) to form a parish library for St. Oswald's (dispersed *c.*1930).
Venn. Perkin, 199–200.

Thomas Townsend d. 1701
Rector of Costock, Nottinghamshire. Bequeathed his books, *c.*300 volumes, to found a parish library for Costock.
Venn. Perkin, 182.

William Hodges 1668?–1702
Rector of St Swithin, London. Library auctioned in London, 23 Feb. 170 (1,594 lots, plus a further 718 'libri omissi' which may or may not have been his).
Venn. Alston, *Inventory.*

Andrew Lortie d. *c.*1702?
French Protestant minister in London. Library sold in London by retail sale, 6 Mar. 1702 (no catalogue survives).
Alston, *Inventory.*

Nathaniel Taylor d. 1702
'Clerk, of Nicholas Lane, near Lombard Street, London'. Library auctioned in London, 14 Dec. 1702 (no catalogue survives).
Venn. Alston, *Inventory.*

William Burkitt 1650–1703
Rector of Milden, Suffolk. Bequeathed *c.*2,000 volumes to found a parish library for Milden.
ODNB. Perkin, 284. *Suffolk parochial libraries: a catalogue* (London, 1977), xv. J. Fitch, 'Three lost Suffolk libraries' [letter to the Editor], *The Library*, 5th ser. 31 (1976): 147–9. G. Moate, 'The "lost" library of William Burkitt', *The Library*, 7th ser. 12 (2011): 119–141.

Peter Clarke d. 1703
Rector of Pickworth, Lincolnshire. Library sold by retail sale in London, 20 Sept. 1703 (no catalogue survives).
Alston, *Inventory.*

Anthony Lybbe d. 1703
Rector of Checkenden, Oxfordshire. Library auctioned in Oxford, 24 Mar. 1707 (joint sale, with one other; no catalogue survives).
Foster. Alston, *Inventory.*

John Merry 1650/1–1703?
Rector of Steepleton Iwerne, Dorset. Library sold by retail sale in London, 5 Oct. 1703 (no catalogue survives).
Foster. Alston, *Inventory.*

Oately d. *c.*1703
The library of 'the learned and reverend Mr Oately, deceased' was sold by retail sale in London, 9 Feb. 1703 (no catalogue survives).
Alston, *Inventory.*

Jordan Tancred 1666?–1703
Rector of Barwick in Elmet, Yorkshire. Used an engraved armorial bookplate dated 1701 (Franks 28876).
Foster.

John Tomkys d. 1703
Vicar of Snitterfield, Warwickshire. Bequeathed his books to found a parish library at Bilston, Staffordshire.
Venn. Perkin, 138–9.

Stephen Camborne *c.*1640–1704
Rector of Lawshall, Suffolk. Bequeathed his books (*c.*140 volumes) to found a parish library for Lawshall. Some of his books were previously owned by his father, Thomas, rector of Campsea Ashe.
Venn. Perkin, 163. *Suffolk parochial libraries: a catalogue* (London, 1977), xv.

Thomas Copping d. 1704
Rector of St Olave's, Hart St, London. Library auctioned in London, 11 Dec. 1704 (888 lots).
Venn. Alston, *Inventory.*

Abraham Pryme 1671–1704
Vicar of Thorne, Yorkshire; antiquary. Listed in Edward Bernard's *Catalogi manuscriptorum* (1697) as owning a small number of manuscripts; many of these passed after his death to the herald John Warburton, and are now in the Lansdowne MSS at the British Library.
ODNB.

Job Brockett *c.*1644–1705
Vicar of Royston, Hertfordshire. Bequeathed 95 volumes, mostly theological, to Dulwich College; the rest of his books went to his brother-in-law Thomas Wood, of Croydon.
Venn. Dulwich College MS VI, fo. 155r.

Thomas Browning d. 1705
Rector of Wickham Bishops, Essex. Involved in the Civil War as a royalist chaplain, sequestrated in 1646, when he was said to have £40 worth of books in his chamber at Cambridge.
Venn. *Walker revised.*

Joseph Kentish d. 1705?
'Late of Bristol, minister'. Library auctioned in London, 19 Nov. 1705 (no catalogue survives).
Alston, *Inventory.*

Abednego Seller 1646/7–1705
Vicar of St Charles, Plymouth, nonjuror, religious author. Edward Bernard's *Catalogi manuscriptorum* (1697) lists him as owning 22 manuscripts. Some of his books were destroyed in a fire in 1700, but Thomas Hearne noted that he had owned a 'vast number' of books.
ODNB.

William Sheppard 1651/2–1705
Rector of Hollington, Sussex. Library auctioned in London, 13 Mar. 1706 (joint sale, with one other; no catalogue survives).
Foster. Alston, *Inventory*.

James Nalton d. *c*.1706?
Minister in Hampstead (presumably not the Nonconformist minister, d. 1662?). Library sold by retail sale in London, 4 Sept. 1706 (no catalogue survives).
Alston, *Inventory*.

John Scamler 1646/7–1706
Rector of Shenfield, Essex. Library auctioned in London, 18 Nov. 1706 (1,457 lots).
Venn. Alston, *Inventory*.

William Umfrevill 1655?–1706
Rector of Bawdsey, Suffolk. Library auctioned in London, 24 June 1706 (1,305 lots).
Venn. Alston, *Inventory*.

Charles Woodward 1618?–1706
Rector of Creeting All Saints, Suffolk. Over 60 books with his signature or that of his father, John, survive at Belton House.
Venn. P. Hoare, The perils of provenance, *Library History* 18 (2002): 225–34.

George Goodall d. 1707
Rector of Padworth, Berkshire. Bequeathed books to Exeter College, Oxford, and to the parish of Padworth. Library auctioned in London, 29 Nov. 1708 (1,302 lots).
Foster. Alston, *Inventory*.

Richard Kingston 1635–1707?
Vicar of Henbury, Gloucestershire, political writer. Library auctioned in London, 17 Apr. 1707 (no catalogue survives).
ODNB. Alston, *Inventory*.

William Pierce 1641/2–1707
Rector of Malton and Heslerton, Yorkshire. Library auctioned in London, 8 July 1708 (joint sale, no catalogue survives).
Venn. Alston, *Inventory*.

Joseph Stillington 1669?–1707
Vicar of Hinxton, Cambridgeshire. Used an engraved armorial bookplate dated 1700.
Venn. Franks *538.

Jacob Asselin d. 1708
Huguenot refugee 1685, minister at the Jewin Street Church, London. Used an early cipher bookplate, made *c*.1690.
R. Gwynn, *The Huguenots in later Stuart Britain*, vol. 1 (2015). Lee, *British*, 21.

John Haslewood 1647/8–1708
Rector of St Olave's, Southwark. Library auctioned in London, 8 Nov. 1708.
Foster. Alston, *Inventory*.

Richard Parr d. 1708
Rector of Ibstone, Oxfordshire. Library sold by retail sale in Oxford, 7 June 1708 (no catalogue survives).
Foster. Alston, *Inventory*.

Cooper d. *c*.1708
The library of 'the Reverend Mr Cooper, late of Epping in Essex' was sold by retail sale in London, 19 Apr. 1708 (no catalogue survives).
Alston, *Inventory*.

Andrew Cranston d. 1708
Vicar of Reigate, Surrey. Founded the parish library of Reigate in 1701, to which he gave *c*.160 books.
ODNB. Perkin, 326–9.

John Daniel d. *c*.1708?
'Late minister of Hartford'. Library auctioned in London, 25 Nov. 1708 (joint sale, with one other; no catalogue survives).
Alston, *Inventory*.

Henry Jones d. 1708
Vicar of Sunningwell, Berkshire. Bequeathed 60 MS vols, mainly 16th/17th c., to the Bodleian Library; some had previously belonged to his uncle John Fell. Library auctioned in Oxford, 7 July 1710 (joint sale, with one other). Listed in Edward Bernard's *Catalogi manuscriptorum* (1697), as owning 100 manuscripts.
Foster. Macray 177–8. Alston, *Inventory*.

John Smith 1667/8–1708
Vicar of West Ham, Essex. Library auctioned in London, 23 May 1709 (1,386 lots).
Foster. Alston, *Inventory*.

Vincent Barry 1660/1–1709?
Vicar of Fulham, chaplain general of the Fleet. Library auctioned in London, 28 Mar. 1709 (991 lots).
Foster. Alston, *Inventory*.

Thomas Beconsall 1663/4–1709
Vicar of Steeple Aston, Oxfordshire. Library auctioned in Oxford, 20 Oct. 1709 (joint sale, with one other).
ODNB. Alston, *Inventory*.

Francis Carswell d. 1709
Vicar of Bray, Berkshire. Noted by Hearne as having 'a very curious study of books'. Library auctioned in London, 9 Jan. 1710 (1,735 lots).
Foster. Alston, *Inventory*.

John Ouseley 1645/6–1709
Rector of Panfield, Essex, historian. Listed in Edward Bernard's *Catalogi manuscriptorum* (1697) as owning 60 manuscripts; his 'choice collections' are referred to in Richard Newcourt's *Repertorium ecclesiasticum...Londinense* (1710) as having 'contributed very much to this work'.
Venn.

John Francklin 1666–1710
Rector of Gressenhall, Norfolk. Inherited the books of his relation Sir John Franklin (d. 1707), which he in turn bequeathed to his wife with the rest of his household goods.
Venn.

Henry Hesketh 1636/7–1710?
Rector of Charlwood, Surrey. Library sold by retail sale in London, 20 June 1712 (no catalogue survives).
ODNB. Alston, *Inventory*.

John Okes 1646–1710
Vicar of Whitegate, Cheshire, 1665–90 (deprived as a nonjuror). Left 300 volumes to form a parish library for his home town of Wotton-under-Edge, Gloucestershire (surviving books now deposited in Christ Church, Oxford).
Venn. Perkin, 402.

Samuel Wells d. c.1710?
Minister at Ferne, Wiltshire. Library auctioned in London, 16 Oct. 1710 (joint sale, with one other; no catalogue survives).
Alston, *Inventory*.

William Assheton 1642–1711
Rector of Beckenham, Kent. Library auctioned in London, 14 Nov. 1711 (2,083 lots).
ODNB. Alston, *Inventory*.

Robert Ferguson d. c.1711?
Library auctioned in London, 14 May 1711 (joint sale, with one other).
Alston, *Inventory*.

Thomas Pococke 1672/3–1711?
Vicar of Chalgrove, Oxfordshire. Library auctioned in Oxford, 28 Feb. 1711.
Foster. Alston, *Inventory*.

Timothy Burrell d. c.1712
Vicar of Slaugham, Sussex. Library sold by retail sale in London, 25 Nov. 1712 (joint sale; no catalogue survives).
Venn. Alston, *Inventory*.

Stephen Skinner d. 1712
Rector of Buckland, Hertfordshire. Library sold by retail sale in London, 30 May 1712 (no catalogue survives).
Venn. Alston, *Inventory*.

Michael Geddes 1647?–1713
Rector of East Hendred, Berkshire; author/translator. Library sold in London, 12 May 1714 (joint sale, with one other).
ODNB. Alston, *Inventory*.

William Haydock 1647/8–1713
Rector of Standish, Lancashire. Library auctioned in London, 14 Nov. 1713 (no catalogue survives).
Venn. Alston, *Inventory*.

John Pigott d. c.1713?
The Library of 'the Reverend Mr John Pigott, deceas'd' was auctioned in London, 8 June 1713 (1,568 lots).
Alston, *Inventory*.

Thomas Whincop d. 1713
Rector of St Mary Abchurch, and St Lawrence Pountney, London. In January 1720 the London bookseller Noel was selling Whincop's books, some of which were bought by Harley.
Venn. Wanley, *Diary*, vol. 1, 16–17. P. L. Heyworth (ed.), *Letters of Humfrey Wanley* (1989), no. 210.

Richard Brocklesby 1634/5–1714
Rector of Folkingham, Lincolnshire (deprived as a nonjuror). Left two libraries, in London and Stamford; the first was sold there as direected by his executors, the second was auctioned in Stamford, 1714.
ODNB. Alston, *Inventory*.

Nathaniel Greenwood d. 1714
Rector of Cottingham, Northamptonshire. 'Part of' his library auctioned in London, 30 Aug. 1714 (340 lots, Latin and English books).
Foster. Alston, *Inventory*.

John Salmon 1689/90-1714
Vicar of St Peter-le-Bayley, Oxford. Library auctioned in Oxford, 9 Nov. 1714 (2,168 lots).
Foster. Alston, *Inventory*.

John Blakey d. *c*.1715
The library of 'the Reverend Mr John Blakey, deceas'd' was auctioned in London, 3 Dec. 1715 (no catalogue survives).
Alston, *Inventory*.

Henry Colman 1670/71-1715
Rector of Foulsham, Norfolk. Bequeathed his library (*c*.1,500 volumes) to found a parish library for Brent Eleigh, Suffolk. The MSS from the library were sold at Sotheby's in 1887, the printed books were dispersed sometime thereafter.
Venn. Perkin, 151-2. *Suffolk parochial libraries: a catalogue* (London, 1977), xv.

John Gamlin d. 1715
Vicar of Faversham, Kent. Library auctioned in London, 24 Nov. 1715 (joint sale, with one other).
Venn. Alston, *Inventory*.

Richard Hook d. 1715
Rector of Great Stanmore, Middlesex. Library sold by retail sale in London, 6 Apr. 1715 (no catalogue survives).
Venn. Alston, *Inventory*.

Francis Thompson 1639/40-1715
Rector of St Matthew, Friday Street, London, President of Sion College. Library sold by retail sale in London, 7 Mar. 1716 (1,950 lots).
Venn. Alston, *Inventory*.

John Bruch d. 1715?
'Doctor, late of Windsor'. Library auctioned in London, 12 Dec. 1715 (joint sale, with one other)
Foster. Alston, *Inventory*.

Curates

Isaac Lowden d. 1612
Perpetual curate of Darlington. Probate inventory listed *c*.70 books, valued at £5 16*s*.
Venn. J. Atkinson et al., *Darlington wills and inventories 1600-1625* (1993), 31-3, 123-4, 215-22. *CHL* I 408-9.

Thomas Devey 1681-1705
Curate of Coleshill, Warwickshire. Probate inventory lists over 130 volumes, valued at £11 12*s*. 5*d*.
Foster. J. L. Salter, 'The books of an early eighteenth-century curate', *The Library*, 5th ser. 33 (1978): 33-46.

Henry Meux 1659/60-1709
Curate of Woodstock, Oxfordshire. Library auctioned in Oxford, 30 Oct. 1710 (no catalogue survives)
Foster. Alston, *Inventory*.

Benjamin Pratt 1677/8–1715
> Curate of St Botolph, Aldgate. Library auctioned in London, 16 May 1717 (no catalogue survives).
> Venn. Alston, *Inventory*.

Roman Catholic clergy

Edward Cary d. 1711
> Roman Catholic priest, chaplain to Sir George Cary at Torre Abbey, Devon, appointed chaplain-general to the army by James II, fled abroad after 1689. Maintained a library for the English Catholic clergy, the books being marked E. C. CL[ericorum] Ang[lorum].
> *ODNB*. J. M. Potter, *Catalogue of the Travers collection* (1990), 55e/p.217.

Engravers

John Dunstan d. *c*.1693?
> Not identified, but the sale catalogue refers to his 'mathematical instruments in brass and wood, his graving and etching tools'. Library auctioned in London, 7 Aug. 1693 (294 lots, plus 111 prints, 65 drawings, tools and instruments).
> Alston, *Inventory*.

Robert White 1645–1703
> Engraver. Library sold in London by retail sale, 15 Dec. 1703 (joint sale, with one other; no catalogue survives).
> *ODNB*. Alston, *Inventory*.

Gardeners

George London d. 1714
> Chief gardener to Queen Anne. Library auctioned in London, 22 Mar. 1714 (750 lots).
> *ODNB*. Alston, *Inventory*.

Gentry

This is one of the largest categories within the listing, and one of the more difficult to define. It generally includes people, or families, who may have had occupations or posts in civil administration—MPs, sheriffs, justices of the peace—but whose livelihood came primarily from their estates, or inherited wealth. They were gentlemen, below the ranks of the peerage, and include knights and baronets. If so inclined, they often had the leisure and opportunity to pursue literary, antiquarian, or historical interests. It has sometimes been difficult to decide whether to include particular owners under this heading, or under another one such as civil servants; a decision was taken based on their biographical profile, but the case could often be made either way.

Swithin Butterfield 1547–1611
> Gentleman, of Cambridge. Bequeathed *c*.60 books to Pembroke College there, including his own MSS compilations, and money to buy books.
> *ODNB*. Sears Jayne, 143.

Sir John Harington 1561–1612
  Of Kelston, near Bath; courtier, author, translator. Booklists survive which show that he had a sizeable library, including many plays.
  ODNB. CELM. J. Scott-Warren, *Sir John Harington and the book as gift* (2001).

Sir Walter Cope 1555?–1614
  Of Cope Castle, Kensington; MP and public official. Gave 46 MSS to the Bodleian Library in 1602, and had many more; owned 'the best-known *Wunderkammer* in England in the late 16th and early 17th centuries' (Watson).
  ODNB. A. G. Watson, 'The manuscript collection of Sir Walter Cope', *BLR* 12 (1987): 262–97. L. Peck, *Consuming splendor* (2005), 156–7.

Robert Booth d. 1615
  Bequeathed books to the parish of Tankersley, Yorkshire, for the use of the rector and his successors; 37 volumes (now in Sheffield University Library) remain today.
  Perkin, 367.

Sir Thomas Parry 1544–1616
  Of Hampstead Marshall, Berkshire; MP and administrator. Books with his armorial stamp survive.
  ODNB. Armorials database.

Henry Savile 1568–1617
  Of Banke, near Halifax. Acquired a significant collection of medieval MSS, many of which were subsequently bought by Sir Robert Cotton and other contemporary antiquaries.
  ODNB. J. Gilson, 'The library of Henry Savile, of Banke', *Transactions of the Bibliographical Society* 9 (1906–8): 126–210. A. Watson, *The manuscripts of Henry Savile of Banke* (1969).

Sir Thomas Knyvett d. 1618
  Of Ashwellthorpe, Norfolk. His library of *c*.70 MSS and 1,400 printed books descended through his family in the 17th c. until the bulk of it was acquired by John Moore, and thence passed to Cambridge University Library.
  D. McKitterick, *The library of Sir Thomas Knyvett* (1978). P. Reid, 'Proto-bibliophiles amongst the English aristocracy, 1500–1700', *Library History* 18 (2002): 25–38.

Sir Walter Raleigh 1552?–1618
  Of East Budleigh, Devon; courtier, explorer, author. A surviving MS list shows that he had a library of at least 500 books during his imprisonment in the Tower of London. Gave £50 to the Bodleian Library *c*.1603.
  ODNB. CELM. Sears Jayne, 148–9. Macray, 29. W. Oakeshott, 'Sir Walter Ralegh's library', *The Library*, 5th ser. 23 (1968): 285–327.

Sir William Sedley, 1st Bart *c*.1558–1618
Sir Charles Sedley, 6th Bart 1639–1701
  Of Aylesford, Kent; barrister, of Lincoln's Inn. Books with an armorial stamp survive, apparently cut for him and possibly used by later members of the family; the books of his descendant Sir Charles, the dramatist, were auctioned in London 23 Mar. 1703 (joint sale, with one other).
  ODNB. Foster. Alston, *Inventory.* Armorials database.

Richard Grosvenor 1583–1619
  Of Eaton Hall, Cheshire. Probate inventory records 38 books.
  P. Reid, 'Proto-bibliophiles amongst the English aristocracy, 1500–1700', *Library History* 18 (2002): 25–38.

Sir Christopher Hatton d. 1619

> Of Kirby Hall, Northamptonshire; cousin and heir of the Lord Chancellor of the same name (d. 1591). Books with his armorial stamps survive.
>
> N. Stacey, 'Antiquarian patronage in the 17th century: Sir Christopher Hatton's library at Kirby Hall', *English Heritage Historical Review* 9 (2014): 66–81. *Fine bindings 1500–1700 from Oxford libraries* (1968), 131.

Sir John Parker 1548–1619

> Of Bekesbourne, Kent; son of Archbishop Matthew Parker. MSS and printed books in his possession around the end of the 16th c. are listed in a memorandum book now in Lambeth Palace Library (MS 737).
>
> Venn. S. Strongman, 'John Parker's manuscripts', *TCBS* 7 (1977): 1–27. Armorials database.

Richard Carew 1555–1620

> Of Antony, Cornwall; landowner, antiquary, author of the *Survey of Cornwall*. Known to be a reader and a linguist; a letter of his to Thomas James, *c.*1610, comments on the nature of his library and the difficulty of obtaining books.
>
> *ODNB*. Bodleian MS Ballard 44, transcribed in *BLQ* 5 (1926): 3–4. F. Halliday, *Richard Carew of Antony* (1953).

Sir Lionel Tollemache, 1st Bt 1562–*c.*1620
Sir Lionel Tollemache, 2nd Bt 1591–1640
Sir Lionel Tollemache, 3rd Bt 1624–69

> Of Helmingham Hall, Suffolk. The Tollemaches were a major East Anglian landowning family, and the family library was well established during the time of the 1st Baronet, including MSS of East Anglian monastic provenance. Some of the books/MSS of John Maitland, 1st Duke of Lauderdale (d. 1682), came into the family's possession through Maitland's marriage to Elizabeth Dysart, widow of Sir Lionel Tollemache (d. 1669). Much of the family library was dispersed at Sotheby's in a series of sales 1961–9.
>
> E. Wilson, 'The book-stamps of the Tollemache family', *BC* 16 (1967): 178–85. J. Freeman, *The post master of Ipswich* (1997), 12–14. A. Edwards & J. Griffiths, 'The Tollemache collection of medieval manuscripts', *BC* 49 (2000): 349–64. Maggs 1324 (2002)/24.

Edward Crashawe d. 1621

> Of Chesterfield, gentleman. Probate inventory lists 'his librarie' in the study, valued at £5.
>
> J. Bestall (ed.), *Chesterfield wills and inventories 1604–1650* (2001), 202.

Thomas Antrobus 1586–1622

> Of Heath House, Petersfield. His father (also Thomas, d. 1611) gave books to Lincoln's Inn. Several books survive with his armorial stamp.
>
> Foster. Armorials database.

John Atkinson d. 1622

> Gentleman, of Bongate, Darlington. Probate inventory lists 'his librarie', valued at £6, although the books are not listed.
>
> J. Atkinson et al., *Darlington wills and inventories 1600–1625* (1993), 173–8.

Sir Nathaniel Bacon 1549–1622
Sir Roger Townshend, 1st Bt 1595–1637

> Of Stiffkey, and Raynham Hall, Norfolk; MPs, landowners, administrators. Bacon's will divided a library of 286 books amongst his family, including many to his grandson Sir Roger Townshend. A list of *c.*300 books in Townshend's possession *c.*1625 (now Folger Library MS L.d. 776) includes many Bacon bequest books.

ODNB. HoP. R. Fehrenbach, 'Sir Roger Townshend's book', in R. Fehrenbach (ed.) *PLRE* 1 (1992): 79–135. West. P. Reid, 'Proto-bibliophiles amongst the English aristocracy, 1500–1700', *Library History* 18 (2002): 25–38.

Nicholas Hare 1582–1622
Wealthy dilettante and minor poet. A number of his books were acquired by John Morris (d. 1658).
T. Birrell, *The library of John Morris* (1976), xvi.

Sir George Buck 1560–1622
Master of the Revels, scholar and author. Noted for having owned a number of contemporary play texts, though this will have been only a small part of his library.
ODNB. L. Erne, *Shakespeare and the book trade* (2013), 199–200.

Sir John Weld 1582?–1623
Humphrey Weld 1612–85
Of Edmonton, Middlesex, and Lulworth, Dorset. Books with their armorial stamps survive.
ODNB. Armorials database.

Sir Edward Dymoke *c.*1557–1624
Of Scrivelsby, Lincolnshire, of a family who for many generations held the office of King's Champion at coronations. Books stamped with the Dymoke badge of a sword are attributed to his ownership.
HoP. Armorials database.

Sir Peter Manwood 1571–1625
Of Hackington, Kent; judge, MP, antiquary. Gave MSS to the Bodleian in 1620; books with his armorial stamp survive.
ODNB. Macray, 424. *CHL* I 531–2. Maggs 1121 (1990)/15. Armorials database.

Sir William Smyth *c.*1550–1626
Sir Thomas Smyth, 1st Bt *c.*1602–68
Of Hill Hall, Essex. A number of books with an armorial stamp attributed to Sir Thomas seem more likely to have belonged originally to Sir William; a family library probably existed at Hill Hall over several generations.
Armorials database.

Arthur Throckmorton *c.*1557–1626
Landowner, MP, ambassador to France. Bequeathed *c.*350 books to Magdalen College, Oxford; some English books were retained by his wife.
HoP. Sears Jayne, 153. Morgan. A. L. Rowse, *Ralegh and the Throckmortons* (1962).

Thomas Glasier d. 1628
Of the Cathedral Close, Lichfield, gentleman. Probate inventory lists 'books with shelves and desks' in the study, valued at £6 13*s.* 4*d.*
D. Vaisey (ed.), *Probate inventories of Lichfield and district 1568–1680* (1969), 55.

Richard Towneley d. 1628
Charles Towneley 1600–64
Christopher Towneley 1604–74
Richard Towneley 1629–1707
Charles Towneley 1631–1712
Of Towneley Hall, Burnley. The library there began to be developed by the first Richard's father John (*c.*1528–1608); it was enlarged by Richard, who used an armorial stamp, and

by his sons Charles and Christopher. Their collections were inherited by Richard, who used an armorial bookplate dated 1702, and his brother Charles. MSS catalogues of the collection made *c.*1702–7 (one in Chetham's Library, one in Manchester University Library) show that the library then contained over 2,000 books. Books and MSS from the Towneley family were sold at Sotheby's in two sales in June 1883.

ODNB. T. Kitto, 'The Towneley family library', *BC* 59 (2010): 399–416. Maggs 1272 (1999)/44. Franks 29653/*207. Armorials database.

Arthur Coke d. 1629

Of Bramfield, Suffolk; 3rd son of Sir Edward Coke. Probate inventory includes 'all the bookes in the library and elsewhere in the house', valued at £86 15*s*.

F. W. Steer, 'The inventory of Arthur Coke, of Bramfield, 1629', *Proceedings of the Suffolk Institute of Archaeology and History* 25 (1951): 265–87. Purcell, 63.

Edward Paston 1550–1630

Of Appleton Hall, Norfolk. His will demonstrates that he had an extensive library, particularly noteworthy for its holdings of printed and manuscript music; many of the music MSS survive today in the British Library, Royal College of Music, and elsewhere.

ODNB. P. Brett, 'Edward Paston…and his musical collection', *TCBS* 4 (1964): 51–69. *CHL* I 505.

Sir Robert Cotton, 1st Bt 1571–1631

Of Conington, Huntingdonshire; MP and antiquary. Best known as the outstanding MSS collector of his generation, but also had a significant library of printed books. The library remained in the custody of his descendants for several generations, and was a valued historical resource; it was sold to the nation after the death of Sir John, the 3rd Bt, in 1701 and ultimately became a foundation collection of the British Museum/Library.

ODNB. CELM. K. Sharpe, *Sir Robert Cotton, 1586–1631* (Oxford, 1979). C. Tite, *The manuscript library of Sir Robert Cotton* (London, 1994). C. Wright (ed.), *Sir Robert Cotton as a collector* (1997). T. Hall, 'Sir Robert Bruce Cotton', in W. Baker (ed.), *Pre-nineteenth-century British book collectors and bibliographers* (1999), 57–69. C. Tite, 'The printed books of the Cotton family and their dispersal', in G. Mandelbrote and B. Taylor (eds), *Libraries within the library* (2009), 43–75. *CHL* I 550–57. Armorials database.

Sir John Kedermister d. 1631

Of Langley Park, Buckinghamshire. Bequeathed *c.*250 vols to found a parish library for Langley Marish; the books were bought for the purpose, over preceding decades, and housed in a specially decorated library room.

Perkin, 259–62. E. Rouse, 'The Kederminster Library', *Records of Buckinghamshire* 13 (1934–40): 369–72; 14 (1941): 50–66. J. Francis, 'The Kedermister Library', *Records of Buckinghamshire* 36 (1996): 62–85. *CHL* I 417–18.

Sir John Shurley 1568–1631

Of Isfield, Sussex; MP. At least one book with his armorial stamp survives.

HoP. Armorials database.

Sir Walter Covert 1549?–1632

Of Slaugham, Sussex; MP. Books with his armorial stamps survive.

HoP. G. D. Hobson, *English bindings in the library of J. R. Abbey* (1940), no. 27. Armorials database.

Sir John Eliot 1592–1632

Of Port Eliot and Cuttenbeake, Cornwall; MP, died in prison. Probate inventory lists books in the study valued at £40.

ODNB. H. Hulme (ed.), *A probate inventory of…Sir John Eliot* (1936).

Sir Isaac Wake 1575–1632
  Diplomat, MP. At least one book with his armorial stamp survives.
  ODNB. Armorials database.

Henry Ferrers 1550–1633
  Of Baddesley Clinton, Warwickshire; antiquary. His inscription is found in books
  associated with St Mary's Church, Warwick; known to have had a library which was
  dispersed soon after his death.
  ODNB. E. Berry, *Henry Ferrers, an early Warwickshire antiquary* (1965). P. Morgan, 'A
  16th-century Warwickshire library', *BC* 22 (1973): 337–55.

Margaret Hoby, Lady Hoby 1571–1633
  Of Hackness, Yorkshire; wife of Sir Thomas Hoby (on her third marriage). Her diary
  contains extensive references to reading in her closet; some of her books, with her
  annotations, survive in Hackness parish library (now in York Minster Library).
  ODNB. A. Cambers, 'Readers' marks and religious practice', in J. King (ed.), *Tudor books
  and readers* (2010), 211–31; Cambers, 50–53, 65–7.

Alban Stepneth 1608/9–34
  Of Prendergast, Pembrokeshire. Bequeathed 23 books to St John's College, Oxford *c.*1634.
  Foster. Sears Jayne, 164.

Sir Robert Naunton 1563–1635
  Of Letheringham, Suffolk; MP, statesman. Books with his armorial stamps survive.
  ODNB. Blatchly. Armorials database.

Sir Thomas Brooke d. 1636
  Of Great Oakley, Northamptonshire. Lists of books (*c.*285 *c.*1615) survive in the Brooke
  of Oakley MSS in Northamptonshire Record Office.
  Sears Jayne, 145.

Sir Peter Legh 1563–1636
Francis Legh 1590–1643
  Father and son, members of a long-established gentry family of Lyme, Cheshire.
  Fragments of their library, of unknown original size, remain at Lyme Park; correspond-
  ence of the late 16th and early 17th c. refers to the obtaining of books.
  Purcell, 80.

Sir Henry Berkeley 1566–1638?
  Of Wymondham, Leicestershire. Books with his armorial stamp survive.
  Armorials database.

Alice Hatton, Lady Hatton 1581–1638
  Daughter of Sir Thomas Fanshawe, wife of Sir Christopher Hatton (d. 1619). Probate
  inventory includes a list of *c.*100 books, typical of a wealthy lady's closet of the time,
  edited as PLRE 273.
  J. L. Black & R. J. Fehrenbach, 'Lady Alice Hatton', PLRE 9 (2017): 209–224.

Sir Dudley Digges 1583–1639
  Of Barham, Kent; MP, diplomat. Books with his armorial stamp—or possibly that of his
  brother Leonard—survive.
  ODNB. Armorials database.

Sir Lewis Tresham, 1st Bt 1578–1639
  Of Rushton, Northamptonshire. Book with his armorial stamp survive at Deene Park, where
  the library is largely founded on that of his father, Sir Thomas Tresham (1547–1605).
  N. Barker and D. Quentin, *The library of Thomas Tresham and Thomas Brudenell* (2006).
  Armorials database.

Andrew Cotton *c*.1564–1640

Of Combermere, Cheshire. Probate inventory lists 'his books' valued at £20, from a total estate valued at £330.

P. Pixton, *Wrenbury wills and inventories 1542–1661* (2009), no. 111.

Sir Thomas Lucy 1583/6–1640

Alice Lucy d. 1648

Richard Lucy *c*.1619–77

Of Charlecote Park, Warwickshire; landowners, MPs and administrators, noted also as patrons of the arts, antiquaries, and scholars. Sir Thomas Lucy and his wife, Alice, are both known to have been active book-lovers who established a significant library, which is featured on Thomas's funeral monument. It was further developed by later family members, including Richard. Some books from the 17th c. survive at Charlecote today, interspersed among later acquisitions, although much of the original library has been lost.

ODNB. J. Cliffe, *The world of the country house in seventeenth-century England* (1999), 166. Purcell, 68–70. Armorials database.

Sir Thomas Mompesson d. 1640

Of Little Bathampton, Wiltshire. Books with his armorial stamp—or possibly that of his son, also Sir Thomas (b. *c*.1630) survive.

Armorials database.

Walter Bartlett 1585–1641

Of Stopham, Sussex; MP for Bramber. Books with his armorial stamp survive.

HoP. Armorials database.

Sir Thomas Bromley *c*.1580–1641

Of Holt Castle, Worcestershire; MP. Probate inventory lists, in the Inner Parlour, 'his library of books, being mostly French and Italian', valued at £4.

HoP. M. Wanklyn (ed.), *Inventories of Worcestershire landed gentry, 1637–1786* (1998), 167.

Sir Henry Spelman 1564?–1641

Sir John Spelman 1594–1643

Clement Spelman 1598–1679

Norfolk gentleman, constitutional and historical scholar, antiquary. Various MS lists of Henry's books and MSS survive, made at various points in the 17th c. Many of his books, together with those of later members of the family, went to Swaffham parish library via the bequest of his son Clement (judge, baron of the exchequer); others were auctioned in London, 28 Nov. 1709, 23 Jan. 1710 (joint sale, with one other).

ODNB. Sears Jayne, 156, 171–2. Perkin, 364–6. A. J. Collins, 'The Blackborough chartulary and the library of Sir Henry Spelman', *Brit. Mus. Q.* 11 (1937): 63–5. W. Rix, *The pride of Swaffham* (1950). H. Cronne, 'The study and use of charters in the seventeenth century: Sir Henry Spelman and Sir William Dugdale', in L. Fox (ed.), *English historical scholarship* (1956), 73–91. M. C. Lyons, *A catalogue, history and analysis of Swaffham Parish Library* (MA thesis, Loughborough University, 1986. Alston, *Inventory*.

Leonard Yeo d. 1641

Of Huish, Devon. Probate inventory lists books in the study, valued at £12 10*s*. The inventory of his son (also Leonard Yeo of Huish, Esq), d. 1687, lists 'all his bookes' valued at £12.

M. Cash (ed.), *Devon inventories of the sixteenth and seventeenth centuries* (1966), 57, 158.

Francis Combe 1583–1641

Of Hemel Hempstead. Bequeathed his library to be divided between Sidney Sussex College, Cambridge and Trinity College, Oxford.

N. Rogers, 'Early history of the library', in D. Beales and H. Nisbet (eds), *Sidney Sussex College, Cambridge* (1996), 82.

Sir Francis Kynaston 1586/7–1642
Of Oteley, Shropshire; MP, poet, translator. Founded an 'academy of learning' in 1635, at his house in London, furnished with books, manuscripts, instruments, etc. for the nobility and gentry.
ODNB. Maggs 1324 (2002)/1.

Robert Wright, alias Reeve d. 1642
Of Thwaite, Suffolk. Books with an armorial stamp attributed to him survive.
Armorials database.

John Fleming 1575–1643
Sir Daniel Fleming 1633–1701
Of Rydal Hall, Cumberland. A number of books with John's armorial stamp survive; his property and library passed to his great-nephew Daniel, who combined local adminis-tration with active historical and antiquarian interests, and who acquired books throughout his life.
ODNB. J. Magrath, *The Flemings in Oxford* (1903–13). B. Tyson (ed.), *The estate and household accounts of Sir Daniel Fleming* (2001). J. Emmerson, 'Dan Fleming and John Evelyn', *BSANZ Bulletin* 27 (2003): 48–61.

Brocase, 'Captain' fl.1643
135 books belonging to Captain Brocase were seized by the London Committee for Sequestration in 1643, and sold.
Roy.

Sir John Bankes 1589–1644
Mary Bankes 1598–1661 (Sir John's wife)
John Bankes 1626–56 (Sir John's son)
Ralph Bankes 1631?–77 (Sir John's son)
John Bankes 1665–1714 (Ralph's son)
Of Corfe Castle and subsequently Kingston Lacy, Dorset. Their books form the foun-dation of the library now at Kingston Lacy. Few of Sir John's books survived Civil War dispersal. Mary, John, and Ralph were all actively acquiring books throughout the Interregnum and Restoration decades, and many remain today, although some were certainly dispersed after Ralph's death, and probably later.
ODNB. A. Mitchell, *Kingston Lacy, Dorset* (1994). N. Barker, *Treasures from the libraries of National Trust country houses* (1999). Y. Lewis, 'Sir Ralph Bankes (?1631–1677) and the origins of the library at Kingston Lacy', *Library History* 18 (2002): 215–23. Purcell, 62, 95.

Sir Thomas Barrington, 2nd Bt *c.*1585–1644
Landowner, MP. A bookseller's bill with 112 entries records his book-buying in the 1630s; books with his armorial stamp survive.
ODNB. M. Bohannon, 'A London bookseller's bill: 1635–1639', *The Library*, 4th ser. 18 (1938), 432–46. Armorials database.

Sir Edward Dering 1598–1644
Of Surrenden Dering, Kent; MP, antiquary. Numerous books survive with his armorial stamp. MSS lists of his library made between *c.*1620 and 1640 are at the British Library, and the Folger Library; he had at least 2,000 volumes. Most of the library was sold at auction between 1811 and 1865.

ODNB. Lee, *British*, 6. T. Lennam, 'Sir Edward Dering's collection of playbooks, 1619–1624', *Shakespeare Quarterly* 16 (1965): 145–53. N. Krivatsy and L.Yeandle, 'Sir Edward Dering', PLRE 1 (1992): 137–269. N. Ramsay, 'The Cathedral Archives and Library', in P. Collinson (ed.), *A history of Canterbury Cathedral* (1995), 379–80. *CHL* I 534–7. P. Reid, 'Proto-bibliophiles amongst the English aristocracy, 1500–1700', *Library History* 18 (2002): 25–38. L. Erne, *Shakespeare and the book trade* (2013), 200–02. I. Green, *Print and Protestantism in early modern England* (2000), 572. Armorials database.

Sir Thomas Roe 1581–1644

Landowner, diplomat, writer. Gave *c.*30 Greek MSS to the Bodleian Library, 1628. Bequeathed the bulk of his books to his nephew Maurice Berkeley of Stoke (d. 1654), with some allowed to his wife; an inventory of the books received by Berkeley runs to *c.*500 titles, edited as PLRE 274.

ODNB. P. Palmer, Sir Thomas Roe, PLRE 9 (2017): 225–308.

Sir Richard Baker *c.*1568–1645

Author, historian, MP; of Highgate, but reduced to poverty and life in the Fleet prison as a debtor. His library was bought for £500 in the 1620s by John Williams, and given to Westminster Abbey.

ODNB. J. A. Robinson & M. R. James, *The manuscripts of Westminster Abbey* (1908), 18.

William Burton 1575–1645

Of Fauld, Staffordshire; antiquary, brother of Robert, the author. Assembled significant antiquarian collections; some books with his inscription are found in Robert Burton's library.

ODNB. Macray, 75. N. Kiessling, *The library of Robert Burton* (1988).

Sir Thomas Jermyn 1573–1644/5

Of Rushbrooke Hall, Suffolk; courtier and soldier. An armorial stamp used by him is also found on a number of books given by his father, Sir Robert Jermyn (1538/9–1614) to Bury St Edmunds church library in 1595.

ODNB. Perkin, 164–5. Armorials database.

Sir John Penington 1584?–1646

Admiral, who became wealthy during a long naval career. More than 61 books were seized from his London house by the London Committee for Sequestration in 1643, and sold.

ODNB. Roy.

Dorothy Cotton 1572–1647

Of Combermere, a member of a Cheshire gentry family. Probate inventory lists 'her books' valued at £3 6s. 8d., from a total estate valued at £374.

P. Pixton, *Wrenbury wills and inventories 1542–1661* (2009), no. 122.

Sir Robert Kemp d. 1647

Of Gissing, Norfolk. Books with his armorial stamp survive. His books passed to his eldest son, Robert (1628–1710).

Armorials database.

Sir Simonds d'Ewes 1602–50

Of Stow Hall, Suffolk; barrister, MP, antiquary. Assembled a significant library, including extensive MSS collections, which remained in his family until sold to Robert Harley by his grandson in 1705.

ODNB. A. Watson, *The library of Sir Simonds d'Ewes* (1966). J. Sears McGee, *An industrious mind: the worlds of Sir Simonds d'Ewes* (2015).

Sir John Isham, 1st Bt 1582–1651
Judith Isham 1590–1625
Sir Justinian Isham, 2nd Bt 1611–75
Elizabeth Isham 1609–54
Judith Isham 1610–36
Sir Thomas Isham, 3rd Bt 1657–81

> Of Lamport Hall, Northamptonshire. Developed the library there over many gener-
> ations, until largely dispersed in the late 19th c. Elizabeth refers in a MS diary to 'the
> bookes which I had in my closet'. Her list of her mother's books, *c.*25 titles, is edited as
> PLRE 270; a separate list of her sister's books, 17 titles, as PLRE 272; and a list of her own
> books, *c.*100 titles, as PLRE 276.
>
> *ODNB*. R. Graves, 'The Isham books', *Bibliographica* 3 (1897): 418–29. W. A. Jackson, 'The
> Lamport Hall–Britwell Court books', in his *Records of a bibliographer* (1967), 121–33. *The
> diary of Thomas Isham of Lamport (1658–81)* (1971). H. Hallam, 'Lamport Hall revisited', *BC*
> 16 (1967): 439–49. Cambers, 47, 65. J. L. Black et al., 'Judith Isham, Judith Isham, Elizabeth
> Isham', PLRE 9 (2017): 179–89, 201–8, 319–45. E. Snook, 'Elizabeth Isham's "own bookes"',
> in L. Knight et al. (eds), *Women's bookscapes in early modern Britain* (2018), 77–93.

Sir John Rivers 1579–1651

> Of Chafford, Kent. Numerous books with his armorial stamp survive.
> Maggs 1075 (1987)/19; 1121 (1990)/14; 1324 (2002)/83. Armorials database.

Sir Simon Clarke 1579–1652

> Of Brome Court, Salford; antiquary, friend of Dugdale. Likely to have had a library, with
> MSS collections (known to have been used by Dugdale), although only one book with his
> armorial stamp is currently recorded.
> P. Styles, 'Sir Simon Clarke', *Transactions and Proceedings of the Birmingham and
> Warwickshire Archaeological Society* 66 (1945–6): 6–34. Armorials database.

Francis Goddard d. 1652

> Of Clyffe Pypard, Wiltshire; high sheriff of Wiltshire. Books with his armorial stamp survive.
> R. Jefferies, *A memoir of the Goddards of north Wilts* [1873]. Armorials database.

Justinian Povey 1580–1652
Thomas Povey 1613/14–1705

> Of London, administrators, politicians, merchants. The library at Dyrham Park,
> Gloucestershire (now partly dispersed) began to be built up by Thomas's nephew and
> heir William Blathwayt (1649?–1717), who bought the estate, and who inherited books
> owned by both Poveys. Thomas was noted as a collector and connoisseur, who gave
> books to the College of Arms.
> *ODNB*. A. Simoni, 'The books at Dyrham Park', *BC* 32 (1983), 171–88.

Sir Robert Coke 1587–1653

> Of Caludon Castle, Warwickshire, and Holkham, Norfolk; MP. Left instructions in his will for
> the establishment of a library at Epsom, but this did not materialize. Many of his books passed
> to his nephew George Berkeley, 1st Earl Berkeley (1628–98), who gave them to Sion College.
> *HoP*. E. Pearce, *Sion College and Library* (1913), 258–60.

Sir Peter Osborne 1584/5–1653

> Of Chicksands Priory, Bedfordshire, governor of Guernsey. Although his fortunes were
> largely ruined after the Civil War, he directed in his will that his library should remain at
> Chicksands as a family heirloom.
> *ODNB*. Purcell, 95.

Sir Thomas Shirley c.1590–1654

Of Botolph's Bridge, Huntingdonshire; recusant antiquary. Many of his MSS collections are in the British Library and Queen's College, Oxford. Books with his armorial stamp survive.

ODNB. R. P. Cust, 'Catholicism, antiquarianism, and gentry honour: the writings of Sir Thomas Shirley', *Midland History* 23 (1998): 40–70. Armorials database.

Thomas Windham d. 1654
William Windham 1647–89
Katherine Windham d. 1704

Of Felbrigg Hall, Norfolk. Thomas left books to his son William, which were subsequently taken by his half-brother's widow; he was compensated with £10. William acquired books himself, and the library at Felbrigg has numerous books with his signature and sometimes date of acquisition. His wife Katherine kept records of her own books in notebooks. Subsequent members of the family (Ashe, 1673–1749, William II, 1717–61, William III, 1750–1810) continued to acquire books, and their inscriptions can also be found across the library.

West. S. West, 'An architectural typology for the early modern country house library, 1660–1720', *The Library*. 7th ser. 14 (2013): 441–64, 451–2.

Sir Thomas Bludder c.1597–1655

Of Flanchford, Reigate; MP, died in prison, in debt. 175 books from his London house were seized by the London Committee for Sequestration in 1643, and sold.

HoP. Roy.

John Gorges 1593–1656

Of Somerset, Coleraine; MP, governor of Londonderry. Books with an armorial stamp of the Gorges family, attributed to him, survive.

Armorials database.

Sir Robert Harley 1579–1656

Of Brampton Bryan, Herefordshire; MP, Master of the Mint. A 1637 library catalogue reveals a quantity of literary works; when the library was lost after pillaging by royalist troops in 1644, Harley estimated the value of the lost books at £200.

ODNB. J. Cliffe, *The world of the country house in seventeenth-century England* (1999), 164–5.

Sir Robert Shirley, 4th Bt 1629–56

Of Eatington, Warwickshire. Books with his armorial stamps survive. The family library is said to have been founded by his grandfather Sir George Shirley, 1st Bt (1559–1622).

ODNB. Maggs 1075 (1987)/53; 1212 (1996)/32. Armorials database.

Sir Richard Wingfield, 2nd Bt d. 1656?

Of Letheringham and Easton, Suffolk. A bookseller's bill of 1654, largely plays, is edited as PLRE 279.

R. J. Fehrenbach, 'Sir Richard Wingfield', PLRE 9 (2017): 371–6.

Henry Bedingfeld 1587–1657
Sir Henry Bedingfeld, 1st Bt 1613–85
Sir Henry Bedingfeld, 2nd Bt 1636–1704

Of Oxburgh Hall, Norfolk. A small number of 17th-c. books survive in the library at Oxburgh Hall today, which are likely to have belonged to these family members. A book with the armorial stamp attributed to the first Henry is in the V&A. Much of the library

of Oxburgh Hall was sold at Sothebys, 26 July 1922/561–612, with a further sale (over 2,500 volumes), 31 Oct. 1951.
ODNB. H. Bedingfeld, *Oxburgh Hall, the first 500 years* (1987). West. Armorials database.

Michael Biddulph d. 1658
Of Lichfield and Elmhurst, Esquire. Probate inventory lists 'his library at Lichfield and Elmhurst', valued at £20.
D. Vaisey (ed.), *Probate inventories of Lichfield and district 1568–1680* (1969), 105.

Sir Thomas Coghill d. 1659
Of Bletchington, Oxfordshire; sheriff of Oxfordshire. Several books survive bearing an armorial stamp which is either his, or that of his elder brother Henry (1589–1672). Armorials database.

John Talbot d. 1659
Of Thornton, Yorkshire; royalist colonel. A mid-17th-c. bookplate, surviving in several copies and at least one book, is attributed to him.
Lee, *British*, 5. Franks 28859.

Sir William Brereton 1604–61
Of Hanford, Cheshire; MP and soldier. Books with his armorial stamp survive.
ODNB. Armorials database.

James Gresham d. 1662
Of Haslemere, Surrey. Books with his armorial stamp survive.
Armorials database.

Sir Robert Pye 1585–1662
Of Faringdon, Berkshire; MP, Remembrancer of the Exchequer. Books with his armorial stamps survive.
ODNB. Armorials database.

Sir Simon Archer 1581–1662
Of Umberslade, Warwickshire; MP, antiquary. His extensive MSS collections, which contributed to Dugdale's *Antiquities of Warwickshire* (1656), are now largely distributed between the Bodleian, the Shakespeare Birthplace Trust, and the Warwickshire Record Office; the extent of his printed book holdings is unknown, but his second son and heir Thomas (1619–85) left a library valued at £350. Books with his armorial stamps survive.
ODNB. P. Styles, Sir Simon Archer, in his *Studies in seventeenth-century West Midlands History* (1978), 1–41. Armorials database.

Henry Townshend 1602–63
Henry Townshend 1652–1707
Of Worcester and Elmley Lovett. Probate inventory of the elder Henry lists 'severall bookes of all sortes att Elmely, and att Worcester', valued at £15; that of the son lists 'a study of books and pamphlets, and other things', valued at £30.
M. Wanklyn (ed.), *Inventories of Worcestershire landed gentry, 1637–1786* (1998), 189, 316.

Sir Ralph Freeman d. 1667
Of Betchworth, Surrey; commissioner of the Mint, translator, author. Books with his monogram stamp survive; at least some of his books descended to Ralph Freeman, Fellow of All Souls College, Oxford (d. 1774), who left them to the College.
ODNB. Armorials database.

Nicholas Acton 1614–64
  Of Bockleton, Worcestershire. Probate inventory lists, in the study, 'two desks, bookes, a cupboard of drawers, a truncke, and other small trifles' valued at £20.
  M. Wanklyn (ed.), *Inventories of Worcestershire landed gentry, 1637–1786* (1998), 196.

Richard Amherst 1599–1664
  Of Bayhall, Kent. Books with his armorial stamp survive (it seems also to have been used by his son William, 1641/2–63).
  Armorials database.

Thomas Godfrey 1586–1664
  Of Hodiford, Kent; MP. Noted in his monumental inscription as 'a great lover of learning'; books with his armorial stamp survive.
  HoP. Armorials database.

Sir Kenelm Digby 1603–65
  Of Gayhurst, Buckinghamshire; courtier, diplomat, scientist, writer. Acquired books throughout his life. His pre-Civil War library was dispersed and possibly destroyed *c.*1643; in exile in Paris he accumulated *c.*3,500 books, left there when he returned to England in 1660. Much of it was purchased after his death by his cousin George Digby, 2nd Earl of Bristol (1612–77) and auctioned in London as part of a mixed sale, 19 Apr. 1680. Gave 233 MSS to Bodleian in 1634, including many left to him by Thomas Allen (1542–1632); gave books to Harvard University in 1655. Many books with his armorial stamps survive.
  ODNB. Macray, 78–81. Philip, 40–42. L. Sheppard, 'A vellum copy of the Great Bible, 1539', *National Library of Wales Journal* 1 (1939–40): 9–19. R. Petersson, *Sir Kenelm Digby: the ornament of England* (London, 1956). C. H. Starks, 'Work in progress: Richard Hunt's revision of the Digby catalogue', in A. C. de la Mare & B. Barker-Benfield (eds), *Manuscripts at Oxford* (1980), 118–21. R. Beadle, 'Medieval English manuscripts at auction, 1676–*c.*1700', *BC* 53 (2004): 46–63. Mandelbrote, 'Auctions'. Alston, *Inventory.* Armorials database.

Francis Willoughby 1614–65
Francis Willoughby 1635–72
  Of Wollaton Hall, Nottinghamshire; members of a long-established gentry family with a library which was continuously developed from the 14th c. onwards (some of the medieval manuscripts survive and are today in Nottingham University Library). The younger Francis was a noted naturalist, and associate of John Ray; the library was reorganized and catalogued at Wollaton in the 1690s by his son, Thomas Willoughby, 1st Baron Middleton (1672–1729).
  ODNB. R. Hanna & T. Turville-Petre (eds), *The Wollaton medieval manuscripts* (2010).

Sir William Parkhurst d. 1667
  Of Richmond, Surrey; MP, warden of the Mint. More than 145 books were seized from his London house by the London Committee for Sequestration in 1643.
  HoP. Roy.

William Richardson d. 1667
  Of North Birney, Yorkshire. Probate inventory lists books in the study, valued at £25.
  P. Brears (ed.), *Yorkshire probate inventories, 1542–1689* (1972), 124.

Walter Smith d. 1667
  Of Sevenoaks, gentleman. Probate inventory lists 'one press and in it a library of bookes', valued at £5.
  H. Lansberry, *Sevenoaks wills and inventories in the reign of Charles II* (1988), 58–60.

Sir Philip Tyrwhitt 1598–1667
Of Stainfield, Lincolnshire. Books with his badge and inscription survive.
Armorials database.

Robert Vaughan 1591/2–1667
Of Hengwrt, Merioneth; antiquary. Assembled a significant collection of early Welsh MSS, many of which are now in the National Library of Wales; his printed books were dispersed in the 19th c. and earlier.
ODNB. N. Lloyd, Meredith Lloyd, *Journal of the Welsh Bibliographical Society* 11 (1975–6): 133–92. D. Huws, 'Robert Vaughan', in W. Baker (ed.), *Pre-nineteenth-century British book collectors and bibliographers* (1999), 365–72.

William Baldwyn d. 1668
Of Longdon in Tredington, Worcestershire. Probate inventory lists 'bookes of all sortes in the studie', valued at £5.
M. Wanklyn (ed.), *Inventories of Worcestershire landed gentry, 1637–1786* (1998), 204.

Sir William Waller c.1597–1668
Of Osterley House, Middlesex; parliamentary general. Probate inventory includes a library valued at £90.
ODNB. Purcell, 115.

Sir William Drake, 1st Bt 1606–69
Of Shardloes, Buckinghamshire; MP. His MSS commonplace books detail the range of his reading and private library; some of his printed books have also been traced.
HoP. K. Sharpe, *Reading revolutions* (2000).

Sir John Harrison c.1589–1669
Of Balls Park, Hertfordshire; MP. 125 books were seized from his home by the London Committee for Sequestration in 1643, and sold.
HoP. Roy.

Sir Nicholas Le Strange, 3rd Bart 1632–69
Of Hunstanton Hall, Norfolk. Probate inventory lists a library valued at £120. A catalogue of books in the library made c.1700, during the lifetime of Sir Nicholas, 4th Bart (1661–1724), lists 2,659 printed books and 37 MSS.
West. P. J. Willetts, 'Sir Nicholas le Strange's collection of masque music', *British Museum Quarterly* 29 (1965): 79–87.

Peter Venables 1603–69
Of Kinderton, Cheshire, MP and landowner (his title 'Baron de Kinderton' was not a peerage). Numerous books with his armorial stamps are known.
HoP. Armorials database.

Henry Oxinden 1609–70
Of Barham, Kent. His library (over 200 volumes at his death), noteworthy for an extensive holding of early drama texts, passed via his daughter Katherine Warly to Lee Warly (d. 1807), who left his books to found a parish library for Elham, Kent. Some remain with the parish library today (now in Canterbury Cathedral), others have been dispersed.
ODNB. G. Dawson, 'An early list of Elizabethan plays', *The Library*, 4th ser. 15 (1934): 445–56. D. Gardiner, *The Oxinden letters 1607–42* (1933). S. Hingley, 'Elham Parish Library', in P. Isaac (ed.), *The reach of print* (1998), 175–90. L. Erne, *Shakespeare and the book trade* (2013), 199. A. Vine, *Miscellaneous order* (2019), 82–92.

Sir Robert Abdy, 1st Bt 1616–70
Of Albyns, Essex; East India merchant. Books with his armorial stamps survive.
Armorials database.

Sir Ralph Hare 1623–72
Of Stow Bardolph, Norfolk; MP. Probate inventory lists books to the value of £20 in his closet (?*c*.200 vols). A parcel of books in his wife's closet is also listed.
HoP. West. S. West, 'An architectural typology for the early modern country house library, 1660–1720', *The Library*, 7th ser. 14 (2013): 441–64, 453.

Anne Sadleir 1585–1672
Daughter of Sir Edward Coke, wife of Ralph Sadleir, of Standon, Hertfordshire. Known to have been an owner of books as well as coins and curiosities; gave MSS to Trinity College, Cambridge and to the Inner Temple.
ODNB. A. Hunt, 'The books, manuscripts and literary patronage of Mrs Anne Sadleir', in V. Burke and J. Gibson (eds), *Early modern women's manuscript writing* (2004), 205–28. S. West, 'An architectural typology for the early modern country house library, 1660–1720', *The Library*, 7th ser. 14 (2013): 441–64, 461.

Sir Roger Twysden, 2nd Bt 1597–1672
Of Roydon Hall, Kent; MP. antiquary, writer. Inherited books from his father, Sir William Twysden (1566–1629); acquired books and MSS throughout his life. He bequeathed his library to his son, hoping that it would remain an heirloom of the Twysden family for ever, but most of it was sold by his grandson in 1715 to Sir Thomas Sebright.
ODNB. F. Jessup, *Sir Roger Twysden* (1965). R. Ovenden, 'Sir Roger Twysden', in W. Baker (ed.), *Pre-nineteenth-century British book collectors and bibliographers* (1999), 350–56.

Sir Thomas Wendy 1614–73
Of Haslingfield, Cambridgeshire; MP. Library (more than 2,000 volumes) given to Balliol College, Oxford, in 1677.
HoP. W. Carless Davis, *A history of Balliol College* (1963), 148. Armorials database.

Henry Brett 1587/8–1674
Of Sandywell Park, Gloucester; MP, alderman of Gloucester. Bequeathed books, including incunabula and medieval MSS, to Gloucester Cathedral Library.
S. Eward, *No fine but a glass of wine* (1985), 266.

Sir Thomas Bendish, 2nd Bt 1607–74
Of Bower Hall, Steeple Bumpstead; ambassador to the Ottoman empire during the Interregnum. Bequeathed *c*.50 volumes to St John's College, Cambridge.
ODNB.

Sir Thomas Prestwich, 1st Bt 1604–74
Of Hulme Hall, Lancashire. Books with his armorial stamp survive.
Armorials database.

Sir Thomas Wentworth, 1st Bt *c*.1611–75
Of West Bretton, Yorkshire; royalist soldier. Probate inventory lists 'certaine books' in the store chamber, valued at £60.
P. Brears (ed.), *Yorkshire probate inventories, 1542–1689* (1972), 145.

Gervase Holles 1606–75
Of Grimsby, Lincolnshire; MP and antiquary. Collected materials relating to the history of Lincolnshire; some of these MSS are now in the British Library. Books with his armorial stamp survive.
ODNB. Armorials database.

Sir William Morice 1602–76
Of Werrington, Devon; MP, Secretary of State. When he retired to his country seat in 1668 'he erected a fair library, valued at £1200, being choice books, richly bound'.
ODNB. J. Cliffe, *The world of the country house in seventeenth-century England* (1999), 168–9.

Frances Wolfreston 1607–77
Of Statfold Hall, near Tamworth; noteworthy as an early English female book owner, who regularly marked her ownership; over 200 with her inscription have been identified. *ODNB*. P. Morgan, 'Frances Wolfreston and "hor bouks"', *The Library*, 6th ser. 11 (1989): 197–219. J. Gerritsen, 'Venus preserved: some notes on Frances Wolfreston', in O. Arngart et al. (eds), *English studies presented to R. W. Zandvoort* (1964), 271–4. A. Hunt, 'Libraries in the archives', in G. Mandelbrote and B. Taylor (eds), *Libraries within the library* (2009), 363–84, 372ff. L. Erne, *Shakespeare and the book trade* (2013), 212–13. S. Lindenbaum, 'Hiding in plain sight', in L. Knight et al. (eds), *Women's bookscapes in early modern Britain* (2018), 193–213. https://franceswolfrestonhorbouks.com/.

Sir Peter Leycester, 1st Bt 1614–78
Of Tabley Hall, Cheshire; antiquary. A library catalogue of *c*.1670, 'shewing how my books stand placed in my study', lists *c*.1,300 titles.
ODNB. J. Cliffe, *The world of the country house in seventeenth-century England* (1999), 164. E. Halcrow (ed.), *Charges to the grand jury . . . 1660–1677 by Sir Peter Leycester* (1953), app. 4 (catalogue of books). S. Webb & P. Reid, 'Sir Francis Leicester's "good library" at Nether Tabley', *Library & Information History* 34 (2018): 1–22.

Robert Thoroton 1623–78
Of Car Colston, Nottinghamshire; physician, author of the *Antiquities of Nottinghamshire* (1677). Used an engraved armorial bookplate.
ODNB. Franks 29403. Maggs 1121 (1990)/48.

Walter Hanford d. 1679
Of Woollas Hall, Eckington, Worcestershire. Probate inventory lists books in his study, together with some jewellery, plate and furniture, valued together at £15.
M. Wanklyn (ed.), *Inventories of Worcestershire landed gentry, 1637–1786* (1998), 221.

Edward Phelipps *c*.1613–80
Of Montacute, Somerset; MP. Books with his armorial stamp survive (although this stamp was evidently used by later members of the family also).
HoP. Armorials database.

Richard Vernon 1615–79
Sheriff of Worcestershire. Probate inventory lists books in the study, but no value is given.
M. Wanklyn (ed.), *Inventories of Worcestershire landed gentry, 1637–1786* (1998), 217.

Sir Ralph Bovey, 1st Bt d. 1679
Of Stowe Hall, Longstowe, Cambridgeshire; Attorney in the Court of Common Pleas. Had libraries of several hundred volumes each in his houses at Stowe Hall, and in Holborn.
J. Cliffe, *The world of the country house in seventeenth-century England* (1999), 164.

John Buxton 1608–80
Of Channonz Hall, Norfolk; Sheriff of Norfolk. The library he assembled was bequeathed in trust for his sons and largely descended through the family before being dispersed by sale in the late 19th c. A notebook recording his expenditure 1627–31 includes detailed accounts of book purchases.
West. D. McKitterick, 'Ovid with a Littleton', *TCBS* 11 (1997): 184–234.

William Lygon *c*.1613–80
Of Madresfield, Worcestershire. Probate inventory lists, in the study, 88 folios, 78 quartos, 195 octavos, 24 12mos, 4 16mos, and 236 pamphlets, all valued at £44.
M. Wanklyn (ed.), *Inventories of Worcestershire landed gentry, 1637–1786* (1998), 228.
J. Cliffe, *The world of the country house in seventeenth-century England* (1999), 164.

John Tregonwell d.1680
Gave c.60 books to the church of Milton Abbas, Dorset, as a thankful acknowledgment of God's mercy in preserving him when he fell from the top of the church; most of these books were destroyed in 1940 as war salvage.
Perkin, 285.

Sir Francis Fane 1612–81
Of Fulbeck, Lincolnshire, third son of Francis Fane, 1st Earl of Westmorland. Books with his armorial stamp survive.
Armorials database.

Sir Thomas Remington c.1612–81
Of Lockington and Lund, Yorkshire. Bequeathed a library of c.1,900 volumes to create a parish library for Lund; no books survive today, but the contemporary catalogue, probably in Remington's hand, was described and offered for sale by Quaritch in 2015. The books probably included ones inherited by Remington from previous generations of his family.
Quaritch 1433 (2015)/17 (now in Cambridge UL, and available in the Cambridge Digital Library)

Sir Henry Blount 1602–82
Sir Thomas Pope Blount, 1st Bt 1649–97
Charles Blount 1654–92
Of Tittenhanger, Hertfordshire. Sir Henry achieved fame by publishing an account of his travels as *A voyage into the Levant* (1636); Aubrey said of him that 'when he was young, he was a great collector of books, as his son is now'. The elder son Thomas was an MP, his brother Charles noted as a radical freethinker. The extent of their libraries is not known but their wills all refer to the disposition of books.
ODNB. Aubrey, *Brief lives*.

James Sale d. 1682
Of Bledlowridge, Buckinghamshire, gentleman. Probate inventory lists 'books of all sorts' in his study, valued at £13.
M. Reed (ed.), *Buckinghamshire probate inventories 1661–1714* (1988), 165.

Elizabeth Brooke, Lady Brooke 1602?–83
Daughter of Thomas Colepeper, wife of Sir Robert Brooke (d. 1646) of Cockfield Hall, Suffolk, where she remained during her long widowhood. Although we have no direct documentation of her library, the biography in her funeral sermon refers not only to the depth and breadth of her reading but also to a body of devotional writings she left behind. She evidently had a closet well-stocked with books.
ODNB. N. Parkhurst, *The faithful and diligent Christian described* (1684).

Sir Richard Browne 1605–83
Of Saye's Court, Deptford; diplomat, clerk to the Privy Council. Used an engraved armorial bookplate and a variety of armorial and monogram stamps. Father-in-law of John Evelyn, to whom he bequeathed his library.
ODNB. Franks 4009. *The Evelyn Library*, Christie's sale catalogue (1977). Armorials database.

Sir John Hobart, 3rd Bt 1628–83
Sir Henry Hobart, 4th Bt 1657–98
Of Blickling Hall, Norfolk. A 'catalogue of books in the green room' at Blickling, made c.1676, lists 380 vols. The probate inventory of Sir Henry, made in 1700, refers to 1,100

volumes and describes the furnishing of the study with walnut bookstands and a reading desk.

ODNB. West. S. West, 'An architectural typology for the early modern country house library, 1660–1720', *The Library*, 7th ser. 14 (2013): 441–64, 450–51.

William Dowdeswell d. 1684

Of Pull Court, Bushley, Worcestershire; sheriff of Worcestershire. Probate inventory lists books in the study, valued at £10.

M. Wanklyn (ed.), *Inventories of Worcestershire landed gentry, 1637–1786* (1998), 237.

Thomas Gore 1631–84

Of Alderton, Wiltshire; antiquary. His will has extensive references to the disposal of books, and although he clearly assembled a significant library, its extent and contents are not known. Used several bookplates; his armorial stamp is known only from a MS family genealogy now in the V&A.

ODNB. J. Jackson, 'The last will of Thomas Gore, the antiquary', *Wiltshire Archaeological Magazine* 14 (1873). Lee, *British*, 13. Franks 12321. Armorials database.

Sir Thomas Peyton, 2nd Bt 1613–84

Of Knowlton, Kent; MP. Books with his armorial stamp survive.

HoP. Armorials database.

Ralph Sheldon 1623–84

Of Weston, Warwickshire; antiquary, member of a wealthy Roman Catholic gentry family. Anthony Wood, who helped to catalogue and organize his library at Weston, noted its size and significance. Numerous books with his armorial stamps survive; he also used 3 bookplates. Gave heraldic MSS to Jesus College, Oxford, and the College of Arms; books which remained in the family were largely dispersed by auction, 7 Sept. 1781.

ODNB. Lee, *British*, 10. Franks 26649–51. I. G. Philip, 'Sheldon's manuscripts in Jesus College Library', *BLR* 1 (1939): 119–23. J. Cliffe, *The world of the country house in seventeenth-century England* (1999), 163–4. Maggs 1075 (1987)/44. Armorials database.

Brome Whorwood 1615–84

Of Holton House, Oxfordshire; MP. Probate inventory includes a library of *c*.100 volumes.

HoP. J. Cliffe, *The world of the country house in seventeenth-century England* (1999), 164.

Sir Jeffrey Burwell 1606–84

Of Rougham Place, Suffolk; lawyer. Books with his armorial stamp survive (several are inscribed by his daughter, Mary, who married Robert Walpole of Houghton, Norfolk).

ODNB. Armorials database.

George Russell d. 1684

Of Aston Abbots, Buckinghamshire, Esquire. Probate inventory lists 'books', in the little parlour and elsewhere, valued at £5.

M. Reed (ed.), *Buckinghamshire probate inventories 1661–1714* (1988), 178.

Sir John Marsham 1602–85

Of Whome's Place, Cuxton, Kent; MP, clerk in chancery, antiquary. Noted as a respected scholar; known to have used two bookplates.

ODNB. Lee, *British*, 8. Franks 19825.

Sir Roger Pratt 1620–85

Of Ryston Hall, Norfolk; architect. Known to have designed a library closet capable of holding *c*.400 vols. Family papers refer to a number of book purchases in the 1650s and

1660s. 69 vols survive at Ryston today, now in later (18th-c.) bindings, annotated with distinctive marginal pencil marks.

ODNB. West. K. Skelton, 'Reading as a gentleman and an architect: Sir Roger Pratt's library', *Transactions of the Ancient Monuments Society* 53 (2009): 15–50. S. West, 'An architectural typology for the early modern country house library, 1660–1720', *The Library*, 7th ser. 14 (2013): 441–64, 449–50.

Sir Norton Knatchbull, 1st Bt 1602–85
Of Mersham Hatch, Kent; MP, theological author. Library auctioned in London, 22 June 1698 (1,452 lots, plus an appendix of MSS apparently owned by someone else, unnamed). *ODNB*. R. Beadle, 'Medieval English manuscripts at auction, 1676–*c*.1700', *BC* 53 (2004): 46–63. D. Pearson, 'Patterns of book ownership in late seventeenth-century England', *The Library*, 7th ser. 11 (2010): 139–67. Alston, *Inventory*.

Sir John Pettus *c*.1613–85
Landowner in Norfolk and Suffolk (but died in debt); politician, author of works on mining. Books with his armorial stamp survive.
ODNB. Armorials database.

Edward Wray *c*.1627–85
Of Barlings, Lincolnshire; probably one of the younger sons of Sir Christopher Wray (1601–46). Library auctioned in London, 20 June 1687 (2,302 lots).
ODNB (other members of the family). Alston, *Inventory*.

Edmund Waller 1606–87
Of Hall Barn, Beaconsfield; poet, MP. His library remained with his family descendants after his death, at Hall Barn, Beaconsfield; the collection was sold in 1832. Part of the library of Maj. Gen. W. N. Waller, 'collected by Edmund Waller the poet and his descendants', was sold at Sothebys, 12 Dec. 1900.
ODNB. Maggs 1121 (1990)/18, 60.

Sir Henry Langley d. 1688
Of The Abbey, Shrewsbury. Listed in Edward Bernard's *Catalogi manuscriptorum* (1697) as owning a number of manuscripts.
Foster.

Sir John Pakington, 3rd Bt *c*.1649–88
Of Westwood, Worcestershire; MP, Anglo-Saxon scholar. Probate inventory lists books valued at £20 in the 'Old Ladyes Closett'.
ODNB. M. Wanklyn (ed.), *Inventories of Worcestershire landed gentry, 1637–1786* (1998), 249.

Josias Geary d. 1689
Of Chesham, Buckinghamshire, gentleman. Probate inventory lists 'a library of books and parchment' in the study, valued at £12.
M. Reed (ed.), *Buckinghamshire probate inventories 1661–1714* (1988), 223.

Sir John Borlase, 2nd Bt *c*.1640–89
Of Bockmore Medmenham, Buckinghamshire; MP. Probate inventory lists 'one chest of drawers thirty four books a nest of drawers [and other furniture]', in the closet adjoining the parlour, valued at £6 4s. 0d.
HoP. M. Reed (ed.), *Buckinghamshire probate inventories 1661–1714* (1988), 209.

Elizabeth Puckering 1621/2–89
Sir Henry Puckering, 3rd Bt 1618–1701
Of Warwick, royalist army officer; they married *c*.1640. Assembled a considerable library, some of it inherited from Sir John Puckering (1544–96) and other ancestors,

with some of the books identifiably associated with Elizabeth. The books were given to Trinity College, Cambridge between *c*.1690 and 1701.

ODNB. D. McKitterick, *The making of the Wren Library* (1995), 56–8. D. McKitterick, 'Women and their books in seventeenth-century England: the case of Elizabeth Puckering', *The Library*, 7th ser. 1 (2000): 359–80.

Sir William Glynne, 1st Bt 1638–90
Of Ambrosden House, Oxfordshire; MP, high sheriff of Flintshire. Inventory made after death shows a library of *c*.800 volumes. Listed in Edward Bernard's *Catalogi manuscriptorum* (1697) as owning 130 manuscripts on English common law.
HoP. J. Cliffe, *The world of the country house in seventeenth-century England* (1999), 164.

Sir Thomas Mostyn, 2nd Bt 1651–92
Of Gloddaeth, Caernarvonshire; antiquary. A catalogue of his MSS made shortly after his death lists over 100 items; founder of what became a Mostyn family library.
HoP. D. Huws, 'Sir Thomas Mostyn and the Mostyn manuscripts', in J. Carley and C. Tite (eds), *Books and collectors 1200–1700* (London, 1997), 451–72. L. Erne, *Shakespeare and the book trade* (2013), 210.

Sir Thomas Tempest, 4th Bt 1642–92
Of Stella, Co. Durham. Over 100 books and MSS with his inscription survive, many in Ushaw College, Durham; the family acquired numerous books from Durham Priory after its dissolution.
A. I. Doyle, 'The library of Sir Thomas Tempest: its origins and dispersal', in G. Janssens & F. Aarts (eds), *Studies in seventeenth-century English literature, history and bibliography* (1984), 83–93. C. Tite, 'Sir Robert Cotton, Sir Thomas Tempest and an Anglo-Saxon gospel book', in J. Carley & C. Tite (eds), *Books and collectors 1200–1700* (1997), 429–39.

Sir Walter Chetwynd 1620?–93
Of Ingestre, Staffordshire; MP, antiquary. Numerous books with his armorial stamps survive. Listed in Edward Bernard's *Catalogi manuscriptorum* (1697) as owning 22 manuscripts. The Chetwynd family library was auctioned in London, 18 May 1821.
ODNB. Maggs 1212 (1996)/39. Armorials database.

Sir Thomas Hervey 1625–94
Isabella Hervey d. 1686
Of Ickworth Manor, Suffolk; MP. Many books survive today, at Ickworth House and elsewhere, inscribed 'Tho: & Isabella Hervey', apparently written by Thomas, although there are numerous books which seem initially to have been Isabella's personally.
HoP. N. Barker, *Treasures from the libraries of National Trust country houses* (New York, 1998), no 31. E. Smith, 'Marital marginalia: the seventeenth-century library of Thomas and Isabella Hervey', in K. Acheson (ed.), *Early modern English marginalia* (2019), 155–72.

Thomas Boothby 1641–96
Of Delfa House, Staffordshire. Books with his armorial stamp survive.
Armorials database.

John Hampden 1653–96
Of Great Hampden, Buckinghamshire, MP and politician. Library auctioned in London, 13 Feb. 1699 (joint sale, with one other).
ODNB. Mandelbrote, 'Auctions', 26. Alston, *Inventory*.

Thomas Preston *c*.1648–97
Of Holker, Lancashire; MP. Bequeathed books to establish a parish library for Cartmel.
HoP. Perkin, 169. D. Ramage, *The ancient library in Cartmel Priory Church* (1959). Armorials database.

Sir John Pye, 1st Bt 1626–97
Of Hone, Devon. Books with his armorial stamp survive.
Armorials database.

Sir Richard Temple, 3rd Bt 1634–97
Of Stowe, Buckinghamshire; MP. Amassed a library of *c.*2,400 books.
ODNB. G. Abernethy, 'Sir Richard Temple and the Stowe Library', *Huntington Library Quarterly* 40 (1976): 45–58.

Mary Wintour, Lady Wintour *c.*1630–97
Wife of Sir John Wintour, of Huddington, Worcestershire (1622–58). Probate inventory lists 'a parcel of bookes', together with a table, a couch and a looking glass, valued together at £6 10*s.*
M. Wanklyn (ed.), *Inventories of Worcestershire landed gentry, 1637–1786* (1998), 262.

George Walsh d. 1698
Of Holt, Worcestershire. Probate inventory lists books, in the study, valued at £8.
M. Wanklyn (ed.), *Inventories of Worcestershire landed gentry, 1637–1786* (1998), 266.

William Blundell 1620–98
Recusant landowner, of Crosby Hall, Lancashire. An inventory of 1675 lists a library of 447 books; his surviving commonplace books reveal extensive evidence of his reading and use of books.
ODNB. G. Baker, *Reading and politics in early modern England* (2010).

Richard More 1627–98
Of Linley Hall, Shropshire; MP. Gave *c.*350 volumes from his library to establish a parish library for More, Shropshire, in 1680.
ODNB. Perkin, 287–9. C. Condren, 'More parish library', *Library History* 7 (1987): 141–62.

Sir Henry Cambell, 3rd Bt 1663–99
Of Clay Hall, Barking. Books with his armorial stamp survive.
Armorials database.

Sir James Langham, 2nd Bt 1621–99
Of Cottesbrooke, Northamptonshire; MP. Library sold by retail sale in London, 26 Jan. 1714 (joint sale, with one other; no catalogue survives).
HoP. Alston, *Inventory.*

Sir Samuel Marrow, 1st Bt 1652/3–99
Of Berkswell, Warwickshire. Library auctioned in Coventry, 21 Sept. 1702 (no catalogue survives).
Venn. Alston, *Inventory.*

Thomas Savage *c.*1622–99
Of Elmley Castle, Worcestershire; sheriff of Worcestershire. Probate inventory lists books in the study at Great Malvern, valued at £30, and 'bookes of all sorts' in the closet at Elmley Castle, valued at £10 10*s.*
Foster. M. Wanklyn (ed.), *Inventories of Worcestershire landed gentry, 1637–1786* (1998), 276.

Andrew Barker 1630?–1700
Of Fairford, Gloucestershire. Used an engraved armorial bookplate, probably made *c.*1680.
Lee, *British*, 15.

Sir Thomas Barnardiston, 3rd Bt, of Kedlington 1674–1700
Ann Barnardiston d. 1701
Sir Samuel Barnardiston, 1st Bt, of Brightwell 1620–1707

Sir Nathaniel Barnardiston, 4th Bt, of Brightwell d. 1712
Members of a prominent Suffolk family who were variously merchants, MPs, and establishers of baronetcies. They each had engraved armorial bookplates, variously dated between 1699 and 1704.
ODNB. Blatchly, 9. Franks 1525/*120/*156/*161–2/*368

Sir Samuel Grimston, 3rd Bt 1643–1700
Of Gorhambury, Hertfordshire; MP. A woodcut bookplate is found in books given by him to St Albans Grammar School.
ODNB. Lee, *British*, 20.

Sir John Aubrey, 2nd Bt d. 1700
Of Lantrithyd, Glamorgan. Used an engraved bookplate dated 1698.
HoP. Franks 955/*150. Lee, *British*, 24.

Francis Fulford 1666–1700
Of Great Fulford, Devon; MP. Used an engraved armorial bookplate dated 1699.
HoP. Franks 11466/*307.

Robert Walpole 1650–1700
Of Houghton Hall, Norfolk; MP. Many of his books survive at Houghton; family accounts show that he actively purchased books in London and at East Anglian fairs. A catalogue of the house collection made in 1717 lists *c.*850 titles.
ODNB. West.

Sir John Barneby 1621–1701
Of Hull, Bockleton, Worcestershire; MP. Probate inventory lists 'six hundred books of severall volumes' in his closet, valued at £12.
HoP. M. M. Wanklyn (ed.), *Inventories of Worcestershire landed gentry, 1637–1786* (1998), 288.

Sir John Bowyer, 3rd Bt 1677?–1701
Of Knipersley, Staffordshire. Used an engraved armorial bookplate.
Franks 3334.

Sir Thomas Willis, 1st Bt 1612–1701
Of Fen Ditton, Cambridgeshire; MP. Library auctioned in King's Lynn, 10 Feb. 1717 (joint sale, with one other).
HoP. M&C. Alston, *Inventory.*

Thomas Cholmondeley 1627–1702
Of Vale Royal, Cheshire; MP. Used an engraved armorial bookplate.
HoP. Franks 5809.

Sir John Hoby, 2nd Bt 1635–1702
Of Bisham, Berkshire. Edward Bernard's *Catalogi manuscriptorum* (1697) lists him as owning 23 manuscripts.
Complete baronetage.

Sir Robert Southwell 1635–1702
Of King's Weston, Gloucestershire; MP, clerk to the Privy Council. Used an engraved armorial bookplate, made *c.*1680.
ODNB. Lee, *British*, 18. Franks 27634.

Stuart Bickerstaffe 1661–1703?
Eldest son of Sir Charles Bickerstaffe of Seal, Kent (d. 1704). Travelled extensively in Europe, during which time he acquired many books. Used an armorial binding stamp,

an ink stamp, and two bookplates. His books were sold in London as an appendix to the auction of Robert Hooke's library, 29 Apr. 1703 (697 lots).

G. Mandelbrote, 'Sloane's purchases at the sale of Robert Hooke's library', in G. Mandelbrote and B. Taylor (eds), *Libraries within the library* (2009), 98–145, 114ff. Armorials database.

Sir Sackville Crow, 2nd Bt 1674?–1703?
Of Laugharne, Carmarthenshire. Library auctioned in London, 15 Nov. 1703 (1,621 lots, probably not his whole library; perhaps including books belonging to his father, also Sackville Crow, *c.*1600–83, diplomat).
ODNB. Alston, *Inventory.*

Charles Dymoke 1667–1703
Of Scrivelsby, Lincolnshire; MP, King's Champion. Used an engraved armorial book-plate dated 1702.
HoP. Franks *320.

Henry Fermor d. 1703
Of Tusmore, Oxfordshire. Listed in Edward Bernard's *Catalogi manuscriptorum* (1697), as owning a number of manuscripts.

Sir William Hayward ca.1617–1704
Of Tandridge Hall, Surrey. A number of mostly 17th-c. books survive bearing an armorial stamp of the Hayward family, which seem most probably to be associated with Sir William (they have also been attributed to his father John, *c.*1571–1631, whose dates look too early).
HoP. Armorials database.

Sir Peter Killigrew, 2nd Bt *c.*1634–1705
Of Arwennack, Cornwall; MP. Used an engraved bookplate made *c.*1700.
HoP. Lee, *British*, 29. Franks 17142. Maggs 1075 (1987)/78.

Sir Paul Pindar, 3rd Bt *c.*1680–1705
Of Idenshaw, Cheshire. Used two engraved armorial bookplates.
Complete baronetage. Franks 23638–9.

John Evelyn 1620–1706
Of Sayes Court, Deptford; scientist, diarist, writer. One of the best-known, and docu-mented, book owners of the later 17th c. Acquired books throughout his life; his MS catalogue of 1687 records *c.*5,000 titles. The library descended through the family until being dispersed at auction in 1977.
ODNB. CELM. Christie's sale catalogue of the Evelyn library, June 1977–July 1978. G. Keynes, 'John Evelyn as a bibliophile', *The Library*, 4th ser. 12 (1931): 175–93. G. Keynes, *John Evelyn: a study in bibliophily* (1937). G. de la Bédoyere, 'John Evelyn's library catalogue', *BC* 43 (1994): 529–48. Special issue of *BC* on John Evelyn in the British Library, vol. 44(2) (Summer 1995). M. Zytaruk, '"Occasional specimens, not compleate systemes": John Evelyn's culture of collecting', *BLR* 17 (2001): 185–212. G. Mandelbrote, 'John Evelyn and his books', in F. Harris & M. Hunter (eds), *John Evelyn and his milieu* (2003), 71–94. M. Foot, 'An Englishman in Paris: John Evelyn and his bookbindings', in *Bibliophiles et reliures: mélanges offerts à Michel Wittock* (2006), 230–45. *CHL* II 28–33. Armorials database.

Sir Hugh Everard, 3rd Bt 1655–1706
Of Much Waltham, Essex; soldier, JP. Library auctioned in London, 20 Oct. 1707 (joint sale, with one other).
Alston, *Inventory.*

Sir Robert Thorold, 3rd Bt d. 1706
Of Haugh-on-the-Hill, Lincolnshire. Library auctioned in London, 7 Jan. 1707 (only a catalogue title page survives).
Alston, *Inventory.*

Sir William Avery d. *c.*1707?
Library sold by auction in London, 15 Oct. 1707 (no catalogue survives, nor has a knight or baronet of this name been traced at this time).
Alston, *Inventory.*

Sir William Boothby, 1st Bt 1637–1707
Of Ashbourne Hall, Derbyshire. His diary and letterbooks, now in the British Library (Add MSS 71689–71692) record his active interest in book buying during the 1680s; his library, reckoned to have been *c.*6,000 volumes, was dispersed sometime after his death. Used a series of armorial stamps.
ODNB. P. Beal, 'My books are the great joy of my life', *BC* 46 (1997): 350–78. *CHL* II 173–4. Armorials database.

Sir Thomas Brograve, 3rd Bt 1670–1707
Of Hamells, Hertfordshire. Library auctioned in London, 28 Aug. 1712 (no catalogue survives).
Alston, *Inventory.*

Cary Coke 1680–1707
Edward Coke 1676/8–1707
Of Holkham Hall, Norfolk, husband and wife, who each used an engraved armorial bookplate dated 1701. Many of their books remain at Holkham (including over 100 with Cary's bookplate), though some books, including numerous bound volumes of plays, were bought by the Bodleian in the 1950s.
Blatchly. D. Rogers, 'The Holkham collection', *Bodleian Library Record* 4 (1953): 255–67. D. P. Mortlock, *The Holkham Library: a history and description* (2006). Franks 6316–17/*186/*297.

Henry Poley 1654–1707
Edmund Poley 1655–1714
Of Badley, Suffolk, brothers; Henry was an MP. Each used engraved armorial bookplates, dated 1703 and 1707 (some of Edmund's may be Henry's reworked).
HoP. Franks 23761–2/23764/*190/*243/*254.

Sir Cyril Wyche 1632?–1707
Of Hockwold Hall, Norfolk; MP, Secretary of State for Ireland. Library auctioned in London, 20 Feb. 1710; the catalogue was apparently compiled from Wyche's own MS catalogue, and includes original shelfmarks (*c.*2,400 titles, housed in 11 cases of 12 shelves each, plus 3 smaller cases).
ODNB. West. Alston, *Inventory.*

Sir Richard Gipps 1659–1708
Of Great Whelnetham, Suffolk, antiquary. Library sold by retail sale in London, 13 Dec. 1728.
ODNB. M. Leach & M. Lockett, 'Sir Richard Gipps' library at Great Whelnetham', *Proceedings of the Suffolk Institute of Archaeology* 43 (2015): 390–411. Alston, *Inventory.*

Sir John Pole, 3rd Bt 1649–1708
Of Shute, Devon; MP. Used an engraved armorial bookplate.
HoP. Franks *125.

Sir Godfrey Copley, 2nd Bt c.1653–1709
  Of Sprotborough Hall, Doncaster; MP. Amassed a library which was increased by his descendants until sold at Sotheby's, 23 Nov. 1925; his estate passed on his death to his cousin Lionel Copley (d. 1720), of Wadworth, Yorkshire. Used an engraved armorial bookplate.
  ODNB. De Ricci, *English collectors of books and manuscripts* (1930), 31. Young, 43.

Sir William Holford, 1st Bt 1663–1709
  Of Welham, Leicestershire. Used an engraved armorial bookplate.
  Complete baronetage. Franks *163.

Emanuel Scrope Howe c.1663–1709
  Soldier and diplomat; envoy to Hanover 1704. Used an engraved armorial bookplate.
  ODNB. Franks 15546/*331.

Sir Thomas Littleton, 3rd Bt 1647–1709
  Of North Ockenden, Essex; MP, Treasurer of the Navy. Used an engraved armorial bookplate dated 1702.
  ODNB. Franks 18416/*147.

Sir George Rooke c.1650–1709
  Of St Lawrence House, Canterbury, and Barham; Admiral of the Fleet. Used an engraved armorial bookplate dated 1702.
  ODNB. Franks *366.

Sir John Wolstenholme, 3rd Bt 1649–1709
  Of Forty Hall, Enfield; MP, commissioner of customs. Library sold by retail sale in London, 13 Apr. 1709 (no catalogue survives).
  HoP. Alston, *Inventory*.

Sir Richard Brooke, 2nd Bt c.1635–1710
  Of Norton, Cheshire; sheriff of Cheshire. Bequeathed his 'study of books and papers' to his son Thomas, 3rd Bt (c.1664–1737).
  J. P. Rylands (ed.), *Lancashire and Cheshire wills and inventories*, Chetham Society n.s. 37 (1897): 65–69.

Christopher Codrington 1668–1710
  Of Dodington, Gloucestershire; governor of the Leeward Islands, soldier. Engaged an agent to amass a library for him, in Oxford, which he bequeathed to All Souls College (c.12,000 volumes), together with £10,000 for building a library and buying more books.
  ODNB. E. Craster, *The history of All Souls College Library* (1971).

Ferrers Shirley 1696–1712
  Of Staunton Harold, Leicestershire; second son of Robert Shirley (1673–99). An engraved armorial bookplate was made for him (not earlier than 1711, the year in which his grandfather was created Earl Ferrers, to which the plate refers).
  Franks 26802.

Sir Charles Lodowick Cotterell 1654–1710
  Of St Martin-in-the-Fields, London; Master of Ceremonies. Library auctioned in London, 8 Jan. 1711 (1,626 lots).
  ODNB. Alston, *Inventory*.

Sir Richard Newdigate, 2nd Bt 1644–1710
  Of Arbury Hall, Warwickshire; MP, mining entrepreneur. Used an engraved armorial bookplate.
  ODNB. Franks 21722.

Richard Spranger 1658/9–1711?
Of Berkhamsted, Hertfordshire. Library auctioned in London, 13 Feb. 1712 (no catalogue survives).
Venn. Alston, *Inventory.*

Sir Cholmondeley Dering, 4th Bt 1679–1711
Of Surrenden Dering, Kent; MP. Used an engraved armorial bookplate.
Complete baronetage. Franks *130.

Charles Bertie 1641–1711
Of Uffington, Lincolnshire; diplomat, MP, younger son of Montague Bertie, 2nd Earl of Lindsey (1607/8–66). Used an engraved armorial bookplate.
ODNB. Franks 2375/*374.

James Buller 1678?–1711
Of Shillingham, Cornwall; MP. Used an engraved armorial bookplate.
HoP. Franks 4293/*184.

Edward Byde 1642/3–1712?
Of Ware Park, Hertfordshire, younger brother of Sir Thomas Byde (1628–1704), MP. Several books with his armorial stamp survive.
T. A. Walker, *Admissions to Peterhouse* (1912). Armorials database.

Sir Henry Fletcher 3rd Bt 1661–1712
Of Hutton in the Forest, Cumberland; MP. Settled his estate on a distant cousin and retired to the English monastery at Douai. Used an engraved armorial bookplate dated 1702.
HoP. Franks 10773/*155.

Sir George Hungerford *c.*1637–1712
Of Cadenham, Wiltshire; MP. Numerous books with his monogram stamps survive. Library sold by retail sale in London, 8 Apr. 1713 (no catalogue survives).
HoP. Alston, *Inventory.* Armorials database.

Arthur Maynwaring 1668–1712
Of Ightfield, Shropshire; MP, author. Library auctioned in London, 4 Feb. 1713 (606 lots).
ODNB. Alston, *Inventory.*

John Sayer d. 1712
Of Hounslow, Middlesex. Used an engraved armorial bookplate dated 1700.
Lee, *British*, 26. Franks 26192/*525.

Francis Cherry 1667–1713
Of Shottesbrooke, Berkshire; antiquary, nonjuror. Patron of Thomas Hearne, and other antiquarian scholars; assembled a significant library. His MSS were bequeathed to the Bodleian by his widow.
ODNB. Macray, 207. Armorials database.

George Herbert d. 1713
Of Eton, gentleman. Probate inventory lists 'one hundred and six old books' in the closet, valued at £5.
M. Reed (ed.), *Buckinghamshire probate inventories 1661–1714* (1988), 309.

Sir Edmund Denton, 1st Bt 1676–1714
Of Hillesden, Buckinghamshire; MP. Used an engraved armorial bookplate (Franks *168).
HoP. Franks *168.

Elizabeth Freke 1642–1714

Daughter of Raphe Freke of Hannington, Wiltshire, married Percy Freke in 1672; her 'autobiographical memoir is an almost entirely secular account of a propertied gentlewoman's complex and unhappy marriage'. Her diaries show that she owned c.100 books. *ODNB*. J. Pearson, 'Women reading, reading women', in H. Wilcox (ed.), *Women and literature in Britain* (1996), 80–99, 83.

Sir Thomas Tyrrell, 2nd Bt c.1670–1714

Of Hanslape, Buckinghamshire. Library auctioned in London, 11 Nov. 1714. Foster. Alston, *Inventory*.

Francis Brydges d. 1714

Younger son of James Brydges, 8th Baron Chandos, of Wilton Castle, Herefordshire (1642–1714); receiver-general of duties on salt. Used two engraved armorial bookplates. *Herefordshire bookplates*, 11. Franks *195/*223.

Robert Byerley 1660–1714

Of Goldesborough Hall, Yorkshire; MP, soldier, racehorse breeder. Used an engraved bookplate dated 1702. *ODNB*. Young 35. Franks 4726/*367/*514.

Matthew Fletcher d. c.1715

Of Chatham, Kent. Library, together with prints, paintings and drawings, sold by retail sale in London, 11 May 1715 (185 lots, plus 481 prints/drawings and 50 paintings). Alston, *Inventory*.

Sir Richard Haddock c.1629–1715

Naval officer, Controller of the Navy. Used an engraved armorial bookplate dated 1702. *ODNB*. Franks *269.

Sir Henry Hunloke, 2nd Bt 1645–1715

Of Wingerworth, Derbyshire; sheriff of Derbyshire. Used an engraved armorial bookplate, made c.1680. *Complete baronetage*. Lee, *British*, 17. Franks 15732.

Sir Thomas Meres 1634–1715

Of Bloomsbury Square, Westminster, and Lincoln; MP. Used an engraved armorial bookplate dated 1705. *ODNB*. Franks *467.

John Wyrley d. c.1715?

Of Hampstead Hall, Warwickshire. Library sold by retail sale in London, 17 Oct. 1715. Alston, *Inventory*.

Heralds

Nicholas Charles 1582–1613

Lancaster Herald. His MSS were sold, after his death, to William Camden for £90. A number of Harleian MSS were previously owned or copied by Charles. *ODNB. Fontes Harleianae*.

William Camden 1551–1623

Clarenceux King of Arms, antiquary, author. A list of significant libraries, drawn up by Selden in 1622, included his. Bequeathed his heraldic books to his successor as Clarenceux, and the rest to Sir Robert Cotton, who gave most to Westminster Abbey (where many survive today). Over 600 books owned by him have been identified.

ODNB. CELM. R. de Molen, 'The library of William Camden', *Proceedings of the American Philosophical Society* 128 (1984): 326–409. E. van Houts, 'Camden, Cotton and the chronicles of the Norman Conquest', in C. Wright (ed.), *Sir Robert Cotton as a collector* (1997), 238–52. W. Herendeen, *William Camden* (2008).

Ralph Brooke *c.*1553–1625
York Herald. Gathered a significant collection of MSS, now scattered between the College of Arms, the BL, and elsewhere. His executrix seems to have sold some of his MSS in 1629; some were acquired by Sir Edward Dering.
ODNB. Fontes Harleianae.

Augustine Vincent *c.*1584–1626
Windsor Herald. His books and MSS passed to his son John (d. 1671), who added to them, before bequeathing the MSS to Ralph Sheldon, who in turn left them to the College of Arms in 1684 (*c.*260 Vincent MSS remain there today).
ODNB. L. Campbell et al., *A catalogue of manuscripts in the College of Arms collections,* vol. 1 (1988). Armorials database.

Sampson Lennard d. 1633
Bluemantle Pursuivant. Some of his heraldic MSS are in the Harleian Collection at the BL; some have his armorial stamp.
ODNB. Fontes Harleianae. Armorials database.

Sir Richard St George 1554/5–1635
Clarenceux King of Arms. His books passed down the family—both his son and grandsons were heralds—and were eventually sold by Thomas Osborne in London, 1738. Books with his armorial stamp survive. Sir Henry St George (1625–1715), his third son, is listed in Edward Bernard's *Catalogi manuscriptorum* (1697) as owning 31 MSS.
ODNB. Armorials database.

Henry Chitting 1580–1638
Chester Herald. Books with his armorial stamp survive.
ODNB. Blatchly, 8. Armorials database.

John Philipot *c.*1589–1645
Somerset Herald. His books passed through several hands after his death but many of his heraldic ones were bought by the College of Arms in the late 17th c., where *c.*130 now survive.
ODNB. Armorials database.

Sir William Le Neve 1592–1661
Clarenceux King of Arms. Acquired many of the books of the herald Sir William Dethick (1543–1612). His library was sold after his death to Sir Edward Walker, Garter King of Arms, who left it to the College of Arms.
ODNB. Fontes Harleianae.

Edward Waterhouse 1619–70
Heraldic and historical author. Books with his armorial stamp survive.
ODNB. Armorials database.

Sir Edward Walker 1611–76
Garter King of Arms. Books with his armorial stamp survive. Bequeathed some heraldic MSS to the College of Arms, together with the books of William Le Neve, but the bulk of his library to his grandson Edward Clopton; it was apparently dispersed soon afterwards.
ODNB. Armorials database.

Sir Edward Bysshe *c.*1610–79
Clarenceux King of Arms (Garter during the Interregnum, but ejected 1660). Library auctioned in London, 15 Nov. 1679 (2,361 lots), with some remaining MSS auctioned 4

July 1681 (joint sale). MS inventory of his library in BL Harl. MS 813 valued it at £300, and listed *c.*2,500 vols.

ODNB. R. Beadle, 'Medieval English manuscripts at auction, 1676–*c.*1700', *BC* 53 (2004): 46–63. Lee, *British*, 16. Mandelbrote, 'Auctions'. T. Birrell, 'Reading as pastime: the place of light literature in some seventeenth-century gentlemen's libraries', in R. Myers (ed.), *Property of a gentleman* (Winchester, 1991), 113–31, 125–6. Alston, *Inventory.*

Sir William Dugdale 1605–85

Garter King of Arms, historian. Bequeathed MSS and papers to the Ashmolean Museum; some of his books sold at auction, 1862.

ODNB. D. Douglas, *English scholars* (1939), ch. 2. H. Cronne, 'The study and use of charters in the seventeenth century: Sir Henry Spelman and Sir William Dugdale', in L. Fox (ed.), *English historical scholarship* (1956), 73–91. Maggs 1272 (1999)/27.

Elias Ashmole 1617–92

Windsor Herald, astrologer, antiquary. Bequeathed his extensive library to the University of Oxford, where it was originally housed in the Ashmolean Museum before being transferred to the Bodleian in 1860. Some of his collections were destroyed by fire in 1679. Over 1,000 books not retained by the museum were auctioned in London, 22 Feb. 1694.

ODNB. Macray. H. A. Feisenberger, *Sale catalogues of libraries of eminent persons*, 11: *Scientists* (London, 1975). W. Black, *A descriptive... catalogue of the MSS bequeathed... by Elias Ashmole* (1845). R. Gunther, 'The Ashmole printed books', *BQR* 6 (1930): 193–5. V. Feola, 'The recovered library of Elias Ashmole for the Ashmolean Museum, *Bibliotheca* 1 (2005): 259–78. Lee, *British*, 210. Alston, *Inventory.* Armorials database.

Sylvanus Morgan 1620–93

Arms-painter and heraldic author. Library auctioned in London, 5 Apr. 1693, with some of the books of Robert Boyle (1,087 lots); many of his manuscripts, which remained in his family, were auctioned 3 Dec. 1759. His notebooks in Cambridge University Library (MS Dd V178) include two lists of his books made in 1646 and 1653, running to *c.*100 titles.

ODNB. Alston, *Inventory.* Armorials database.

Lawyers

Sir John Paulet b. 1576

Lawyer, illegitimate son of William Paulet, 3rd Marquis of Winchester (d. 1598). Books with his armorial stamp survive.

Armorials database.

George Anton *c.*1550–*c.*1615?

MP for, and Recorder of Lincoln. Gave MSS to Lincoln's Inn; books survive with his armorial stamp.

HoP. Armorials database.

William Rich 1567–*c.*1620?

Member of the Middle Temple, 1605. A number of surviving books with his armorial stamp suggest a library that was dispersed *c.*1620. His books are often annotated, and two have an unusual printed ownership label naming the bookbinder.

A.W. Pollard, 'An English bookbinders' ticket, c.1610?', *The Library*, 3rd ser. 12 (1931): 332–5. Armorials database.

Alexander Rigby d. 1621
Of Wigan and Poole, Lancashire, lawyer; clerk of the peace for Lancashire 1612–21. His law books—about 80 titles, reckoned to be two-thirds of his total library—were listed in a 1624 inventory, edited as PLRE 269.
J. Black & R. Fehrenbach, 'Alexander Rigby', PLRE 9 (2017): 163–78.

Paul d'Ewes 1567–1631
One of the Six Clerks in Chancery. List of 122 books owned c.1610, mainly legal, in British Library MS Harl.70.
ODNB. Sears Jayne, 141. J. S. McGee, *An industrious mind: the worlds of Sir Simonds d'Ewes* (2015).

Paul Ambrose Croke 1561–1631
Barrister of the Inner Temple. Bequeathed books and MSS to his son-in-law Edward Heath, listed in British Library Egerton MS 2983 fo. 28v. His personal account books for the 1610s/20s include some references to book purchases.
Sears Jayne, 159, 163. J. H. Bloom, 'Paulus Ambrosius Croke: a seventeenth-century account book', *Notes & Queries*, 12th ser. 4 (1918): 36–8. P. Kopperman, *Sir Robert Heath* (1989), 66–70.

Humfrey Dyson 1582–1633
Notary public. Amassed a sizeable library, of over 1,000 volumes; some of them are listed in a number of notebooks now All Souls College, Oxford MS 117. Most of his books were sold after his death, and many which were acquired by Richard Smith (1590–1675) re-entered the market in his 1682 auction sale; Dyson's books are now widely spread around the world's libraries.
ODNB. Sears Jayne. R. L. Steele, 'Humphrey Dyson', *The Library*, 3rd ser. 1 (1910): 144–51. W. A. Jackson, 'Humphrey Dyson and his collection of Elizabethan proclamations', *Harvard Lib. Bull.* 1 (1947): 76–89. W. A. Jackson, 'Humfrey Dyson's library', *PBSA* 43 (1949): 279–87. A. H. Nelson, *The library of Humfrey Dyson* (forthcoming, Oxford Bibliographical Society).

Sir Edward Coke 1552–1634
Lord Chief Justice. A MS catalogue of his library in 1634, now at Holkham Hall, Norfolk, lists 1,237 MSS/books; many of his books survive there today, and elsewhere.
ODNB. Sears Jayne, 163. W. Hassall, *A catalogue of the library of Sir Edward Coke* (1950). D. Rogers, 'The Holkham collection', *BLR* 4 (1953): 255–67.

Thomas Edwards 1555–1634
Lawyer and MP for Calne, Wiltshire. Several books with his armorial stamp survive.
HoP. Armorials database.

Sir Julius Caesar 1558–1636
Judge, Chancellor of the Exchequer, Master of the Rolls. Noted as the owner of a travelling library; his will reveals an extensive library divided between home and office. Shelflist of his MSS in British Library Lansdowne MS 124; much of his MSS collection was auctioned in London, 14 Dec. 1757.
ODNB. Sears Jayne, 167. W. Sherman, *Used books* (2008), ch. 7.

William Platt d. 1637
Barrister, of Lincoln's Inn. Bequeathed his library, together with London property and money for scholarships, to St Johns College, Cambridge (c.40 books survive there today). Venn. Armorials database.

Richard Brownlow 1553–1638
Sir John Brownlow 1594–1679
Sir William Brownlow 1595–1666
Sir Richard Brownlow 1628–68
Sir John Brownlow 1659–97

> The first Richard, Chief Prothonotary of the Court of Common Pleas, made his fortune and established the Brownlow family seat at Belton House, Lincolnshire; the library there was continuously developed from his time onwards, and contains books associated with many subsequent generations.
> ODNB. P. Hoare, 'The perils of provenance', *Library History* 18 (2002): 225–34. A. Brundin & D. Roberts, 'Book-buying and the grand tour: the Italian books at Belton House', *The Library*, 7th ser. 16 (2015): 51–79.

Robert Ashley 1565–1641

> Barrister, of the Middle Temple; literary translator. Bequeathed his library, *c.*5,000 volumes, to the Middle Temple.
> ODNB. CHL I 459–60. K. Whitlock, 'The Robert Ashley founding bequest to the Middle Temple Library and John Donne's library', *Sederi* 14 (2004): 153–75.

Thomas Sanderson 1569/70–1642

> Barrister, of Lincoln's Inn; originally from Gainsborough, Lincolnshire. A book with his armorial stamp is tentatively attributed to him; his lengthy will (The National Archives PROB 11/190/438) contains many directions regarding books and it is clear that he had a sizeable library.
> Foster. Armorials database.

Richard Colchester 1600–43

> Of Gray's Inn, one of the Six Clerks in Chancery. His surviving account book for the late 1630s/early 1640s (Gloucester Record Office, D36 A1) records the purchase and binding of a number of books.
> Foster.

John Norton b. 1612/13

> Civil lawyer. More than 84 books were seized from his London house by the London Committee for Sequestration in 1643, and partly sold.
> Venn. Roy.

Sir Edward Littleton 1589–1645

> Chief Justice of the Common Pleas. A large engraved armorial plate is known to have been used by him sometimes as a bookplate, and books with his armorial stamp survive. His books in London were seized after his death, by parliamentary order, and apparently then dispersed.
> ODNB. Lee, *British*, 7. Armorials database.

Sir John Lambe 1566?–1647

> Dean of the Arches. Gave 21 MSS to William Laud in 1632, which he passed on to the Bodleian. More than 115 books were seized from him by the London Committee for Sequestration in 1643, and partly sold.
> ODNB. J. Fuggles, 'Sir John Lambe's manuscripts in the Bodleian Library', *BLR* 10 (1979): 109–12. Roy.

Edward Gwynn d. 1649?

> Barrister, of Middle Temple. About 200 books of his survive, found in many libraries, with his name and initials tooled on the covers. Bequeathed his books to his legal friend Alexander Chorley; the library appears to have been dispersed later in the 17th c.

W. A. Jackson, Edward Gwynn, in his *Records of a bibliographer* (1967), 115–19. List of books owned by Edward Gwynn, on Folgerpedia: https://folgerpedia.folger.edu/Main_Page.

Sir Robert Heath 1575–1649
Lady Margaret Heath d. 1647
Francis Heath 1622–83
John Heath 1614–91
   MP and judge, Recorder of London. Presented books to St John's College, Cambridge in 1630; an armorial stamp is recorded from these books. A catalogue of the books belonging to his wife Margaret, made *c*.1647, is in British Library Egerton MS 2983, fo. 79; the same MS has a list of Francis's books (fos 155, 156). More than 120 books were seized from the London home of his son John by the London Committee for Sequestration in 1643, and sold.
   ODNB. Roy. P. Kopperman, *Sir Robert Heath* (1989). M. Empey, 'Lady Margaret Heath', in PLRE 11 (forthcoming). Armorials database.

Sir Thomas Gardiner 1591–1652
   Barrister, Recorder of London. 42 books were seized from his London house by the London Committee for Sequestraion in 1643, and sold.
   ODNB. Roy.

John Selden 1584–1654
   Lawyer, scholar, writer. His library of *c*.8,000 volumes, one of the largest of his generation, was given to the Bodleian after his death (some duplicates were given to Gloucester Cathedral Library).
   ODNB. Macray 110–23. Philip, 47–9. Toomer, 64–71. D. Barratt, 'The library of John Selden and its later history', *BLR* 3 (1951), 128–42, 208–12, 256–73. C. Tite, 'A "loan" of printed books from Sir Robert Cotton to John Selden', *BLR* 13 (1991): 486–90. S. Naiman, 'John Selden', in W. Baker (ed.), *Pre-nineteenth-century British book collectors and bibliographers* (1999), 297–306. *CHL* I 315–21.

Thomas Cory d. 1656
   Chief Prothonotary of the Court of Common Pleas. Books with his armorial stamp survive.
   ODNB. Armorials database.

Sir John Dodderidge 1555–1628
John Dodderidge 1610–58
   The elder John was a successful lawyer, and judge at the Court of King's Bench. He left most of his books to his nephew John, who was also a lawyer and MP, who gave 112 volumes from their libraries to Barnstaple as the foundation of a town library, which was built 1665–7.
   ODNB. Perkin, 130. S. Dodderidge, *The Dodderidges of Devon: with an account of the Bibliotheca Doddridgiana* (1909).

John Bradshaw 1602–59
   Judge, regicide, President of the Council of State. Bequeathed all his law books, and selected other books, to his nephew Henry Bradshaw (d. 1698); the collection appears to have been dispersed in, or at least by, the early 19th c.
   ODNB. Maggs 1324 (2002)/76.

Charles Tooker 1598–1660
   Civil lawyer. More than 110 books were seized from his London house by the London Committee for Sequestration in 1643, and sold.
   Foster. Roy.

John Egiocke c.1616–64
Of Feckenham, Worcestershire; barrister and MP for Evesham. Probate inventory lists in his chamber and study, 'implementes and bookes amounting to £8'.
M. Wanklyn (ed.), *Inventories of Worcestershire landed gentry, 1637–1786* (1998), 199.

Thomas Pury 1589/90–1666
Gloucester lawyer, parliamentarian civil servant. Helped refound Gloucester Cathedral Library in the 1640s; gave £145 and 'many books'.
ODNB. S. Eward, *A catalogue of Gloucester Cathedral Library*, 1972.

Erasmus Earle 1590–1667
Frances Earle 1592–1671
Barrister, of Lincoln's Inn, Recorder of Norwich. Probate inventory on the death of his wife, Frances, lists 51 books in the study.
ODNB. West. S. West, 'An architectural typology for the early modern country house library, 1660–1720', *The Library*, 7th ser. 14 (2013): 441–64, 452–3.

Robert Nicholas 1595–1667
Judge of the Upper Bench and Baron of the Exchequer during the Interregnum. Gave books to Queen's College, Oxford. About 25 legal MSS from his collections—mostly 17th-c. copies of law reports, for use in his legal practice—survive among John Moore's books in Cambridge University Library. His library may have been dispersed during the time of his grandson, the MP Oliver Nicholas (1651–1716).
ODNB. Morgan. J. Baker, *Catalogue of English legal manuscripts in Cambridge University Library* (1996), li–lii.

Sir Edmund Pierce d. 1667
Lawyer, MP. More than 86 books were seized from his London house by the London Committee for Sequestration in 1643, and partly sold.
ODNB. Roy.

Francis Baber 1600–69
Chancellor of the diocese of Gloucester. Gave books to Gloucester Cathedral Library in 1661.
Foster. S. Eward, *No fine but a glass of wine* (1985), 253.

Sir William Meyrick 1595/6–1669
Civil lawyer and judge. 130 books were seized from him by the London Committee for Sequestration in 1643.
ODNB. Roy.

William Prynne 1600–69
Parliamentarian lawyer, pamphleteer, keeper of the records at the Tower of London. Donated books to Lincoln's Inn Library; bequeathed any of his books they wanted to Oriel College, Oxford.
ODNB. Morgan.

Godfrey Clarke d. 1670
Lawyer, of Somersall, near Chesterfield. His 'Library in the study' was valued for probate at £30.
Foster. *CHL* II 176.

Sir Justinian Lewin 1613–73
Lawyer, Master in Chancery. More than 54 books were seized from him by the London Committee for Sequestration in 1643, and sold.
ODNB. Roy.

John Theyer 1597–1673
Lawyer and antiquary. His library, including *c*.800 MSS, was sold after his death to Robert Scot, who in turn sold it to the Royal Library (hence many MSS are now in the British Library). List of his MSS in BL MS.Royal App.70. Listed in Edward Bernard's *Catalogi manuscriptorum (1697)*, as owning 312 manuscripts.
ODNB. M. R. James, 'The history of Lambeth Palace Library', *TCBS* 3 (1959): 1–31.

Sir Andrew Henley, 1st Bt 1622–75
Barrister, of Middle Temple, and MP. A book with his armorial stamp survives in the Clements Collection in the V&A. Library auctioned in London, 1700 (joint sale, with one other).
HoP. Alston, *Inventory*. Armorials database.

Sir Matthew Hale 1609–76
Judge, Chief Justice of the Court of King's Bench. Left detailed instructions in his will for the disposal of his books; a list of MSS and books given by him to Lincoln's Inn, 1676, is in British Library Stowe MS 1056, fos 86–8; the manuscripts are listed in Edward Bernard's *Catalogi manuscriptorum (1697)*.
ODNB. *CHL* I 453.

John Godolphin 1617–78
Judge of the Admiralty Court during the Interregnum; ejected at the Restoration, after which he continued in practice as a barrister. Library auctioned in London, 11 Nov. 1678 (joint sale, with one other).
ODNB. R. Beadle, 'Medieval English manuscripts at auction, 1676–*c*.1700', *BC* 53 (2004): 46–63. Alston, *Inventory*.

George Ent *c*.1644–79
Barrister, of the Middle Temple. Bequeathed his library to the Royal Society (listed in *Bibliotheca Norfolciana* (1681), 154–67; *c*.360 books, plus *c*.150 unbound tracts).
Venn. J. Buchanan-Brown, 'The books presented to the Royal Society by John Aubrey', *Notes and Records of the Royal Society* 28 (1974): 167–93.

John Hopkinson 1610–80
Antiquary, of Lofthouse,Yorkshire, assistant herald, deputy clerk of the peace; accumulated MSS collections relating to Yorkshire.
ODNB. J. M. Potter, *Catalogue of the Travers Collection*, 1990, 255a/p. 227.

Sir Robert Croke 1611/12–81
Barrister, of the Inner Temple. Library auctioned in London, 23 Feb. 1682 (joint sale; no catalogue survives).
Foster. Alston, *Inventory*.

William Howell d. *c*.1681?
Possibly the barrister of Lincoln's Inn, Master in Chancery 1673? Library auctioned in London, 7 Nov. 1681 (joint sale, with 2 others).
Foster. Alston, *Inventory*.

Henry Parker d. *c*.1681?
Lawyer, of Gray's Inn. Library auctioned in London, 5 Dec. 1681 (joint sale, with one other).
Alston, *Inventory* (his attribution to Henry Parker, 1604–52, seems uncertain).

Sir Richard Weston 1620–81
Baron of the Exchequer. His 'Compleat library of law' auctioned in London, 24 June 1686 (305 lots, all legal; we do not know how many non-legal books he owned).
ODNB. R. Beadle, 'Medieval English manuscripts at auction, 1676–*c*.1700', *BC* 53 (2004): 46–63. Alston, *Inventory*.

John Parsons d. *c*.1682?
Lawyer, of the Middle Temple. Library auctioned in London, 30 Nov. 1682 (918 lots).
Alston, *Inventory*.

Sir Thomas Raymond 1627?–83
Judge, of the Court of Common Pleas, and King's Bench. Library auctioned in London, 3 Dec. 1683 (joint sale, with one other).
ODNB. Alston, *Inventory*.

John Collins d. 1682
Lawyer, of Gray's Inn. Library auctioned in London, 2 July 1683 (joint sale, with one other).
Alston, *Inventory*.

Sir Robert Wiseman 1609/10–84
Lawyer, Dean of the Arches. Legal content of his library auctioned in London, 18 Feb. 1686 (634 lots; we do not know how many non-legal books he owned).
ODNB. Alston, *Inventory*.

Henry Winford 1642–85
Barrister, of the Inner Temple; of Astley, Worcestershire. Probate inventory lists books valued at £12.
Foster. M. Wanklyn (ed.), *Inventories of Worcestershire landed gentry, 1637–1786* (1998), 239.

Charles Perrott 1642–86
Barrister, of Doctor's Commons, MP for Oxford University. Bequeathed books to St John's College, Oxford.
HoP. Morgan.

Anscel Beaumont 1621–86
Lawyer, of Middle Temple. Library auctioned in London, 21 Mar. 1687 (joint sale, with one other).
Alston, *Inventory*.

Samuel Jeake 1623–90
Lawyer, Nonconformist preacher, political activist. The contents of his private library of *c*.2,100 volumes are known from his MS catalogue, now in the Jeake MSS at Rye Museum.
ODNB. M. Hunter et al., *A radical's books: the library catalogue of Samuel Jeake* (1999). *CHL* II 182–4. Cambers, 127.

Sir John Maynard 1604–90
Barrister, judge, MP. Noted as having possessed a large library.
ODNB. *CHL* I 453.

Sir Robert Henley *c*.1624–92
Chief prothonotary of the King's Bench, MP. Books with his armorial stamp survive.
HoP. Armorials database.

John Hoyle d. 1692
Lawyer, tried for homosexual practices in 1687; lover and muse of Aphra Behn. Library auctioned in London, 14 Nov. 1692 (1,196 lots, only *c*.600 may be Hoyle's).
S. H. Mendelson, *The mental world of three Stuart women* (1987). P. A. Hopkins, 'Aphra Behn and John Hoyle', *Notes & Queries* 239 (1994): 176–85. Alston, *Inventory*.

Henry Powle 1630–92
Barrister, of Lincoln's Inn, politician and MP, Master of the Rolls. His extensive MSS collection are now largely distributed between the British Library and the Bodleian; a catalogue of MSS probably belonging to him is in British Library Add. MS.11754.
ODNB.

Roger Belwood d. 1694
Of the Middle Temple; barrister in York. Library auctioned in London, 4 Feb. 1695 (1,600 lots).
Venn. R. Beadle, 'Medieval English manuscripts at auction, 1676–c.1700', BC 53 (2004): 46–63. Alston, *Inventory*.

Sir William Thompson d. 1695
Serjeant at law, of the Middle Temple. Used a large engraved armorial bookplate.
Franks 29303.

Sir John Trenchard 1649–95
Chief justice of Cheshire, MP. Library auctioned in London, 25 Nov. 1695 (joint sale, with one other).
ODNB. Alston, *Inventory*. Armorials database.

Richard Wallop 1616–97
Baron of the Exchequer. Library auctioned in London, 22 Nov. 1697 (joint sale, with one other).
ODNB. Alston, *Inventory*.

Andrew Farrington d. *c.*1699?
Barrister, of the Inner Temple; Recorder of St Albans. Library auctioned in London, 6 July 1699 (joint sale, with one other; no catalogue survives).
Foster. Alston, *Inventory*.

Ralph Hough 1649/50–99
Of the Inner Temple, examiner in the Court of Chancery. Library auctioned in London, January 1700? (2077 lots).
Foster. D. Randall & J. Boswell, *Cervantes in seventeenth-century England* (2009), 626. Alston, *Inventory*.

Sir Peter Pett 1630–99
Advocate-general for Ireland, founder member of the Royal Society. Library auctioned in London, 6 July 1699 (joint sale, with one other; no catalogue survives).
ODNB. Alston, *Inventory*.

Charles Vincent 1649/50–*c.*1701
Of the Middle Temple. Library auctioned in London, 15 May and 2 June 1701.
Foster. Alston, *Inventory*.

Thomas Brotherton *c.*1656–1702
Barrister, of Gray's Inn, MP. Listed in Edward Bernard's *Catalogi manuscriptorum* (1697) as owning 12 manuscripts.
HoP.

Nathaniel Brown d. *c.*1702
Lawyer, of Worcester. Library auctioned in London, 18 Feb. 1702 (no catalogue survives).
Foster. Alston, *Inventory*.

Walter Prat d. 1703?
Of Thavies Inn. Library auctioned in London, 22 Nov. 1703 (no catalogue survives).
Alston, *Inventory*.

Sir Samuel Astry *c.*1631–1704
Clerk of the Crown in King's Bench. A late 17th-c. bookplate is attributed to him.
Lee, *British*, 8.

Thomas Lane *c*.1660–1704? (or later)
Barrister, of Doctors' Commons. Library auctioned in London, 5 Feb. 1710 (joint sale, with one other).
ODNB. Alston, *Inventory*.

Roger Meredith d. *c*.1704?
Master in Chancery. Library sold by retail sale in London, 14 July 1704 (joint sale, with one other; no catalogue survives).
Alston, *Inventory*.

John Brydall 1635–1706?
Lawyer. A collection of pamphlets assembled by him is now in Lincoln's Inn Library.
ODNB. A. Day, 'Pamphlets, protestants and pragmatics', *BC* 35 (1986): 443–62.

Edward Munday d. 1706?
Attorney General of Ireland. Library auctioned in London, 8 Nov. 1706 (no catalogue survives).
Alston, *Inventory*.

Sir Thomas Jenner 1637–1707
Recorder of London, Baron of the Exchequer. Library auctioned in London, 23 May 1707 (no catalogue survives).
ODNB. Alston, *Inventory*.

William Petyt 1636/7–1707
Lawyer, antiquary, Keeper of the Tower Records. Gave books to the Middle Temple in 1698; left MSS to be kept in trust as a collection (now in the Inner Temple). A list of his MSS, *c*.1700, is in British Library Lansdowne MS 989, fos 99–101. Listed in Edward Bernard's *Catalogi manuscriptorum* (1697) as owning numerous manuscripts.
ODNB. J. C. Davies, *Catalogue of manuscripts in the . . . Inner Temple* (1972). Maggs 1293 (2000)/45.

Henry Poley 1654–1707
Barrister, of Middle Temple, MP; of Badley, Suffolk. Used engraved armorial bookplates dated 1703.
HoP. Franks 23764/*254.

Edward Chilton 1658–1707
Attorney General of Barbados. Library auctioned in London, 6 Mar. 1710 (joint sale, no catalogue survives).
J. Kneebone et al. (eds), *Dictionary of Virginia biography* (1998–). Alston, *Inventory*.

Anthony Calcott d. 1708?
Lawyer, of Gray's Inn. Library sold by retail sale in London, 7 Dec. 1708 (joint sale, with one other; no catalogue survives).
Alston, *Inventory*.

Thomas Gleave d. 1708?
Lawyer, of the Inner Temple. Library auctioned in London, 24 Feb. 1709 (joint sale, no catalogue survives).
Alston, *Inventory*.

Sir Robert Atkyns 1621–1709
Lawyer, judge, Baron of the Exchequer. Library sold by retail sale in London, 13 July 1717 (joint sale, with one other).
ODNB. Alston, *Inventory*.

John Richardson d. 1709?
>   Lawyer, of the Inner Temple. Library auctioned in London, 30 May 1709 (no catalogue survives).
>   Alston, *Inventory*.

William Dobyns 1646/7–1709
>   Lawyer, of Lincoln's Inn. Used an engraved armorial bookplate.
>   Venn. Franks 8788/*267.

Draper Donynge 1682?–1710
>   Barrister, of the Inner Temple. 'Part of' his library auctioned in London, 17 Jan. 1712.
>   Foster. Alston, *Inventory*.

Richard Freeman 1646–1710
>   Barrister, of Middle Temple, Lord Chancellor of Ireland. Used an engraved armorial bookplate.
>   Foster. Franks 11343/*452.

Sir John Holt 1642–1710
>   Recorder of London, Chief Justice of King's Bench. Used an engraved armorial bookplate dated 1702. Library auctioned in London, 29 May 1729 (526 lots).
>   *ODNB*. Franks 15179/*273. Alston, *Inventory*.

Thomas Alured d. 1708
>   Barrister, of Gray's Inn; Recorder of Beverley. Gave several hundred volumes to BevErney parish library *c*.1700–08.
>   Venn. Perkin, 137.

Edward Bellamy 1678/9–*c*.1710
>   Lawyer, of Gray's Inn. Library sold by retail sale in London, 16 Feb. 1711 (joint sale, with one other; no catalogue survives).
>   Venn. Alston *Inventory*.

Robert Bertie 1676–1710
>   Barrister, of Middle Temple, MP; 4th son of James Bertie, 1st Earl of Abingdon. Used an engraved armorial bookplate dated 1702.
>   Foster. Franks 2382/*369.

George Bramston d. 1710
>   Deputy judge of the Admiralty; Master of Trinity Hall, Cambridge. Used an engraved armorial bookplate. Library auctioned in London, 18 Dec. 1710 (no catalogue survives).
>   Venn. Franks 3526/*239. Alston, *Inventory*.

Sir John Cooke 1666–1710
>   Advocate-general, Dean of the Arches. Library sold by retail sale in London, 4 Dec. 1710 (no catalogue survives).
>   *ODNB*. Alston, *Inventory*.

Richard Parsons 1641/2–1711
>   Chancellor of the diocese of Gloucester, antiquary. Listed in Edward Bernard's *Catalogi manuscriptorum* (1697) as owning 7 manuscripts.
>   *ODNB*.

Rice d. 1711?
>   Lawyer, of Furnival's Inn. Library auctioned in London, 22 Feb. 1712 (joint sale, with one other; no catalogue survives).
>   Alston, *Inventory*.

Henry Trinder *c.*1640/45–*c.*1711
Barrister, of Furnival's Inn. Library auctioned in London, 22 Feb. 1712 (joint sale, with one other; no catalogue survives).
Foster. Alston, *Inventory.*

Sir John Powell 1645–1713
Judge in the Court of Common Pleas, and Queen's Bench. Used an engraved armorial bookplate dated 1702.
ODNB. Franks *262.

Thomas Rymer 1641–1713
Barrister, of Gray's Inn, historian (appointed to edit the *Foedera* series), poet, critic. Library sold by retail sale in London, 10 Mar. 1714 (joint sale, with one other)
ODNB. Alston, *Inventory.*

Christopher Constantine d. 1714?
Lawyer, of the Inner Temple. Library sold by retail sale in London, 11 June 1714 (joint sale, with one other; no catalogue survives).
Alston, *Inventory.*

Sir Charles Hedges 1650–1714
Ecclesiastical judge, politician. Used engraved armorial bookplates, dated 1702.
ODNB. Lee, *London*, 200. Franks 14399/*384/*427.

John Farrington d. 1714?
Lawyer, of Middle Temple. Library sold by retail sale in London, 19 Feb. 1715 (English books; no catalogue survives), 9 Mar. 1715 (law books, 345 lots).
Alston, *Inventory.*

Wise d. 1714?
Lawyer, of the Inner Temple. Library sold by retail sale in London, 25 June 1714 (no catalogue survives).
Alston, *Inventory.*

John Bridgman d. 1715?
Lawyer? Library sold by retail sale in London, 14 July 1715 (no catalogue survives).
Alston, *Inventory.*

Medics

Physicians

Timothy Bright 1549/50–1615
Physician to St Bartholomew's Hospital, and developer of shorthand. His will refers to books in Italian, Greek, Latin, and other languages, divided between his brother and son.
ODNB. G. Keynes, *Dr.Timothie Bright* (1962).

William Butler 1535?–1618
Physician in Cambridge. Bequeathed the bulk of his books to Clare College, Cambridge
ODNB. C. H. Cooper, *Annals of Cambridge*, vol. 3 (1845), 119–24.

Thomas Hopper d. 1624
Physician in Oxford. Bequeathed *c.*400 books, mostly medical to New College, Oxford.
Foster. Sears Jayne, 151. Morgan.

Theodore Gulston 1575–1632
   Physician in Leicestershire and London. Many of his books given to Merton College, Oxford by his widow; some of his books were also given to Peterhouse, Cambridge.
   ODNB. Morgan.

Sir William Paddy 1554–1634
   Physician in London. Gave *c*.1,100 books to St John's College, Oxford in 1602, largely medical, and made further gifts and bequests of books to the College. Books survive (not only at St John's) with his armorial stamp.
   ODNB. Sears Jayne, 164. *CHL* I 468–9. J. Fuggles, *A history of the library of St John's College, Oxford* (BLitt. thesis, University of Oxford, 1975). Armorials database.

Benjamin Turner d. 1639
   Physician, of Bristol. Probate inventory lists 'a study of books' valued at £6 13*s*. 6*d*.
   E. George (ed.), *Bristol probate inventories 1542–1650* (2002), 107.

Richard Brace d. 1642
   Physician, of Bristol. Probate inventory lists, 'in the study', 'one hundred and twenty several books of several volumes', in various formats, valued together at £6.
   E. George (ed.), *Bristol probate inventories 1542–1650* (2002), 125.

Sir Theodore de Mayerne 1573–1655
Sir John Colladon 1608–75
Sir Theodore Colladon 1643–1712
   De Mayerne was a Geneva-born physician, who became physician to James I and developed a very successful practice in London. His books passed to his niece after his death and were ultimately auctioned in London, 2 Feb. 1713 (joint sale, with additions from his niece's husband Sir John Colladon, and his son Sir Theodore, also physicians). Many of his MSS and papers are in the Royal College of Physicians, the British Library, and Cambridge University Library.
   ODNB. D. McKitterick, *Cambridge University Library: a history*, vol. 2 (Cambridge, 1986), 93. Alston, *Inventory*.

William Harvey 1578–1657
   Physician, author of *De motu cordis*. Amassed a considerable library which he bequeathed to the Royal College of Physicians, largely destroyed in the Great Fire of 1666.
   ODNB. Thornton. G. Keynes, *The life of William Harvey* (Oxford, 1966).

John Goodyer *c*.1592–1664
   Botanist, physician, land steward. Bequeathed *c*.240 books/MSS to Magdalen College, Oxford.
   ODNB. R. Gunther, *Early English botanists and their gardens* (1922).

Sir Francis Prujean 1597–1666
   Physician. More than 160 books were seized from his London house by the London Committee for Sequestration in 1643, and sold.
   ODNB. Roy.

Henry Power *c*.1626–68
   Physician in Halifax. A catalogue of his library, mostly scientific, made in 1664, is in British Library Sloane MS 1346, fos 1–16.
   ODNB.

William Allott d. 1670
   Physician, of Chesterfield. Inherited medical books from his uncle Robert Allott (d. 1642), Linacre Professor of Physick at Cambridge. His books were valued for probate at £15.
   CHL II 176.

Henry Stanley d. 1671
> Physician. A number of books with his armorial stamp survive. His library was auctioned in London, 12 Feb. 1723 (2,070 lots).
> Munk I, 247–8. Alston, *Inventory*. Armorials database.

Christopher Terne 1620/1–73
> Physician in London. Library auctioned in London, 12 Apr. 1686 (joint sale, with two others).
> *ODNB*. Alston, *Inventory*.

Richard Inglett 1632–73
> Fellow of Exeter College, Oxford (ejected 1662); afterwards moved to Plymouth, where he practised medicine. Probate inventory lists books valued at £10.
> Foster. *Calamy revised*.

Jonathan Goddard 1617–75
> Physician in London, founder member of the Royal Society. According to Aubrey, he intended to leave his appreciable library to the Royal Society, but it was inherited instead by his nephew, as he died intestate.
> *ODNB*. Aubrey, *Brief lives*.

Thomas Sherley 1638–78
> Physician in London. Library auctioned in London, 2 June 1679 (joint sale, with one other).
> *ODNB*. Alston, *Inventory*.

Nathan Paget 1615–79
> Physician in London. Library auctioned in London, 24 Oct. 1681 (2,178 lots).
> *ODNB*. Thornton. J. M. Hanford, 'Dr. Paget's library', *Bulletin of the Medical History Association* 33 (1945): 90–97. Alston, *Inventory*.

Henry Corbet 1624–80
> Physician in Hull and Lincoln. Probate inventory lists 'his library' in the red chamber, valued at £30.
> Venn. J. Bestall (ed.), *Chesterfield wills and inventories 1604–1650* (2001), 202.

Sir Robert Tabor 1643?–81
> Physician to Charles II; medical author. Library auctioned in London (medical books), 12 Apr. 1686 (joint sale, with two others).
> *ODNB*. Alston, *Inventory*.

Sir Thomas Browne 1605–82
Edward Browne 1642–1708
> Physicians, father and son (the father the author of *Religio medici*, etc., the son President of the Royal College of Physicians). An auction catalogue of their joint library, 8 Jan. 1711 lists 2,377 lots. Edward Bernard's *Catalogi manuscriptorum* (1697) lists Edward Browne as owning 28 manuscripts.
> *ODNB*. *CELM*. J. Finch, *A catalogue of the libraries of Sir Thomas Browne and Dr Edward Browne, his son. A facsimile reproduction with introduction* (Leiden, 1986). G. Richmond, 'Sir Thomas Browne's library', *ABMR* 4 (1977): 2–9. J. Thornton, 'Dr Edward Browne (1642–1708) as a bibliophile', *Library World* 54 (1952–3): 69–73. L. Gwynn, *The library of Sir Thomas Browne* (PhD thesis, Queen Mary University London, 2016). Alston, *Inventory*.

Simon Rutland 1659?–82
> Physician, of Brentwood. His 'medical library' auctioned in London, 23 Apr. 1683 (joint sale, with one other).
> Venn. Alston, *Inventory*.

John Webster 1611–82
> Schoolmaster and physician at Clitheroe, Yorkshire, radical theologian. Probate inventory valued his library at £400; a MS catalogue, now in Chetham's Library, lists c.1,500 books.
> *ODNB*. P. Elmer, *The library of Dr John Webster* (1986).

Thomas Allen d. 1684
> Physician to Bethlehem Hospital. Library auctioned in London, 12 Apr. 1686 (joint sale, with two others).
> Venn. J. Andrews et al., *The history of Bethlem* (1997). Alston, *Inventory*.

Christian Bathurst d. c.1684
> Physician (?the Christopher Bathurst, MD Padua 1653, who practised in Lincolnshire?). Library auctioned in London, 24 Mar. 1684 (joint sale, with two others).
> Foster. Alston, *Inventory*.

William Croone 1633–84
> Physician in London. Bequeathed his mathematical books to Emmanuel College, Cambridge, and his medical books to the Royal College of Physicians.
> *ODNB*. Thornton. F. Stubbings, *Forty-nine lives* (Cambridge, 1983).

Jasper Gunter 1623/4–72
> Physician, of Chichester? Library auctioned in London, 20 Mar. 1684 (joint sale, with one other).
> Foster. Alston, *Inventory*.

George Tonstall 1617/18–c.1684
> Physician. Library auctioned in London, 24 Mar. 1684 (joint sale, with two others).
> Foster. Alston, *Inventory*.

Willoughby, Percival 1596/7–1685
> Physician, of Derby; this identification is not certain. English books (only) auctioned in London, 18 Oct. 1708 (660 lots).
> Munk I, 241. Alston, *Inventory*.

Cornelius Callow 1660–87?
> Physician in London. Library auctioned in London, 21 Nov. 1687 (joint sale, with one other).
> Venn. Munk I, 473–4. Alston, *Inventory*.

Nathaniel Fairfax 1637–90
> Physician in Woodbridge, Suffolk; antiquary. Library auctioned in London, 3 June 1695 (joint sale, with one other).
> *ODNB*. Alston, *Inventory*.

Walter Needham 1632–91
> Physician to the Charterhouse. Library sold by retail sale in London, 25 Oct. 1708 (no catalogue survives).
> *ODNB*. Alston, *Inventory*.

Samuel Thurnor d. 1691
> Physician. Bequeathed c.200 books, largely medical, to Magdalen Hall (now Hertford College), Oxford.
> Foster. Munk I, 292. Morgan.

Andrew Clench d. 1692
> Physician in London. Library auctioned in London, 1 June 1692 (292 lots, medical and scientific, possibly not his entire library).
> *ODNB*. Alston, *Inventory*.

Sir Charles Scarburgh 1616–94

Physician in London. His library, noted for its strength in mathematics, was auctioned in London, 8 Feb., 18 Feb., and 1 Mar. 1695 (1,097 lots in the first two parts, no catalogue for the third part survives).

ODNB. C. Newman, 'Sir Charles Scarburgh', *BLJ* 3 (1980): 429–30. Alston, *Inventory.*

John Betts *c.*1623–95

Physician in ordinary to Charles II. Library auctioned in London, 3 June 1695 (joint sale, with one other).

ODNB. Alston, *Inventory.*

Christopher Merrett 1614–95

Physician in London, founder member of the Royal Society. Library auctioned in London 20 Sept. 1695 (no catalogue survives).

ODNB. Alston *Inventory.*

Luke Rugeley 1617–96

Physician, in London. Son of the physician Thomas Rugeley (*c.*1576–1656), from whom he inherited books. His library was auctioned in London 9 Feb. 1697 (2,426 lots, plus an appendix of 301 lots, i.e. 2,727 in all); a number of his books were acquired by Hans Sloane.

Munk I, 267–8. W. Thompson, 'Some aspect of the life and times of Sir Hans Sloane', *Ulster Medical Journal* 7 (1938). A. Walker, 'Sir Hans Sloane and the library of Dr Luke Rugeley', *The Library*, 7th ser. 15 (2014): 383–409.

Francis Bernard 1627–98

Physician in London. His library, 'the most extensive to be sold at auction in the 17th century', was auctioned in London 4 Oct. 1698 (14,947 lots). Edward Bernard's *Catalogi manuscriptorum* (1697) lists him as owning 127 manuscripts.

ODNB. R. Beadle, 'Medieval English manuscripts at auction, 1676–*c.*1700', *BC* 53 (2004): 46–63. A. Freeman, 'Some notes on Francis Bernard', *BC* 61 (2012): 65–9. Alston, *Inventory.*

Ralph Bathurst 1620–1704

Physician, and President of Trinity College, Oxford. Gave books to Trinity; also gave books to the Bodleian Library in 1657. Gave *c.*30 vols to Wells Cathedral Library (of which he was Dean).

ODNB. Morgan. Macray, 125. C. Church, 'Notes on the . . . Library of the Dean and Chapter . . . of Wells', *Archaeologia* 57 (1901): 201–28. C. Hopkins, *Trinity: 450 years of an Oxford college* (2005).

John Windebanke 1618–1704

Physician in Guildford. Library sold by retail sale in London, 29 Nov. 1704 (joint sale, with three others; no catalogue survives).

Munk I, 409. Alston, *Inventory.*

Roger Howman 1640–1705

Physician, of Norwich. Used an engraved bookplate, also used in adapted form by his son and grandson.

Venn. Blatchly. Franks 15569.

Nathaniel Johnston 1629?–1705

Physician in Pontefract and London, political author, antiquary. Listed in Edward Bernard's *Catalogi mansucriptorum* (1697) as owning 130 manuscripts, many of them his own MS collections.

ODNB.

John Lawson d. 1705
Physician in London, President of the Royal College of Physicians. Bequeathed 1,100 volumes to Sion College.
Munk I, 367. E. Pearce, *Sion College and Library* (1913), 263–4.

John Harborough d. 1705
Physician, of Norfolk, practised in London? Used an engraved armorial bookplate.
Venn. Franks 13656/*296.

Patrick Adair d. 1706?
Physician, who specialized in treating seamen. Library sold by retail sale in London, 12 June 1706 (joint sale, no catalogue survives).
Alston, *Inventory*.

John Harrison d. *c*.1706?
Physician, of Colchester. Library auctioned in London, 5 Mar. 1706 (871 lots).
Venn. Munk I, 456. Alston, *Inventory*.

Walter Charleton 1620–1707
Physician in London, medical author. Books with his inscription are found in various collections, but the size of his library is not known.
ODNB. D. McKitterick, *Cambridge University Library: a history*, vol. 2 (1986), 93–4.

Edward Hooker *c*.1617–1707
Licenciate of the Royal College of Physicians. His will includes extensive bequests of specific books to officers of the Charterhouse, and others; the rest of his library was dispersed in a series of sales in London in 1708 (continuation sale advertised 10 May 1708, subsequent sale 8 July 1708; no catalogues survive).
Alston, *Inventory*.

Joseph Gaylard 1657/8–1707?
Surgeon, military physician in the West Indies. Library auctioned in London, 28 Jan. 1708 (1,230 lots).
Venn. Munk I, 504. Alston, *Inventory*.

Leonard Plukenet 1642–1706
Medical practitioner in London, botanist. Library auctioned in London, 20 Oct. 1707 (joint sale, with one other).
ODNB. Alston, *Inventory*.

Joshua Palmer d. 1708
Physician in London. Library auctioned in London, 11 Apr. 1709 (819 lots)
Venn. Munk I, 429. Alston, *Inventory*.

Humphrey Ridley 1653–1708
Physician in London, medical author. Library auctioned in London, 21 June, 8 July 1708 (no catalogue survives).
ODNB. Alston, *Inventory*.

Edward Tyson 1651–1708
Physician in London. Left the bulk of his books to his nephew, though some also went to the Bodleian. Listed in Edward Bernard's *Catalogi manuscriptorum* (1697) as owning 26 manuscripts.
ODNB. Thornton.

Sir Edmund King 1629–1709
Surgeon and physician in London. Library auctioned in London, 28 Nov. 1709 (joint sale, with one other).
ODNB. Alston, *Inventory*.

Lewis Pau d. 1709
Physician in London, originally of Montpellier. Library auctioned in London, 10 Oct. 1709 (1,454 lots).
Alston, *Inventory*.

Phineas Fowke 1639–1710
Physician in London; gave 49 books to Christ Church, Oxford in 1704.
ODNB.

Samuel Wall d. *c*.1710
Physician and medical experimenter in London. Library auctioned in London, 7 Sept. 1710 (no catalogue survives).
J. Heilbron, *Electricity in the seventeenth and eighteenth centuries* (1979), 235–6. Alston, *Inventory*.

William Creed 1659/60–1711
Physician in Oxford. Bequeathed books to Corpus Christi College, Oxford, including many medical books.
Foster. Morgan.

Charles Goodall *c*.1642–1712
Physician in London, President of the Royal College of Physicians. The extent of his library is not known, but in a letter of 1693 to Anthony Wood he wrote that 'the books you mention I have by me and many more relating to K. Ch. I & those unhappy times'.
ODNB. H. Beecham, 'A notebook and a collection of manuscripts: originally the property of Dr Charles Gooddall', *BLR* 7 (1967): 312–17.

Nehemiah Grew 1641–1712
Physician in London, botanist, secretary to the Royal Society. Library sold by retail sale in London, 19 June 1712 (no catalogue survives).
ODNB. Alston, *Inventory*.

Martin Lister 1639–1712
Physician in London, naturalist. Donated many books, antiquities and specimens to the Ashmolean Museum in 1682.
ODNB.

Bigge, Dr d. *c*.1713?
Of High Wycombe; unidentified, possibly the William Bigge, b. 1645/6, who matriculated at Magdalen Hall, Oxford, 1661? 'Libraries' auctioned in London, 1713 (continuation sale, 9 Mar. 1713; joint sale, with one other).
Foster Alston, *Inventory*.

William Salmon 1644–1713
Physician in London, medical author. Library auctioned in London, 16 Nov. 1713, 10 Mar. 1714 (5,836 lots).
ODNB. Thornton. Alston, *Inventory*.

Christian Harel d. *c*.1714
Royal physician, originally from the Netherlands. Library sold by retail sale in London, 7 Apr. 1714 (joint sale, with one other).
Munk I, 452. E. Furdell, *The royal doctors, 1485–1714* (2001). Alston, *Inventory*.

Stephen Hunt d. 1714?
Physician, of Canterbury. Gave or bequeathed his library to Canterbury Cathedral in 1714, 'in wch were a great many curiositys purposely purchased … a little before his death'.
Venn. Munk I, 503–4.

John Ker 1648/9–c.1714

Physician, originally Irish or Scottish, author of a textbook on Latin prose. Library auctioned in London, 19 Apr. 1714 (1,647 lots, probably not his entire library).

R. W. Innes-Smith, *English-speaking students of medicine at Leyden* (1932), 133. Alston, *Inventory*.

William Brewster 1665–1715

Physician, of Hereford. Bequeathed his books to St John's College, Oxford (*c*.200 volumes), the Bodleian, and All Saints' Church, Hereford (*c*.300 volumes). A catalogue of his library, made by him in 1706, is in Bodleian MS Eng.misc.c.405 (lists 1,069 titles). Listed in Edward Bernard's *Catalogi manuscriptorum* (1697) as owning a small number of manuscripts.

Foster. Perkin, 239. Macray, 195. F. Morgan, 'Dr William Brewster of Hereford', *Medical History* 8 (1964): 137–48. Wanley, *Diary*, vol. 1 p. 8.

Thomas Lawrence d. 1715?

Physician to William III, and Queen Anne. Library auctioned in London, 29 June 1715. Foster. Munk I, 347. Alston, *Inventory*.

Paul Rotier d. 1715

Physician (?surgeon; described in his will as a doctor of physic) in London. Library auctioned in London, 24 Mar. 1715, with a further portion sold by retail sale, 27 June 1716 (367 + 706 lots).

Alston, *Inventory*.

Surgeons

Herman van Otten d. 1611

Surgeon, of Banbury. Probate inventory lists 'seven of the bigger books', valued at 13*s.* 4*d.*, and 'threescore and five smaller books', £1 13*s.* 4*d.*

J. Gibson (ed.), *Banbury wills and inventories 1591–1620* (1985), 221.

Richard Woodson d. 1623

Surgeon, of Bristol. Probate inventory lists 'all his books belonging to chururgery' valued at 30*s.*

E. George (ed.), *Bristol probate inventories 1542–1650* (2002), 36.

Joseph Fenton d. 1634

Surgeon at St Bartholomew's Hospital. Several hundred volumes from his library survive in the British Library (in the Sloane collection) and elsewhere.

D. Pearson, 'Illustrations from the Wellcome Library: Joseph Fenton and his books', *Medical History* 47 (2003): 239–48.

Ralph Launder d. 1638

Surgeon, of Chesterfield. Probate inventory lists 'one Bible, 35 other books great and small', valued with instruments and other objects at £2.

J. Bestall (ed.), *Chesterfield wills and inventories 1604–1650* (2001), 327.

John Deighton d. 1640

Surgeon, of Gloucester. Probate inventory lists 187 books.

Sears Jayne, 170. E. Barnard & L. Newman, 'John Deighton of Gloucester, surgeon', *Transactions of the Bristol and Gloucestershire. Archaeological. Society* 64 (1943): 71–88.

Edward Courthop d. 1666

Surgeon, of Sevenoaks. Probate inventory lists 'the library of books in the shop', together with 180 other books (listed only by size, 20 books in folio etc.), valued at a little under £15.

H. Lansberry, *Sevenoaks wills and inventories in the reign of Charles II* (1988), 41–3.

Philip Frith d. 1670

Surgeon-apothecary in Rye. Bequeathed his books to Samuel Jeake (1652–99).

M. Hunter et al, *A radical's books: the library catalogue of Samuel Jeake* (1999).

John Knight 1622–80

Sergeant surgeon to Charles II. Bequeathed heraldic and geneaological MSS to Gonville & Caius College, Cambridge, and historical works to Ipswich Town Library.

ODNB. J. Blatchly, *The Town Library of Ipswich* (1989), 40–44. Armorials database.

Thomas Hobbes 1648–98

Surgeon and physician in London. Library sold by retail sale in London, 3 Apr. 1712 (279 lots, plus 'many more not here mentioned').

ODNB. G. Morris, 'The household goods of Thomas Hobbs', *Transactions of the London and Middlesex Archaeological. Society* 23 (1972): 204–8. Alston, *Inventory*.

George Horsnell d. *c.*1698

Surgeon, of London. Library sold by retail sale in London, 16 June 1698 (joint sale, with one other; no catalogue survives).

Alston, *Inventory*.

Charles Bernard 1650–1711

Sergeant-surgeon to Queen Anne. Gave a Tacitus MS to the Bodleian in 1705; late 17th-c. catalogues of his library survive in British Library Sloane MSS 1770, 1694. Library auctioned in London, 22 Mar. 1711 (3,467 lots).

ODNB. Macray, 174. Alston, *Inventory*.

Apothecaries

Edward Bassett fl. 1678

BL Sloane MS 2392 is a small octavo blank book (in a later binding) with the name 'Edward Bassett May 3d [16]76' near the front. The first half of the book is filled with medical/apothecary's recipes, while the second half is a library list, 'Catalogus librorum', comprising 885 books in various languages/formats. There are numerous medical books but many other subjects besides. The two parts of the book are in different hands, and it is not apparent that Bassett was the owner of the books. There are also some details of books loaned or exchanged.

Samuel Case d. 1699

Apothecary, alderman and mayor of Stratford-upon-Avon. Probate inventory lists 'a parcel of books', valued at £6.

J. Jones (ed.), *Stratford-upon-Avon inventories*, vol. 2: *1626–99* (2002), 321.

Oculists

Richard Banister *c.*1570–1626

Lincolnshire oculist. Gave books in his lifetime, and bequeathed money to buy books, to Stamford parish library. His personal library was bequeathed between his sons (medical and Latin books) and daughters (English books).

ODNB. Perkin, 353–4. A. Sorsby, 'Richard Banister and English opthalmology', in *Science, medicine and history: essays in honour of Charles Singer*, vol. 2 (1953), 17–18, 50–51.

Nonconformist clergy

Men listed here were mostly appointed to parochial or other ecclesiastical positions during the Civil War or Interregnum period, but ejected at or shortly after the Restoration in 1660 (largely in 1662, following the Act of Uniformity, which required adherence to the *Book of common prayer*). Theologically, they held a range of views across the Dissenting spectrum; many of them continued to minister to loyal congregations, often licensed to do so after the Indulgence of 1672. Some were poor, but others had family wealth; they were often deeply learned, sometimes significant authors (e.g. Baxter), and many of them had considerable libraries. Much of the information here derives from A. G. Matthews's *Calamy revised*, in which he systematically noted references to books in probate documents. The significance of the Nonconformist clergy in this landscape can be seen by scanning the list of English book auctions in the first decade of their existence, down to the mid-1680s, when around a quarter of the names will be found to be such men. They were sometimes supporters of the nascent Dissenting academies, whose libraries are being documented by the *Dissenting Academies Project*.[1]

Hugh Peter 1598–1660
> Minister in New England 1635–41, parliamentary agent and preacher in the 1640s, chaplain to the Council of State 1650. Executed as a regicide. Was given books from William Laud's library, after Laud's execution, valued at £140.
> *ODNB*. R. P. Stearns, *The strenuous puritan* (Urbana, IL, 1954), 221–2.

Henry Field 1621/2–62
> Fellow of Christ's College, Cambridge 1645–8, Rector of Uffington, Lincolnshire 1645, ejected 1660, imprisoned for seditious preaching 1661. A number of books survive with distinctive manuscript book labels in red ink, 'Henry Feilde', with running numbers suggesting a sizeable library. An entire calligraphic MS of his, dated 1642, was in the Pirie sale at Sotheby's (NY), 2 Dec. 2015/368, and a manuscript volume of Donne's sermons made by him is now Bodleian MS Eng.th.c.71.
> *Calamy revised*. Pearson, *Provenance research*, 46–7.

John Horsham 1595/6–1664
> Vicar of Staverton, Devon 1630 (ejected 1662). Probate inventory lists books valued at £65, from an estate valued at £506 17s.
> *Calamy revised*.

John Machin 1624–64
> Minister at Astbury, Cheshire, in the 1650s, curate of Whitley 1661 (ejected 1662). Probate inventory lists books valued at £16, from an estate valued at £120.
> *ODNB. Calamy revised*.

Thomas Hall 1610–65
> Schoolmaster (1629) and curate (1641) of King's Norton, Warwickshire (ejected 1662). Left books to found a parish library for King's Norton, and one for Birmingham; had a personal library of *c*.1,000 vols.
> *ODNB*. Perkin, 255. J. E. Vaughan, *The parish church and ancient grammar school of King's Norton* (Gloucester, 1973). D. Thomas, 'Collecting and godly reading in mid-seventeenth century Worcestershire', *Midland History* 40 (2015): 24–52; D. Thomas (ed.), *The autobiography and library of Thomas Hall* (2016).

---

[1] http://www.qmulreligionandliterature.co.uk/research/the-dissenting-academies-project/ (accessed 1 Feb. 2019).

John Maynard 1600–65
Vicar of Mayfield, Sussex 1624 (ejected 1662). Library auctioned in London, 13 June 1687 (2,190 lots).
ODNB. Calamy revised. Alston, *Inventory.*

Josiah Packwood 1601/2–66
Vicar of Hampton in Arden, Warwickshire 1647 (ejected 1660). Probate inventory lists books valued at £20, from an estate valued at £282 16s. 10d.
Calamy revised.

Henry Raymond d. 1666
Vicar of Denford with Ringstead, Northamptonshire 1647 (ejected 1660). Probate inventory lists books valued at £14, from an estate valued at £220 4s. 6d.
Calamy revised.

John Massey 1614/15–68
Rector of Patney, Wiltshire 1647 (ejected 1662). Probate inventory lists books valued at £20, from an estate valued at £204.
Calamy revised.

Thomas Larkham 1602–69
Parliamentary chaplain in the 1640s, minister in Devon, Cumberland, and elsewhere, vicar of Tavistock *c.*1648 (resigned 1660). Probate inventory lists books valued at £20, from an estate valued at £78 3s. 4d.
ODNB. Calamy revised.

George Mainwaring d. 1670
Rector of Malpas, Cheshire *c.*1648 (ejected 1660); subsequently lived in Chorlton, Lancashire. Probate inventory lists books (bequeathed to his sons) valued at £20, from an estate valued at £50 14s.
Calamy revised. J. P. Rylands (ed.), *Lancashire and Cheshire wills and inventories,* Chetham Society n.s. 37 (1897), 38–9.

Robert Sherborn 1635–70
Curate of Cawood, Yorkshire *c.*1660 (ejected 1662). Probate inventory lists books valued at £16, from an estate valued at £38 0s. 6d.
Calamy revised.

Samuel Austin 1605/6–71
Vicar of Menheniot, Cornwall 1646 (ejected 1660), apparently lived and preached in Plymouth thereafter (briefly imprisoned). Published a poem, *Urania, or, the heavenly muse,* 1629. Probate inventory lists books valued at £25 3s. 6d, from an estate valued at £68 16s.
ODNB. Calamy revised.

William Bridge 1600/01–71
Town preacher at Yarmouth, Norfolk 1641 (ejected 1661). Bequeathed his library (apart from any manuscripts fit to be printed) to his son Samuel (b. 1643).
ODNB. Calamy revised.

William Greenhill 1591?–1671
Vicar of Stepney, Middlesex 1652 (ejected 1660). Bequeathed his library to his cousin Zacharie Bourne; it was auctioned in London, 18 Feb. 1678 (686 lots).
ODNB. Calamy revised. Alston, *Inventory.*

John Lydston 1613–71
Chaplain in the parliamentary army; Rector of St Mellion, Cornwall 1648 (ejected 1662); subsequently moved to Saltash. Probate inventory lists books valued at £30, from an estate valued at £347 4s.
Calamy revised.

Humphrey Saunders 1604/5–72
Rector of Holsworthy, Devon, 1632 (ejected 1662). Probate inventory lists books valued at £70, from an estate valued at £313 14s. 8d.
Calamy revised.

Nathaniel Barton 1615/16–73
Curate of Cauldwell, Derbyshire (ejected 1662); served in the parliamentary army during the Civil War. Probate inventory lists books valued at £60, from an estate valued at £437 3s. 6d.
Calamy revised.

Stephen Watkins d. 1673?
Chaplain of St Saviour's, Southwark from at least 1647 (ejected 1660); schoolmaster in Kent in the 1660s. Library auctioned in London, 2 June 1679 (joint sale, with at least one other).
Calamy revised. Alston, *Inventory.*

John Langford d. 1674
Vicar of Gwennap, Cornwall from at least 1653 (ejected 1660); licensed to preach at Falmouth, 1672. Will refers to 'my history notes and heraldry manuscripts'; probate inventory lists books and other goods in his study valued at £40, from an estate valued at £285.
Calamy revised.

Thomas Holland 1623–75
Curate of Blackley, Manchester, 1655 (ejected after the Restoration). Probate inventory lists books valued at £15, from an estate valued at £106 2s. 10d.
Calamy revised.

Lazarus Seaman d. 1675
Minister at All Hallows, Bread Street, London by 1638 (ejected 1662), Master of Peterhouse, Cambridge 1644 (ejected 1660), President of Sion College 1651–2. Library sold at auction in London, 31 Oct. 1676 (5,610 lots); the first English auction with a surviving catalogue.
ODNB. Calamy revised. Alston, *Inventory.*

John Bryan d. 1676
Vicar of Holy Trinity, Coventry 1644 (ejected 1662); licensed to preach at Coventry, 1672. Probate inventory lists books valued at £60, from an estate valued at £263 2s. 11d.
ODNB. Burden. Calamy revised.

Robert Fogg d. 1676
Rector of Bangor Isycoed, Flintshire 1646 (ejected 1661); licensed to preach at Nantwich, Cheshire 1672. Probate inventory lists books valued at £10, from an estate valued at £44 13s. 4d.
Calamy revised.

Thomas Kidner d. 1676
Vicar of Hitchin, 1648 (elected 1662). Library auctioned in London, 6 Feb. 1677 (2,782 lots, all English-language books, suggesting this is only a part of his library).
Foster. *Calamy revised.* Alston, *Inventory.*

Thomas Pyke 1610/11–76
Rector of Radcliffe, Lancashire from at least 1646 (ejected 1662); licensed to preach at Blackley, 1672. Probate inventory lists books valued at £20, from an estate valued at £76 17s. 6d.
Calamy revised.

Peter Atkinson 1602/3–77
Curate of Ellel, Lancashire from at least 1646 (ejected after the Restoration); licensed to preach at Cockerham 1672. Probate inventory lists his library, valued at £10, from an estate valued at £33 13s. 10d.
Calamy revised.

Thomas Cawton 1636?–77
Orientalist, independent minister in London. Library auctioned in London, 29 Nov. 1680 (joint sale, with 4 others).
ODNB. Alston, *Inventory.*

Gaspar Hickes 1604/5–77
Vicar of Landrake, Cornwall 1632 (ejected 1662); licensed to preach there, 1672. Probate inventory lists his library, valued at £80, from an estate valued at £722 4s.
ODNB. Calamy revised.

Thomas Manton 1620–77
Rector of St Paul's Covent Garden 1656 (ejected 1662); thereafter, a leading member of the Nonconformist community in London. Library auctioned in London, 25 Mar. 1678 (2,043 lots).
ODNB. Calamy revised. Alston, *Inventory.*

Thomas Trurant d. 1677
Vicar of Ovingham, Northumberland from at least 1645 (ejected 1662); licensed to preach there 1672. Probate inventory lists books valued at £10, from an estate valued at £73 0s. 4d.
Calamy revised.

Bartholomew Ashwood 1622–78
Vicar of Axminster, Devon 1656 (ejected 1660); licensed to preach there, 1672. Probate inventory lists books to the value of £20, from an estate valued at £41 17s.
ODNB. Calamy revised.

Gabriel Sangar 1608?–78
Vicar of St Martin in the Fields, London, c.1650 (ejected 1660); licensed to preach there, 1672. Library auctioned in London, 2 Dec. 1678 (joint sale, with one other).
ODNB. Calamy revised. Alston, *Inventory.*

Henry Stubbes 1605/6–78
Vicar of St Philip & St Jacob, Bristol 1647 (ejected 1662); licensed to preach in London, 1672 (unless his son of the same name, d. 1676, author and physician?). Library auctioned in London, 29 Nov. 1680 (joint sale, with 4 others).
ODNB. Calamy revised. Alston, *Inventory.*

Thomas Vincent 1634–78
Rector of St Mary Magdalen, Milk Street, London 1656 (ejected 1662); licensed to preach in London, 1672. Library auctioned in London, 29 Nov. 1680 (joint sale, with 4 others).
ODNB. Burden. *Calamy revised.* Alston, *Inventory.*

Robert Wild 1615/16–79
Rector of Aynho, Northamptonshire 1646 (ejected 1660) and poet. In his will, he bequeathed £50 to buy Bibles, to be distributed to children to win them through a dice game.
ODNB. Calamy revised. Cambers, 182.

Theophilus Gale 1628–79
Fellow of Magdalen College, Oxford 1650, preacher at Winchester Cathedral 1657 (ejected 1660); later became pastor to a Congregational church in Holborn. Bequeathed his library of c.1,000 vols to Harvard College (many were destroyed by fire in 1764).
ODNB. Burden. *Calamy revised.* Cambers, 128.

Thomas Brooks 1608–80

Minister at St Margaret's, New Fish Street, London 1648 (ejected 1660). Library auctioned in London, 30 May 1681 (joint sale, with 3 others).
ODNB. *Calamy revised.* Alston, *Inventory.*

Ralph Button 1611/12–80

Canon of Christ Church, Oxford 1648 (ejected 1660); thereafter, undertook various tutoring roles. Library auctioned in London, 7 Nov. 1681 (joint sale, with one other).
ODNB. *Calamy revised.* Alston, *Inventory.*

Stephen Charnock 1628–80

Independent minister in Ireland during the Interregnum, pastor in London after the Restoration. Lost books in the Great Fire of 1666; library sold at auction in London, 4 Oct. 1680 (1,330 lots).
ODNB. *Calamy revised.* D. Pearson, 'Patterns of book ownership in late seventeenth-century England', *The Library*, 7th ser. 11 (2010): 139–67. Alston, *Inventory.*

Owen Stockton 1630?–80

Lecturer at Colchester, 1658 (ejected 1662); licensed to preach at Ipswich, 1672. Library auctioned in London, 30 May 1681 (joint sale, with 3 others); also left books to Gonville & Caius College, Cambridge.
ODNB. *Calamy revised.* Alston, *Inventory.*

George Fawler 1607–80

Chaplain of Bridewell, London 1643 (ejected 1662); licensed to preach in Islington, 1672. Library auctioned in London, 30 May 1681 (joint sale, with 3 others).
Calamy revised. Alston, *Inventory.*

Randal Guest 1607/08–81

Rector of Pulford, Cheshire 1648 (ejected 1662). Probate inventory lists books valued at £30 7s. 2d , from an estate valued at £49 19s. 8d.
Calamy revised.

John Malden 1621/2–81

Curate of Newport, Shropshire 1656 (ejected 1662); licensed to preach at Whitchurch, 1672. Probate inventory lists books valued at £10, from an estate valued at £135.
Calamy revised. Burden.

Thankfull Owen 1620–81

President of St John's College, Oxford 1650 (ejected 1660); thereafter, lived mostly in London. Library auctioned in London, 7 Nov. 1681 (joint sale, with one other).
ODNB. *Calamy revised.* Alston, *Inventory.*

Bartholomew Webb d. 1681

Vicar of Ogbourne St Andrew, Wiltshire 1646 (ejected 1662); subsequently continued to preach in the area. Probate inventory lists books valued at £60, from an estate valued at £482 10s. 10d.
Calamy revised.

Stephen Baxter 1620/1–82

Rector of Harvington, Worcestershire 1654 (ejected 1662); afterwards practised as a physician. Probate inventory includes books valued at £20, from an estate valued at £69 18s.
Calamy revised.

Hugh Henshaw 1629/30–82

Curate at various parishes in Lancashire and Cheshire from 1646 (ejected 1662); licensed to preach at Knutsford 1672. Probate inventory lists books valued at £60, from an estate valued at £318 7s. 9d.
Calamy revised.

John Hill 1612/13–82
> Rector of Newton Ferrers, Devon 1652 (ejected 1660); licensed to preach at Exeter, 1672. His will refers to 'all my French books'.
> *Calamy revised.*

Thomas Willesby 1618–82
> Vicar of Wombourn, Staffordshire 1652 (ejected 1662). Directed in his will that his books should be sold for the benefit of ejected ministers or their widows.
> *Calamy revised.*

John Arthur d. 1683?
> Rector of Clapham, Surrey (ejected 1662; his death date may be 1663). Library auctioned in London, 12 Feb. 1683 (2,195 lots).
> Venn. *Calamy revised.* Alston, *Inventory.*

John Milward 1619/20–1683?
> Rector of Darfield, Yorkshire 1655 (ejected 1661); licensed to preach at Farncombe, Somerset 1672. Bequeathed books to John James and John King, fellow Nonconformists, and money to Corpus Christi College, Oxford and the Bodleian to buy books.
> *ODNB. Calamy revised.*

Samuel Wright d. 1683
> Vicar of Heanor, Derbyshire from at least 1650 (ejected 1662). Probate inventory lists 145 books valued at £8, from an estate valued at £84 1s. 8d.
> *Calamy revised.*

John Owen 1616–83
> Dean of Christ Church, Oxford 1651 (ejected 1660); a significant figure, preacher, and publisher in Nonconformist affairs after the Restoration. Library auctioned in London, 26 May 1684 (3,024 lots).
> *ODNB. Calamy revised.*

Thomas Lye 1621–84
> Rector of All Hallows, Lombard Street, London 1658 (ejected 1662); licensed to preach in Clapham, 1672. Library auctioned in London, 17 Nov. 1684 (joint sale, with one other).
> *ODNB. Calamy revised.* Alston, *Inventory.*

Timothy Staniforth 1628/9–84
> Curate of Allestree, Derbyshire 1657 (ejected 1662); licensed to preach at Chaddesden 1672. Probate inventory lists books valued at £20, from an estate valued at £77 4s.
> *Calamy revised.*

Michael Briscoe 1625/6–85
> Curate and preacher at Walmsley, Lancashire from *c.*1648, subsequently spent some time in Ireland; licensed to preach at Toxteth Park, 1672. Probate inventory lists books valued at £100, from an estate valued at £789 16s. 11d.
> *Calamy revised.*

Jeremiah Scholes 1629–85
> Vicar of Norton, Derbyshire 1657 (ejected 1662); licensed to preach at Chorlton 1672. Probate inventory lists books valued at £44, from an estate valued at £84 6s. 8d.
> *Calamy revised.*

Richard Bell 1615/16–86
> Vicar of Polesworth, Warwickshire 1654 (ejected 1662); licensed to preach at Walsall, 1672. Probate inventory includes a library valued at £80, from an estate valued at £336 0s. 4d.
> *Calamy revised.*

Thomas Jacombe 1623/4–87
Rector of St Martin, Ludgate, London 1654 (ejected 1662); thereafter, chaplain to the dowager Countess of Exeter, and licensed to preach in Little Britain, 1672. His library, which he said cost him £2,000, was auctioned in London, 31 Oct. 1687 (5,007 lots, made £1,114 12s. 6d.).
ODNB. Calamy revised. Mandelbrote, 'Auctions'. Alston, *Inventory.*

John Oakes d. 1688
Vicar of Boreham, Essex 1657 (ejected 1662); pastor in New Broad Street, London 1678. Library auctioned in London 20 May 1689 (1,106 lots).
Calamy revised. Alston, *Inventory.*

John Bingham 1612/13–89
Vicar of Marston upon Dove, Derbyshire 1656 (ejected 1662); thereafter, taught and preached in Derbyshire. Noted for his oriental and classical scholarship. Probate inventory lists books valued at £13 6s. 8d., from an estate valued at £66 13s. 6d.
ODNB. Calamy revised.

Edmund Moore d. 1689
Fellow of Trinity College, Cambridge 1656 (ejected 1661). Library auctioned in London, 29 July 1689 (495 lots).
Calamy revised. Alston, *Inventory.*

Richard Baxter 1615–91
Vicar of Kidderminster, Worcestershire 1648 (ejected 1662); licensed to preach in London, 1672. A hugely influential devotional author, and a leading figure in late 17th-c. English Nonconformity. His surviving library catalogue shows him to have had c.1,500 volumes.
ODNB. G. Nuttall, 'A transcript of Richard Baxter's library catalogue', *JEH* 2 (1951): 207–21; 3 (1952): 74–100. *Calamy revised. CHL* II 179–80. Cambers, 131.

Thomas Bromley 1630–91
Nonconformist minister and mystical writer, of Upton upon Severn, Worcestershire, and London. Lost c.£30 worth of books in the Great Fire in 1666. Library auctioned in London, 26 Aug. 1691 (1,007 lots).
ODNB. Alston, *Inventory.*

Samuel Lee 1625?–1691
Fellow of Wadham College, Oxford, licensed to preach at Newington Green 1672, emigrated to America 1686. His library was auctioned in Boston, 1693.
ODNB. W. Poole, *Wadham College books in the age of John Wilkins* (2014).

James Creswick 1616–92
Rector of Freshwater, Isle of Wight 1654 (ejected 1662). 'Had a very noble library, which he shipp'd off at the Isle of Wight in casks for Yorkshire. By mistake these casks were delivered at a wrong port, where he heard nothing more of them, till all or most of the books were spoil'd or rotten.'
Calamy revised.

Henry Hickman 1629–92
Rector of St Aldate's, Oxford 1657 (ejected 1661). Subsequently moved to Holland and became pastor of the English church at Leiden. Built a library at Stourbridge Grammar School, and presented books, c.1665; the size of his library is not known, but his will refers to his 'whole library' divided between England and the Netherlands.
ODNB. Burden. *Calamy revised.*

John Reynolds d. 1692
> Vicar of Roughton, Norfolk 1654 (ejected 1662); licensed to preach in London, 1672. Library auctioned in London, 6 Dec. 1693 (1,627 lots).
> *Calamy revised*. Alstion, *Inventory*.

John Bennet 1623/4–93
> Rector of Whitwick, Leicestershire (ejected 1662); licensed to preach in Littleover, Derbyshire 1672. Library auctioned in London, 18 May 1694 (1,613 lots).
> Venn. *Calamy revised*. Alston, *Inventory*.

Joseph Eccleshall d. 1693
> Vicar of Sedgley, Staffordshire 1657 (ejected 1662); licensed to preach there, 1672. Probate inventory lists 180 books valued at £12, from an estate valued at £239 12s. 1d.
> *Calamy revised*.

Samuel Martyn d. 1693
> Nonconformist minister, pastor to a congregation at Liskeard, Cornwall in 1690. Probate inventory lists books valued at £35, from an estate valued at £358.
> *Calamy revised*.

Anthony Palmer 1613–93
> Rector of Bratton Fleming, Devon 1645 (ejected 1662); licensed to preach at Barnstaple, 1672. Probate inventory lists books valued at £50, from an estate valued at £562 15s. 4d.
> *ODNB. Calamy revised*.

John Starkey 1627?–94
> Lecturer at Grantham, Lincolnshire 1655 (ejected); licensed to preach at Ormskirk, 1672. Library auctioned in London, 11 Oct. 1694 (619 lots).
> *Calamy revised*. Alston, *Inventory*.

Samuel Annesley 1620–96
> Vicar of St Giles Cripplegate, London, 1658 (ejected 1662); licensed to preach in Spitalfields, 1672. Library auctioned in London, 18 Mar. 1697 (1,256 lots).
> *ODNB. Calamy revised*. Alston, *Inventory*.

Michael Drake 1622–96
> Rector of Pickworth, Lincolnshire 1646 (ejected 1662); licensed to preach at Fulbeck, 1672. Probate inventory lists 'his library', valued at £10.
> *Calamy revised*.

Samuel Beresford d. 1697
> Vicar of St Werburgh's, Derby 1657 (ejected 1662); licensed to preach in Shrewsbury, 1672. Bequeathed half the proceeds of the sale of his books, after his death, to benefit the poor in his native parish of St Alkmund's, Shrewsbury.
> *Calamy revised*. Burden.

George Day d. 1697
> Vicar of Wiveliscombe, Somerset 1661 (ejected 1662); licensed to preach there 1672. Later moved to London and acted as pastor to a congregation at Ratcliff, Middlesex. Bequeathed part of his library to be divided among 7 poor scholars designed for the ministry.
> *Calamy revised*.

Charles Sagar 1636–98
> Master of Blackburn School, Lancashire 1656 (ejected 1666); subsequently became a Nonconformist minister, licensed to preach at Blackburn 1672. Probate inventory lists books valued at £40, from an estate valued at £102 15s. 11d.
> *Calamy revised*.

Richard Adams d. 1698
  Rector of St Mildred's, Bread Street, London 1655 (ejected 1662); subsequently lived in Southwark, and in Cheapside, where he was licensed to preach in 1672. Gave *c.*400 volumes to Woodchurch School, 1676–81.
  ODNB. Calamy revised.

William Bates 1625–99
  Vicar of St Dunstan's in the West, London, *c.*1654 (ejected 1662). Said to have lost £200 worth of books in the Great Fire of London, 1666. His library was bought after his death by Daniel Williams for £500, and became the nucleus of what is now Dr Williams' Library.
  ODNB; Calamy revised.

Daniel Shelmerdine 1637–99
  Vicar of Barrow on Trent, Derbyshire 1657 (ejected 1662); licensed to preach at Twyford 1672. Probate inventory lists books valued at £10, from an estate valued at £39 6*s.* 8*d.*
  Calamy revised.

John Woodhouse *c.*1627–1700
  Presbyterian minister; established a Nonconformist academy at Sheriffhales, Shropshire, in the 1670s, where he developed a library for the use of his students.
  ODNB. Calamy revised. Burden. Cambers, 128.

Robert Carel d. 1701
  Rector of Uplowman, Devon *c.*1660 (ejected 1661); subsequently became a Nonconformist preacher in Devon. Probate inventory lists books valued at £50, from an estate valued at £183 0*s.* 10*d.*
  Calamy revised.

Samuel Clarke 1626–1701
  Rector of Grendon Underwood, Buckinghamshire 1657 (ejected 1662); licensed to preach at Leighton Buzzard, 1672. Library auctioned in High Wycombe, 10 June 1701.
  ODNB. Calamy revised. Alston, *Inventory.*

Oliver Heywood 1630–1702
  Curate of Coley, Yorkshire 1650 (ejected 1662); licensed to preach in Halifax 1672. His diaries reveal extensive references to the use of books, and loaning of books to students and others.
  ODNB. Calamy revised. Cambers.

Roger Morrice 1628/9–1702
  Vicar of Duffield, Derbyshire, 1658 (ejected 1662); afterwards chaplain to Baron Holles. His library catalogues of the 1680s and 1690s reveal a collection of *c.*1,700 volumes; his will includes detailed instructions regarding his books and historical collections.
  ODNB. Calamy revised. Cambers, 130–31.

Vincent Alsop 1630–1703
  Rector of Wilby, Northamptonshire 1662 (ejected the same year); licensed to preach in Geddington, 1672, later minister at Tothill Street, Westminster. Library sold by retail sale in London, 9 July 1703 (no catalogue survives).
  ODNB. Calamy revised. Alston, *Inventory.*

Robert Moore d. 1704
  Curate of Brampton, Derbyshire from *c.*1658 (ejected 1662); licensed to preach there 1672. Probate inventory lists 405 books valued at £30, from an estate valued at £135 6*s.* 6*d.*
  Calamy revised.

Thomas Rowe 1656/7–1705
Pastor to the independent congregation in Holborn, 1679. Library 'of near 5000 volumes' auctioned in London, 13 June 1715 (no catalogue survives; presumably this Thomas Rowe, and not the author, 1687–1715).
ODNB. Alston, *Inventory.*

John Quick 1636–1706
Vicar of Churchstow, Devon 1658 (ejected 1660); licensed to preach at Plymouth, 1672. Library auctioned in London, 10 Mar. 1707 (the only known copy is defective).
ODNB. Calamy revised. Alston, *Inventory.*

Samuel Stancliffe 1631–1706
Rector of Great Stanmore, Middlesex, 1658 (ejected 1662); later a Nonconformist minister at Rotherhithe, Surrey. Library auctioned in London, 6 Mar. 1706 (no catalogue survives).
Calamy revised. Alston, *Inventory.*

Thomas Goodwin c.1650–1708
Independent minister in London, who also ran a Dissenting ministers' academy at his estate in Pinner. Library sold at auction in London, 27 Nov. 1710, 3 Nov. 1712 (over 6,000 volumes). His father (also Thomas Goodwin, 1600–80) said he lost half his library, valued at over £1,000, in the Great Fire of 1666.
ODNB. Cambers, 122. Alston, *Inventory.*

John Spademan 1648/9–1708
Vicar of Swaton, Lincolnshire; resigned to be pastor of the English church at Rotterdam, later a Nonconformist minister in England. Library auctioned in London, 21 Feb. 1709 (3,067 lots).
Venn. *Calamy revised.* Burden. Alston, *Inventory.*

Edward Veel 1632/3–1708
Fellow of Trinity College, Dublin, 1654 and minister at Dunboyne 1655 (ejected 1661); licensed to preach in Wapping 1672. Library auctioned in London, 25 Nov. 1708 (a joint sale, with one other).
ODNB. Calamy revised. Burden. Alston, *Inventory.*

Richard Stretton 1632/3–1712
Nonconformist minister in Leeds and London. Library auctioned in London, 13 Oct. 1712.
Calamy revised. Alston, *Inventory.*

John Gidley d. 1711
Nonconformist minister in Exeter, ordained in 1660, licensed to preach there 1672. Bequeathed some books, and money to buy Bibles ('without the Apocrypha or Common Prayer') to the parish of St Thomas, Exeter.
Calamy revised.

James Forbes 1629?–1712
Independent minister in Gloucester. Bequeathed his library of c.1,300 volumes and 300 pamphlets to the Congregational Church in Gloucester (Southgate Chapel), deposited in Gloucester City Library 1954, sold to the University of Toronto c.1968.
ODNB. Calamy revised. Burden. P. Heyworth, 'Unfamiliar libraries XVI: the Forbes Library', *BC* 19 (1970): 317–27. Cambers, 128–9.

Joseph Stennett 1663–1713
Baptist minister in London, and hymn writer. Library sold by retail sale in London, 4 May 1715 (no catalogue survives).
ODNB. Alston, *Inventory.*

Edward Boucher d. 1715
> Rector of Churchill by Kidderminster, Worcestershire from at least 1655 (ejected 1661); licensed to preach at Shuttington, Warwickshire 1672. Probate inventory lists books valued at £10, from an estate valued at £51 10s. 2d.
> *Calamy revised.*

Painters

John Michael Wright 1617–94
> Painter, picture drawer in ordinary to Charles II, acquired books and prints during time in Italy. Library, including prints and antiquities, auctioned in London, 4 June 1694 (185 lots, plus 198 prints, and rings/seals).
> *ODNB*. Alston, *Inventory*.

Henry Cook 1642–1700
> Painter. Library auctioned in London, 30 Dec. 1700 (253 lots).
> *ODNB*. Alston, *Inventory*.

Robert Streater d. 1711
> Serjeant-painter to Charles II, James II, and William III. Library auctioned in London, 29 Nov. 1711 (joint sale, with one other).
> *ODNB* (see entry for his father, also Robert, d. 1679). Alston, *Inventory*.

Jacobus Wilson d. 1713
> 'late of Bread Street, painter, deceased in Barbadoes'. Library (with prints, drawings and models) auctioned in London, 19 May 1713 (no catalogue survives).
> Alston, *Inventory*.

Printers and booksellers

Entries in this section are limited to examples where we have information on the personal libraries of members of the book trade, rather than inventories listing their business stock.

George Thomason 1600?–66
> Bookseller; assembled the collection of Civil War pamphlets now known as the Thomason Tracts. These were eventually purchased for the British Museum by George III in 1761.
> *ODNB*. L. Spencer, 'The professional and literary connexions of George Thomason', *The Library*, 5th ser. 13 (1958): 102–18. L. Spencer, 'The politics of George Thomason', *The Library*, 5th ser. 14 (1959): 11–27. D. Stoker, 'George Thomason's intractable legacy', *The Library*, 6th ser. 14 (1992): 337–56. D. Stoker and M. Kingston, 'George Thomason', in W. Baker (ed.), *Pre-nineteenth-century British book collectors and bibliographers* (1999), 344–9. M. Mendle, 'George Thomason's intentions', in G. Mandelbrote and B. Taylor (eds), *Libraries within the library* (2009), 171–86. *CHL* II 39.

John Spencer c.1610–80
> Bookseller, and Librarian of Sion College. Donated over 200 books to Sion College, 1631–58.
> E. Pearce, *Sion College and Library* (1913), ch. 13.

William Anderton d. 1693
> Printer in London, executed for printing treasonable pamphlets. Library auctioned in Oxford, 1 Mar. 1699.
> Alston, *Inventory*.

Benjamin Motte d. 1710
>Printer, of Aldersgate, London. Library auctioned in London, 14 May 1711 (joint sale, with one other).
>*ODNB.* Alston, *Inventory.*

Thomas James d. 1711
>Bookseller and printer in London. Grandson of Thomas James, Bodley's Librarian. He bequeathed his collection of *c.*3,000 vols to public uses; in 1711 they were offered to, and accepted by, Sion College.
>E. Pearce, *Sion College and Library* (1913), 197, 266. Plomer.

Schoolmasters and teachers/tutors

Reginald Bainbrigg 1544/5–1612/13
>Headmaster of Appleby Grammar School. Bequeathed his library of *c.*295 volumes to the school; *c.*150 survive today (now in Newcastle University Library).
>*ODNB.* E. Hinchcliffe, *The Bainbrigg Library of Appleby Grammar School* (1996). R. Ovenden, 'The manuscript library of Lord William Howard of Naworth', in J. Willoughby and J. Catto (eds), *Books and bookmen in early modern Britain* (Toronto, 2018), 278–318, 300–01.

John Harrison d. 1642
>Head Master of Eton. Bequeathed to the College his books, sextant, and dials; the books constitute 'one of the earliest English scientific libraries which is still kept together' (Birley).
>R. Birley, 'Robert Boyle's Head Master at Eton', *Notes & Queries of the Royal Society of London* 13(2) (1958): 104–14. R. Birley, *The history of Eton College Library* (1970), 27–30.

Thomas Hayne 1581/2–1645
>Schoolmaster in London, and author. Bequeathed his books (*c.*400–600 volumes?) to Leicester Town Library.
>*ODNB.* C. Deedes et al., *The Old Town Hall Library of Leicester* (1919).

Timothy Key d. 1676
>Schoolmaster, of Lichfield. Probate inventory lists 'books in his study', valued at £2.
>D. Vaisey (ed.), *Probate inventories of Lichfield and district 1568–1680* (1969), 258.

Owen Phillips d. 1678
>Under-master of Winchester College. Library auctioned in London, 11 Nov. 1678 (joint sale, with one other).
>Foster. Alston, *Inventory.*

Thomas Watson d. 1679
>Headmaster of Charterhouse. Library auctioned in London, 8 Oct. 1680 (1,106 lots).
>Alston, *Inventory* (where the wrong Watson is identified).

John Rosewell *c.*1635–84
>Head master of Eton. Bequeathed his books to Corpus Christi College, Oxford.
>Foster. Morgan.

Seth-Mountley Buncle d. *c.*1695
>Master of the Mercer's School, London. Library auctioned in London, 9 Apr. 1695 (joint sale, with one other).
>Foster (Boncle). Alston, *Inventory.*

Richard Busby 1606–95
Headmaster of Westminster School, canon of Wells, rector of Cudworth, Somerset. Bequeathed his books to Westminster School (*c.*450 volumes; 350 survive today) and to found a parish library for Cudworth. Also bequeathed some books to the parish of Martock, Somerset, and to Willen, Buckinghamshire (*c.*150 volumes). Gave books to Wells Cathedral Library during his lifetime.
ODNB. Perkin 187, 282, 390. C. Church, 'Notes on the . . . Library of the Dean and Chapter . . . of Wells', *Archaeologia* 57 (1901): 201–28. Armorials database.

Thomas Baulgy d. 1697?
Headmaster of the Free School, Sheffield. Library auctioned there 26 May 1697
Alston, *Inventory*.

Mr Hodgson d. 1698?
Schoolmaster. Library sold by retail sale in London, 29 Apr. 1698 (294 lots).
Alston, *Inventory*.

Du Prat d. *c.*1699?
?François du Prat, tutor in the Cavendish and other households, correspondent of Thomas Hobbes? Library auctioned in London, 2 May 1699 (2,509 lots).
N. Malcolm (ed.), *The Clarendon edition of the works of Thomas Hobbes*, vol. 7: *The correspondence*, vol. 2: *1660–1679* (Oxford, 1994), 881–5. Alston, *Inventory*.

Venterus Mandey 1646–1702
Teacher of mathematics, author/translator of books on mechanics and measuring. Library auctioned in London, 21 Feb. 1709 (no catalogue survives), 13 Mar. 1714.
Alston, *Inventory*.

John Ayres d. *c.*1705
Writing master, author of works on calligraphy and penmanship. Listed in Edward Bernard's *Catalogi manuscriptorum* (1697) as owning a number of manuscripts.
ODNB.

John Thornton d. 1704
Tutor and chaplain to the Duke of Bedford. Library auctioned in London, 11 July 1705 (no catalogue survives).
Venn. Alston, *Inventory*.

Mr Smart d. 1711?
'Late schoolmaster at the Two White Balls in Marylebone-Street'. Library sold by retail sale in London, 22 Dec. 1711 (no catalogue survives).
Alston, *Inventory*.

William Hardesty 1653?–1712
Master of the Free School at Ashbourne, Derbyshire; rector of Fenny Bentley. Library auctioned in London, 20 Feb. 1716 (no catalogue survives).
Venn. Alston, *Inventory*.

John Postlethwaite 1651/2–1713
High master of St Paul's School, London. Library auctioned in London, 13 Apr. 1714 (1,582 lots).
Foster. Alston, *Inventory*.

Humphrey Ditton 1675–1714
Mathematician, master of the mathematical school at Christ's Hospital. Library auctioned in London, 9 Mar. 1715.
ODNB. Alston, *Inventory*.

Scientists and mathematicians

As with the section on authors, people are listed here if they are primarily remembered today as scientists, although they might be categorized under other headings.

Thomas Harriot 1560–1621

Mathematician, in the service of Sir Walter Ralegh, and Henry Percy, 9th Earl of Northumberland. His will reveals a sizeable library; his extensive papers, left to Percy, survive in the British Library and at Petworth.

ODNB. J. Shirley (ed.), *Thomas Harriot: Renaissance scientist* (1974). J. W. Shirley (ed.), *A source book for the study of Thomas Harriot* (1981).

Nathaniel Torporley 1564–1632

Mathematician; resident of Sion College, though also a holder of ecclesiastical livings. Gave 18 MSS and 215 printed books to Sion College between 1629 and 1633.

ODNB. Sears Jayne, 162. E. Pearce, *Sion College and Library* (1913), 234. *CHL* I 393.

Thomas Allen 1542–1632

Mathematician, antiquary, fellow of Gloucester Hall, Oxford. Bequeathed 250 MSS to Kenelm Digby, who gave them to the Bodleian. Also gave 20 MSS to the Bodleian in 1601, and printed books in 1604; books/MSS from his collection are also found in other libraries.

ODNB. Sears Jayne 135, 160. N. R. Ker, 'Thomas Allen's manuscripts', *BLR* 2 (1948): 211–15. A. G. Watson, 'Thomas Allen of Oxford and his manuscripts', in A. Watson & M. Parke (eds), *Medieval scribes, manuscripts and libraries* (1978), 279–314.

Robert Kellum fl. 1680

A catalogue of books on chemistry in his library, made *c*.1680, is found in BL MS Sloane 3798; another list survives in Sloane MS 3686.

Robert Boyle 1627–91

Youngest son of Richard Boyle, 1st Earl of Cork; became a leading member of scientific circles in Oxford and London in the 1650s and 1660s, published many scientfic and philosophical works. Possessed an extensive library, which was sold after his death partly by auction (5 Apr. 1693, a mixed sale with the books of Sylvanus Morgan) and partly by dispersal through the trade.

ODNB. J. F. Fulton, *A bibliography of the Honourable Robert Boyle*, 2nd edn (1961), iv–vi. H. Feisenberger, 'The libraries of Newton, Hooke and Boyle', *Notes and Records of the Royal Society of London* 21 (1966): 42–55.

Robert Hooke 1635–1703

Scientist, surveyor, curator of experiments for the Royal Society. Library auctioned in London, 29 Apr. 1703 (2,585 lots).

ODNB. L. Rostenberg, *The library of Robert Hooke* (1989). H. A. Feisenberger, *Sale catalogues of libraries of eminent persons*, 11: *Scientists* (London, 1975; catalogue reproduced). G. Mandelbrote, 'Sloane's purchases at the sale of Robert Hooke's library', in G. Mandelbrote and B. Taylor (eds), *Libraries within the library* (2009), 98–145. Alston, *Inventory*. Website on his library: http://www.hookesbooks.com/.

John Ray 1627–1705

Naturalist, theologian. Library auctioned in London, 11 Mar. 1708 (1.350 lots).

ODNB. H. A. Feisenberger, *Sale catalogues of libraries of eminent persons*, 11: *Scientists* (London, 1975; catalogue reproduced). Alston, *Inventory*.

Yeomen/Farmers

John Bromhall d. 1630

Yeoman farmer, of Sound, Cheshire. Probate inventory includes 'all his books with book frame', valued at £5 6s., from a total estate valued at c.£270.

P. Pixton, *Wrenbury wills and inventories 1542–1661* (2009), no.82.

George Browne 1596–1689

George Browne 1626–1703

Of Townend, Troutbeck. Developed the foundations of the Browne family library which continued to be developed through the 18th c.

N. Barker, *Treasures from National Trust country house libraries* (New York, 1998), no. 54. M. Purcell, 'Books and readers in eighteenth-century Westmorland: the Brownes of Townend', *Library History* 17 (2001): 91–106.

Bibliography

This selective list of relevant literature used in compiling this book mostly covers books and journal articles published during the last 40 years or so, which deal with topics relating to some or all of the themes of the chapters. It does not include references to studies of particular owners or libraries, which will be found listed under the appropriate name in the Appendix.

Acheson, Katharine (ed.), *Early modern English marginalia* (New York: Routledge, 2019).
Andersen, Jennifer, and Sauer, Elizabeth (eds), *Books and readers in early modern England* (Philadelphia, PA: University of Pennsylvania Press, 2002).
Babcock, Robert G. et al, *A book of her own: an exhibition of manuscripts and printed books in the Yale University Library that were owned by women before 1700* (New Haven, CT: Beinecke Rare Book and Manuscript Library, 2005).
Balsamo, Luigi, *Bibliography* (Berkeley, CA: B. M. Rosenthal, 1990).
Barnard, John, and McKenzie, D. F. (eds), *The Cambridge history of the book in Britain*, vol. 4 (Cambridge: Cambridge University Press, 2002).
Beal, Peter, '"Lost": the destruction, dispersal and rediscovery of manuscripts', in Robin Myers, Michael Harris, and Giles Mandelbrote (eds), *Books on the move* (London: The British Library, 2007).
Berg, Maxine, and Clifford, Helen (eds), *Consumers and luxury: consumer culture in Europe, 1650–1850* (Manchester: Manchester University Press, 1999).
Bermingham, Ann, and Brewer, John (eds), *The consumption of culture 1600–1800: image, object, text* (London: Routledge, 1995).
Blagden, Cyprian, 'The distribution of almanacs in the second half of the seventeenth century', *Studies in Bibliography* 11 (1958): 107–16.
Boran, Elizabethanne (ed.), *Book collecting in Ireland and Britain 1650–1850* (Dublin: Four Courts Press, 2018).
Braunmuller, A. R., 'Robert Carr, Earl of Somerset as collector and patron', in Linda Levy Peck (ed.), *The mental world of the Jacobean court* (Cambridge: Cambridge University Press, 1991), 230–50.
Brewer, John, and Porter, Roy (eds), *Consumption and the world of goods* (London: Routledge, 1993).
Bryan, Jennifer, *Looking inward: devotional reading and the private self in late medieval England* (Philadelphia, PA: University of Pennsylvania Press, 2008).
Bucholz, R. O., 'Going to court in 1700: a visitor's guide', *Court Historian* 5 (2000): 181–215.
Burke, Victoria, 'Women and early seventeenth century manuscript culture', *Seventeenth Century* 12 (1997): 135–50.
Burke, Victoria, 'Ann Bowyer's commonplace book (Bodleian MS Ashmole 51): reading and writing among the "middling sort"', *Early Modern Literary Studies* 6 (2001): 11–28.
Burke, Victoria, 'Recent studies in commonplace books', *English Literary Renaissance* 43 (2013): 153–77.

Cambers, Andrew, 'Readers' marks and religious practice: Margaret Hoby's marginalia', in John N. King (ed.), *Tudor books and readers* (Cambridge: Cambridge University Press, 2010), ch. 10.

Cambers, Andrew, *Godly reading* (Cambridge: Cambridge University Press, 2011).

Capp, Bernard, *The world of John Taylor the water-poet* (Oxford: Clarendon Press, 1994).

Chaney, Edward, *The evolution of English collecting: the reception of Italian art in the Tudor and Stuart periods* (New Haven, CT: Yale University Press, 2003).

Clark, Peter, 'The ownership of books in England, 1560–1640', in Laurence Stone (ed.), *Schooling and society: studies in the history of education* (Baltimore, MD: Johns Hopkins University Press, 1976), 95–111.

Cliffe, J. T., *The world of the country house in seventeenth-century England* (New Haven, CT: Yale University Press, 1999).

Conlon, James, 'Men reading women reading: interpreting images of women readers', *Frontiers: A Journal of Women Studies* 26 (2005): 37–58.

Connolly, Margaret, *Sixteenth-century readers, fifteenth-century books* (Cambridge: Cambridge University Press, 2019).

Cooper, Nicholas, *The houses of the gentry 1480–1680* (London: Paul Mellon Centre, 1999).

Cormack, Bradin, and Mazzio, Carla, *Book use, book theory 1500–1700* (Chicago: University of Chicago Library, 2005).

Cox, Nancy, 'Objects of worth, objects of desire', *Material History Review* 39 (1994): 24–41.

Craik, Katharine, *Reading sensations in early modern England* (Basingstoke: Palgrave, 2007).

Crawford, Julie A., 'Reconsidering early modern women's reading: or, how Margaret Hoby read her de Mornay', *Huntington Library Quarterly* 73 (2010): 193–223.

Crawford, Patricia, *Women and religion in England 1500–1720* (London: Routledge, 1993).

Crawford, Patricia, and Gowing, Laura, *Women's worlds in seventeenth century England* (London: Routledge, 2000).

Cressy, David, *Literacy and the social order* (Cambridge: Cambridge University Press, 1980).

Cressy, David, 'Books as totems in seventeenth-century England and New England', *Journal of Library History* 21 (1986): 92–106.

Dacome, Lucia, 'Noting the mind: commonplace books and the pursuit of self in eighteenth century Britain', *Journal of the History of Ideas* 65 (2004): 605–25.

d'Addario, Christopher, 'Echo chambers and paper memorials', *Textual Cultures* 7 (2012): 73–97.

Davis, Natalie Zemon, 'Beyond the market: books as gifts in sixteenth-century France', *Transactions of the Royal Historical Society*, 5th ser. 33 (1983): 69–88.

Davis, Natalie Zemon, *The gift in sixteenth-century France* (Oxford: Oxford University Press, 2000).

DiMeo, Michelle, and Pennell, Sara (eds), *Reading and writing recipe books, 1550–1800* (Manchester: University of Manchester Press, 2013).

Earle, Peter, *The making of the English middle class: business, society and family life in London, 1660–1730* (Berkeley, CA: University of California Press, 1989).

Erler, Mary C., *Women, reading and piety in late medieval England* (Cambridge: Cambridge University Press, 2002).

Erickson, Amy, *Women and property in early modern England* (London: Routledge, 1993).

Ezell, Margaret, 'The politics of the past: restoration women writers on women reading history', in Rebecca Crump and Sigrid King (eds), *Pilgrimage for love* (Tempe: Arizona Center for Medieval and Renaissance Studies, 1999), 19–40.

Ferch, David L., '"Good books are a very great mercy to the world": persecution, private libraries and the printed word in the early development of the dissenting academies, 1663-1730', *Journal of Library History* 21 (1986): 350–61.

Flather, Amanda, *Gender and space in early modern England* (Woodbridge: Boydell Press, 2007).

Foot, M. M., *The history of bookbinding as a mirror of society* (London: The British Library, 1998).

Fox, Adam, *Oral and literate culture in England, 1500–1700* (Oxford: Clarendon Press, 2000).

Fox, Robert, and Turner, Anthony (eds), *Luxury trades and consumerism in ancien regime Paris* (Aldershot: Ashgate, 1998).

Galinou, Mireille, *City merchants and the arts 1670–1720* (London: City of London Corporation, 2004).

Gardiner, Dorothy, 'The Tradescants and their times *c.*1600–1662', *Journal of the Royal Horticultural Society* 53 (1928): 308–17.

Gibson-Wood, Carol, 'Classification and value in a seventeenth century museum: William Courten's collection', *Journal of the History of Collections* 9 (1997): 61–77.

Ginzburg, Carlo, *The cheese and the worms: the cosmos of a sixteenth-century miller* (London: Routledge and Kegan Paul, 1980).

Girouard, Mark, *Life in the English country house* (New Haven, CT: Yale University Press, 1978).

Glomski, Jacqueline, 'Book collecting and bookselling in the seventeenth century: notions of rarity and identifications of value', *Publishing History* 1 (1996): 5–21.

Goldberg, P. J. P., 'Lay book ownership in late medieval York: the evidence of wills', *The Library*, 6th ser. 16 (1994): 181–9.

Green, Ian, *Print and Protestantism in early modern England* (Oxford: Oxford University Press, 2000).

Griffiths, Fiona, 'Susan Groag Bell's "Medieval women book owners" after 35 years', *Journal of women's history* 29 (2017): 208–13.

Guerci, Manolo, 'The construction of Northumberland House and the patronage of its original builder, Lord Henry Howard, 1603-14', *Antiquaries Journal* 90 (2010): 341–400.

Gwynn, Lucy, 'The architecture of the English domestic library 1600–1700', *Library and Information History* 26 (2010): 56–69.

Hackel, Heidi, *Reading material in early modern England* (Cambridge: Cambridge University Press, 2005).

Hackel, Heidi Brayman, and Kelly, Catherine E. (eds), *Reading women: literacy, authorship and culture in the Atlantic world, 1500–1800* (Philadelphia: University of Pennsylvania Press, 2009).

Halasz, Alexandra, *The marketplace of print: pamphlets and the public sphere in early modern England* (Cambridge: Cambridge University Press, 1997).

Hamling, Tara, and Richardson, Catherine (eds), *Everyday objects: medieval and modern material culture and its meanings* (Farnham: Ashgate, 2010).

Harris, Frances, 'The Englishwoman's private library in the seventeenth and eighteenth centuries', in Peter Vodosek and Graham Jefcoate (eds), *Bibliotheken in der literarischen Darstellung* (Wiesbaden: Harrassowitz, 1999), 189–203.

Heal, Felicity, and Holmes, Clive, *The gentry in England and Wales 1500–1700* (Basingstoke: Macmillan, 1994).

Hepple, Leslie W., 'William Camden and early collections of Roman antiquities in Britain', *Journal of the History of Collections* 15 (2003): 159–73.

Houghton, Walter E., Jr., 'The English virtuoso in the seventeenth century', *Journal of the History of Ideas* 3 (1942): 51–73, 190–219.

Hull, Suzanne, *Chaste, silent, and obedient: English books for women, 1475–1640* (San Marino, CA: Huntington Library, 1982).

Impey, Oliver, and MacGregor, Arthur (eds), *The origins of museums: the cabinet of curiosities in sixteenth- and seventeenth-century Europe* (Oxford: Clarendon Press, 1985).

Inmann, Christine, *Forbidden fruit: a history of women and books in art* (Munich: Prestel, 2009).

Jacobsen, Helen, *Luxury and power: the material world of the Stuart diplomat, 1660–1714* (Oxford: Oxford University Press, 2012).

Jardine, Lisa, and Grafton, Anthony, 'Studied for action: how Gabriel Harvey read his Livy', *Past and Present* 129 (1990): 30–78.

Jensen, Kristian, *Revolution and the antiquarian book* (Cambridge: Cambridge University Press, 2011).

Juel-Jensen, Bent, 'Musaeum Clausum, or Bibliotheca Abscondita', *Journal of the History of Collections* 4 (1992): 127–40.

Justice, George L., and Tinker, Nathan (eds), *Women's writing and the circulation of ideas: manuscript publication in England 1550–1800* (Cambridge: Cambridge University Press, 2002).

Kelly, Thomas, *Early public libraries* (London: Library Association, 1966).

Kishlansky, Mark, *A monarchy transformed: Britain 1603–1714* (London: Allen Lane, 1997).

Knight, Leah, White, Micheline, and Sauer, Elizabetheth (eds), *Women's bookscapes in early modern Britain* (Ann Arbor: University of Michigan Press, 2018).

Laurence, Anne, *Women in England 1500–1760: a social history* (London: Weidenfeld and Nicolson, 1994).

Leedham-Green, Elisabeth, and Webber, Teresa (eds), *The Cambridge history of libraries in Britain and Ireland*, vol. 1 (Cambridge: Cambridge University Press, 2006).

Leong, Elaine, 'Collecting knowledge for the family: recipes, gender and knowledge in the early modern household', *Centaurus* 55 (2013): 81–103.

Leong, Elaine, *Recipes and everyday knowledge: medicine, science and the household in early modern England* (Chicago: Chicago University Press, 2018).

Levy, F. J., 'How information spread among the gentry, 1550–1640', *Journal of British Studies* 21 (1982): 11–34.

Levy, Michelle, 'Do women have a book history?', *Studies in Romanticism* 53 (2014): 297–317.

Love, Harold, *Scribal publication in seventeenth-century England* (Oxford: Clarendon Press, 1993).

MacGregor, Arthur (ed.), *Tradescant's rarities: essays on the foundation of the Ashmolean Museum* (Oxford: Clarendon Press, 1983).

McKitterick, David, 'Women and their books in the seventeenth century: the case of Elizabeth Puckering', *The Library*, 7th ser. 1 (2000): 359–80.

McKitterick, David, *The invention of rare books* (Cambridge: Cambridge University Press, 2018).

Mandelbrote, Giles, and Manley, K. A. (eds), *The Cambridge history of libraries in Britain and Ireland*, vol. 2 (Cambridge: Cambridge University Press, 2006).

Mendelson, Sara, and Crawford, Patricia (eds), *Women in early modern England, 1550–1720* (Oxford: Clarendon Press, 1998).

Millstone, Noah, *Manuscript circulation and the invention of politics in early Stuart England* (Cambridge: Cambridge University Press, 2016).

Moss, Ann, *Printed commonplace-books and the structuring of Renaissance thought* (Oxford: Clarendon Press, 1996).

Moss, Ann, 'The *Politica* of Justus Lipsius and the commonplace-book', *Journal of the History of Ideas* 59 (1998): 421–36.

Needham, Paul, 'The late use of incunables and the paths of book survival', *Wolfenbütteler Notizen zur Buchgeschichte* 29 (2004): 35–59.

Nevitt, Marcus, *Women and the pamphlet culture of revolutionary England 1640–1669* (Aldershot: Ashgate, 2006).

Orr, Leah, 'Prices of English books at auction *c*.1680', *The Library*, 7th ser. 20 (2019): 501–26.

Pearson, David, 'The libraries of English bishops, 1600–40', *The Library*, 6th ser. 14 (1992): 221–57.

Pearson, David, 'Patterns of book ownership in late seventeenth-century England', *The Library*, 7th ser. 11 (2010): 139–67.

Pearson, David, 'The English private library in the seventeenth century', *The Library*, 7th ser. 13 (2012): 379–99.

Pearson, David, *Provenance research in book history* (New Castle, DE, and Oxford: Oak Knoll and Bodleian Library, 2019).

Pearson, Jacqueline, 'Women reading, reading women', in Helen Wilcox (ed.) *Women and literature in Britain* (Cambridge: Cambridge University Press, 1996), 80–99.

Peck, Linda Levy, *Consuming splendor: society and culture in seventeenth-century England* (Cambridge: Cambridge University Press, 2005).

Pennell, Sara, 'Consumption and consumerism in early modern England', *Historical Journal* 42 (1999): 549–64.

Perkin, Michael, *A directory of the parochial libraries of the Church of England* (London: Bibliographical Society, 2004).

Pointon, Marcia, *Strategies for showing: women, possession, and representation in English visual culture 1665–1800* (Oxford: Oxford University Press, 1997).

Poole, William, 'Book economy in New College, Oxford in the later seventeenth century', *History of Universities* 25 (2010): 56–127.

Pratt, Aaron T., 'Stab-stitching and the status of early English playbooks as literature', *The Library*, 7th ser. 16 (2015): 304–28.

Prior, Mary (ed.), *Women in English society* (London: Methuen, 1985).

Prior, Mary, 'Wives and wills 1558–1700', in John Chartres and David Hey (eds), *English rural society 1500–1800* (Cambridge: Cambridge University Press, 1990), 201–25.

Purcell, Mark, *The country house library* (New Haven, CT: Yale University Press, 2017).

Ramsay, Nigel (ed.), *Heralds and heraldry in Shakespeare's England* (Donington: Shaun Tyas, 2014).

Raven, James (ed.), *Lost libraries: the destruction of great book collections since antiquity* (Basingstoke: Palgrave Macmillan, 2004).

Raven, James, *The business of books* (New Haven, CT: Yale University Press, 2007).

Raven, James, Small, Helen, and Tadmor, Naomi (eds), *The practice and representation of reading in England* (Cambridge: Cambridge University Press, 1996).

Raymond, Joad, *Pamphlets and pamphleteering in early modern Britain* (Cambridge: Cambridge University Press, 2002).

Raymond, Joad (ed.), *The Oxford history of popular print culture*, vol. 1: *Cheap print in Britain and Ireland to 1660* (Oxford: Oxford University Press, 2011).

Reid, Peter, 'Proto-bibliophiles among the British aristocracy', *Library History* 18 (2002): 25–38.

Roberts, Sasha, 'Reading in early modern England: contexts and problems', *Critical Survey* 12(2) (2000): 1–16.

Rowell, Christopher, 'A seventeenth-century cabinet restored: the green closet at Ham House', *Apollo* 143 (1996): 18–25.

Schurink, Fred, 'Manuscript commonplace books, literature, and reading in early modern England', *Huntington Library Quarterly* 73 (2010): 453–69.

Scott-Warren, Jason, 'News, sociability and bookbuying in early modern England: the letters of Sir Thomas Cornwallis', *The Library*, 7th ser. 1 (2000): 381–402.

Scott-Warren, Jason, *Sir John Harington and the book as gift* (Oxford: Oxford University Press, 2001).

Sharpe, Kevin, *Reading revolutions: the politics of reading in early modern England* (New Haven, CT: Yale University Press, 2000).

Simpson, Murray, 'Housing books in Scotland before 1800', *Journal of the Edinburgh Bibliographical Society* 4 (2009): 11–31.

Slights, William W. E., 'The edifying margins of Renaissance English books', *Renaissance Quarterly* 42 (1989): 682–716.

Smith, Helen, *Grossly material things: women and book production in early modern England* (Oxford: Oxford University Press, 2012).

Smith, Woodruff, *Consumption and the making of respectability* (London: Routledge, 2002).

Smyth, Adam, *Material texts in early modern England* (Cambridge: Cambridge University Press, 2018).

Snook, Edith, *Women, reading, and the cultural politics of early modern England* (Aldershot: Ashgate, 2005).

Spufford, Margaret, *Small books and pleasant histories* (London: Methuen, 1981).

Spufford, Margaret, *The great reclothing of rural England: petty chapmen and their wares in the seventeenth century* (London: Hambledon Press, 1985).

Stewart, Alan, 'The early modern closet discovered', *Representations* 50 (1995): 76–100.

Stone, Laurence, *The crisis of the aristocracy, 1558–1641* (Oxford: Clarendon Press, 1964).

Toomer, G. J., *Eastern wisedome and learning: the study of Arabic in seventeenth-century England* (Oxford: Clarendon Press, 1996).

Vine, Angus, *Miscellaneous order: manuscript culture and the early modern organization of knowledge* (Oxford: Oxford University Press, 2019).

Wayne, Valerie, *Women's labour and the history of the book in early modern England* (London: Arden Shakespeare, 2020).

Weatherill, Lorna, 'A possession of one's own: women and consumer behaviour in England, 1660–1740', *Journal of British Studies* 25 (1986): 131–56.

West, Susie, 'An architectural typology for the early country house library, 1660–1720', *The Library*, 7th ser. 14 (2013): 441–64.

Wiggins, Alison, 'What did Renaissance readers write in their printed copies of Chaucer?', *The Library*, 7th ser. 9 (2008): 3–36.

Williams, Abigail, *The social life of books: reading together in the eighteenth-century home* (New Haven, CT: Yale University Press, 2017).

Woudhuysen, H. R., *Sir Philip Sidney and the circulation of manuscripts, 1558–1640* (Oxford: Clarendon Press, 1996).

Wrightson, Keith, 'Estates, degrees and sorts', in Penelope J. Corfield (ed.), *Language, history and class* (Oxford: Basil Blackwell, 1991), 30–52.

Index

Note: The index largely focuses on references to personal names, both in the main text and the Appendix. Institutions are indexed when they are mentioned, significantly, in the main text, but not when they occur in the Appendix (there would be too many). For more sophisticated searching of the Appendix, use the search functions of *Book Owners Online*.